Karl Polanyi

New Dynamics of Innovation and Competition

This series, published in association with the ESRC Centre for Research in Innovation and Competition at the University of Manchester, emanates from an engagement of the Centre's research agenda with a wide range of internationally renowned scholars in the field. The series casts new light on the significance of demand and consumption, markets and competition, and the complex inter-organisational basis for innovation processes. The volumes are multidisciplinary and comparative in perspective.

Series editor:
Mark Harvey, Senior Research Fellow at CRIC

Already published:

Innovation by demand: an interdisciplinary approach to the study of demand and its role in innovation   Andrew McMeekin, Ken Green, Mark Tomlinson and Vivien Walsh (eds)

Qualities of food   Andrew McMeekin, Mark Harvey and Alan Warde (eds)

Market relations and the competitive process: new dynamics of innovation and competition   Stan Metcalfe and Alan Warde (eds)

Karl Polanyi

New perspectives on the place of the economy in society

edited by
Mark Harvey
Ronnie Ramlogan
Sally Randles

Manchester University Press

Copyright © Manchester University Press 2007

While copyright in the volume as a whole is vested in Manchester University Press, copyright in individual chapters belongs to their respective authors, and no chapter may be reproduced wholly or in part without the express permission in writing of both author and publisher.

Published by Manchester University Press
Altrincham Street, Manchester M1 7JA, UK
and Room 400, 175 Fifth Avenue, New York, NY 10010, USA
www.manchesteruniversitypress.co.uk

British Library Cataloguing-in-Publication Data is available

Library of Congress Cataloging-in-Publication Data is available

ISBN 978 0 7190 7333 5 paperback

First published by Manchester University Press in hardback 2007

This paperback edition first published 2014

The publisher has no responsibility for the persistence or accuracy of URLs for any external or third-party internet websites referred to in this book, and does not guarantee that any content on such websites is, or will remain, accurate or appropriate.

Printed by Lightning Source

Contents

List of figures and tables	*page* vii
List of contributors	ix
Series foreword	x
Preface: the English experience in the life and work of Karl Polanyi *Kari Polanyi-Levitt*	xi
1 Working with and beyond Polanyian perspectives *Mark Harvey, Sally Randles and Ronnie Ramlogan*	1

Part I Working within the legacy of Polanyi

2 The forgotten institutions *Michele Cangiani*	25
3 Institutions, politics and culture: a Polanyian perspective on economic change *John Harriss*	43
4 The enforcement of contracts and property rights: constitutive versus epiphenomenal conceptions of law *Geoffrey Hodgson*	58
5 Karl Polanyi and the instituted process of economic democratisation *Marguerite Mendell*	78
6 Reinstituting the economic process: (re)embedding the economy in society and nature *Fikret Adaman, Pat Devine and Begum Ozkaynak*	93
7 Moral philosophy and economic sociology: what MacIntyre learnt from Polanyi *Peter McMylor*	113

Part II New Directions

8 Issues for a neo-Polanyian research agenda in economic sociology *Sally Randles*	133
9 Instituting economic processes in society *Mark Harvey*	163

10 Labour markets as instituted economic process: a comparison of France and the UK *Nathalie Moncel* 185

11 Telephone transactions: instituting new processes of exchange and distribution *Miriam Glucksmann* 208

12 Instituted economic processes in the telecommunications sector *Andrea Mina* 233

13 Corporate merger as dialectical double movement and instituted process *Sally Randles and Ronnie Ramlogan* 254

Index 281

Figures and tables

Figures

4.1	A coordination game and a Prisoners' Dilemma game	page 70
4.2	The previous Prisoners' Dilemma game transformed	71
6.1	Historical society	97
6.2	Visions of the future	98
9.1	Configuration of four instituted economic processes	171
9.2	The interaction of four multiple causal domains	174
10.1	Working time patterns	199
10.2	Wage distribution	200
10.3	Labour cost components	203
10.4	The instituted employment system	204
11.1	The caller–operator dyad	215
11.2	Providing information to callers	215
11.3	Connecting consumers to third parties	217
11.4	Selling goods or products	218
11.5	Selling services	220
11.6	Emergency services and helplines	221
13.1	Interdependent instituted markets and the merger process	260
13.2	Internal and external dialectics of the four key objects of Polanyi's concern and ontological framework	263

Tables

1.1	Polanyi citations and association with the tags 'embeddedness' and 'embedded'	5
10.1	Activity, employment and unemployment evolution in France and the UK	188

10.2 Determination of the share of GDP going to compensation of employees	189
10.3 Youth labour force supply: 1997	190
10.4 Women's participation in France and the UK: 1994	191
10.5 Inactive population willing to work	192
10.6 Occupational labour market vs. internal labour market	193
10.7 Non-standard employment forms in France and in the UK	198

Contributors

Fikret Adaman, Professor, Department of Economics, Bogazici University, Turkey
Michele Cangiani, Professor, Department of Historical Studies, University of Venice, Italy
Pat Devine, Honorary Research Fellow, Economics, School of Social Science, University of Manchester, UK
Miriam Glucksmann, Professor, Department of Sociology, University of Essex, UK
John Harriss, Professor, Development Studies Institute, London School of Economics, UK
Mark Harvey, Senior Research Fellow, CRIC, University of Manchester, UK
Geoffrey Hodgson, Research Professor in Business Studies, University of Hertfordshire, UK
Peter McMylor, Lecturer, Sociology, School of Social Science, University of Manchester, UK
Marguerite Mendell, Associate Professor and Vice-Principal, School of Community and Public Affair, Concordia University, Canada
Andrea Mina, Research Fellow, CRIC, University of Manchester, UK
Nathalie Moncel, Senior Research Fellow, Centre for Research on Education, Training and Employment (Céreq), Marseilles, France
Begum Ozkaynak, Istanbul, Turkey
Kari Polanyi-Levitt, Emeritus Professor, McGill University, Canada
Ronnie Ramlogan, Research Fellow, CRIC, University of Manchester, UK
Sally Randles, Research Fellow, CRIC, University of Manchester, UK

Series foreword

The CRIC–MUP series New Dynamics of Innovation and Competition is designed to make an important contribution to this continually expanding field of research and scholarship. As a series of edited volutes, it combines approaches and perspective developed by CRIC's own research agenda with those of a wide rage of internationally renowned scholars. A distinctive emphasis on processes of economic and social transformation frames the CRIC research programme. Research on the significance of demand and consumption, on the empirical and theoretical understanding of competition and markets, and on the complex inter-organisation basis of innovation processes, provides the thematic linkage between the successive volumes of the series. At the interface between the different disciplines of economic, sociology, management studies and geography, the development of economic sociology lends a unifying methodological approach. A strong comparative and historical dimension to the variety of innovation processes in different capitalist economies and societies is supported by the international character of the contributions.

The series is based on international workshops hosted by CRIC which have encouraged debate and diversity at the leading edge of innovation studies.

CRIC is an ESRC funded research centre based in the University of Manchester.

Preface: the English experience in the life and work of Karl Polanyi

Kari Polanyi-Levitt

Introduction

My congratulations to the ESRC Centre for Research on Innovation and Competition at the University of Manchester for organising the conference on which this volume is based. To the best of my knowledge, this was the first academic event dedicated to a critique of the work of my father, ever held in the UK. In this contribution, I have attempted to address the significance of *The Great Transformation* (Polanyi, 1944), a work so obviously influenced by his re-reading of English social and economic history. This is also the work most closely related to my own academic interest in International Political Economy and Development.

He would, I think, have been delighted at the attention his work is now receiving in British academic discourse and would certainly have been surprised that this event is taking place in a centre devoted to research on innovation and competition. Innovation in the conventional sense of product or process design was not a subject which attracted his interest, and competition, in the context of 'Manchester' was a code for the 'self-regulating market' of nineteenth century laissez-faire capitalism, central to his critique of market economy and market society. In a more profound sense, however, he was indeed concerned with innovation, not in production technology, marketing or business organisation, but rather in the area of economic and social institutions. His life work was devoted to understanding the place of the economy in society.

Polanyi and the Great Transformation

Karl Polanyi came to England from Vienna in 1933, and in 1937 obtained employment with the Workers' Education Association (WEA) teaching courses on international relations and English social and economic history, a subject entirely new to him. His encounter with the conditions of working-class life on overnight stays with the families who accommodated him was a profound culture shock. The lecture notes for his WEA classes, available in the archive of the Karl Polanyi Institute of Concordia University in Montreal, are the skeleton upon which he later developed *The Great Transformation* (Polanyi, 1944), published in England as *The Origins of Our Times* (Polanyi, 1945).

For Polanyi, an almost personal sense of the responsibility of his generation for the war and all its fateful consequences motivated his search for the 'origins of our times' – the original title of *The Great Transformation*. The central problem addressed in this book was the ultimate cause of the collapse of nineteenth-century civilisation and the consequent dramatic events of the inter-war years. Although written in Vermont between 1941 and 1943, it was in England, the birthplace of the Industrial Revolution that he found the origins of the disasters that befell Europe from 1914 to 1945 – 'the great transformation' that terminated the long nineteenth century and eventuated in the institutional reforms of the post-World War II era.[1] His thesis was that the economic and social upheavals and political tensions resulting from the utopian attempt to restore the nineteenth-century liberal economic order after the World War I were the essential cause of the world economic crisis and of the demise of democracy in most of the states of continental Europe.

The exposition of the narrative in *The Great Transformation* was underpinned by three distinctive concepts: the fictitious commodities of land, labour and money; the disembedded economy; and the 'double movement'.[2] For Polanyi the truly revolutionary innovation behind *The Great Transformation* was the positive rejection of poor relief and the introduction of a price-making market for the fictitious commodity of labour by the new Poor Law of 1834. This gave legal sanction to the degradation of working men and women, forcing them to choose between work, however miserably remunerated, and the stigma of the workhouse. The result was the unleashing of productive forces and capitalist accumulation on a scale never before experienced in human history and was accompanied by massive dispossession, displacement, unemployment, and the destruction of social relations in which economic livelihood, social status, pride in craft, and cultural expression were embedded. As the nexus of market relations expanded and became denser, social relations of community and extended family are subordinated to the logic of the market, and the market economy assumes a life of its own, governed by economic laws, whether neoclassical or Marxist. Polanyi insisted that these so-called laws were neither natural nor historically inevitable. He rejected all varieties of economic determinism.

Polanyi's view of the economy as *an instituted process* is central to his discussion of the relationship of economy and society. In a seminal article on the economy as an instituted process entitled 'Aristotle Discovers the Economy', Polanyi returned to a central theme of *The Great Transformation*:

> The conceptual tool with which to tackle this transition from namelessness to a separate existence [of the economy] we submit, is the distinction between the embedded and the disembedded condition of the economy in relation to society. The disembedded economy of the nineteenth century stood apart from the rest of society, more especially from the political and governmental systems. (Polanyi, 1957, p. 68)

The market economy was now organised in specific institutions based on the assumption of economic motives and 'propensities' and society had to be re-engineered to enable the economy to function according to its own laws.[3]

This is not, however, the only sense in which Polanyi employed the conceptual tool of the distinction between the embedded and the disembedded condition of the economy. His concern was less with the evident necessity of market economy to be embedded in institutions, than with the larger issue of the relation of economy to society. In Polanyi's account of the rise of market economy, the embedding of the market economy in specific economic institutions subordinates the substance of society to the laws of the market. The economy is thus *dis*embedded from society.

The self-regulating market, according to Polanyi was a utopian project. It 'could not exist for any length of time without annihilating the human and natural substance of society; it would have physically destroyed man and transformed his surroundings into a wilderness. Inevitably, society took measures to protect itself'. Interestingly, the text continues 'but whatever measures it took impaired the self-regulation of the market, disorganized industrial life and thus endangered society in yet another way' (*The Great Transformation*, Polanyi, 1944, pp. 3–4).

According to Polanyi, laissez-faire liberalism intent on the spread of the market system was met by a protective counter-movement of legislation regarding public health, factory conditions, social insurance, public utilities, municipal services, and trade union rights. In Germany, France, and Austria governments of widely different political complexions enacted similar measures. The Great Depression of 1873–95, which was in effect a deflation of prices and profits, was an economic earthquake which dislocated the lives of scores of millions in rural Europe. Within a few years, with the singular exception of Britain, free trade was a matter of the past. The continued expansion of market economy took place under new conditions set by the 'double movement' of expansion of trade accompanied by protectionist institutions designed to check the social dislocation of the market (*The Great Transformation*, Polanyi, 1944, p. 223). Intensified national competition and imperialist rivalries brought this first globalization to a precipitous end in 1914.

Europe emerged from the war impoverished, burdened by reparation and war debts, fractured by the creation of small and fragile states carved out of the derelict Hapsburg Empire, with civil war and famine in post-revolutionary Russia. It leapt from crisis to crisis until an unsustainable pyramid of debt collapsed in 1931. In Polanyi's view the Great Depression was the final act in a series of financial and economic crises and failed stabilization programs imposed by the victorious Western powers:

> In the early thirties, change set in with abruptness. Its landmarks were the abandonment of the gold standard by Great Britain; the Five Year Plans in Russia; the launching of the New Deal; the National Socialist Revolution in Germany; the collapse of the League in favour of autarchist empires. While at the end of the Great War nineteenth-century ideals were paramount, and their influence dominated the following decade, by 1940 every vestige of the international system had disappeared. (*The Great Transformation*, Polanyi, 1944, p. 24)

When the world emerged from World War II to construct the international institutions which dominated the post-war era it was generally accepted that the market economy would have to serve national objectives of full employment and be complemented by progressive taxation and the welfare state. Only the United States, it seemed, maintained its belief in universal capitalism. The long nineteenth century was history. The economy it seemed would now serve the social objectives of nations. The tide, it appeared, had turned against the unrestricted domination of the economy by capital. The historical swing of the pendulum had restored social control over the economy. This was the 'great transformation' which closed the book on the disembedded economy of the English classical political economists of the early nineteenth century.

From 1945 to the mid-1970s Europe and North America experienced high growth, full employment, rising productivity, rising wages and extensive programmes of social security. As Polanyi reminded us, however, the measures taken by society to protect itself could impair the functioning of the market and set in motion a counter-attack by capital to free itself from social constraints. This indeed is what has happened since the early 1980s when the Reagan and Thatcher administrations reversed the historical pendulum to dismantle gains made by labour in the first three post-war decades. The 'double movement' is not a self-correcting mechanism which moderates excesses of market fundamentalism but a contradiction in the Marxian sense of the word. Although historical analogies are always dangerous, there are widespread fears that the neo-liberal tide is sweeping the world toward disasters possibly more devastating than the breakdown of the economic and financial system of the 1930s.

Final reflections

The Great Transformation was published in England in 1945. It received few reviews and attracted little attention. It was the wrong place and the wrong time for this book. Forty years had to pass before the pioneering role of Britain in instituting policies of deregulation and privatisation in the 1980s and more generally the Anglo-American attempt to impose the market principle on the world under the rubric of globalisation brought fresh relevance to his work.

In the United States, *The Great Transformation* met with a favourable reception. It attracted the attention of American sociologists and institutional economists in the tradition of Thorsten Veblen, John. R. Commons, Wesley C. Mitchell and others. A remarkable introduction was written by Robert M. MacIver and the book was widely reviewed.

On retirement from teaching in 1953, Polanyi co-directed, with Conrad M. Arensberg, an interdisciplinary research project on the economic aspects of institutional growth, financed by the Ford Foundation. The project terminated in 1957. In this context, he directed a number of studies by graduate students including Paul Bohannan, Walter C. Neale, Harry W. Pearson, Rosemary Arnold, Daniel B. Fusfeld and Charles S. Silberman. The results of the project were published as *Trade and Market in the Early Empires* (Polanyi et al., 1957). The book includes Polanyi's celebrated contribution on 'The Economy as Instituted Process', 'Aristotle Discovers the Economy', and (with Arensberg and Pearson) 'The Place of Economics in Society'. In 1957 he retired from Columbia University to Pickering, Ontario, where he continued to work until his death in 1964.

For many years, academic interest in the work of Karl Polanyi was almost exclusively directed to his work on economic anthropology, where his rejection of formal economics as a useful tool in anthropological research was challenged and hotly debated. *The Great Transformation*, however, continued to have a life of its own. It is now translated into fifteen languages. In the 1970s World Systems Theory in sociology attracted new interest in *The Great Transformation*, which became essential reading in international political economy. In recent years critics of economic globalisation, including environmentalists, have found in Polanyi a trenchant critique of market fundamentalism, while people engaged in community development are attracted to the concept of reciprocity in support of not-for-profit economic activity.

The socially embedded economy and Polanyi's approach to the role of economic and social institutions in shaping modern economic life is also receiving increasing attention. The market is not a natural phenomenon and the rapidly changing technology in an ever more interdependent world gives rise to complex sets of institutional change. If the work of Polanyi has contributed to elevating the institutional approach in British academic discourse, we welcome the delayed return of Karl Polanyi to England, the source of so much of his creative thinking. For this I congratulate and thank the organisers of the conference and the editors of this volume.

Notes

1 This was made clear in a concluding passage of the second chapter of *The Great Transformation* in which he stated that 'in order to comprehend German

fascism, we must revert to Ricardian England' (*The Great Transformation*, Polanyi, 1944, p. 32).

2 Commodities are 'fictitious' because by definition they are produced for sale. But natural resources including land, are God-given; humans do not reproduce to provide workers for the labour market, and money is a social convention. While commodities like cattle, cowry shells, gold and silver have been used as money, modern money is essentially a book-keeping entry validated by the sanctity of contract and embodied in law. Historically money was the first to be 'liberated' from regulations prohibiting usury, for centuries deemed sinful by Christian doctrine. The commercialisation of land, including the enclosures, extended over centuries, but the threat of social instability created by the dispossession of peasant cultivators was moderated by measures to protect the poor and to maintain standards of workmanship and quality of craft.

3 A price-making market economy is a complex mechanism which requires specific institutions, to constrain and guide the behaviour of individuals to conform to market behaviour as producers, consumers, savers, investors, etc. In this sense the economy is always embedded in institutions. Attempts to introduce instant capitalism in post-Soviet Russia failed because they were not underpinned by the essential legal and social institutions of civil society. The lesson of Russia and more generally the instability and insecurity associated with globalisation in the 1990s, has led scholars and policy makers, including the World Bank, to embrace institutional reform and good governance, and the 'embedded economy' has gained currency in policy discourse.

References

Polanyi, K. (1944), *The Great Transformation*, New York, Rinehart and Co.
Polanyi, K. (1945), *Origins of Our Time: The Great Transformation*, London, Gollancz.
Polanyi, K. (1957), 'Aristotle Discovers the Economy', in K. Polanyi, C. M. Arensberg and H. W. Pearson (eds), *Trade and Market in the Early Empires*, New York, Free Press.

Working with and beyond Polanyian perspectives

Mark Harvey, Sally Randles and Ronnie Ramlogan

When Karl Polanyi (1886–1964) wrote *The Great Transformation* (1944), it was in the middle of World War II, with great powers espousing two major ideologies of the century confronting Nazism, fascism and an imperial Japanese dictatorship. Preceding the war, capitalism had witnessed probably its most turbulent phase: depression throwing millions of out work across the world, extensive industrial restructuring and the emergence of new technologies, financial and monetary chaos, hyperinflation, and early phases of European welfare states and the New Deal in the USA. Quite a background! He wrote, it appears, with urgency, hoping to get his word in early to address the world as and when it emerged from war (Block, 2003).

The fundamental challenge that he posed was to understand the nature of such catastrophic crises that led to war, slaughter and the disruption of the most basic elements of everyday life. Moreover, it was not just crisis that needed explaining, but how such crisis could have emanated from one hundred years of (intra-European) peace.[1] His answer was to rethink the relationship between polity and economy and, more profoundly, to suggest that the economy can historically shift its place in society and boundaries can be more or less blurred or distinct. Both turbulence and tranquillity can only be understood within this frame: there is no such thing as a purely economic crisis or a purely economic order, of which his prime example was the 'self-regulating market' running like a planetary system, with its own natural laws, beyond human, and especially political intervention. All economic order and crisis, all market order and crisis, are at once economic and institutional.

This is not to say that he was the first to raise such questions, and indeed, he was politically and intellectually formed in the Austrian cauldron of ideas from Hayek and von Mises to the Red Vienna of the 1920s (McRobbie and Polanyi-Levitt, 2006). But with his great historical sweep, later expanded by anthropological studies (Polanyi et al., 1957; Polanyi and Dalton, 1968), he revitalised and broadened the terms of earlier ways of political and economic thinking. *The Great Transformation* itself exemplified a mode of thinking about the relation between polity and economy. Instead of proceeding abstractly (in the manner of classical or neo-classical political economy) to define the essence of industrial capitalism, the model of its workings, he analysed the historically changing role of the state especially in developing laws concerning the sale of labour, exemplified by the Speenhamland system and the 1834 New Poor Law (Block and Somers, 2003), and hence the institutional conditions for labour market functioning. He looked at the institutions of the gold standard, first its importance for peace, binding economies with an interest of mutual advantage gained through trade under a common exchange rate standard, and its eventual collapse. Money cannot be a taken-for-granted medium for exchange. It is not an economic phenomenon, but a politico-economic institution, of critical significance in any market economy. It is also a historical institution, hence inherently mutable, prone to politico-economic crisis. His anthropological studies, whether of trade in the Trobriand Islands, or Dahomey and the slave trade (Polanyi, 1966; Polanyi and Dalton, 1968), gave him some material with which to compare institutions of reciprocal exchange, or monarchically orchestrated redistributive exchanges, with market exchanges, and thereby grasp the latter as specific historical institutional arrangements. By such contrasts, he was also able to problematise the place of the economy in society, illuminating what is so distinctive about the market economies of contemporary capitalisms.

Contemporary resonances

And this leads us to reflect on why Polanyi has enjoyed periods of resonance with different historical presents – during the turbulent years of the late 1960s, and again over the last decade or so. For such an influential thinker, his oeuvre is relatively small and 'unfinished', reflecting a disrupted life whose imperatives were far from those of a standard academic career, or indeed of an intellectual dedicated to writing 'major works'.[2] Many of his most seminal ideas have been open to very different interpretations, and there are many unresolved inconsistencies, and internal contradictions. A more settled or narrowly focused life might have led to greater closure, and more certainty about how different concepts hung together. But just this openness has enabled different strands and implications to have been drawn out, shaped by the historical circumstances that gave his ideas their renewed interest.

In the 1960s, Polanyian ideas were recruited to counter universalist ideas that capitalist economic market motives and concepts applied to all societies and all possible futures. Subsequently, one main focus of interest has been on the place of markets as *the* central institution of contemporary capitalism, and its 'embedding' in other social relations and institutions. There was an 'absorption' of Polanyi into economic sociology (Granovetter,

1985; Granovetter and Swedberg, 2001). Another main strand, linked to debates about the role of the nation state in an era of globalisation, has been in the central Polanyian idea concerning 'regulated' versus 'self-regulated' capitalism. There is a sense that economic scales have become detached from political scales, restricting the possibilities of national governmental, or indeed any scale of political economic management. This dislocation also feeds into counter-ideologies of 'de-regulation' promoted vigorously in the 1980s–1990s by the Chicago School–Regan–Thatcher axis. Scandals spawned by de-regulation – such as Enron – then stimulate counter-pressures for re-regulation. Finally, drawing again on Polanyian anti-universalist arguments, and especially following the collapse of Soviet-style socialism, variety is sought *within* capitalism, emphasising alternative, even their deeply divergent political economies, in Anglo-Saxon or Nordic countries, continental Europe, or Japan. So changed historical circumstances amplify or attenuate different Polanyian themes.

Some core Polanyian ideas

Embeddedness and disembeddedness

Turning to a brief examination of some key Polanyian concepts, perhaps one of the strangest 'amplifications' has been Polanyi's idea of the 'embeddedness' of markets, or more broadly, of the economy, in social relations or institutions. This concept is now probably the single most obvious Polanyi identifier. Yet, in *The Great Transformation*, as Barber (1995) has noted, the word only appears twice, is not indexed, and has a quite minor role in the overall argument. In *Trade and Market in the Early Empires*, when it is used a bit more extensively, it also plays a subordinate role in the general account of 'the economy as instituted process' (see below). Hopkins (1957), in co-developing Polanyi's ideas of the institutionalisation of the economy, does not use it at all, but, commenting on its meaning in a footnote suggests that embeddedness is similar to a (Parsonian) sociologist's notion of indifferentiation of economic institutions from other social institutions (as, for example, the household), whereas 'unembeddedness' (Hopkins, 1957, p. 299) is applied to markedly differentiated economic institutions (the stock market, a factory).[3]

It is also curious that Polanyi scholars frequently speak of Polanyi using a concept of 'dis-embedded' economies (cited 27 times, Web of Science).[4] So far as we are aware, the term dis-embedded appears only once in Polanyi in *Aristotle discovers the Economy* (Polanyi, 1957, p. 68), but subsequently in a context otherwise using identical language, he replaces it with the term 'institutionally distinct' in *Livelihood of Man* (Polanyi, 1977, p. 47). So for 'embedded' and even more for 'dis-embedded', this suggests a quite fluid and limited role for the concept within Polanyi's own conceptual framework, which is not to say, of course, that the full import of an idea is necessarily recognised by its 'author'. In later works, 'embeddedness' does emerge more strongly but in a broader problematic of understanding the shifting place of the economy in society.[5] Here two things seem to be going on, not always distinguished by those who seek to thoroughly sociologise the economy (Krippner, 2001). On the one hand, there is the *concept* of the 'economic', strongly defended by Polanyi for *all* societies, but requiring *analytical* work to be done in deciphering, and distinguishing the economic processes for societies in which economic processes are deeply embedded in institutions (political, civic, religious) rather than differentiated or dis-embedded. So for Polanyi, it was important to retain a well-defined concept of the specifically 'economic', 'and thereby make reasonably sure that we know what we mean when we so confidently talk about "the economy" '. (Polanyi, 1966, p. 307), even when 'the process is not embedded[6] in "economic" institutions alone – *a matter of degree, anyway* (our emphasis)' (*ibid.*). The examples given in his work include tribal kinship organisations or the household in archaic societies, central institutional forms at once religious, political, cultural, socially reproductive and economic with the latter embedded in the former (Polanyi, 1977, 1966). On the other hand, there is a societal and historical process whereby economic processes become 'dis-embedded', in the sense of differentiated, in distinctively economic institutions (a matter of degree, as we have seen). The primary example here was the emergence of the self-regulating market in nineteenth-century England. Here, the term dis-embedded does *not* mean detached from society and its other more or less differentiated institutions. Although there may be some inconsistency and lack of clarity, the qualifier disembedded applied to economy does not mean an economy separated from, let alone independent or autonomous, *from society*, at most from other institutions within society. This interpretation would be quite inconsistent with Polanyi's oft-repeated critique of the 'economistic fallacy' advanced by classical political economy after Smith, and especially Malthus and Ricardo, where the economy ceases to be 'societal' and operates according to independent Law of Nature (Polanyi, 1968, 1977).[7] Indeed, the embeddedness/disembeddedness continuum is about the 'shifting place of the economy *in* society'. The historical processes of differentiation, and then subsequently critical asymmetries and tensions of impact, influence or even domination of the economy over society is an implicit rather than fully developed dimension of even Polanyi's later work. But it is certainly already immanent in the narrative of *The Great Transformation*, notably the emergence of the 'self-regulated market', with its dominance of relatively differentiated economic motives of human action, the pursuit of gain.

The strong identification of Polanyi with the concept of embeddedness, however, appears only to have arisen, ironically, as a consequence of Granovetter's famous 1985 article, where it is recruited to a quite different purpose. Here embeddedness is linked with a 'new economic sociology', and in particular his double critique of under-socialisation that views economic man primarily in terms of individualised agency, and oversocialisation, where individuals are stamped in the mould of structures and institutions (including norms and roles). Embeddedness here denotes the connectedness of individuals in social networks of interpersonal relations, an idea quite remote from Polanyi's (Block, 2003; Peck, 2005), where, as we have seen, it is primarily deployed to account for and describe characteristics of institutions, not individuals. In other words, the Polanyi concept of embeddedness only emerged as an important Polanyian concept as a consequence of an association first highlighted by a quite alien Granovetterian concept.

The evidence from citations, although limited to text appearing in titles and abstracts, is quite powerful. It should also be emphasised that number counts tell us nothing about uses and meanings, and so even if the evidence is 'hard', it is also 'poor'. Table 1.1 demonstrates that Polanyi, in spite of a very extensive citation record before 1985, only became associated with the concept of embeddedness after 1985. Moreover, of the 85 times Polanyi is cited in combination with the tag 'embeddedness', he is co-cited with Granovetter 66 times, hence only 19 times in his own right. The

Table 1.1 Polanyi citations and associations with the tags 'embeddedness' and 'embedded'

	Text count	Polanyi cited	Granovetter 1985 paper cited	Granovetter and Polanyi co-cited	Polanyi cited pre-1985
Author citation only		2706	2395	215	
Author *and* embeddedness	1076	85	477	66	0
Author *and* embedded	73722	77			1
Embeddedness work cited Great Transformation (1944)		82			
Trade and Market (1957)		16			
Primitive, Archaic, Modern (Dalton, 1968)		8			
Livelihood (1977)		4			
All others		12			

Source: Institute for Scientific Information (ISI)

overwhelming Polanyi work cited in combination with the tag is the Great Transformation. Granovetter himself makes explicit the derivation of the concept (Granovetter, 1985, p. 482), only to immediately distance himself from that school of thought (*ibid.*). The other Polanyi works that show how Polanyi himself developed the concept are relatively lowly cited.

But there is another ironic twist in the history of the Polanyian concept of 'embeddedness'. Perhaps in reaction to the Granovetterian appropriation of the term, Polanyi followers then went to work developing the concept into something very much more important than appears in Polanyi's own work. Notably Lie (1991, 1992) attempted to recuperate the term, suggesting that its originator failed to take it to its 'logical conclusion'. He thus argues against any notion of dis-embedded economic institutions, especially markets, on the grounds that this simply gave ground to neoclassical economists, assuming that analytical or real dis-embedding granted markets or economies an 'asocial' and 'noncontextual' status (Lie, 1991, p. 223) . Similarly Block (2003) pursues the theme of the 'always embedded market economy', and, dismissing the concept of 'disembeddedness' as an internal contradiction within Polanyian conceptual framework, suggests that institutions and above all the state are always at the foundation of any market economic process. He suggests that Polanyi left the concept 'unachieved' and theoretically underdeveloped, because he was unable to sufficiently break from Marxist influences that presupposed the economy as a separate sphere with its own inherent logic, ultimately determining all aspects of social and political life. Block thus develops embeddedness as a concept within a different political economy, viewing the economy as continuously shaped by political agency, thus eventually opening the possibility of a democratisation of capitalism.[8]

More widely, other perspectives have drawn upon and expanded the Polanyian notion of embeddedness, insisting that its real significance lies in a critical institutional analysis of markets. Hollingsworth and Boyer (1997) embrace this much broader concept of embeddedness to equate to generalised processes of institutionalisation of the economy, and in particular explore the kinds of regularities and forms that are necessary for any 'really existing markets'. Commodities require institutionalised norms defining quality, a set of rules of the game for any routinised trading, monetary systems, and policing arrangements. These in turn depend on a broader institutional framework, such as those that underpin any monetarisation of exchanges, and enforcement of contract (Boyer, 1997). So, laws of contract and property rights are necessary. Within a broader regulationist perspective, there are different modes of governance, different relations between state and market at different historical periods. Jessop (2001, pp. 223–6) argues for the concept of embeddedness to be differentiated and enlarged to account for different 'levels' of societal articulation, from networks, to inter-organisational articulations, to 'societal' embeddedness of economic institutions with institutional frames of the state, law, culture. He also emphasises that any historical economic embedding involves a 'spatio-temporal fix', an institutionalisation of spatial scale and temporality, a point developed further by Peck (2005), evoking macro-social embedding of scales.

Fictitious commodities, self-regulating markets and the double movement

After tracing the amplifications and attenuations of the Polanyian idea of 'embeddedness/disembeddedness', it is worthwhile turning to some core concepts that have had less controversial if also less renowned careers. There is a triad of interconnected concepts that appear in *The Great Transformation*, and arguably these ideas were much more central to Polanyi's own way of thinking at the time. These are the concept of 'fictitious commodities', 'self-regulated markets', and the 'double movement'. Together, they form the central explanatory force of the argument behind the historical period of a Hundred Year's Peace, and its eventual collapse. A 'new civilisation' emerged in the nineteenth century primarily through the progressive marketisation of land and labour. Increasingly these became absorbed into price-making markets that determined their economic and human fate. But for Polanyi, land and labour are 'fictitious commodities'. That is to say, if we follow his argument, they are naturally given, not produced by human labour. Polanyi adds a third fictitious commodity of money, clearly a different category, because self-evidently not only a human artefact, but a quite specifically economic one. There is an elision that occurs in the argument from 'not produced'[9] to 'not produced for sale'[10] (one passed over by subsequent appropriators of the concept of 'fictitious commodities') (e.g. Jessop, 2001; Block, 2003; Boyer, 1998). Money enters the category of a fictitious commodity in that it is not produced for sale, but, in market societies, for the purposes of operating as a medium of exchange. If it becomes an object of sale, a commodity like any other, it destabilises all exchanges, loses its proper economic function, and creates disastrous and destructive economic turbulence. The case of land and labour is again different: unrestrained commoditisation of these fictitious commodities leads to natural rather than economic destruction: pollution and environmental degradation; stunted human lives and death. The early period of industrialisation was the historical proof: factory lives, uncontrolled use of child labour, unlimited working hours and life-threatening working conditions laid waste to human life, and early industrialisation resulted in urban pollution spilling over even into middle-class areas.

The growth of the factory system above all drove a dynamic expansion of the market system to include the three fictitious commodities, and especially labour. Given that Polanyi has already identified labour with life itself, and the existence of humans in society, marketisation of labour resulted in 'a change in the organisation of society. All along the line, human society had become an accessory of the economic system' (*The Great Transformation*, Polanyi, 1944, p. 75). This subordination of humanity to a self-regulatory market system (part of the embeddedness/disembeddedness argument), was however also accompanied by a conceptual shift, with a new generation of political economists and politicians advocating an ideology of self-regulating markets, as a quasi-natural phenomenon. Polanyi identified Malthus and Ricardo as the first of a long line of ideologues, continuing to this day.[11]

Polanyi branded this ideology utopian,[12] because ultimately it was either impossible or too destructive to subjugate the three fictitious commodities to self-regulating laws of the price-making market system. So, to counter the dynamism of the ever-expanding self-regulating market, society, in particular the state, steps in to mitigate its worst effects, and limit its scope. Monetary stability, especially the Gold Standard, became a framework for international trade with supra-national institutionalised norms, or, as Silver and Arrighi (2003) have argued, as an expression of British economic hegemony. Laws to protect child labour, control factory safety, eventually limit working hours, and so on, emerged to counter the effects of the self-regulation that was most notably promoted by the 1834 New Poor Law. These countermeasures, however, were in constant tension with the dynamism of the self-regulated market, which, when combined with ideological and political advocates, resisted and might even push back state regulation. The resulting toing-and-froing constituted the double movement characteristic of market society development.[13] Self-regulation was impaired by regulation (Block, 2005; *The Great Transformation*, Polanyi, 1944, pp. 201–8). As already hinted, this triad of concepts (fictitious commodities, self-regulating markets, double movement), exemplify Polanyi's most historical and dynamic account of the 'shifting place of economy in society', especially if one interprets the double movement as a process of de- and re-regulation, ultimately reflecting a shifting relationship of polity and economy. It resonates with recent times of aggressive de-regulation followed by phases of more regulated capitalism. What is most conspicuously missing – except for a merest hint in a lecture given in Budapest in 1963 by Polanyi shortly before his death – is a realisation of the post-war growth of welfare states, and, more than that of elements of a non-market economic dynamic of capitalism.

> Now, it would be capitalism seeing itself constrained to introduce elements of planning into its over-marketised realm, now, again, socialism would be considering enhancing its achievements in economic planning by the introduction of certain market elements. (cited in Ilona Polanyi, 'Notes on His Life', in Polanyi, 1977, p. xix)

But apart from a very few traces, most of Polanyi's published writings after *The Great Transformation* left the conceptual frame of the dynamics of the double movement undeveloped. The role of the contemporary state remains as it was in *The Great Transformation*, primarily one of regulation and protection of the three fictitious commodities against uncontrolled market forces. Fictitious commodities disappear from the later works, as a consequence, one may speculate, of his extensive study of slavery, a trade *par excellence* in humans as commodities without consideration for the preservation of life.[14] The concept of the self-regulated market remains firmly located in his established reference point of nineteenth-century England.

The economy as instituted process

There is certainly a re-foundation of his thinking apparent in *Trade, and Markets in the Early Empires*, even if many themes from before are carried forward, and many new ones clarify and enhance interpretation of the earlier work. The central idea that emerged in this later work, based now firmly on the comparative, historical and anthropological study of tribal, archaic and modern economies, was that of 'the economy as instituted process' (Polanyi, 1957b). This elliptical phrase needs unpacking. Firstly, Polanyi posited that there were in *all* societies two fundamental, and specifically *economic* processes. This too needs unpacking. Process here means motion, a continuous activity over time. So the theory is a process-based theory. There are two processes, changes in location and changes in appropriation, which are distinctively economic, and in combination provide the basis of *all* economic systems. Moreover, for Polanyi, they are the only two.[15] No extended discussion or justification of this delimitation is offered in his work, and this leads to some strange language of even the production process being equated to transportation, described in terms only of changes in location, where 'things move in relation to other things' (Polanyi, 1968, p. 307).

However, these are not universal or abstract processes, but only real processes insofar as they are historically and societally instituted. In some societies they are instituted in such a way as to be embedded in other processes and subordinated to other institutional forms. In modern market societies, however, these processes are instituted in separate and differentiated institutions, workplaces, markets and so on. In his later work, the focus has shifted to analysing the instituting of processes according to three different 'modes of integration': reciprocity, redistribution and exchange.[16] Different types of society are integrated through the instituting of processes of distribution and appropriation of goods according to these modes of integration. Tribal societies typify societies that are integrated through processes of reciprocation between subgroups. But for reciprocation to be an effectively integrating economic process, these societies must be organised into symmetrical groupings, each complementary to each other. Archaic societies are characterised by monarchical or central state modes of redistributing goods, especially between different status groups. Markets and exchanges certainly exist in archaic societies, but prices are fixed by rule. But equally, modern welfare states could be interpreted in the same light as centrally redistributive, with taxation and social insurance the contemporary (very different) counterparts of monarchical taxes on all market transactions in Dahomey. Polanyi's argument is that these redistributive processes are constitutive of a state-centred integrative process for societies. In archaic societies economic integration is subordinated to state integration.

Finally, markets exemplify processes of distribution and appropriation governed by exchange, forming their own 'self-regulating' societal integration between scattered buyers and sellers of goods. Price-fluctuation and the 'law of supply and demand' only emerge in historical conditions where the exchange process governs price in a price-making market. But these markets too need to be seen as 'instituted processes' with organised rules of the market, the 'supply crowd' and the 'demand crowd', embracing how and in what terms prices are set, in what exchange medium, under what competitive conditions, in short, in a whole complex and variable set of instituting processes of distribution and appropriation. In this perspective, even the most extreme example of a 'self-regulating' market is an outcome of the societal and historical instituting of the processes of distribution and appropriation. Price-making markets are modes of societal integration requiring stability and order, so that they 'run on ruts', with institutional conditions of shared conceptual frames, motives, understandings of what constitutes pertinent information, as well as the more conspicuously 'institutional' character of formal market rules.[17] It has to be said, however, that almost the whole corpus of empirical examples provided for economies as instituted process are the rich and varied accounts of primitive and especially archaic economies (Polanyi, 1957b, 1977). Here a fascinating array of hybrid and transitional forms, in Ancient Athens, Mycaenae, Dahomey, Alalakh, among many others, provide a fertile source for understanding institutional variation. No such attention was paid to exploring the variety of the market modes of integration, and we are primarily left with that provided by *The Great Transformation*, unanalysed by his subsequent conceptual development. There is a poverty of thinking about the variety of instituted markets, that might have qualified or developed further concepts of regulation and self-regulation (Jessop, 2001), as well as different modes of institutionalising exchange and distribution (Harvey and Randles, 2002).

However, with this new comparative framework, it is clear that economic processes are always societally and historically instituted whether they are extremely 'embedded' or extremely 'disembedded'. Polanyi's emphasis and interest in the institution of money is paradigmatic of this approach: he argues against any concept of money that accords it an intrinsically and universally 'catallactic' property, generating exchanges by virtue of its role in exchange. This projects the modern institution of money into societies where money (units of gold, cowrie shells, etc.) has quite different functions, such as constituting a hoard or treasure, acting merely as a standard to facilitate bartering of goods, or as a unit of state accounting and taxation. Archaic money is contrasted with price-making market money as different societal modes of integration, the one redistributive and status-confirming, the other indeed 'catallactic', coordinating buyers and sellers. Yet in both cases, money is *par excellence* an economic institution, even though, in archaic societies it is embedded in, or undifferentiated from, other societal processes involved in the creation of social status and monarchical order.

This re-founding of Polanyian thought on the idea of the economy as instituted process, and the shifting place of economy in society, throws some back-light on to his earlier writings. In particular, it consolidates the central role of distribution and exchange in analysing the economy, and hence in understanding the role of the economy in society. Societies were economically distinguished by their modes of integration through distribution and property-exchange, their circulating principle. Markets made capitalism, rather than capitalism made markets – and, as Block (2003) has observed, Polanyi seemed to prefer the term 'market society' over 'capitalism'. The dynamics of the *Great Transformation* were thus given in retrospect a new force, by virtue of a double movement centred on the regulation and self-regulation of markets. In this way, having excluded any other possible candidate economic processes, dynamics relating to distribution and exchange are given exclusive privilege.

Although the re-foundation of Polanyian concepts in the later work leaves open many alternative interpretations, and indeed, adds a further layer of conceptual puzzles or new openings for future development, it is clear that for Polanyi at least, neither the critique nor the analysis of self-regulated markets of *The Great Transformation* later led to his abandoning the concept of the specifically economic. Embedded does not mean social *as against* economic. Economic processes do not become less economic when they are embedded, or more economic when disembedded. So also, 'disembedded' does not reduce to 'self-regulated'. Even less does 'market-economic' equate to 'asocial economic'. In the light of later works, it is therefore implausible to have an interpretation of the 'double movement' as a toing-and-froing between embeddedness and dis-embeddedness. The double movement makes more sense, in this retrospective re-fashioning, as a dialectic of regulation and de-regulation within a historical process resulting in differentiated modes of economic governance as a particular domain within contemporary governance structures. The idea of de-differentiating economic processes, and re-embedding them into archaic or primitive norms of redistribution and reciprocity, linked to religious or status-maintaining orders, would be quite alien. Historically, it is difficult to conceive of a return to embeddedness (although see Chapter 6 below), let alone the creation of a new form of embeddedness, understood as re-integration or de-differentiation of instituted economic processes – unless, contra-Polanyi, one wishes to conceptually abandon all talk of 'economy'. Both the concept and the historical reality of modernity is one of relative differentiation of the economy *within* society. Thus also, the redistribution of modern welfare states is a (relatively) *dis-embedded* and economic-management form of redistribution, complementing the distributive effects of historically instituted (but relatively dis-embedded) market processes. It contrasts with the embedded redistribution of archaic societies, and has more to do with concepts of economic, rather than religious or monarchical, justice. So, the later works enable us to disentangle some previously conflated concepts, and give us new ways of thinking about 'the shifting place of the economy in society'. Whether or not one wishes to adopt Polanyi's two processes, he at least has said what he specifically means by the term 'economic' when using it, and implicitly asks us to do the same.

New disciplinarities

From this brief overview of some of Polanyi's key concepts, it is clear that his approach presented a challenge to a disciplinary autonomy, or any neat carving up of the world into ontologies that sustain disciplinary separation. How else could one study the shifting place of economy in society other than in a transdisciplinary and comparative way? The preceding discussion of his understanding of the economy presents as much of a challenge as a stimulus to the new economic sociology, in that it affirms the specificity of the economic, and hence a need to study the institution of economic processes, as it does to mainstream disciplines of economics and sociology. In that respect, it accords with Weber's concept of economic sociology, and especially the need for an economic sociology to analyse the central economic activities of any society as such, as well as their social, political, cultural contexts (Swedberg, 1998). Moreover, his combination of historical, anthropological and comparative methodologies has been exemplary of collaboration and cross-leveraging between disciplines.

Polanyi's major contribution to the revival of economic sociology has been well recognised (Smelser and Swedberg, 1994; Swedberg, 1994; Granovetter and Swedberg, 1992), and it is clear from the above discussion that this influence has overflowed into developments in political economy and economic geography. His influence persists across these different historical conceptual trajectories no doubt partly because of the persistence of the problematic he opened up, left open, even ambiguous, and for that very reason stimulating to further working and re-working, to the generation of new empirics as well as new theoretical developments. The present volume reflects this conceptual polysemy, in which different aspects are drawn on and developed.

The book

The chapters in this volume have been developed from papers given at an international workshop that took place in Manchester toward the end of

2002, organised by the Centre for Research on Innovation and Competition (CRIC).[18] According to the guest of honour at the workshop, Emeritus Professor Kari Polanyi-Levitt (McGill University), the daughter of Karl Polanyi, this was the first event of its kind in the UK to consider the relevance and importance of his work in the country where Polanyi had been domiciled for several years after emigrating from Hungary in the pre-World War II period.

It is divided into two parts. The first, entitled 'Working within the legacy of Polanyi', develops some of the key ideas and draws upon the legacy of Karl Polanyi. It explores major questions concerning the institutionalisation of the economy in society, and the role of markets. Moreover, the authors raise some of the key political and moral themes that arise from the legacy, issues of the democratisation of the economy, of the moral import of market ethics as a historical phenomenon, and the need for a developed theory of the relation between law and the economy. The second sets out from the more neglected aspect of his work, the instituting of economic processes. Here there is a range of empirical and theoretical development around this conceptual node, that explicitly *goes beyond* this Polanyian point of origin, and in directions not foreshadowed by Polanyi himself. Thus the book provides no single overall coherent Polanyian standpoint, but offers different avenues of development, more or less distant from their common source of origin. It would be mistaken to seek synthesis, particularly as the editors would ill conceal their partisan intentions. In that respect, this book stands as a further example of the vicissitudes of conceptual development, already noted in the discussion of the peculiar history of the concept of embeddedness. *In this respect*, contrary developments of ideas are generated within the complex historical shifting around of the place of the economy in society, in ways that Polanyi himself highlighted.

Part I: working within the legacy of Polanyi

Part I, working within the legacy of Polanyi, develops a number of major themes: a discussion of institutionalisation of the economy within a holistic societal approach; the politics that can be drawn from Polanyi's critique of the self-regulating market within the contemporary context; the transformation of moral categories embedded in social practices; and an explicit concept of legal regulation as a distinct and separate level of analysis of institutionalisation of the economic.

Cangiani (Chapter 2) and Harriss (Chapter 3) both discuss the relationship between the Polanyian ideas of institutionalisation and those of 'new institutional economics' and contemporary economic sociology. Cangiani emphasises the similarity between Polanyi and the classic institutionalists, such as Veblen and Weber, where a holistic and societal view enables markets to be situated in the wider context, as a particular historical manifestation rather than a universal context. This provides him with a powerful critical tool both to critique approaches that take market society for granted, and an empirical analytical tool for interpreting the diverse societal conditions of market functioning, taking Italian industrial districts as an exemplary case. Harriss complements Cangiani, and gives the critique of neo-institutionalists and classical economists a particular twist with his focus on the limitations of their conception of institutions of property rights in developing countries. He also adds a strong historical dimension, by assessing these accounts, and contrasting them with a Polanyian perspective, in relation to historical institutional change. The strength of the classical institutionalist perspective is that it enables a holistic account of power, politics and social structure and its impact on institutional economic forms.

Geoffrey Hodgson (Chapter 4), coming from an evolutionary and institutional economic perspective, critically examines the limitations of a Polanyian perspective – limitations, he argues, shared by many – that treat the legal frameworks that underpin and are necessary for economic functioning as their epiphenomenon. He insists – as for example Deakin and Wilkinson have done – that legal institutional development requires analysis in its own right, even when that development occurs in a co-evolutionary way to economic institutional change. Although the chapter does not do so, this argument can be brought to bear on the debate over embeddedness and disembeddedness, in that he affirms the need to consider both legal and economic institutions (such as firms and markets) as distinct if interacting institutional domains, with their own distinctive dynamisms. His chapter reinforces the views developed by Cangiani and Harriss by arguing that this institutional approach draws on the much richer classical tradition of which Polanyi provides one important variant.

The next two chapters pick up the political theme already signaled by Harriss, but now with advocacy combined with analysis. These are two contributions that most overtly carry the Polanyian political torch forward to contemporary circumstances. Mendell (Chapter 5) traces Polanyi's interest in economic democracy and his attempts to develop a model of functional democracy (functional socialism) which was influenced to a great extent by the guild socialism of G. D. H. Cole, the writings of Robert Owen, but especially by the experience in 'Red Vienna' in the 1920s. Today, we might refer to Polanyi's writings in this period as part of the contemporary interest in *associational democracy* or *democratic associationalism*. This chapter attempts to place these emergent alternative forms of socio-economic organisation within a larger context of institutional transformation occurring within contemporary society and the rearrangement of state–society relations in new organisational forms that result from this transformation. By linking the analysis of institutional transformation of contemporary theorists such as J. Rogers Hollingsworth to the question of *agency*, that is, to the role of actors in constructing institutional settings, the impact of civil society organisations on institutional innovation and transformation is explored as it manifests in contemporary society.

Adaman, Devine and Ozkaynak (Chapter 6) develop this same perspective to give Polanyian politics a contemporary reference, and argue that participatory planning is an essential device for attaining the Polanyian objective of re-embedding economy in society. They develop their case from an argument that the central critical Polanyian ideas of the double movement and fictitious commodities, implies a political objective of re-embedding. In particular, they expand on the seminal idea of an environmentalist politics contained in *The Great Transformation*. Taking the environment, and the economy of nature as their focal point, free markets are compared with various forms of intervention, state regulation up to and including socialist solutions. The authors contend that participatory planning is superior to the self-regulating market and to market socialism. Participatory planning is essentially a process of negotiated co-ordination involving the social owners at the relevant level. A degree of self-organisation is envisaged to result in the formation of the necessary voluntary associations as well as politically authorised representative assemblies. One desired outcome is that wages, rents and profits are determined by social processes of negotiation, negating the status of resources, labour and capital as fictitious commodities.

The final chapter (Chapter 7) of this first part develops the moral dimension to Polanyian thought, which, as Sayer (2005) has observed, is implicit in much of the analysis of *The Great Transformation*: it is in the tradition, heralded by Adam Smith's *The Theory of Moral Sentiments* of a moral political economy, where moral norms are immanent in, and condition, economic relations and practices, even in the most marketised economies. Peter McMylor develops this moral theme through exploring the influences and connections between the work of Polanyi and that of the moral philosopher MacIntyre. He argues that MacIntyre's account of moral change and Polanyi's account of the social context of economic change provide conceptual and empirical substance about the nature of historical and social processes. MacIntyre indeed acknowledged that his thought was partly shaped by his admiration of the Polanyian method. The concepts of embeddedness and disembeddedness played a major role in MacIntyre's understanding of the transformation of moral categories displayed in social practices. McMylor argues that Polanyi's commitment to social justice was deeply influenced by his Christian upbringing and his association with an intellectual elite driven by the desire to bring about social and moral transformation of Hungary. Along with the workers movement, Polanyi is perceived to have seen Christianity as the locus of moral respect for the individual noting that it would provide the moral drive for transcending the Western society.

Part II: new directions
The second part of the book takes off from the later Polanyi of 'instituting the economy in society', but addresses its main attention to developments

within contemporary capitalism, so providing more differentiated analyses of markets whilst at the same time expanding the scope of the framework beyond identifying capitalism in terms of market society. In this respect, recognising the limits of the Polanyian legacy, the contributions in this part take Polanyian concepts into new directions. Processes of production and consumption are added to those of appropriation and distribution. Market and non-market forms of economic organisation are seen as integral to a multi-modal concept of contemporary capitalism. In greatly varying ways, the state, in addition to regulating economic activity, is seen as centrally engaging in economic activity. The themes of regulation, what is meant by instituting of economic processes, the role of the state and social forces, new market formation, and the transformation of economic processes, are explored to varying degrees in the different contributions.

To set the scene, Sally Randles (Chapter 8) picks up and develops further the points made in this introduction, by interpreting the Polanyian legacy. She combines a historical analysis of its emergence, vicissitudes, and recovery with a critical analysis of the core conceptual framework. Locating Polanyi's own writings in time and shifting place – Vienna, London, the USA from pre- to post-World War II, she emphasises how the political context and motivations are interwoven with the anthropological method in the study of pre-modern societies. Having situated the legacy, Randles then takes some of the central conceptual ideas (the self-regulated market, the causality behind regulation, embeddedness, institutionalisation, and transformation) and subjects them to a discriminating critical analysis, for their strengths, limitations and contradictions. This enables her to open out the potential for an empirical and theoretical programme of a Polanyi-inspired research that characterises the remaining contributions.

The chapter by Harvey (Chapter 9) lays the theoretical ground for an 'instituted economic process' (IEP) analysis of contemporary capitalisms. In doing so he distances this approach from the 'embeddedness' problematic, arguing for the need to retain and develop a concept of the specifically economic, within a societal perspective. Developing further a 'process' analytical basis, he argues for four fundamental processes that only in combination define 'economies', transformational processes of quality, space and time, appropriation, and use. Along with the instituting of specifically economic processes, he argues that specific economic causalities are also historically instituted, delimiting the scope of any explanatory framework. In this respect, an IEP approach radicalises further the idea present in Marx of causalities distinctive to the capitalist modes of production. This theoretical framework, first developed in the historical and comparative work *Exploring the Tomato: Transformations of Economy, Society and Nature* (Harvey et al., 2002), is grounded in a broad range of empirical research including work on biotechnology, medical services and technological innovation, and contemporary welfare states.

Nathalie Moncel (Chapter 10) develops the IEP approach in a comparative analysis of French and UK labour markets – tackling the core Polanyian issue of the marketisation of labour in capitalism. In ways distant from any essentialist notion of labour as a fictitious commodity, she analyses the distinctiveness of labour as an object of exchange, by contrasting societally different labour markets. These are shown to entail deep historical differences in the exchange itself, in how labour supply and labour demand is instituted, and most importantly how the social parties to the exchange, both employers and employees, are differently organised. She demonstrates how both the quality and price of labour and their articulation are markedly contrasted in different market institutions. Last, but by no means least, the different role of the state, the role of law and of regulation, involve different articulations between economic and political processes in society.

Miriam Glucksmann (Chapter 11), developing her own theoretical framework of the 'total social organisation of labour' (Glucksmann, 1995), uses a case study of the contemporary development of call centres to explore the two original Polanyian economic processes of appropriation and distribution. Call centres vary in their economic activities in their connection between production and consumption, whether they are engaged in selling financial services, innovating in the delivery of public services, and acting as various forms of intermediation between producers, distributors, and end consumers. She argues that the emergence of call centres as a new form of economic organisation above all demonstrates that processes of distribution and exchange are both transformed and articulated in relation to each other in different ways. Moreover, in so doing, new markets for distribution and transaction services emerge. So the process of market development involves a dynamic concept of transformation and institution, distant from any essentialist or universalist ideas of economic process.

Connected only contingently by telephone, in his chapter Andrea Mina (Chapter 12) develops the IEP approach in an empirical investigation of the European market for mobile telephony that emerged through the interplay of innovation, regulation and competition. The formation of a market at a new geographic scale involved the interaction between market and non-market processes, notably for standardisation, where different economic agents and governments were engaged in long and complex interaction. Competition and innovation are both analysed as emergent instituted properties linking equipment production with the creation of an infrastructure for market exchange and the shaping of demand for transnational interoperability. Moreover, Mina stresses that alternative technologies and processes of market formation contested for market growth and expansion at the global scale, where the units of competition are systems of production and exchange that comprise both market and non-market aspects. This analysis, by going beyond dualisms of market and regulation, demonstrates the potential for new Polanyi-inspired approaches.

The final development of new Polanyian perspectives on contemporary capitalism is provided by Randles and Ramlogan (Chapter 13), taking a 'mega-merger' of a giant pharmaceutical company as their case study. As with the previous chapter, there is a particular focus on the dynamic relation between market formation and regulation. On a theoretical basis they extend and bring new insights into the interdependence *between* markets (capital, pharmaceutical, corporate control) in contemporary capitalism as exemplary of 'instituted process'. They develop the concept of the 'double movement' in new directions, insisting on its dialectical character (already intimated in the Polanyi archive), by exploring new forms of state regulation but also regulation by private market institutions and actors.

A concluding note

Taken as a whole, this volume illustrates some of the complexities of conceptual trajectories, demonstrating how from the same fertile stock of seminal ideas, quite different growths proliferate in different conceptual and institutional ecologies – and indeed changing historical circumstances. The various authors have come to Polanyi with different conceptual baggages, from different directions, and from different disciplinary formations. Yet, in all these contributions there has been at some point a decisive encounter with elements of the Polanyian legacy. We have seen how the concepts of embeddedness and disembeddedness became the ideas most identified with him many years after the author's death. This volume bears witness to the continued struggle and contestation that these ideas have unwittingly triggered. Other strands of the Polanyian legacy, firmly buried for some fifty years, suddenly bear fruit, notably the concept of specifically economic processes, and their societal and historical institution. It was the absence of closure, the presence of so many questions left hanging, and indeed of ambiguities and inconsistencies, combined with a rare historical and comparative anthropological sweep, that has stimulated all the authors of this volume, in their own ways, to pursue the fundamentally significant Polanyian problem of the shifting place of economy in society.

Notes

1 From today's perspective, this appears quite a Euro-centric perception, especially in terms of aggressive European expansionism and colonialisation of the 'new imperialism' that preceded World War I.
2 Until writing *The Great Transformation* in his late fifties, he had been primarily a journalist, editing the Austrian equivalent to *The Economist*, and then a teacher in England for the Workers Education Association.

3 Polanyi himself supports this interpretation when, in 'Aristotle Discovers the Economy' (1957), he accounts for the emergence of the concept of the distinctively 'economic': 'The prime reason for the absence of any concept of the economy is the difficulty of identifying the economic process under conditions where it is embedded in non-economic institutions. Only the concept of the economy, not the economy itself, is in abeyance, of course' (Polanyi, 1957, p. 71).
4 Indeed, the most frequently used text to support the concept actually shies away from it, by arguing for a reverse embedding of social relations in economic institutions: 'Instead of economy being embedded in social relations, social relations are embedded in the economic system... For once the economic system is organised in separate institutions, based on specific motives and conferring special status, society must be shaped in such a manner as to allow that system to function according to its own laws... A market economy can function only in a market society' (*The Great Transformation*, Polanyi, 1944, p. 57). Where it does appear, in 'Aristotle Discovers the Economy' (Polanyi, 1957a), however, it is very clear: 'The conceptual tool with which to tackle this transition from namelessness to a separate existence... is the distinction between the embedded and the disembedded condition of the economy in relation to society. The disembedded economy of the nineteenth century stood apart from the rest of society, more especially from the political and governmental system. In a market economy the production and distribution of material goods in principle is carried on through a self-regulating system of price-making markets.' (*ibid.*, p. 68). 'This, then, is the nineteenth-century version of an independent economic sphere in society. It is motivationally distinct, for it receives its impulse from the urge of monetary gain. It is institutionally separate from the political and governmental centre. It attains an autonomy that invests it with laws of its own. In it we possess that extreme case of a disembedded economy which takes its start from the widespread use of money as a means of exchange' (*ibid.*, p. 68).
5 The posthumous (1977) *The Livelihood of Man* has a sub-section entitled 'The Economy Embedded in Society', when dealing with the transition between tribal and archaic societies.
6 This usage of the term 'embedded' appears much more generic, referring to the stabilisation, or sedimentation, of activities or processes into recognisable institutions, be they social, cultural, political *or* economic.
7 'Society was now imbedded in the economic system, rather than vice versa... The place of the economic system in society was now defined by the "economic motives" of hunger and gain... Society was ruled by the laws governing the market, and these, in their turn, were determined by Nature herself. This theoretical shift in the place of the economic system in society was, of course, accompanied by a great development of actual markets, which did not yet exist to a similar extent in Adam Smith's time.' Appendix to the 'Place of the Economy in Society' (Polanyi, 1968, pp. 131–2).
8 'The concept of the always embedded economy suggests that there are no inherent obstacles to restructuring market societies along more democratic and egalitarian lines' (Block, 2003, p. 300).
9 'Labour and land are no other than the human beings themselves of which every society consists and the natural surroundings in which it exists. To

include them in the market mechanism means to subordinate the substance of society itself to the laws of the market' (*The Great Transformation*, Polanyi, 1944, p. 71). Labour 'is only another name for human activity which goes with life itself' (*ibid.*, p. 72).

10 'None of them is produced for sale' (*ibid.*, p. 72). 'As the development of the factory system had been organised as part of a process of buying and selling, therefore labour, land and money had to be transformed into commodities in order to keep production going. They could, of course, not be really transformed into commodities, as actually they were not produced for sale on the market. But the fiction of their being so produced became the organising principle of society' (*ibid.*, p. 73).

11 'The origins of the cataclysm lay in the utopian endeavour of economic liberalism to set up a self-regulating market system. Such a thesis seems to invest that system with almost mythical powers; it implies no less than that the balance of power, the gold standard, and the liberal state . . .' (*ibid.*, 29–30). See also note 6 above, the citation coming from unpublished memoranda circulated to students at the University of Columbia in 1947, and so closely following the writing of *The Great Transformation*.

12 'The concept of a self-regulating market was utopian, and its progress was stopped by the realistic self-protection of society' (*ibid.*, p. 141).

13 'Social history in the nineteenth century was thus the result of a double movement: the extension of the market organisation in respect to genuine commodities was accompanied by its restriction in respect to fictitious ones . . . A network of measures and policies was integrated into powerful institutions designed to check the action of the market relative to labour, land, and money' (*ibid.*, p. 76).

14 Indeed, it is striking that when the term 'fictitious money' is used in a chapter on 'Dahomey and the Slave Trade'; it is stripped of its earlier theoretical meaning. Here it is used in the conventional sense of an artificial rate of exchange between the 'modern' money of Europe and the 'archaic' money of Dahomey. A unit of account was established in the 'ounce trade' at half the established Dahomeyian rate of exchange between gold and cowries, that effectively gave European slavers a huge advantage when purchasing slaves. But it became an established rate of exchange, and there was no question of money itself being traded as a commodity in money markets, or of money as a fictitious *commodity*, in earlier Polanyian terms.

15 'The movements refer to changes in location, or in appropriation, or both . . . Material elements may alter their position either by changing place or by changing 'hands' . . . Between them, these two kinds of movements may be said to *exhaust the possibilities* [our emphasis] comprised in economic process as a natural and social phenomenon' (Polanyi, 1957b, p. 248).

16 Swedberg (2003) emphasises the significance of this economic sociological concept of the societally integrative aspect of economic processes.

17 'The instituting of the economic process vests that process with unity and stability; it produces a structure with a definite function in society; it shifts the place of the process in society, thus adding significance to its history; it centres interest on values, motives and policy' (*ibid.*, 1957, pp. 249–50).

18 Earlier versions of several of the papers in this volume have been previously published in the *International Review of Sociology*, 2003, 13(2).

References

Barber, B. (1995), 'All Economies Are "Embedded": The Career of a Concept and Beyond', *Social Research*, 62(2), pp. 387–413.
Block, F. (2003), 'Karl Polanyi and the Writing of the Great Transformation', *Theory and Society*, 32, pp. 275–306.
Block, F. and Somers, M. (2003), 'In the Shadow of Speenhamland: Social Policy and the Old Poor Law', *Politics and Society*, 31(2), pp. 283–323.
Boyer, R. (1997), 'The Variety and Unequal Performance of Really Existing Markets: Farewell to Doctor Pangloss', in J. R. Hollingsworth and R. Boyer (eds), *Contemporary Capitalism: The Embeddedness of Institutions*, Cambridge, Cambridge University Press, pp. 55–93.
Dalton, G. (ed.) (1968), *Primitive, Archaic and Modern Economies: Essays of Karl Polanyi*, New York, Anchor Books, Doubleday.
Deakin, S. and Wilkinson, F. (2005), *The Law of the Labour Market: Industrialisation, Employment and Legal Evolution*, Oxford, Oxford University Press.
Glucksmann, M. (1995), 'Why "Work"? Gender and the "Total Social Organisation of Labour" ', *Gender, Work and Organisation*, 2(2), pp. 63–75.
Granovetter, M. (1985), 'Economic Action and Social Structure: The Problem of Embeddedness', *American Journal of Sociology*, 91(3), pp. 481–510.
Granovetter, M. and Swedberg, R. (2001), *The Sociology of Economic Life*, Boulder, Westview Press.
Harvey, M. and Metcalfe, S. (2005), 'The Ordering of Change: Polanyi, Schumpeter and the Nature of the Market Mechanism', *Journal des Economistes et Etudes Humaines*, 14(4), pp. 87–114.
Harvey, M. and Randles, S. (2002), 'Market Exchanges and "Instituted Economic Process": An Analytical Perspective', *Revue d'Economie Industrielle*, 101, pp. 11–30.
Harvey, M., Quilley, S. and Beynon, H. (2002), *Exploring the Tomato: Transformations in Nature, Economy and Society*, Cheltenham, Edward Elgar.
Hollingsworth, J. R. and Boyer, R. (eds) (1997), *Contemporary Capitalism: The Embeddedness of Institutions*, Cambridge, Cambridge University Press.
Hopkins, T. K. (1957), 'Sociology and the Substantive View of the Economy', in K. Polanyi, C. M. Arensberg and H. W. Pearson (eds), *Trade and Market in the Early Empires*, New York, Free Press.
Jessop, B. (2001), 'Regulationist and Autopoieticist Reflections on Polanyi's Account of Market Economies and Market Society', *New Political Economy*, 6(2), pp. 213–32.
Krippner, G. (2001), 'The Elusive Market: Embeddedness and the Paradigm of Economic Sociology', *Theory and Society*, 30, pp. 775–810.
Lie, J. (1991), 'Embedding Polanyi's Market Society', *Sociological Perspectives*, 34(2), pp. 219–35.
Lie, J. (1992), 'The Concept of Mode of Exchange', *American Sociological Review*, 57(2), pp. 508–23.
McRobbie, A. and Polanyi-Levitt, K. (eds) (2006), *Karl Polanyi in Vienna: The Contemporary Significance of the Great Transformation*, 2nd edn, Montreal, Black Rose Books.
Peck, J. (2005), 'Economic Sociologies of Space', *Economic Geography*, 81(2), pp. 129–75.

Polanyi, K. (1944), *The Great Transformation*, Boston, Beacon Press.
Polanyi, K. (1957a), 'Aristotle Discovers the Economy', in K. Polanyi, C. M. Arensberg and H. W. Pearson (eds), *Trade and Market in the Early Empires*, New York, Free Press.
Polanyi, K. (1957b), 'The Economy as Instituted Process', in K. Polanyi, C. M. Arensberg and H. W. Pearson (eds), *Trade and Market in the Early Empires*, New York, Free Press.
Polanyi, K. (1966), *Dahomey and the Slave Trade: An Analysis of an Archaic Economy*, American Ethnological Society Monograph, 42, University of Washington Press.
Polanyi, K. (1977), *The Livelihood of Man*, ed. Harry W. Peason, New York, Academic Press.
Polanyi, K. and Dalton, G. (eds) (1968), *Primitive, Archaic and Modern Economies: Essays of Karl Polanyi*, New York, Anchor Books, Doubleday.
Polanyi, K., Arensberg, C. M. and Pearson, H. W. (eds) (1957), *Trade and Market in the Early Empires*, New York, Free Press.
Sayer, A. (2005), 'Moral Economy', University of Lancaster Department of Sociology, on-line paper available at www.comp.lancs.ac.uk/sociology/papers/sayer-moral-economy.pdf.
Smelser, N. J. and Swedberg, R. (eds) (1994). 'Introduction' in *The Handbook of Economic Sociology*, Princeton, Princeton University Press.
Swedberg, R. (1994), 'Markets as Social Structures', in N. J. Smelser and R. Swedberg (eds), *The Handbook of Economic Sociology*, Princeton, Princeton University Press.
Swedberg, R. (1998), *Max Weber and the Idea of Economic Sociology*, Princeton, Princeton University Press.
Swedberg, R. (2003), *Principles of Economic Sociology*, Princeton, Princeton University Press.

Part I
Working within the legacy of Polanyi

2
The forgotten institutions

Michele Cangiani

Polanyi's institutional method

Karl Polanyi writes that the forms of economic integration – reciprocity, redistribution and exchange – are to be understood as signifying 'more than simple aggregates of corresponding forms of behaviour on the personal level'; the 'integrative effect' – that is the organisation of the economic system as a whole – is to be attributed to 'the presence of definite institutional arrangements such as symmetrical organisations, central points and market systems, respectively' (Polanyi, 1957, p. 251). Polanyi's institutional analysis does not, then, start from the individuals as basic units, to study how their inborn economic rationality finds its opportunities and its constraints in the institutional context. Polanyi's method, on the contrary, is based on the principle that economic systems as such are the object of the analysis and are to be considered as historical, socially instituted processes, which 'integrate' consistently and durably the individual activities. The economic behaviour of the individuals is in general adapted, and therefore peculiar, to each system.

The main reason for distinguishing among the three 'forms of integration', according to Polanyi, is to understand the historical uniqueness of the market society. The first part of *The Great Transformation* deals with the general features and the historical development of a form of economic system and of society whose radical and irreversible novelty is explained also through the comparison with primitive and pre-modern societies. Modern capitalist society ('market society' in a wider sense) is represented as a specific mode of organisation, of 'integration' of the economy: a peculiar way of integrating individual activities into a system, and of reproducing the system in the time. The market constitutes the 'institutional arrangement' of this kind of society. Polanyi accurately explains this concept. He distinguishes firstly among external, local and internal markets. He deals then with the historical development of the internal market, up to the emergence of a market competition at a national level and, eventually, the achievement of the 'self-regulating market'.

Polanyi's comparative analysis is intended to stress the discontinuities in the 'evolution of the market pattern'. 'The market', as an institution that organises the economic life, appears as a radical novelty, as a mutation: 'this structure represented a violent break with the conditions that preceded it' (Polanyi, 1977, p. 10). Previously the trades and the (local) markets were regulated and controlled by other social institutions; they never included unconditionally land and labour, and were 'considered as incidental since they did not provide to the necessaries of life' (Polanyi, 1957, pp. 60–1). The market system not only represented a 'complete reversal' of that trend (Polanyi, 1957, p. 68), but showed a 'staggering capacity for organising human beings ... together with the surface of mother earth, which could now be freely marketed, into industrial units under the command of private persons mainly engaged in buying and selling for profit' (Polanyi, 1977, p. 9).

Moreover, this *'market economy'* – whose congenital capitalistic relations of productions are clearly mentioned in the just quoted sentence – 'gave rise to yet another, even more extreme development, namely a whole society embedded in the mechanism of its own economy – *a market society'* (*ibid.*, p. 9). 'While social classes were directly determined, other institutions were indirectly affected by the market mechanism' (*ibid.*, p. 12). 'A whole culture – with all its possibilities and limitations – and the picture of inner man and society induced by life in a market economy necessarily followed from the essential structure of a human community organised through the market' (*ibid.*, p. 10). In particular, the motives and attitudes of the individuals assumed that 'economising' character, which is represented in the myth of Robinson Crusoe and is, in fact, adequate to the modern form of social organisation of the economy.

The result is a typically 'economic' way of organising *and conceiving* the economy, based on the reality of an 'economically' instituted economy. In pre-modern societies, the economic action was, according to Polanyi, 'embedded' within social institutions of diverse sorts; it was, as Marcel Mauss said, a *'fait social total'*, conveying manifold cultural meanings, expressing the whole culture as a symbolic system. The concept of the market as an 'institutional arrangement' connotes a totally different situation. Market exchanges are necessarily aimed to a monetary gain and don't follow rules other than those of the institutional context they presuppose: a generalised system of 'price-fixing markets'. In the market society, then, the economic behaviour stands out as such and the economic system appears to be autonomous, following rules of its own. Here lies the real basis of the ideological generalisations of the economic theory and of its tendency to consider the economic system as a closed system.

The differentiation of diverse aspects and functions of social life – first of all of the economic activity, which led the process of differentiation – is a fundamental aspect of the modern society. With the disruption of traditional totality, the individuals conceive themselves as such and society as problematic: not as a given (natural, i.e. divine) reality to be interpreted, but as a human and historical reality to be analysed and changed. The circularity of determination between individuals and social institutions – that Marx points out in his 'Eleven Theses on Feuerbach', in the third of them in particular – should simply be accepted as such: as the core of modern liberty. The problem is rather that the individuals, on the one hand, carry on the tendency to conform to social norms and to the powers that be, which phylogenetically proved to be a successful survival strategy. On the other hand, as Karl Mannheim observes, individual freedom in a complex industrial society would demand a dramatic increase and diffusion of 'substantive rationality', defined as 'the capacity of acting intelligently in a given situation': but this, besides being difficult in itself, doesn't match with the concentration in a few hands of the means of production and therefore of the knowledge and the power of making choices (Mannheim, 1954, I, Ch. 2).

Polanyi's conception of the exchange as a 'form of integration' and of the market as its supporting 'institutional arrangement' conveys the same meanings, at the same level of abstraction, as the analysis of the 'simple circulation', which Marx set forth in the first chapter of *The Capital*. We find there – not only implicit in the analysis of exchange, value and fetishism, but also explicitly declared – the basic concept of the institutional method, as well as of the 'critique of political economy': the economists worry about the quantitative rates, the relative prices of commodities, but do not perceive the price system as a system of social relations, as a social structure. Marx observes that the determination of the value by abstract labour is typical of 'a social epoch'; moreover, the 'unfolded form' of the value – that is, the general exchangeability of commodities, which in Polanyian terms is the expression of the 'price-fixing market' – considered as such, reveals itself to be a social structure. This structure is a historically specific way of institutionalising the relations of the human beings with each other and their environment. The individual's labour is thus socially validated ('integrated'); correspondingly, from a societal point of view, labour and other resources are allocated and needs faced.

The 'simple circulation' is the first step of Marx's analysis; the general, abstract concept of capitalist mode of production will be completed by the two following steps, money and capital. The first step requires by its own logic the second. The model of a society of individual producers and consumers, whose social relations are constituted exclusively by the exchange of commodities, does not represent, in fact, any historically existed society. Capitalism is the object of Marx's theory, which develops through different levels of abstraction, dialectically linked to one another. So, on the one hand, we can see that the general circulation of commodities expresses value in the form of money; money acquires then an autonomous existence, and, in turn, aims to overcome its own contradiction, of being, like Balzac's *Peau de chagrin*, capable of fulfilling any desire, but at the 'price' of shrinking and eventually disappearing: money must therefore become capital. The purchase of labour, instead of simply resulting in a reduction of the pre-existent monetary value, as happens when any other commodity is purchased and consumed, allows its valorisation. On the other hand, while at the most abstract level, the first stage of the theory leads to its subsequent development, it also conveys meanings that do not disappear later.

We could consider Polanyi's concept of the market as an 'institutional arrangement', which corresponds to Marx's concepts of value of exchange and 'simple circulation', in a similar way. Polanyi's concept too is an abstract one, and it is precisely this quality that makes it useful, indeed necessary, for grasping the reality of the market economy and understanding some basic characteristics of the market society beyond its actual complexity and its transformations. It is at this abstract level that Polanyi – who was familiar with the first chapter of *Das Capital* – works out his concept of a 'disembedded', autonomous economy, and of an 'economic' society where the social relations are essentially relations of exchange of commodities, and the organisation of the social division of labour and the allocation of resources are provided by 'price-making markets'. The historical specificity of the market-capitalistic society can thus be acknowledged together with the constraints that its survival as a system implies for the development of its institutions and the free choices of the individuals.

Polanyi's concept of the market ties up also with that of the 'market situation' as the only one where, according to Max Weber, the economic rationality and, more precisely, the 'capitalistic calculation' can be properly achieved. These concepts are of great importance as regards Weber's aim of defining the specificity of the 'modern capitalism' in comparison to the preceding social systems. The idea of a 'disembedded' economy too can be traced back to Weber's vision of a world 'disenchanted' in consequence of the breakdown of traditional cultures, and, more in general, to his analysis of the process of 'rationalisation'. The economy becomes 'rational' in the sense that its functioning follows norms of its own, and thus differentiates itself from other realms of social life. All that means, for Weber as well as for Polanyi, was that the purpose and the procedure of every economic activity are no longer laid down within traditional cultures. Producers aim for monetary gain and individuals, to the extent that their livelihood ceases to be organised within their community and their culture, become – to quote Marx – 'naked labourers'. Polanyi, in his turn, seems once again inspired by Weber in saying that 'hunger and gain' become the motives – merely and brutally 'economic' motives – of the economic behaviour (Polanyi, 1977, p. 11; Weber, 1980, I, p. 106). When 'the principle of gain and profit' spreads 'as the organising force in society', Polanyi notes the institution of the labour market implies both 'the smashing-up of social structures in order to extract the element of labour from them' and 'the penalty of starvation' for people refusing to offer their labour: 'what the white man still occasionally practice in remote regions today' (Polanyi, 1957, pp. 170, 164).

In that situation, money, either as capital or as wages, becomes in general the means and the universal medium: scarce by definition and requiring a choice among different uses. On the one hand it becomes not only lawful, but institutionally possible (in the 'market situation') to employ money in order to get more money; and on the other, individuals cannot any longer unconditionally rely on their community for their needs, which, besides, cease to be culturally predetermined. As a consequence of this social mutation, *scarcity* too acquires a new meaning in addition to the 'substantive' one. The latter can be referred both to the general condition of the human being of depending 'for his livelihood upon nature and his fellows' (Polanyi, 1977, p. 20), and to an emerging penury, whose reduction or compensation is the object of social and individual activities. The new meaning has instead an institutional character: it is inherent in the economic organisation itself, in the historically specific way of employing the resources and meeting the needs; it becomes systematic and *systemic*. Everybody must 'economise'; furthermore, as profit becomes 'the organising force in society', economising is carried out for its own sake. Scarcity is generally considered by economics a presupposition of the economic behaviour: according to its new meaning, it is in reality a consequence of the economic activity, when the latter, in the market society, is *institutionalised* as 'economising'.

Facts and concepts

The aim of the above interpretation of Polanyi's institutional method is to show the convenience of keeping and employing the abstract concepts that belong to the most general level of the analysis of the social system as a historical whole. Naturally, Polanyi's theory is itself a complex whole, where it is possible (and, again, convenient) to distinguish different levels of abstraction. We find for example, in *The Great Transformation*, the wide-range comparison with primitive economies as well as the monetary vicissitudes of the early 1930s. The central issue of that book, the market system, is itself dealt with through an interplay between more general and less general concepts. At a less general level, the 'market system' has to be understood, in its strict sense, as one of the forms of the capitalistic organisation of society: as that peculiar stage or 'institutional structure' of capitalism that Polanyi calls sometimes 'the nineteenth century civilisation' or 'the Victorian system'. This kind of capitalism – whose pivotal 'four institutions': the balance-of-power system, the gold standard, the self-regulating market and the liberal state are indicated by Polanyi at the beginning of his book – has undergone an inevitable and irreversible transformation, giving place to a new institutional structure, which could be synthetically denoted as corporate (corporative) capitalism. However as we have seen above, the analysis of the 'market system' in a wider sense too, is carried on by Polanyi, not only in *The Great Transformation*, but also subsequently. We could say that a system of a higher order – market (or capitalistic) society – is thus defined by defining the common characteristics of its different 'institutional structures'.

Continuing on the problem of the utility of the most abstract concepts, we can observe, at first, that the very method of institutional analysis asks for pushing to the utmost the demonstration that what was deemed to be general and natural is instead historical and social, in one word *institutional*. We have seen that method at work in regard to the issue of 'scarcity'; in general, Polanyi's critique of economic theories follows the same path. Thus in order to get these results, an analysis at an adequate level of abstraction is required.

The institutional concept of the 'market', as the above outlined general concept of a historical social system, makes it possible to understand this form of organisation of the economy as one element of a set: to locate it – Polanyi would say – within the 'frame of reference' of the 'substantive' definition of the economy. This theoretical achievement at a very high level of abstraction allows the criticism of the 'formal definition' of the economy in terms of 'scarcity plus economising' (Polanyi, 1977, p. 20). It becomes, in fact, apparent that this definition mistakes a given institutional arrangement of the economy for the economy in general, a species for its genus, an element of a set for the set. This is, according to Polanyi, the 'economistic fallacy'. As Marx put it: 'all the learning of modern economists' consists in 'the representation of the *bourgeois* relations as immutable laws of the society *in abstracto*'; 'all the historical differences' are thus dissolved (Marx, 1976, p. 9).

A similar criticism can be addressed also to that way of interpreting the economic history in the *'longue durée'*, which is based on the distinction between the institutional change and the permanence of the norms and motives of the economic behaviour. To Fernand Braudel the market appears as the most proper expression of the economy and is essentially the same in all societies; only its dimensions and bounds vary. Furthermore, 'market' and 'capitalism' are considered by Braudel as different phenomena; capitalism is characterised by an acquisitive and even speculative attitude, fundamentally invariable in its different personifications, from the medieval peddler to the global corporation. No wonder that Braudel reproaches Polanyi for his concept of the market as a new kind of economic organisation and of society, a concept that would derive from a *'goût théologique de la définition'* rather than from historical evidence (Braudel, 1979, pp. 195–6; Braudel, 1986).

Douglass North is more radical than Braudel in building his economic history on a general definition of the economy, which is, as Polanyi would say, 'catallactic', traced upon the market system. Following North's economistic and functionalist view, the aim of institutions would always be that of 'maximising wealth'. The existence of institutions different from the market would fundamentally be explained by their function of allowing lower 'transaction costs' when 'well defined and enforced property rights' are missing (North, 1977, pp. 710–11). North accepts 'the challenge of Polanyi', but the 'new economic history' he proposes goes simply in the opposite way. For example, the 'ports of trade', whose existence demonstrates, according to Polanyi, that the economy has in antiquity a 'place', a social organisation, different from the market system, are instead, according to North, a functional equivalent of the market, an expedient for granting safe exchanges. The generalisation of the transaction costs theory seems here to lead either to a mere tautology or to a nineteenth-century evolutionistic conception of the economy as market economy, that makes all historical differences disappear. To the extent that the 'new economic history' is fundamentally and predominantly concerned with the problem of economic development through individual profit-seeking activities, pre-modern institutions cannot be interpreted but as functionally equivalent to the economic and political institutions of the market system. Thus the object of comparison are not different forms of social organisation of the economy, only one of which has 'economising' as its most general and typical institutional character. North's historical-comparative analysis is concerned, on the contrary, with different institutional contexts of the same 'rational' and even profit-seeking economic activity; and the gap of (market) efficiency of pre-modern institutions compared with the market system appears as the central problem.

Let us consider now another aspect of North's method, which is complementary to his 'economistic' conception of the economy. The specificity of the exchange as a 'form of integration' and the uniqueness of the market society tend to vanish also as a consequence of the idea that systems of allocation and modes of transaction different from the market are prevalent in contemporary as well as in previous societies. As it has become usual on this subject, North makes reference to the famous article by Ronald Coase, 'A Theory of the Firm' (1937). This reference is, in my view, as improper as it is revealing: Coase's theory cannot be displaced from the level of the analysis of the firm and its choices to the level of comparative analysis of social systems.

Today's institutional analyses of the market, both by institutional economists and economic sociologists, afford the complex reality of norms, values, motives, networks of social relations, forms of governmental intervention, forms of governance, purposeful strategies, power struggles and so on, that constitute not simply the boundary of the market, but the market itself, and affect its evolution. We could add the more traditional issues of the 'forms of the market' from competition to monopoly, and of their complementarity in given situations, as well as of the intertwining between economic and political power (which has only its most visible and spectacular manifestation in the passage of the same persons from managerial positions in industry and finance, to governmental positions, and vice versa). Even Coase's remains of market would be hardly traceable, and anyway distorted by rationality's bounds, asymmetrical information, opportunist and free-rider attitudes. Finally, nobody could deny the existence in contemporary societies of non-market relations such as reciprocity, gift and governmental redistribution.

Are then the very concepts of 'market system' and of the exchange as a 'form of integration' devoid of meaning, since they seem lacking of empirical evidence? Are the abstract models of economics mere fancy? Is the 'economistic fallacy' without any connection with reality, in spite of its wide diffusion in the social sciences, from economics to anthropology and historiography? Is the interest for concreteness, empirical data and generically social-cultural phenomena sufficient to mark the institutional method and the critique of the basic assumptions of mainstream economics? No, they are not. To study the complex reality of the market, in its concrete varieties, developments and implications, is useful, indeed necessary: however, a survey at higher levels of abstraction, concerned with the general and typical characteristics of the social system and its history, is also necessary. I'll try to deal below with a few arguments in favour of this thesis.

1. As we have seen, the confutation of the 'economistic' generalisations requires a higher level of generalisation.

2. If 'the essence of institutional economics' is to be found, as Geoffrey Hodgson stresses, in the concern for the 'web of partially durable and self-reinforcing institutions', in which the agents are 'mutually entwined' (Hodgson, 2000, p. 325), no reason can be given for neglecting the most general characteristics of that web. Of course, it is possible to object that the general concept of market or capitalist society – at the level of abstraction at which Veblen, Weber and Polanyi, not to mention Marx, dealt with it – does not belong to institutional *economics* more than to historiography, to sociology or to an anthropological vision of the social system as a whole. Clearly there is need for various perspectives and different kinds of research; thus the following points are only meant to suggest some considerations in favour of a multifarious analysis at different levels, together with some cautions.

(a) The more abstract concepts should not be entangled in the less abstract. Let's consider for instance the famous essay in which Mark Granovetter deals with 'the embeddedness of economic behavior' (Granovetter, 1992, p. 53). There he explicitly refers to Polanyi, but he neglects to specify that the object of his study and the problems he puts forth are not at all the same as Polanyi's. Granovetter's survey does not involve the definition of modern society with respect to previous societies; the history and the society in which he wants to situate economic behaviour are the history of personal relations between individuals, such as the social relations intertwined in neighbourhoods, colleges and country clubs. Studies on how this type of 'concrete patterns of social relations' (*ibid.*, p. 63) influence personal success and economic calculation, trust or malfeasance, morality or opportunism in economic transactions may be useful and brilliant. One may even christen this type of research 'the embeddedness approach'. But to make reference to Polanyi or to quote Hobbes while doing so seems inappropriate and misleading. More importantly, Granovetter's method is at risk of conflicting with institutional method in two basic respects. Firstly, it remains an individualistic and micro-sociological method. Secondly, and consequently, it comes to an empiristic generalisation of the 'embeddedness' that belittles the difference between the 'market system' and other 'institutional arrangements' of the economy, between modern market-capitalistic society and all the previous forms of social organisation. Besides, even at the level of individual behaviour, behind the manifold drives and influences, and 'social relations' in Granovetter's sense, we should not forget the motives of 'gain and hunger', which belong to a more general frame of social relations. We could refer to all this as the risk of a 'sociological fallacy'; again, the institutional specificity of the economy, its general characteristics as market and capitalistic economy, tend to vanish.

(b) Every analysis is meaningful at its own level of abstraction. As regards the concept of market, and in particular the distinction between firm and market, it should be obvious that the firm (as a hierarchical organisation) can be opposed to the market (as the set of exchanges between individual actors more or less capable of a rational choice) as long as we analyse concrete situations, given in space and time, within a market-capitalistic system. However, when the evolution of the market structure is under consideration, it is impossible not to consider it as a result of the strategies of the firms and of their power struggles. At a more general level of reasoning, it is also obvious that the development of the market in the modern sense *presupposes* the existence of capitalist firms. Oliver Williamson's instance of a steel mill composed by thousands of individual producers (Williamson, 1985) can be understood as a rhetorical expedient for the sake of his argument. Williamson himself is probably aware that, from a historical and institutional point of view, his instance is totally devoid of evidence, and can only have the sense of a proof *ab absurdo*. On the contrary, such an institutional concept as Polanyi's distinction between the market as a general form of economic organisation and the previous forms of exchange, though very abstract, can be (and has been, from *Trade and Market in the Early Empires* onward) confirmed by empirical evidence. What matters here is, anyway, that we are in presence of two different levels of abstraction. Williamson explains the firm on the ground of its economic efficiency, compared with the efficiency of the market considered in the real, concrete terms of its functioning. In particular, it is in given situations – to be explained also with reference to a historical conjuncture of capitalist development and 'regulation' (Aglietta, 1976) – that given firms make their choice of either internalising given productive and distributive processes or relying on other firms. As for Polanyi, his enquiry concerns the very concept of economic efficiency; he traces its origin back to the development of the market system and capitalist firms: the object of his analysis is the most general institutional frame, which economic analyses such as Williamson's do not consider as such, but take for granted.

I will mention only one among many possible examples concerning this issue. Some sociological researches pointed out a particular aspect of the development, in central Italy, of an 'industrial district', which enjoyed of a remarkable success in the market of quality shoes. Not only have the usual characteristics of the district model, such as specialisation and flexibility, been important in this respect, but also some social and cultural traits of the entrepreneurs. One of those traits is the custom of collaboration among the members of enlarged families that was rooted in the peasant culture, probably as an attitude adopted to cope with the local system of share-cropping (see e.g. Paci, 1980).

At a first glance, the results of those researches contrast with Harry Braverman's thesis of the decay of the family as a unity of production, both in the sense of a familiar business and of familiar production or transformation of consumption goods. This is, according to Braverman, a consequence of the development of the 'universal market': the individuals no longer tend to satisfy their wants inside their family (or, we could add, their community), but by means of an ever growing variety of commodities to be bought on the market by individually earned wages (Braverman, 1974, Ch. 8). In reality, the two analyses not only are not contrasting, but are complementary, because they consider the reality of the development of the market at two different levels of abstraction. Moreover, the general tendency indicated by Braverman suggests a verification of the persistence of the traditional cultural traits that support initially the success of several industrial districts. In fact, industrial development, even in the form of clusters of small firms in local communities, tends everywhere to undermine the traditional cultural contexts in the course of one or two generations.

(c) The previous example suggests that empirical analyses cannot substitute for more abstract conceptual levels; moreover, they can also be fruitfully grounded on them. Generally speaking, it is thanks to the selection of relevant facts and the questions that abstract concepts make possible, that the results of our researches can be rich in meaning, rather than unilateral or trivial.

For instance, Polanyi, in his articles of 1934 about the crisis of the British cotton industry, questions the reasons for the growing success of the Japanese industry. Alongside the technical, organisational and commercial factors, he compares the sociological features of the Lancashire workers – breadwinner males, with a century of class consciousness behind them

– with those of the young women who constituted the bulk of labour supply to Japanese cotton factories. Owing to the still rural and traditionalistic background of that workforce, Polanyi observes, the Japanese entrepreneurs have at their disposal, as though it were a millennial deposit, that corporative mentality that European industrialists and politicians are trying to reintroduce with difficulty, since it is not easy to erase the 'liberal intermezzo' from history. It was then natural and easy for Japanese employers to base both the organisation of the factories and the industrial relations on discipline, paternalism and a 'corporate culture' (to use a more recent expression) (cf. Polanyi, 1934). We can notice in this analysis not an entanglement, but a stratification of more and less abstract concepts. Beyond the case under observation, we discern a larger and deeper perspective on the shift from one 'institutional structure' (or form of regulation) of capitalism to another and on the historically varying connection between capitalism and modern ideals of liberty and democracy. The case studied appears in its turn more thoroughly investigated and significant.

3. Pushing the theory to very high levels of abstraction allows not only a deeper analysis of the functioning and evolution of the market system, but also the consideration of the market system as such. What this means could be clarified in regard to the issue of efficiency. Beyond the 'economic' problem of efficiency *within* the market society, there are both the problems, at which I hinted above, of (a) the historical-institutional nature of the problem itself, and (b) of the efficiency of the market system as such from a 'substantive' point of view. The following section is dedicated to the latter problem in particular, through the reference to 'old' or 'classic' institutional thought.

The efficiency of the market system

Both classical sociology and classical institutional economics were characterised by their concern for the capitalist or market system in general. The repression of that issue characterises the mainstream developments of sociology and economics, especially after World War II. In order to appreciate the full meaning of the old-style thinking, and its distance from that we are used to nowadays, it would be worth relating it to its historical context, but it is not possible to do so here. Suffice it to say that it was the epoch of the crisis of liberal capitalism, culminating with World War I. The optimistic outlook of utilitarianism was on the wane, the institutional reality of the market was evidently and irreversibly departed from its theoretical model, numerous projects for a new organisation of the economy were emerging. The different kinds of socialist visions could be situated between two poles. There is, on the one hand, the radical transition proposed by Otto Neurath, from a monetary economy to a 'natural' one, without money, without market, where needs and resources would be consciously and purposefully handled (Neurath, 1919). On the other hand, Walther Rathenau devised a 'socialisation' of the economy, which would be realised, of course, by capitalists themselves (Rathenau, 1918). In England, G. D. H. Cole (1920) re-stated Guild Socialism, Bertrand Russell reflected on the best 'road to freedom' among different socialist and anarchist projects (Russell, 1918). Richard Tawney (1920) pleaded the cause for a reversal of the control that, in the 'acquisitive society', the economic function has on cultural and political functions. John Hobson maintained that the future peace would depend on democracy, interpreted as the transition from class supremacy to an effectively democratic government, founded on the development of 'intelligent co-operation' with a view to 'clearly defined ends'. Only this kind of government, having overthrown the 'strong business organisations', could pursue a peaceful foreign policy (Hobson, 1919, pp. 8, 75, 87, 143). In the USA, Wesley Mitchell also suggested that the economic theory should face the fact that the individuals modify their behaviour according to current institutions, and that these change and hence the organisation of economic activity. This institutional point of view in 1914, according to Mitchell, was still regarded as 'a rare form of mental aberration', but the catastrophe of the war was an incentive to change perspective (Mitchell, 1924, pp. 25–8).

For Polanyi the after-war '*Rote Wien*' was a crucial period for his intellectual and political formation. In Vienna he participated in the debate on the feasibility and the possible forms of socialism. In his 1922 essay about this subject – in which he outlines, in opposition to Ludwig Mises, the traits of a non-centralised socialist organisation – the problem of the objectives pursued by the economic system is central. The economy should be 'framed' by a social, conscious and democratic process of choice about its goals and constraints. Within that frame monetary exchanges and markets could find place, but would have a different meaning than in a 'market economy'. We can perhaps relate to this distinction the later Polanyian distinction between the 'market' as the central institution (and the general concept) of a given economic organisation, and the 'markets' in premodern, differently instituted economies.

The starting point in Polanyi's essay is that in a market economy – that is, a capitalist economy more or less characterised by big business, as, in those times, it was universally acknowledged – the economic system tends to be self-referential. Since the choices and the very selection of information are determined or biased by 'the principle of gain and profit', 'economic' efficiency cannot be immediately and in general considered as coinciding with efficiency from the point of view of society. Capitalist economy, writes Polanyi, 'by nature' cannot be guided towards 'social utility'. Indeed it lacks 'the sense organ' in order to perceive social needs and evaluation. Not only that, but the production has a 'retroactive effect on the community' and on individual needs, which can be changed, corrupted or artificially created (Polanyi, 1922).

Polanyi's 'substantive definition' of the economy makes it possible to understand the market system as a specific 'institutional arrangement' of the economy, and, at the same time, to raise the question of the substantive rationality of that system: that is, to weigh its efficiency from the point of view of 'social utility'. In terms of the systems theory, we could say that this is the problem of the orientation and control of the economic system, of its insertion in a wider system. Between the end of the nineteenth century and the first decades of the twentieth, it was the time of the downfall of the utilitarian utopia together with the illusory freedom it promised. At the same time, it seemed obvious that modern achievements of liberty and civil rights should be irreversible, and the economy would – should – never more be 'embedded' in the same way and sense as in pre-modern societies. The conviction was spreading then, that a social – in the first place political, hopefully democratic – process of choice should orient and control the economy.

One of the reference points about this question – which, as we shall see in a while, is typically raised also by institutional economists – can have been for Polanyi the distinction made by Max Weber between 'formal' rationality and 'material' or 'substantive' rationality of the economy. Already in *The Protestant Ethic and the Spirit of Capitalism*, where the rise of rational economic behaviour is analysed, the risk of a congenital irrationality is singled out in that behaviour, for becoming an end in itself instead of being aimed at personal happiness. In *Economy and Society* the distinction between 'formal' rationality and the 'material' ends – the ends that come from political, ethical or personal exigencies – is systematically traced. The theme of the 'irrationality' of (capitalistic) economic rationality is taken up again and generalised. It is a rationality which, according to Weber, is 'bounded on principle', that is, by its own nature and at the level of the entire system. There are two 'causes of irrationality'. The first is that the great majority of people are excluded from exerting rational choices, owing to the need of concentrating them in the capitalistic direction of production. In Weber's words: that exclusion is an objective necessity if the 'formal rationality in capital accounting' has to be maximised. That necessity constitutes a constraint for the organisation of productive processes and also of the social system as a whole, and is then, at least for this reason, a 'specific element of substantive irrationality' (Weber, 1980, p. 138).

The second cause of irrationality depends precisely on the 'formal' quality of the (market, capitalistic) rationality, which renders it 'indifferent ... as to any material postulate' (*ibid.*, p. 104). It is interesting to note that the 'indifference' as such could not – according to the meaning given by Weber himself to the process of 'rationalisation' – be a cause of irrationality. The distinction between 'formal' and 'material' or 'substantive' economic rationality is historically grounded on the differentiation or 'dis-embedding' of the economy. The 'formal' rationality appears to Weber in this historical situation as the typical character of the economic system. The latter, on the other hand, should provide the means for ends that are an expression of a series of more or less rational, but not formally economic motives. As a consequence, in a modern, complex, differentiated society a further problem arises, that of the political function of designing a frame of the economic activity, of institutionalising a (hopefully democratic) social process of rational choice concerning the material or substantive economic rationality.

Lionel Robbins, in his 1932 *Essay* (Robbins 1962), justifies the 'formal definition' of the economy, and the economic rational choice as perfectly instrumental to goals determined from outside, also by making reference to Weber's distinction between formal and substantive rationality. If we stop here, however, we misinterpret Weber's intention, which is of raising the problem of the entanglement of the two sorts of rationality he conceptually distinguishes. Here lies the irrationality: logically, the formal rationality cannot have anything to do with the solution of the problem of the (final) aims of the economic activity: but the 'indifference' of the formal rationality to 'material postulates' implies, according to Weber, the possibility of, indeed an inherent tendency to, a reverse relation of instrumentality, by which 'material' ends would be paradoxically determined by the 'formal' rationality of 'capital accounting'.

This is precisely the point of Weber's deep criticism of neoclassical economics. Rational capital investment oriented to 'profitability' implies that the needs to be satisfied will be chosen among those 'endowed of purchasing power' and those allowing a greater profitability. Technology and the organisation of labour processes too will be chosen in the same way. Moreover, not only is the market competition the seat of a 'struggle', on which the distribution of purchasing power depends, but the needs are 'stirred up' and 'directed' by the producers. Finally, the orientation of consumers (on the grounds of marginal utility) and that of producers (on the grounds of profitability) are 'basically different', and the consumers are not 'sovereign' (*ibid.*, pp. 88–90). Weber thus bases his criticism of the general equilibrium theory on the analysis of the general characteristics of the market or capitalist system as an 'institutional arrangement'. Through this analysis, he discovers the paradox of the 'material' efficacy of 'formal' rationality. Needless to say, the resulting bounds of rationality do not concern the individual behaviour, as in current institutional economics, but depend on the general features of the economic system as a market and capitalistic 'instituted process'.

The Weberian two 'causes of irrationality' are interdependent, as it is also clear in Polanyi's statement that when 'the use of labour power could be universally bought and sold' it became evident that 'the broader range of vital social interests' was deeply affected and restricted by the market mechanism and the profit motive (Polanyi, 1957, pp. 131, 145). Just as the quality of subjects of choice is removed from the majority of workers, the power to finalise the economic system and the freedom to define its constraints is removed from the whole of society. In fact, in accordance with the above mentioned Polanyian concept of 'market society', the inverse relationship is true; not only, for example, the amount of unemployment benefits, but also the extent to which political democratic institutions are admissible, tend to be a dependent variable with respect to the independent necessity of growth of the economic system and of reproduction of its (capitalist) organisation.

These sorts of problems represent the typical core of 'classical' institutional economics. It is not possible here to explore this issue at length. I would however like to recall Veblen's distinction between 'industrial and pecuniary employments'. The 'pecuniary' or 'business' form of the economic activity in the course of capitalistic development ceases to be simply the 'method' of achieving social good through individual interest, but becomes 'the controlling factor about which the modern economic process turns' (Veblen, 1994, p. 286). Together with the 'business enterprise', the tendency to 'commercialize' personal relations and social criteria establishes itself. Industrial processes are controlled by managerial evaluations referred to profit rather than to 'material utility' (Veblen, 1954, p. 263). 'Character, scope and growth' of production (i. e. of 'industry') are 'conditioned' by fundamental institutions, linked to one another: on the one hand, 'under existing circumstances of ownership, the discretion in economic matters ... ultimately rests in the hands of the business men'. On the other hand, 'industrial processes and plants adapt themselves to the exigencies of the market', which are 'pecuniary exigencies'. As a result, in a society organised 'on a pecuniary basis' 'the aggregate of discrete individual interests nowise expresses the collective interest'. 'The ground of survival in the selective process is fitness for pecuniary gain, not fitness for serviceability at large' (Veblen, 1994, pp. 297, 305, 299).

As a final example, consider J. M. Clark's reflection in the time of World War I; the war offers, according to him, the chance to question both nineteenth-century liberalism and marginal utility theory in general. Clark believes that 'collectivist policies', apart from meeting war-related needs, also reveal some, such as the need for a vast and organic social organisation of the economy, which are independent of the war. With the attainment of such organisation, production output would not be defined simply in terms of subjective preference and social production would no longer be estimated in terms of private profit. Social benefit would not be accessory and contingent as regards profit, but indeed would become central (Clark, 1917, pp. 772–3).

What society demands, writes Clark, results from the desires of those of its members that are better endowed, first of all with money. There are so some with enormous power and other who totally lack any form of influence. How does one arrive at a given distribution of purchasing power? Does it depend solely on the initiative of the individual or also on the social institutions that make up the context? What guarantee do we have that resources will in fact be used efficiently to create the greatest happiness for the greatest number of individuals? (*ibid.*, pp. 774–5)

Clark goes on to criticise more specifically alleged market efficiency: the waste in 'conspicuous consumption' and in advertising, the appropriation by private interests of commodities such as knowledge, the impossibility of repaying costs sustained by groups of individuals and society as a whole, and the 'efficiency' (in business terms) of social parasite forms. The problem is in general, according to Clark, that competition stimulates the individuals to be as efficient as possible in given conditions, but only society can undertake the task of deciding such conditions so as to maximise the prospect of satisfaction and development.

It seems clear in what sense, for the 'old' institutional vision, institutions should become an object of analysis. When Mitchell (1924) asks for a more realistic form to be adopted by the economic science, he refers to the institutions, as the result of historical processes and constituting the general features of the economic system. That is the object of the empirical knowledge that Mitchell and institutional economists of the same sort deem necessary. Statistical data, and in general any kind of information, would be the instruments of a social process of self-consciousness and of 'social engineering', without excluding the most general institutional characteristics of social relations and economic behaviour.

As the history is made by victors, so the distinctive traits of classical institutional thought tend not to be acknowledged. That current of thought is often narrowly interpreted. Its demand for empirical research is stressed, as if bolstering up theory with statistics would have been the main problem (see e.g. Yonay, 1998). Typical institutionalist exigencies – such as the research on institutions as a way of socially controlling and reorganising the economy, and the questioning the very presuppositions of economic theory – are often ignored, just as they are neglected when actual economic reality is to be analysed.

The foregoing examples make clear, in my opinion, the discontinuity, the gap, the shift of paradigm between old-style and the greater part of present-day institutional thought. My opinion is, besides, that the 'old' kind of method would be indispensable for the analysis of present-day problems.

References

Aglietta, M. (1976), *Régulation et crises du capitalisme*, Paris, Calmann–Lévy.
Braudel, F. (1979), *Civilisation matérielle, économie et capitalisme, II*, Paris, Colin.
Braudel, F. (1986), *La dynamique du capitalisme*, Paris, Arthaud.

Braverman, H. (1978), *Labor and Monopoly Capital: The Degradation of Work in the Twentieth Century*, New York and London, Monthly Review Press.

Clark, J. M. (1917), 'The Basis of War-time Collectivism', *American Economic Review*, 7(4), pp. 772–90.

Coase, R. (1937), 'A Theory of the Firm', *Economica*, 4, pp. 386–405.

Cole, G. D. H. (1920), *Guild Socialism Re-stated*, London, Parsons.

Granovetter, M. (1992), 'Economic Action and Social Structure: The Problem of Embeddedness', in M. Granovetter and R. Swedberg (eds), *The Sociology of Economic Life*, Boulder and Oxford, Westview Press (first published in 1985 in the *American Journal of Sociology*, 91(3), pp. 481–510).

Hobson, J. (1919), *Democracy after the War*, London, George Allen & Unwin; New York, Macmillan (first edition 1917).

Hodgson, G. M. (2000), 'What is the Essence of Institutional Economics?', *Journal of Economic Issues*, 34(2), pp. 317–29.

Mannheim, K. (1954), *Man and Society in an Age of Reconstruction*, London, Routledge & Kegan Paul.

Marx, K. (1976), Notebook M ('Introduction', 1857), in *Lineamenti fondamentali di critica dell'economia politica*, Turin, Einaudi.

Mitchell, W. C. (1924), 'The Prospects of Economics', in R. G. Tugwell (ed.), *The Trend of Economics*, New York, A. A. Knopf.

Neurath, O. (1919), 'Durch die Kriegswirtschaft zur Naturalwirtschaft' (partially translated into English in *Empiricism and Sociology*, by M. Neurath and R. S. Cohen (eds), Dordrecht and Boston, 1973).

North, D. C. (1977), 'Markets and Other Allocation Systems in History: The Challenge of Karl Polanyi', *Journal of European Economic History*, 6(4), pp. 703–16.

Paci, M. (ed.) (1980), *Famiglia e mercato del lavoro in un'economia periferica*, Milan, F. Angeli.

Polanyi, K. (1922), 'Sozialistische Rechnungslegung', *Archiv für Sozialwissenschaft und Sozialpolitik*, 2.

Polanyi, K. (1934), 'Lancashire als Menschheitsfrage', and 'Lancashire als Menschheitsproblem', *Der Österreichische Volkswirt*, 23 and 30 June.

Polanyi, K. (1957), *The Great Transformation*, Boston, Beacon Press (first published 1944).

Polanyi, K. (1977), *The Livelihood of Man*, ed. H. W. Pearson, New York, Academic Press.

Polanyi, K., Arensberg, C. M. and Pearson, H. W. (eds.) (1957), *Trade and Market in The Early Empires: Economies in History and Theory*, Glencoe, IL, Free Press.

Rathenau, W. (1918), *Die neue Wirtschaft*, Berlin, Fischer.

Robbins, L. (1962), *An Essay on the Nature & Significance of Economic Science*, London, Macmillan (first published 1932).

Russell, B. (1918), *Roads to Freedom: Socialism, Anarchism and Syndicalism*, London, George Allen & Unwin.

Tawney, R. (1920), *The Acquisitive Society*, New York, Harcourt, Brace & Co.

Veblen, T. (1934/1954), 'The Opportunity of Japan (1915)', in *Essays in Our Changing Order*, New York, Viking Press (reprinted from *The Journal of Race and Development*, 1915).

Veblen, T. (1994), 'Industrial and Pecuniary Employments', in T. Veblen, *The Place of Science in Modern Civilisation and Other Essays*, London, Routledge/Thoemmes Press (first published 1961).

Weber, M. (1980), *Economia e società*, Milan, Edizioni di Comunità.

Williamson, O. E. (1985), *The Economic Institutions of Capitalism: Firms, Markets, Relational Contracting*, New York, Free Press.

Yonay, Y. P. (1998), *The Struggle over the Soul of Economics*, Princeton, Princeton University Press.

3

Institutions, politics and culture: a Polanyian perspective on economic change

John Harriss

> Such terms as 'values' and 'culture' are not popular with economists, who prefer to deal with quantifiable (more precisely definable) factors. Still, life being what it is, one must talk about these things. (David Landes)[1]

Karl Polanyi's *The Great Transformation* (Polanyi, 1944) is a powerful historical and moral critique of those great changes in societies that he sought to characterise and to explain in terms of the attempt to establish self-regulating markets. The notion of a 'self-regulating market economy' is a utopian one, he argued, and attempts to realise it necessarily depend upon the fictions that land (which means the natural environment), labour (which means people) and money (a symbol of value) are commodities like others. Polanyi would have been a robust critic of present-day attempts to realise the market utopia, and there are indeed passages in *The Great Transformation* that strikingly anticipate – in a critical vein – arguments that have been advanced by the World Bank and other agencies in the 1980s and 1990s in support, for instance, of structural adjustment programmes.

The attempt to establish a self-regulating market economy requires that economic activities be 'disembedded' from their other facets, but the strong implication of Polanyi's critique is that economic activity is never finally disembedded (an insight that has of course been picked up and developed by economic sociologists). He went on to devote the later part of his life to the analysis of 'pre-modern' economies, and with his students and associates founded what came to be known as the 'substantivist' view of economics. The whole implication of Polanyi's scholarly work, I think, is fundamentally to question the idea that forms of economic organisation can be explained by the application of the 'economising' calculus of mainstream, choice-theoretic economics. Yet this is precisely what is claimed by the exponents of 'new' or neo-classical institutional economics. The aim of this chapter is, in the spirit of Karl Polanyi, to subject these claims to critical scrutiny.

The new institutional economics (NIE) and its analytical claims

Institutions are, as Jeffrey Nugent (2002) explains, humanly devised rules that affect behaviour, constraining certain actions, providing incentives for others, and thereby making social life more or less predictable.[2] They are as Geoffrey Hodgson (2001, p. 302) puts it, 'the stuff of socio-economic reality'. It is in a way rather curious that so fundamental an aspect of social life should not have been a more important focus of study in the social sciences (outside anthropology) until relatively recently. This reflects the facts that, as Nugent says, mainstream, choice-theoretic economics has not previously problematised institutions, such even as those that are necessary for markets to function – and the expansionary pre-eminence of this kind of economics amongst the social sciences. Hodgson, however, reminds us that the dominance of this particular style of economics, with its pretensions to universality, has overlain and led to the forgetting of a rich tradition of thought about institutions, associated both with the German historical school (in which he includes Polanyi) and with American scholars such as Veblen and John Commons. I shall pick up some of his arguments in this chapter.

Nugent distinguishes between the 'demand' for institutions and their 'supply', pointing out that the former involves in particular problems due to informational asymmetries, and the latter problems of collective action. He then shows us how it is possible to explain, parsimoniously, within the framework of neo-classical economics, why particular institutions are the way they are and why they differ from each other, and how they influence productivity, taking great care as he does so to point out the dangers of making tautological, functionalist assumptions (on the lines of the following: these are the institutions that exist; they must therefore reduce transactions costs; thefore they exist – and they must be efficient).

Institutional theorists recognise that it is perfectly possible for a society to get 'locked in' to an inefficient set of institutions because of the interests of power-holders in their reproduction.[3] An example from some of my own work would be the existence of socially inefficient agrarian institutions, such as those that obtained in Eastern India, and which made usurious money-lending and speculative trading in food grains privately profitable for a small class of landowners to the extent that, for a long time, there was little or no incentive for them to make productive investments in agriculture, and certainly not those that required collective action, as in the organisation of irrigation. I think it can be shown that the institutional arrangements that under-pinned this kind of rural economy were socially inefficient and that they supported and were supported by the power of the landowning oligarchy which had a strong interest in their reproduction. This is one way, at least, whereby 'historical path dependence' may arise.[4]

How good is the kind of institutional theory that Nugent describes when it comes to explaining change in institutions? How valuable or effective is it, therefore, in theorising change in human societies? Nugent is explicit about the limitations of the NIE: most of it is rather static, he says, and 'because of the interdependencies among different institutional arrangements within a given institutional structure, it is often difficult to isolate the most relevant institutional change for hypothesis testing'. The examples that he gives of NIE explanations of important institutional changes are all interesting, but each of them confirms the modesty of his claims for the NIE as a way of explaining historical change. NIE explanations provide an interesting gloss on current understandings of the emergence of the factory system of production during the Industrial.

Revolution: the factor of the danger of asset misuse helps to explain why capital owners hired workers in, rather than hiring machines out; the demand for skilled labour probably made the tying of workers into relatively long-term contracts advantageous; there were probably advantages in terms of knowledge and information sharing and the building of trust and cooperation, when workers were brought together in factories. But Nugent says that he would not argue 'that evidence exists to suggest that the traditional economies of scale argument for the rise of the factory system is entirely dominated by these transaction cost and NIE considerations'. The second of his cases, about the emergence and distribution of private property rights involves an interesting study of property rights and coffee production in Central America and the contrasts between Guatemala and El Salvador on the one hand, and Costa Rica and Colombia on the other. The argument is that the latter pair of countries 'developed coffee quite early thanks to the rapid development of private property rights for mostly smallholders', and the reason for this is said to be 'elite schism' or in other words the fragmentation and consequent development of competition amongst the elites of the two countries – whereas Guatemala on the other hand 'was dominated by a conservative alliance of church and monopolistic merchants that did not fission'. The argument is an interesting one. The application of the NIE in this case, however, does not in itself explain change. It serves to highlight the importance of power considerations and of politics, but it does not in itself explain them at all. Rather it raises interesting questions about the political context which have to be answered through some other, historical [and political] analysis. Thinking of E. H. Carr's (Carr, 1961) metaphor of fishing, in his classic study of the nature of history, the NIE is a useful net that directs our attention to particular facts that then need to be explained historically. It is not in itself a theory of historical change. I believe that John Toye's (Toye, 1995, p. 64) judgement that the NIE has no theory of history ('The main weakness of the NIE as a grand theory of socio-economic development is that it is empty')[5] is substantially correct.

I refer back to my East Indian example again. As I said, I think it can be shown that an inefficient set of agrarian institutions persisted over a long period; and it can be shown that this in turn explains the long run stagnation in the agriculture of Bengal. This stagnation came to an end in the early mid-1980s, and since that time the rate of growth of agricultural output in West Bengal has been amongst the highest, perhaps the highest, in the country. The explanation of this historic change is of course, complex, and exactly as Nugent says 'it is difficult to isolate the most relevant institutional change for hypothesis testing'. The precise role of the modest agrarian reforms implemented by the Marxist-led government of the state remains controversial; but they were certainly instrumental in changing the socially inefficient institutions that I have referred to. Institutional change here followed from the rise to state power of a (moderate) left wing political party.[6]

It is not too long a jump, then, to argue that the relationships between social classes, and the nature of power structures, which themselves have to be analysed historically, are of particular significance in explaining change or alternatively the lack of it over long periods of time. If we wish to explain the different historical trajectories of Guatemala and Costa Rica, for example, amongst the cases referred to by Nugent, we will also have to take account of the specifics of class relationships, for it is these which appear to underlie the institutional differences that are his focus. As Pranab Bardhan has said: 'The history of evolution of institutional arrangements and of the structure of property rights often reflects the changing relative bargaining power of different social groups', and he points out that, 'North [who won the Nobel Prize for Economics in 1993, for his contributions to institutional economics] unlike some other transaction cost theorists, comes close to the viewpoint traditionally associated with Marxist historians' (Bardhan, 2001, p. 261). North's work, indeed, can be seen as reflecting a constant tension between his commitment to the framework of choice-theoretic economics and his awareness of the limitations, which it imposes when it comes to the analysis of change. This is reflected in his admission that there is 'much to learn' from 'the 'old economic historian', the institutionalists of Vebel and C. E. Ayres' persuasion, or the Marxist';[7] and in his concern, as Lazonick has pointed out, to graft onto 'mainstream economics a theory of *political* change'.

If I may extend my point, I have long been interested in the differences between the historical trajectories of the major Indian states, in terms of rates of economic growth and of levels of development. Contrary to the theoretical presuppositions of many economists, in regard to both growth and human development, the Indian states have continued to diverge rather than to converge (Rao et al., 1999). A large number of different indices show that in many respects the states of the Hindi Heartland in the North, notably Bihar and Uttar Pradesh, lag far behind those of the South and the West. It is a much longer story than I can conceivably do justice to here: but there is a lot of evidence to suggest that a major part of the explanation has to do with the persistence of hierarchical social relationships, and of the fairly extreme social fragmentation associated with them, in the Hindi Heartland, while these have been more or less successfully challenged by the political mobilisations for over more than a century of lower caste and class people in the South and the West. I can offer an institutional explanation for different patterns of change, if you will, but one which focuses on the persistence (or not) of what I have referred to as 'hierarchy', or what Francine Frankel and M. S. A. Rao call the (traditional) 'dominance' of upper caste/class people who exercise authority that is sanctioned by religious beliefs. With a group of co-authors these writers have shown how the particular political histories of the major states reflect the workings out of the persistence or not of this upper caste dominance, which is of course linked with the history of lower caste/class mobilisations.[8] Now, in terms of this framework, it becomes difficult to explain how and why two of the states of the Hindi Heartland, Rajasthan and Madhya Pradesh, should have started to grow much more vigorously and to improve levels of human development, clearly distancing themselves from Uttar Pradesh and Bihar. The answer, I think, still lies in political factors, in this case having to do with the nature of party political competition in these two states, by comparison with Bihar and Uttar Pradesh, and with political leadership. In Madhya Pradesh, in particular, a reforming chief minister, with a definite vision of development for the state, has created a kind of a local version of the 'developmental state'.[9]

Limits of the NIE: politics and culture

The question is whether new institutional economists, and notably North, have succeeded in 'grafting a theory of political change onto mainstream economics'. For North, 'a dynamic model of economic change entails as an integral part of that model analysis of the polity'. But it is not at all clear that the NIE actually has a theory of how and why polities differ. It offers no explanation of the fact that the same economic institutions can have very different consequences in distinct contexts. As Robert Bates has argued this shows 'the necessity of embedding the new institutionalism within the study of politics', for the reasons for the differences observed – for example between the outcomes of the establishment of coffee marketing boards in Kenya and Tanzania – have to do with the political context.[10] Ultimately this means studying institutions historically and so integrating theory building and the study of reality.

I have described my analysis of different patterns of change across the various major Indian states as positing an 'institutional' explanation – but, *pace* North's attempts at grafting together an analysis of political change with choice-theoretic economics, I do not think that it is one that fits within the frame of the 'new institutional economics' outlined by Jeffrey Nugent. This is described as 'new' because, unlike the older traditions of thought about institutions in the German historical school and in early American institutionalism, it operates with the same basic assumptions about scarcity and individual choice, as mainstream neo-classical economics.[11] The institutions to which my analysis of political regimes across Indian states refers are those of caste, and they involve ideas about authority rooted in religious belief. They have to do, then, with what is commonly referred to as 'culture'. This is one of the most awkward words in the English language, not least because it is polysemic. Here I am referring to culture in the sense of 'the (historically specific) habits of thought and behaviour of a particular group of people', or of 'the ideas, values and symbols – more generally, 'meanings' – in terms of which a particular group of people act'.[12] 'Culture', in this sense, is quite often used as a kind of a residual in explanations for social change, or the lack of it, to account for what appears to be 'irrational', or in other words what is not readily explained in terms of the basic model of utility maximisation. The NIE engages with the problem of culture, as it does with politics, but with difficulty. Douglass North (North, 1990, p. 42) argues that 'culture defines the way individuals process and utilise information and hence may affect the way informal constraints get specified', which at least adds to the factors involved in explaining the nature of institutions in any particular case but leaves culture as exogenous to explanation. It remains a residual.

Taking serious account of those aspects of social life and experience that are labelled in English as 'culture' (in the particular sense just described) starts to expose the limitations of the universalising pretensions of neoclassical economics, which depend in part upon quite simplistic assumptions about the preferences that individuals are supposed to be maximising, and upon a simplified notion of human rationality. Even rather cursory empirical examination of human behaviour shows that people very often act habitually – that is, in ways which are characteristic of their 'culture' – and that preferences too are culturally specific. Of course these preferences and actions may be subjected to rational thought by the social actors themselves, but they are very often not.[13] The strength of the 'old' institutionalism is that it does not treat culture as an awkward (though sometimes convenient) residual, but rather makes it central in analysis. My own analysis of variation in the patterns of change between the Indian states is, it follows, much more in line with the 'old' institutionalism than it is with the NIE.

The 'old' institutionalism has been criticised as being 'descriptive' and lacking in the formal rigour of mainstream economics and its off-shoot in the NIE,[14] but as Hodgson has argued there was more to it than this for scholars from the German historical school, and the Americans like Veblen and Commons, at least *sought* to tackle the problem of historical specificity, and the serious limitations of attempts at producing universal theory in the face of the sheer complexity of society and the historical variation between different 'societies'. In doing so they did not retreat into empiricism, but aimed rather to develop 'middle range' theory, or a particular historiography, based – in Hodgson's own exploration of the tradition of the 'old' institutionalism – on certain general propositions concerning the importance for understanding of socio-economic systems of 'the laws ... that dominate the production and distribution of vital goods and services. Such laws would concern property rights, contracts, markets, corporations, employment and taxation'. These legal rules and contracts, it is held, are always and necessarily 'embedded in deep, informal social strata, often involving such factors as trust, duty and obligation (so that) a formal contract always takes on the particular hue of the informal social culture in which it is embedded'. Further, it is clear that 'The emergence of law, including property rights, is never purely and simply a matter of spontaneous development from individual interactions (but rather) is an outcome of a power struggle between citizens and the state.' Politics and power, as I argued earlier, thus become of central significance in this approach.[15]

Culture matters: trust and Indian economic development

Let me illustrate the argument further, referring again to India.[16] We may recognise that 'shared habits of thought and behaviour' (i.e. a particular culture) associated with caste are central to what it means to be Indian – though we should also recognise both that caste is an important aspect of a dominant ideology (that of orthodox Brahminical Hinduism, resisted by subordinated groups over more than two millennia),[17] and that it is a historical phenomenon. Notably, caste underwent significant restructuring under colonial rule. It is not true that caste is a colonial creation, but there is no doubt that the meaning of caste was changed by the ways in which the colonial rulers used it to classify the population (Dirks, 2001). All cultures, though by definition they involve enduring habits, are both contested within the field of power, and they are all the time being reflexively reworked or reinvented.

The values and practices of caste have tended to create relatively tight, closed social networks, so that Indian society, it has been said, is pronouncedly segmented or 'cellular'.[18] This in turn has important implications for economic action. As we know, from some of the new institutional economists indeed, most transactions involve uncertainty, arising from any one actor's incomplete knowledge about the future actions of others with whom s/he is transacting. Trust is one way of coping with this uncertainty – uncertainty that is occasioned by the freedom of others – that is never entirely removed, as Hodgson has argued (see above), even in the presence of legal rules and contracts. But where does trust come from? One important source of or basis for trust is the sharing of key characteristics with others, or from knowledge of them in particular social networks (predictability comes with familiarity). Caste relations, involving both shared characteristics and particular social networks, are an important source of trust in Indian society – and it may be said of certain caste communities that they constitute an economic organisation. A South Indian caste community, for instance, the Nattukottai Chettiars, has functioned very much like a bank, and Nattukottai Chettiars have transacted vast sums of money across long distances relying on the specific trust to which their caste relationships have given rise (Rudner, 1994). But there is a significant difference between such *specific trust* based on particular shared characteristics or social networks, or that which depends upon personalised transactions, and *generalised trust* running through society as a whole (beyond such networks/relations as caste). Generalised trust can be shown to be desirable for an effectively and efficiently functioning market economy (Platteau, 1994). As David Landes (1998, p. 218) has put it '[The] ideal society would ... be honest [or, in other words, "generalised trust" would prevail]. Such honesty would be enforced by law, but ideally the law would not be needed. People would believe that honesty is right (also that it pays) and would live and act accordingly.' I think that it can also be shown that the very strength of the specific trust that is generated in caste relationships stands counterposed to such generalised trust or morality, and that this has constrained India's economic development.

In order to develop the argument I refer to some recent research of mine on trust in the corporate sector in the country, in the context of economic globalisation. The private sector of the Indian economy has been dominated for a long time by a small number of powerful family business groups, which have been secretive and non-transparent, and have relied heavily on personalised, family and kinship networks – on 'specific trust', therefore – resisting the professionalisation of management. Now, in the context of India's increased integration into the global economy these great family firms are finding themselves disadvantaged, and they are having to open themselves up more to scrutiny, in order to attract investors. The big family-controlled business groups are in 'crisis' – in their own estimation as well as in that of the financial press. The crisis is reflected in the declining market capitalisation of family businesses, in contrast with multinational corporations and professionally run Indian companies.[19] It has been in response to this sense of crisis that three Chennai-based family business houses have sponsored an annual 'Family Business Conclave' for the Confederation of Indian Industry (CII), facilitated by a professor from one of the top US business schools who has also been advising the Chennai families.

The theme of the Conclave in 2000, set by the CEO of one of the great Chennai business houses, was that of 'the need to expand the radius of trust' by distinguishing more clearly than has historically been the case, between family interest and business interests.[20] It has come to be recognised, though clearly the argument is resisted in many family businesses, that in addition to the generic problems of family business that have to do with the problems of coordination and collective action between siblings in successor generations,[21] as well as the so-called 'Buddenbrooks Phenomenon' (referring to the declining commitment to business observed in the second and third generations in many business families), Indian family business now confronts new and specific problems in the context of economic globalisation. In the highly protected industrial economy of the period up to 1991 the big business houses rarely faced much competition, they did not need to be customer-oriented,[22] they were not much subject to shareholder scrutiny,[23] and they invested very little either in product development or in their employees. Joint-ventures with foreign companies enabled the big houses to reap monopoly profits.[24]

With these features of Indian business there went highly centralised decision-making by senior family members, organisational informality, and reliance on personal loyalty and on seniority (or personal connections) rather than on competence. Low trust on the part of family members in professional executives became a self-fulfilling prophecy.[25] As companies attempt to meet the demands of a newly competitive business environment[26] so these organisational characteristics are having to be changed – and it is often proving to be very painful process. At last many family businesses are replacing family members with professional managers, and a clearer separation is being made between family and business interest, to the extent that in a few cases family members have withdrawn from operational charge of group companies in an organisational set-up in which there is a clear distinction being made between corporate boards and the family board.[27] Part of the context of these changes is not only the changed business environment but also the loosening of family and kinship organisation amongst these elite families, with an increasing incidence of cross-caste marriage amongst children who have very often lived for long periods in the United States. What is involved in these organisational moves is a shift away from a heavy reliance upon 'selective trust' deriving from networks centred in close kin groups to a greater reliance on formal institutions of corporate governance. This is what was meant by the theme of 'expanding the radius of trust' at the Family Business Conclave.

In summary, there is a shift taking place, both in the way family businesses are organised, and in industrial organisation, depending upon institutional innovation, from a reliance on personalised relationships or 'specific trust' to a reliance upon abstract principles and professional codes. The problem of trust in India, ironically, is that norms of trust are so strong. The kind of trust that is strong is what I have called 'selective trust', amongst groups of people within specific social networks. It depends upon what Satish Saberwal, whom I quoted earlier, speaks of as 'segmented codes for conduct'. Such selective trust has made possible the development of great business enterprises, as Rudner (1994) has shown so well, with regard to the Nattukottai Chettiars. Selective trust has to be relied upon when institutionalised sanctions and incentives are weak, as they are in India. But the weakness of the latter – the fact that the enforcement of laws is so poor in India – also has to do with the strength of selective trust. This is reflected now in the problems of corporate governance. At the centre of these is 'the culture of compliance', a boardroom culture shaped by traditions of deference and promoter/management control of boards – a culture which is very resistant to external scrutiny. Business families have not liked to trust outsiders, but have always sought to retain control within a tight circle of kin. They have resisted the claims of what was referred to at the CII Conclave as 'explicitly stated principles and ethical norms'; but then the lack of consistently applied principles in the external environment justifies or leads to reliance on selective trust. There is a kind of a vicious circle in operation. Institutionalised sanctions and incentives are weak because of the absence, or the weakness, of generalised morality in Indian society. The problem of business management in India in the context of economic globalisation is that of bringing about a change in the institutional framework and in business behaviour, but in a context in which these changes confront the culture of 'selective trust'. Change is taking place now, but only against the resistance that derives from the strength of 'selective trust'.[28] In a sense the contest is now on, with different champions on either side from within the business world, between 'traditional', informal institutions, linked to family, caste and kinship, and formal institutions of corporate governance involving laws and codes of practice.

Conclusion

The case of trust in Indian business shows up key points which together help to support the argument that I am making for an approach deriving from the 'old' institutionalism in the analysis of social change, as against the static nature of the NIE. First it shows up the inter-relations of formal institutions with the 'deep informal social strata' in which they are embedded, and hence the importance of those historically specific 'shared habits of thought and behaviour' (or culture). These are not at all easily or satisfactorily explained in the would-be universal theory of mainstream economics – and they remain exogenous in the NIE. Yet they may be central to understanding what is happening! David Landes, after all, concludes his magisterial history of economic development over the last millennium by saying that 'If we learn anything from the history of economic development, it is that culture makes all the difference' (though he also points out that 'culture does not stand alone ... monocausal explanations will not work').[29] Second – though I have only been able to suggest the argument here, and in my earlier examples – explaining institutional change, and hence social change, requires that we take account of power, as Hodgson implies and as Pranab Bardhan explicitly stated in the commentary that I cited earlier. Power is missing from the NIE. Whether or not the rules of corporate governance in India will be changed in such a way as to be effective will depend upon the outcome of a power struggle between different fractions of Indian business and their political supporters, and on 'deeper' changes in habits of thought and behaviour. The two are inter-related and the outcomes cannot be predicted. Change in human societies can only be satisfactorily explained when these historically specific factors are taken into consideration, as they are in an approach, like Polanyi's, based on the 'old' institutionalism – while they are not in the NIE.

Acknowledgements

I would like to thank Jeffrey Nugent for his courtesy in allowing me to quote from the paper that he presented at the conference on Paradigms of Change, held at the University of Bonn in May 2002; Ronnie Ramlogan for his comments and gentle forbearance; and my colleagues James Putzel and Jonathan DiJohn for their comments on an earlier draft. The research reported on briefly in the final part of this paper was supported by the Economic and Social Research Council of the UK.

Notes

1 See Landes (1998, p. 215).
2 Note that one of the leading figures of new institutional economics, Douglass North, emphasises constraints on behaviour. With Nugent I believe it is important also to recognise the incentive effects of institutions.
3 Compare North (1990, p. 99) 'unproductive paths [can] persist. The increasing returns characteristic of an initial set of institutions that provide disincentives to productive activity will create organisations and interest groups with a stake in the existing constraints'. And see also Ha-Joon Chang's historical review of 'Institutions and Economic Development' from which he concludes that 'in many cases institutions were not accepted... because of the resistance from those who would (at least in the short run), lose out from the introduction of such institutions' (Chang, 2002, p. 117).
4 My own work on this, Harriss (1982), in part refers to the classic study by Bhaduri (1973). An authoritative study that substantiates my argument is Boyce (1987).
5 Douglass North (one of the leading exponents of the NIE) and Lance Davis conceded in their work on American economic growth that their 'model is not dynamic, and we know very little about the path from one comparative static equilibrium to another' (Davis and North, 1971, p. 263). It is a moot point as to whether North has been able to develop a dynamic theory in his subsequent work, as I explain later in the main text.
6 See amongst other sources Harriss (1993) and Rao's (1995) critical comments on this paper; and for a contrasting view, Lieten (1992).
7 See North (1978, p. 974). For an elaboration of the points I have raised here see the critical discussion of North's work by Lazonick (1991, pp. 310–18).
8 See Frankel and Rao (1989). They define 'dominance' as follows: 'the exercise of authority in society by groups who achieved socio-economic superiority and claimed legitimacy for their commands in terms of superior ritual status'. See also my development of the Frankel–Rao analysis in Harriss (1999).
9 On the recent growth performance of Rajasthan and Madhya Pradesh see some passing commentary in Rudolphs and Rudolphs (2001). On the theory of the

'developmental state', elaborated for Japan and other states in East Asia see White (1988).
10 Quotations here are from the 'Introduction' to the collection edited by Harriss et al. (1995) which includes essays by Douglass North and Robert Bates.
11 Douglass North has written of NIE that it 'builds on, modifies and extends neo-classical theory'. See Harriss et al. (1995, p. 17).
12 I am not implying that these two definitions of culture have absolutely the same meaning (see Hodgson, 2001, pp. 292–4), but both assert the historical specificity of cultural patterns. As Platteau (1994, p. 534) has argued: 'Ultimately, the cultural endowment of a society plays a determining role in shaping its specific growth trajectory, and history therefore matters.'
13 Amartya Sen shows this in his commentary on identity politics in *Reason Before Identity*, Delhi Oxford University Press, 1999.
14 See, for example, the comments of Harriss et al. (1995, pp. 4–5).
15 Hodgson (2001, pp. 301, 304, 312). Hodgson notes the continuities with Marx's approach, but argues that 'the analysis goes further than Marx, by grounding property relations in shared habits and by also emphasising the concept of culture' (p. 309).
16 The following discussion draws on my paper 'On Trust, and Trust in Indian Business', *Working Paper*, 02-35, Development Studies Institute, London School of Economics, 2002.
17 See Ramanujan's (1973) introduction to his translations of Veerasaivite poems, many of which expressly ridicule and repudiate caste.
18 This idea appears in some of Marx's writings on India; in Moore's 1966 classic; and most expressly in Saberwal (1996).
19 *The Economic Times*, for example, reported in August 2000 that 'Bourses signal gloom for family biz: The harsh truth emerging from the floor of the bourses is blowing away the last bit of hope for India's family owned businesses. The New Economy is steadily taking over the mettle from the Old Economy is a reality [sic] ... The family-owned businesses have performed poorly in the bourses, but worse they are failing to steer investors' interest. In contrast, the multinational corporations and the professionally-run Indian companies not only have succeeded in raising their market capitalisation through price accretion, but have added to their investors' base too ... The average market cap [on the other hand] of the Tatas [the biggest family group] declined by 43.5 per cent [between January and August 2000].' A. V. Birla group witnessed a decline of over 28 per cent and the Thapars, 36 per cent (*Economic Times*, 21 August 2000). Earlier the same business newspaper reported that between the end of 1997 and the end of 1998 the market capitalisation of the nine leading Indian business houses fell by 23 per cent, while that of the biggest MNC groups increased by the same percentage (*Economic Times*, 1 January 1999).
20 It seems likely that these attempts on the part of some family businessmen to set their own house in order represents one particular continuation of the debates about corporate governance in the country that were stimulated by the Cadbury Report – the report on corporate governance in the UK by Sir Adrian Cadbury – which has been addressed in meetings and conferences by the CII from 1996. As Jairus Banaji has said 'corporate governance is at the heart of the drama of liberalisation'. See Banaji (2001).

21 Even the biggest and most successful Indian business houses have experienced major problems because of tensions especially between siblings. It is a public secret that the TVS Group, the biggest based in Chennai, was divided between two factions, the members of which scarcely spoke to each other for twenty years, until a recent rapprochement occasioned by a shared concern about the abilities of TVS firms to be globally competitive.

22 As one senior businessman said to me it was the time of the 'handkerchief-on-the-seat' culture as customers queued up to wait to be supplied.

23 One of the great Chennai business houses, Amalgamations, remains largely private. In 1999–2000 the group as a whole, which includes 37 companies, only 3 of them listed on the stock exchange, had a turnover of Rs3,000 crores (around 7,000 million dollars). The companies are owned through an elaborate set of cross-holdings, by a holding company in which there are only five shares, belonging to the wife (now deceased) and the four children of the founder of the group. In circumstances like these there is little pressure for transparency. See *Business World*, 28 February 2000, for an account of the Amalgamations Group. The structure of cross-holdings, and their effects, closely resembles what is described as 'the pyramids' in East Asian family business holdings (see *The Economist*, 7 April 2001). The complex chains of control that still exist in many big family business groups in India, as well, make for a lack of transparency. This is one of the aspects of corporate governance which discourages foreign investors.

24 In these circumstances Indian companies became locked into a 'golden cage', as Suresh Krishna of Sundram Fasteners Ltd, puts it, meaning that they were powerfully discouraged from developing globally competitive businesses, whilst enjoying monopoly profits in the Indian market.

25 See Cohen (1974), for an analysis of this nexus of factors in Indian big business in the 1960s. In many ways family and kinship organisation, and the organisation of businesses in India, resemble those of China and Korea, rather than those of Japan, as these are described by Fukuyama (1995, Chs 8, 9, 12 and 15). China and Korea, he says, are 'low trust, family-oriented societies with weak intermediate organisations [between family and state]' whereas family ties are weaker in Japan and there is a much stronger emphasis on loyalty to those in authority rather than on family obligations.

26 The CEO of one the great families said to me: 'In my thirty years in business I never knew what competition is till now.'

27 See *Business India*, 21 February–5 March 2000 for an account of the Murugappas' organisation. The clear separation of business management and of family management is the line strongly advocated by John Ward, the Kellogg School professor who has assisted the Murugappa Group and who now facilitates the CII's Family Business Conclaves. It corresponds, too, with the emphasis that is being placed in recommendations concerning the reform of corporate governance in India, on securing the independence of company boards (see Banaji, 2001).

28 See Rudner (1994) on the Nattukottai Chettiars. My points here about boardroom culture are supported in the work of Banaji (2001). My argument may seem to be broadly supportive of that concerning generalised morality advanced by Platteau (1994), but I think that his approach is too one-sided and misses the inter-relationships of institutions and societal systems of values that I have drawn attention to here.

29 Landes (1998, p. 516). The point about culture 'not standing alone' is an extremely important one, in the light of the current vitality of cultural determinism – reflected, for example, in Francis Fukuyama's 1995 book on trust. On this point, as in other ways, Landes follows Max Weber, who of course also argued that culture does not stand alone in his classic *The Protestant Ethic and the Spirit of Capitalism*

References

Amit, B. (1973), 'A Study in Agricultural Backwardness under Semi-feudalism', *Economic Journal*, 83(329), pp. 120–37.
Banaji, J. (2001), *Corporate Governance and the Indian Private Sector: A Report*, Oxford, Queen Elizabeth House.
Bardhan, P. (2001), 'Institutional Impediments to Development', in S. Kahkonen and M. Olson (eds), *A New Institutional Approach to Economic Development*, Delhi, Vistaar Publications.
Boyce, J. (1987), *Agrarian Impasse in Bengal: Institutional Constraints on Technological Change*, Oxford, Oxford University Press.
Carr, E. H. (1961), *What Is History?*, London, Penguin Books.
Chang, Ha-J. (2002), *Kicking away the Ladder: Development Strategy in Historical Perspective*, London, Anthem Press.
Cohen, A. (1974), *Tradition, Change and Conflict in Indian Family Business*, The Hague, Mouton.
Davis, L. and North, D. (1971), *Institutional Change and American Economic Growth*, Cambridge, Cambridge University Press.
Dirks, N. (2001), *Castes of Mind: Colonialism and the Making of Modern India*, Princeton, Princeton University Press.
Frankel, F. and Rao, M. S. A. (eds) (1989), *Dominance and State Power in Modern India: Decline of a Social Order*, Vol. 1, Delhi, Oxford University Press.
Fukuyama, F. (1995), *Trust: The Social Virtues and the Creation of Prosperity*, London, Penguin Books.
Harriss, J. (1982), 'Making out on Limited Resources; Or, What Happened to Semi-feudalism in a Bengal District', *CRESSIDA Transactions II*, pp. 16-76.
Harriss, J. (1993), 'What Is Happening in Rural West Bengal? Agrarian Reform, Growth and Distribution', *Economic and Political Weekly*, 28(24), 12 June 1993.
Harriss, J. (1999), 'Comparing Political Regimes across Indian States: A Preliminary Essay', *Economic and Political Weekly*, 34(48), pp. 3367–77.
Harriss, J. (2002), 'On Trust, and Trust in Indian Business', *Working Paper 02–35*, Development Studies Institute, London School of Economics.
Harriss, J., Hunter, J. and Lewis, C. (eds) (1995), *The New Institutional Economics and Third World Development*, London, Routledge.
Hodgson, G. (2001), *How Economics Forgot History: The Problem of Historical Specificity in Social Science*, London, Routledge.
Landes, D. (1998), *The Wealth and Poverty of Nations*, New York, W. W. Norton.
Lazonick, W. (1991), *Business Organisation and the Myth of the Market Economy*, Cambridge, Cambridge University Press.

Lieten, G. K. (1992), *Continuity and Change in Rural West Bengal*, Delhi, Sage.
Moore, B. (1966), *The Social Origins of Dictatorship and Democracy*, New York, Beacon Press.
North, D. (1978), 'Structure and Performance: The Task of Economic History', *Journal of Economic Literature*, 16(3), pp. 963–78.
North, D. (1990), *Institutions, Institutional Change and Economic Performance*, Cambridge, Cambridge University Press.
North, D. (1995), 'The New Institutional Economics and Third World Development', in J. Harriss, J. Hunter and C. Lewis (eds), *The New Institutional Economics and Third World Development*, London, Routledge.
Nugent, J. (2002), 'The New Institutional Economics: Can It Deliver for Development and Change?', paper presented at the Conference on Paradigms of Change, University of Bonn, May.
Polanyi, K. (1944), *The Great Transformation*, Boston, Beacon Press.
Platteau, J. P. (1994), 'Behind the Market Stage Where Real Societies Exist', *Journal of Development Studies*, 30(3), pp. 533–77 (Part 1); and 30(4), pp. 753–817 (Part 2).
Pranab, B. (2001), 'Institutional Impediments to Development', in S. Kahkoren and M. Olson (eds), *A New Institutional Approach to Economic Development*, Delhi, Vistaar Publications.
Ramanujan, A. K. (1973), *Speaking of Siva*, Harmondworth, Penguin Books.
Rao, J. M. M. (1995), 'Agrarian Forces and Relations in West Bengal', *Economic and Political Weekly*, 30(30), 29 July.
Rao, M. G., Shand, R. and Kalirajan, K. (1999), 'Convergence of Incomes across Indian States: A Divergent View', *Economic and Political Weekly*, 27 March.
Rudner, D. W. (1994), *Caste and Capitalism in Colonial India: The Nattukottai Chettiars*, Berkeley, University of California Press.
Rudolphs, L. and Rudolphs, S. (2001), 'Iconisation of Chandrababu: Sharing Sovereignty in India's Federal Market Economy', *Economic and Political Weekly*, 5 May.
Saberwal, S. (1996), *The Crisis of India*, Delhi, Oxford University Press.
Sen, A. (1999), *Reason Before Identity*, Delhi, Oxford University Press.
Toye, J. (1995), 'The New Institutional Economics and Its Implications for Development Theory', in J. Harriss, J. Hunter and C. Lewis (eds), *The New Institutional Economics and Third World Development*, London, Routledge.
Weber, M. (1976), *The Protestant Ethic and the Spirit of Capitalism* (translation by Talcott Parsons), London, Allen & Unwin.
White, G. (ed.) (1988), *Developmental States in East Asia*, London, Macmillan.

4

The enforcement of contracts and property rights: constitutive versus epiphenomenal conceptions of law

Geoffrey Hodgson

Introduction

By what means are property rights sustained and contracts enforced? The purpose of this chapter is to consider the role and ontological status of law and legal systems in modern, complex socio-economic systems. Are such laws mere reflections of other socio-economic relationships between individuals or social classes, or is law itself a part of the underlying socio-economic reality? This enquiry raises general questions concerning the relationship between legal and economic institutions, and the relationship between markets and the state in particular.

The first and second sections of this chapter address, respectively, Marxism and a doctrine that I broadly describe as 'individualism'. It is argued that Marxism treats law as an expression (or epiphenomenon) of underlying (and inadequately defined) social relations. Individualism treats law as a mere formalisation of spontaneous outcomes of individual interactions. Hence, in different ways, both Marxists and individualists have typically favoured the idea that law is an epiphenomenon.

In contrast, it is argued in the third section that legal relations are partly constitutive of reality. The next section considers some general aspects of institutions, among which legal institutions are included. This prepares the ground for the discussion in the final section of different types of mechanism of institutional emergence and rule enforcement. It is argued that individualists have given too much relative emphasis to spontaneously emerging institutions and many legal institutions are not of this type. As a result, many legal institutions, including contracts and property rights, cannot be generally enforced in a complex society without 'third party' institutional intervention, such as by the state. This argument is extended to support Karl Polanyi's proposition that markets cannot function properly without some intervention by the state.

Marxism: law as an epiphenomenon of underlying structures

An epiphenomenal conception of law is one that regards laws and legal systems as expressions of another more fundamental level of reality, which itself does not include juridical relations. In other words, laws and legal systems are regarded as mere surface phenomena. This view of law is found among a wide variety of thinkers, adopting diverse methodological positions and political stances. This diversity will be manifest in the selection of writers considered below.

In the famous Preface to the *Contribution to the Critique of Political Economy* of 1859, Karl Marx (1971, p. 20) saw legal relations as part of the 'superstructure' built on 'the economic structure':

> The totality of these relations of production constitutes the economic structure of society, the real foundation, on which arises a legal and political superstructure and to which correspond definite forms of social consciousness.

Marx (1971, p. 21) saw 'property relations' as 'merely' an expression 'in legal terms' of the 'relations of production' in society. He continued:

> it is always necessary to distinguish between the material transformation of the economic conditions of production, which can be determined with the precision of natural science, and the legal, political, religious, artistic or philosophic – in short, ideological forms in which men become conscious of this conflict and fight it out.

Here law for Marx was an 'ideological form' of a relatively superficial character and lower epistemological status than the 'material' and 'economic conditions of production', which allegedly but inexplicably are more subject to scientific dissection. A similar treatment of legal relations is found in the first volume of *Capital*, which initially appeared in 1867. There Marx (1976, p. 178) wrote:

> The juridical relation, whose form is the contract, whether as part of a developed legal system or not, is a relation between two wills which mirrors the economic relation. The content of this juridical relation (or relation of two wills) is itself determined by the economic relation.

This again suggests that such changes in the legal form of the contract are surface phenomena. The grain of truth in this argument is that legal formalities are never adequate or accurate summaries of economic or social relationships. The flaw in the argument is to fail to recognise that economic content is affected by legal relations, as well as vice versa. Each direction of causality requires us to recognise the reality and importance of the legal form. Accordingly, the legal form of the contract gives use clues about the underlying economic relation, even if the mirror to which Marx alludes is always in fact a distorting one.

What is striking in Marx's diverse writings on this question is his failure to define adequately key terms such as 'economic structure', 'relations of production', 'economic conditions of production', or 'economic relations'. The meaning of these terms is not self-evident and they cry out for definition. Furthermore, a clear meaning has to be given to these terms to give meaning to Marx's strict dichotomy between 'economic' and 'legal' relations. His failure to define the 'economic' deprives his argument of analytical force.

Lack of clarity is not confined to Marxism. In the literature in the social sciences as a whole, the term 'economic' carries a multiplicity of meanings. Meanings range from connotations of 'material production' to being concerned with 'economy' in a sense of cost-reduction or efficiency. Marx hinted at the first meaning, but few economists today would see the economy as essentially the sphere of material production. 'Economics' is regarded by mainstream economists as the study of choice under conditions of scarcity, wherever they may apply. I am not defending this definition here. I am simply pointing out that no consensus exists over the meaning of terms such as 'economy', 'economic' or 'economic relation'. This consensus has been lacking during the nineteenth and the twentieth centuries. Neither is there a commonly accepted definition of the term 'relations of production'. Hence, when we find these terms in the writings of Marx or anyone else we cannot take them as self-evident.

Whatever, 'the economy' might mean, for Marx its essential structures do not include legal relations. The law is seen as an expression or reflection of these 'economic relations' or 'relations of production'. What Marx rules out is the possibility that laws may be a necessary and essential part of these 'economic relations' or 'relations of production'. Certainly, for Marx and subsequent Marxists, the presumption has often been that changes in fundamental 'economic relations' or 'relations of production' would of themselves lead to more superficial or confirmatory changes in the law. The danger here is that the importance of law is itself downgraded, in both analytical and policy terms.

At root here are questions of social ontology. Marx and Engels (1976, p. 59) wrote in the *German Ideology* in about 1845–47: 'ruling ideas are nothing more than the ideal expressions of the dominant material relations'. Again, the meaning of 'material relations' is never defined, but it is clear that Marx and Engels regard them as fundamental, while law is epiphenomenal and in the secondary realm of ideas and ideologies. In emphasising matter over ideas, Marx and Engels were clearly reacting against German idealism, but in doing so they developed formulations that were extreme in some respects and ill-defined in others.

Within their social ontology, legal relations are secondary to an unelaborated 'material' essence. The closest that Marx and Engels (1976, pp. 41–2) get to a clarification and justification of this 'materialist' position is their statement that

> men must be in a position to live in order to be able to 'make history'. But life involves before everything else eating and drinking, housing, clothing and

various other things. The first historical act is thus the production of the means to satisfy these needs, the production of material life itself.

There is an important element of truth here. Basic human needs, such as food and shelter, must be satisfied to make human life possible. However, as Marx and Engels themselves emphasised, production and consumption are social processes, involving social structures and relations between individuals. Social relations and institutions are just as necessary for human society as production itself.

Even in early and primitive human societies, social relations, including those linked to the production of human needs, involved social rules. Some of these rules could be described as laws. Hence it does not follow from the above argument by Marx and Engels that social rules and legal relations necessarily have a secondary status. The production of human needs involves social relations, social rules and ideas, as well as material objects. On this basis there is no convincing argument to give the latter priority or ontological primacy.

Individualism: law as an epiphenomenon of individual interactions

Marxism differs substantially from both ontological and methodological individualism (Heijdra et al., 1988; Sensat, 1988). Ontological individualism upholds that social reality consists of nothing else but individuals. Methodological individualism is the idea that all social phenomena should be explained only in terms of individuals, individual preferences or individual goals. In the case of ontological individualism, law has no status other than an attribute of individuals, including their attitudes or beliefs. In other cases of methodological individualism it would be possible to see law as epiphenomenal to relations or interactions between individuals, but explicable completely in the terms of the individuals themselves.

Without going into further details, we may bear these nuances in mind when considering the broad type of approach that I shall describe in general terms as 'individualist'. The following examples should help to clarify what I mean by this term in this context.

Robert Sugden (1986, p. 5) spoke for many sharing his individualist preconceptions when he argued that legal codes 'merely formalize . . . conventions of behaviour' that have evolved spontaneously out of individual interactions. Others downgrade the reality of legal structures in the manner in which they define such concepts as property and exchange. Ludwig von Mises (1949) and others have defined production as an 'exchange with nature' thus downgrading the concept of exchange by ignoring the fact that nature itself cannot own or enforce property rights. Armen Alchian (1977, p. 238) defined the property rights of a person in the universal terms of 'the probability that his decision about demarcated uses of the resource will determine the use'. The upshot of this definition is that if a thief manages to keep stolen goods then he acquires a substantial property right in them, even if, on the contrary, legal or moral conclusions would suggest that they remain the rightful property of their original owner.

The individualist approach to the understanding of legal relations is generally exemplified in the work of some 'new institutional economists' who attempt to explain all institutions – including legal institutions – in terms of individuals and their interactions.[1] This methodological individualism is applied to legal institutions such as property and the state. For example, Richard Posner (1980) developed a theory of the emergence of property in primitive societies that depended on elaborate 'insurance' arrangements between parties.

In terms similar to Posner, Oliver Williamson (1983) wrote of a system of 'hostages', where both parties to an agreement are committed to non-salvageable costs. This argument suggests that a system of contract is possible and sustainable without the intervention of a legal system. The morsel of truth here is that it is sometimes more costly for parties to break a contract than to complete it. Accordingly, there can be strong incentives for contract compliance other than legal sanctions alone. Nevertheless, the 'hostages' idea is implausible as a general mechanism for governing contracts. Contracts are vulnerable to default when new circumstances, perceptions or information arise. Committed costs are insufficiently substantial and widespread to deal with all such eventualities, many of which are unforeseen.

Williamson rightly emphasised that most contractual disputes are resolved without direct recourse to the courts. However, this does not mean that the legal or quasi-legal institutions have no place in the everyday process of contract. As Avner Greif et al. (1994, p. 746) put it, 'the effectiveness of institutions for punishing contract violations is sometimes best judged like that of peacetime armies: by how little they must be used'. Where the rule of law prevails, the mere possibility of access to the courts is sufficient for the legal system to bear down upon contractual agreements. The threat of legal action can be silent. A very small frequency of successful litigations is required to act as a credible check on the dealings of the whole trading population.

Other authors have suggested that the state and an entire legal system can evolve spontaneously. This suggestion is bolstered by historical studies of circumstances in which contract enforcement evolved in medieval times through the efforts of trading coalitions or town guilds (Greif, 1989, 1993, 1994; Greif et al., 1994; Landa, 1994; North, 1991) or even in more modern circumstances in the absence of an adequate international political or legal authorities (Clay, 1997). These studies show that in the absence of a strong (international) legal authority, quasi-legal institutions emerged to help police and enforce contracts. The historical evidence shows that quasi-legal institutions such as trading coalitions can develop in the absence of legal and statutory ones. We can conclude that trade generally may rely on extra-legal as well as legal powers of contract enforcement. However, it would be wrong to conclude from these studies that extra-legal institutions are always adequate or efficient, or that legal authorities generally play a minor or dispensable role in all trade.

The individualist conception of law that is examined here is one that regards the law as a mere formalisation of outcomes of interactions between individuals. Many of the authors cited above do not consistently take this extreme view, for instance by accepting elsewhere that laws have significant and real effects. Nevertheless, the stated positions of Sugden and others are consistent with an individualist conception of law, and from this evidence I posit this conception as an 'ideal type'.

The individualist conception of law typically depends upon the argument that legal rules and mechanisms evolve spontaneously, without state intervention. This opens up the possibility of treating the law as an epiphenomenon of individual interactions, although some proponents of wholly spontaneous legal evolution may argue that the law is more than merely epiphenomenal. Nevertheless, by showing the limits of spontaneous legal evolution we undermine a key component of the individualist conception.

Interestingly, some of the more powerful recent criticisms of these individualist treatments of law have come from those who are in original and other respects close to the 'new institutional economics'. Against Posner's (1980) theory of the emergence of property, Jack Knight (1992, p. 120) argued convincingly that relatively complex institutional rules concerning property are unlikely to emerge and be widely accepted in such circumstances: 'It is hard to see how such complicated rules could emerge from a decentralized process.'

In response to the idea of the entirely spontaneous evolution of legal structures, two types of question emerge. First, the models and historical examples used to support this idea involve the evolution of relatively simple legal rules. Would such a spontaneous evolution be possible if more complex rules were involved? Knight answered this question in the negative. Second, the models and historical examples rely on cases either (1) where a small number of traders is involved, and hence it is likely that those that renege on contracts can be recognised and punished, or (2) where traders belong to an identifiable family or ethic group and all members of this group are punished if any of its members break agreements. Would such a spontaneous evolution of legal systems be possible if there were a large number of traders, and group punishment was disallowed?

The second question has been addressed in the work of Itai Sened (1995, 1997). Several authors, including Greif (1993), have used game theory to illustrate these arguments. In response, Sened (1995, p. 162) observed:

> Like traditional economists, most game theorists systematically overlook the role of law enforcement... Many important social institutions do not emerge as equilibria in games among equal agents, but as equilibria in games among agents who control old institutions and agents who challenge such institutions

with new demands. In particular, governments play a crucial role in the evolution of institutions that protect individual rights.

In his extended critique of the notion of property without law, Sened (1997) argued that true individual rights are established only when a territorial institution establishes its monopoly over the use of force. However, to accept the role of the state in the evolution of property and contract is not to romanticise this institution. Sened sees the state not as a benevolent and disinterested legislator but as an institution whose members pursue their own interests. For Sened, governments weight the benefits of granting rights against the cost of enforcement. Sened (1997, p. 123) further wrote:

> Governments do not erect such structures out of benevolence or moral concern. They grant and protect rights in order to promote their own interests. But in doing so, they fulfil two crucial social functions. The function of maintaining law and order that is a necessary condition for economic growth and affluence, and the function of arbitrage between conflicting interests.

In addition, Sened showed the limitations of the aforementioned type of game theoretical model involving a few agents. With a larger number of players it is more difficult for individuals to establish mutual and reciprocal arrangements that ensure contract compliance. If trading coalitions do emerge, then these themselves take upon state-like qualities to enforce agreements and protect property. In a world of incomplete and imperfect information, high transaction costs, asymmetrically powerful relations and agents with limited insight, powerful institutions are necessary to enforce rights. These institutions result from a complex bargaining process. Sened uses an n-person prisoners' dilemma to show that the introduction of a government, enforcing rights, can often improve on a sub-optimal outcome.

It is an open question as to whether another strong institution, apart from the state, could fulfil this necessary role. However, it is not to endorse or glorify the state if we start analytically from the assumption that a state will emerge, and analyse its possible role on the process of establishment of property. It is proposed here that the emergence of a powerful institution like the state is a necessary but not a sufficient condition for the protection of property and other individual rights.

Individualist writers, from David Hume to Friedrich Hayek over-emphasised the spontaneous element in the emergence of law, as largely an outcome of individual interactions. Marxists, on the other hand, see law as an inessential epiphenomenon, which can be stripped away to reveal the 'true' a-legal, social reality beneath. Neither individualism nor Marxism is correct. In civilised societies the law is part of the essential social reality, yet at the same time it is more than the outcome of interactions between individuals. It is also an outcome of a power struggle between citizens and the state. The state benefits by maintaining its power, while citizens benefit from a regime of law and order in which they can produce and trade.

Although there are major differences between the individualist writers discussed here, there are also common features. For individualist writers, of the type discussed above, social reality consists fundamentally of individuals, individual purposes and relations between individuals. Legal relations are mere expressions of individual preferences and the payoffs pertaining to individual interactions. As in Marxism, the law itself plays no constitutive role in the formation of modern society.

Contracts and property rights: the constitutive role of law

Individual property is not mere possession; it involves socially acknowledged and enforced rights. Individual property, therefore, is not a purely individual matter. It is not simply a relation between an individual and an object. It requires some kind of customary and legal apparatus of recognition, adjudication and enforcement. Such legal systems made their first substantial appearance within the state apparatuses of ancient civilisation. Since then the state has played a major role in the establishment, enforcement and adjudication of property rights.

At the same time, the development of any state apparatus carries the omnipresent danger that individual private property would be wilfully appropriated by the state, perhaps using the ancient norms and precedents of communal tenure. The state has the capacity to appropriate, as well as to protect and enforce, private property. For private property to be relatively secure, a particular form of state had to emerge, countered by powerful and multiple interest groups in civil society. This meant that a pluralistic state with some separation of powers, backed up by a plurality of group interests in the community at large. With such a balance of power, a framework of constitutional law could be established, in which the interests of both the state and the citizenry could be protected to some degree.

What concerns us more here is the logical and causal, rather than the historical priority of a legal apparatus over contracts and property. Some individualists uphold that contract and property are potentially spontaneous developments, not requiring a state. The valuable nugget of truth here is that these institutions always involve elements of spontaneity and social interaction, and outcomes cannot result entirely from decree. The realisation that social orders can arise without design or decree is a major insight. The particular flaw is to fail to recognise that some kind of legal or quasi-legal apparatus, however rudimentary, is necessary to preserve property rights in complex societies. The preservation of internal property rights requires sanctions against theft or fraud. Furthermore, enduring contracts rely upon systems of adjudication in the case of dispute, often using written records of precedents and rules.

To accept the role of the state in the evolution of property and contract is not to romanticise this institution. The existence of a state does not automatically give rise to private property. It is a necessary but not sufficient condition for its full development. The legal system has also to be grounded in the customs and practices of civil society. Without other checks, property is always vulnerable to state sequestration.

Clearly, trade will not develop unless there is specialisation in production and a division of labour. In addition, the rise of the state is historically and logically prior to the emergence of exchange and markets: state bureaucracies and codified legal systems are necessary preconditions for developed and enduring markets. Contrary to Williamson's (1975, p. 20) famous remark that 'in the beginning there were markets', the evolution of the market required a prior legal system. Hence we may concur with Geoffrey Ingham (1996, p. 264) that 'both historically and analytically speaking, in the beginning there were bureaucracies!'

Once contracts and property became established, regularised internal trade was possible. Markets appeared in places where a number of such exchanges could regularly take place. A market was 'a place set apart' from the traditional, ceremonial and political activities of state or society. But often the city or national state was involved in the creation, organisation and regulation of such markets (Polanyi, 1944; Polanyi et al., 1957).

This does not mean that legal systems are all that matters nor that they are always effective. In many societies, legal rules were or are ineffective. As Douglass North (1991) has pointed out, the adoption in the nineteenth century of an amended version of the US Constitution by the newly independent South American countries did not lead to democracy. There was not an adequate civil basis for decrees of popular power. Sometimes the influences of religious and other beliefs are so strong that they negate the formal declarations of the law. In India, for instance, discrimination according to social caste has been illegal since 1948. Yet such discrimination is still widespread and is sustained by Hindu religious beliefs. The formal declaration of a law is not enough to make it a reality. Laws have to be rooted in the customs and observances of the people.

However, in cases where legal rules are ignored or defied, there are always other social rules that are generally being observed. Even when the law is generally observed, effective formal law can only be a representation of a subset of these underlying rules. Other social rules, not specified in law, are always important. In addition, formal legal rules are potent in societies where the rule of law prevails.

In any case, legal rules are always incomplete. Émile Durkheim (1984, p. 158) argued in 1893 that every contract itself depends on factors other than full, rational calculation: 'For in a contract not everything is contractual.' He explained that whenever a contract exists there are factors, not reducible to the intentions or agreements of individuals, which have regulatory and binding functions for the contract itself. These factors consist of rules and norms that are not necessarily codified in law. In a complex world, no complete and fully specified contract can be written. The parties to the agreement are forced to rely on institutional rules and standard patterns of behaviour, which cannot for practical reasons be established or confirmed by detailed negotiation. Typically, each person takes for granted a set of rules and norms, and assumes that the other party does the same.

Even the simplest economic activities rely on a taken-for-granted network of institutional supports. Ludwig Wittgenstein (1953) used the example of signing a cheque. Such an act depends upon the prior existence of many institutions, routines and conventions – banks, credit and law – that are the antecedents and frameworks of socio-economic action. Without such institutions all human activity would be hopeless. Similar remarks apply to other everyday activities, such as mailing a letter or waiting for a bus. In every case, we habitually and unthinkingly depend upon a dense network of established institutions and routines. It is to these deeper and more general issues that we now turn.

On institutions in general, and law in particular

At the root of the problem of the nature of legal relations is the more general issue of social ontology, concerning the nature of society, social structures and their relations with individuals. What is crucial is the ontological status of institutions in general, and property, markets and law in particular. Although in all cases they are underdeveloped, the implicit ontologies in both Marxism and the individualist writers in this respect are found wanting.

By social institutions I mean durable systems of established and embedded social rules that structure social interactions. In short, institutions are socially embedded systems of rules. Language, money, law, systems of weights and measures, traffic conventions, table manners, firms (and other organisations) are all institutions. All institutions involve some shared conceptions, expectations and ways of thinking.

In what sense are such rules embedded? Pragmatist philosophers and 'old' institutional economists such as Thorstein Veblen (1919) argue that institutions work only because the rules involved are embedded in shared habits of thought and behaviour. The prevailing rule structure helps to create habits and preferences that are consistent with its reproduction. By reproducing shared habits of thought, institutions create strong mechanisms of conformism and normative agreement. Hence 'custom reconciles us to everything' – as Edmund Burke put it – and customary rules acquire the force of moral authority. In turn, these moral norms help to further reinforce the institution in question. Hence institutions are emergent social structures, based on commonly held habits of thought. Upon these structures, actual or potential patterns of social behaviour arise. Habits are the constitutive material of institutions, providing them with enhanced durability, power and normative authority.

As John Searle (1995) argued at length, the mental representation of an institution is partly constitutive of that institution since an institution can only exist if people have the necessary beliefs and mental attitudes. Accordingly, legal and other social rules are not merely formal expressions of an underlying reality but a major constitutive part of that reality. Consequently, institutions are simultaneously both objective structures 'out there', and subjective springs of human agency 'in the human head'. Institutions are in this respect like Klein Bottles: the subjective 'inside' is simultaneously the objective 'outside'.

Marxism has little to say about social rules. There is a strong emphasis on social structure; but structure is described rather vaguely in terms of relations of class and production, without further definition of those terms. Individualism sees social rules as emerging through individual interactions, while overestimating the possibilities of emergence of complex rule systems.

Two vital features are missing in both accounts. First, neither Marxism nor individualism provides an adequate picture of the institutionalised individual. Neither shows how institutions may help to reconstitute the mentality or preferences of the individuals involved. I argue elsewhere that the mechanism involved in such a reconstitution is one of institutional constraints or conventions altering habits of cognition or behaviour (Hodgson, 2002a, 2003). Second, neither Marxism nor individualism provides an adequate account of institutional change. Marxism sees institutional changes as surface expressions of other deeper – but inadequately defined – structural changes. Individualism concentrates on the spontaneous emergence of institutions from individuals but overlooks the fact that the emergence of many institutions depends on *other institutions*, and not all institutions can spring spontaneously from individuals alone (Hodgson, 2002b). It is specifically to the limits of spontaneous institutional emergence and self-regulation that we now turn.

Self-enforcement versus external enforcement

Of course, it is important to understand the significance of self-organising institutions and spontaneous orders. A focus on self-organising aspects of the social system can be traced back to David Hume and Adam Smith, and it is a major theme in the Austrian school of economics from Carl Menger to Friedrich Hayek. The literature on self-organisation and spontaneous orders provides the essential insight that institutions and other social phenomena can arise in an undersigned way through structured interactions between agents.

However, this does not mean that the concepts of self-organisation or spontaneous order are sufficient for an understanding of all institutions. They do not tell us the whole story. Indeed, it can be argued that much of the literature on institutions is disfigured by a relatively excessive emphasis on these (albeit essential) ideas, to the detriment of other vital issues. These issues are briefly introduced here.

It is important not to overlook the extent to which processes of institutional formation or self-organisation depend on specific types of rule, incentive structure, preference stability or normative salience. Consider first some important distinctions between different types of incentive structure. The first relevant distinction is between coordination rules and outcomes, on the one hand, and other types of incentive structure and outcomes, on the other hand. Additional issues, such as moral pressure and endogenous preference functions, will be considered later. At first we assume individuals with given preference functions.

Coordination rules typically provide incentives for everyone to conform to the convention. For this reason, a coordination outcome can be relatively stable and self-policing. Language is an example. Willard van Orman Quine (1960) made the point that language has an error-correcting regime. Individuals have an incentive to make their words clear. As an essential condition of communication, the coding itself (the signifier) must be unmistakable, even if the meaning (the signified) remains partly ambiguous. In communication we have strong incentives and inclinations to use words and sounds in a way that conforms as closely as possible to the perceived norm. Although languages do change through time, there are incentives to conform to, and thus reinforce, the linguistic norms in the given region or context. Norms of language and pronunciation are thus largely self-policing.

Similarly, some (but not all) legal rules have a strong self-policing element. For example, there are obvious incentives to stop at red traffic lights and to drive on the same side of the road as others. Although infringements will occur, these particular laws can be partly enforced by motorists themselves, because infringements can increase perceived personal risks. But even here some variations are possible. Motorists in a 'macho' culture may relish taking such risks. The possibility of self-policing institutions depends on perceived payoffs, and such perceptions can sometimes be moulded by cultural circumstances. This important issue is raised again later below; prior to that point we continue to assume exogenously given preference functions.

A coordination outcome can be self-enforcing; because not only does each player lack any incentive to change strategy, but also each player wishes that other players keep to their strategy as well (Schotter, 1981, pp. 22–3). If agents have compatible preferences and strategies in this sense, then coordination rules can often emerge spontaneously and be self-regulating. For example, if the rule 'drive on the right-hand-side' of the road emerges, then each driver has an incentive to stick to this rule and also wishes that other drivers would do likewise. Even if I prefer to drive on the left, but I find myself in a country where driving on the right is the convention, then I will drive on the right, and others will prefer that I do

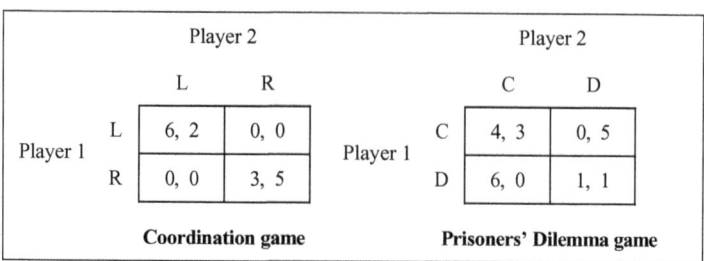

Figure 4.1 A coordination game and a Prisoners' Dilemma game

this. I do this because my second-best option is itself much better than a head-on collision! A coordination outcome has characteristics of stability and self-enforcement, even when the outcome is not ideal for everyone involved. An example of this is illustrated in Figure 4.1.

As an example of a contrasting case, consider the famous Prisoners' Dilemma game, as also illustrated in Figure 4.1. At least in a one-shot play of this game, each player has an incentive to defect. The situation of mutual cooperation (C–C) is not a Nash equilibrium because each player can gain an advantage by shifting from (C) cooperation to (D) defection. The Nash equilibrium is (D–D), where each player gets less than she would if both players cooperated (C–C). A 'spontaneous order' may emerge but it is clearly sub-optimal, by any reasonable criterion. Although a Nash equilibrium may emerge, its social and individual suboptimality always brings it into question.

Robert Axelrod (1984) has famously argued that with repeated (indefinite or infinite) plays of the Prisoners' Dilemma game, enduring cooperation (C–C) can emerge because each player can learn to reciprocate attempts to cooperate by the other, and punish defection when it occurs by further defection. But this result is not universal and Axelrod's 'tit-for-tat' strategy can be out-competed by alternative behavioural rules (Binmore, 1998). There is no guarantee that cooperation will emerge or be enduring even in repeated games of this type.

Compare some of the key differences between a coordination game and a Prisoners' Dilemma game. In the case of a coordination game the incentives to conform to the emergent convention are strong and enduring, even if it is not everyone's first choice. Furthermore, as in the representative cases of languages and rules of the road, normative issues are often secondary to the straightforward incentives and disincentives involved. This partly because the incentive structure involved is normally sufficient to reach an enduring and acceptable outcome. In a Prisoners' Dilemma game there is also a Nash equilibrium. The equilibrium is stable in the one-shot case, but it will not necessarily endure if the game is repeated. Furthermore, the transparent sub-optimality of the Nash equilibrium, from both the individual and the social point of view, by Paretian and other plausible

Contracts and property rights

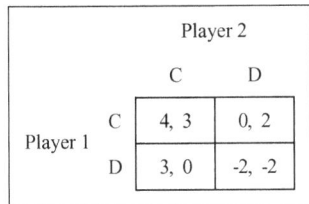

Figure 4.2 The previous Prisoners' Dilemma game transformed

criteria, raises normative questions including the desirability of third-party intervention to improve the situation for everyone involved. We make a big mistake of we treat these two types of situation as the same, or if we concentrate on models of self-organisation based on coordination-type incentive structures, while neglecting other equally important incentive configurations.

With its potential for sub-optimal outcomes, a Prisoners' Dilemma situation would be a candidate for intervention by a third party such as the state. It is conceivable that such a third party could intervene to deter or prevent defection. For example, if the state made defection illegal and subject to a fine of 3 units (or alternatively taxed defection by 3 units), then the Prisoners' Dilemma game in Figure 4.1 would be transformed to the different type of game in Figure 4.2. Clearly, this is no longer a Prisoner's Dilemma game. Both players have an incentive to cooperate, irrespective of the strategy of the other.[2]

Note also that a similar structure of payoff incentives may be attainable by an alteration in the preferences of the players, as well as by a tax or a fine. If a view prevailed that defection was intrinsically bad or immoral, then agents might internalise such ideas in their own preferences. If these changes in preferences were strong enough, they could lead to changes in perceived payoffs similar to those represented in Figure 4.2, and mutual cooperation would result. Arguably, such changes in preferences could result from a period of mutual cooperation in repeated plays of the game. Without propaganda or coercion, individuals might become freely persuaded that cooperation has a greater relative moral superiority over defection. This would be a case of systemically endogenous enforcement, rather than enforcement from outside. Alternatively, or in addition, a powerful third party could help by example, persuasion or propaganda to shift individual preferences. For example, a democratic state might implore us to fasten seat belts in cars or recycle our garbage, or a totalitarian regime could adopt more sinister methods of propaganda or coercion to reach similar goals.

Of course, such a practical transformation of incentives and outcomes would be very difficult to engineer in complex, real world circumstances. But this does not mean that state intervention is always dysfunctional. The transformation in Figure 4.2 dramatically oversimplifies the real world complexities and problems of knowledge involved. But it does show that payoff manipulations can have important qualitative effects. The practical possibility of efficacious state intervention is a matter for detailed theoretical and empirical enquiry in specific circumstances.

A key point here is that while self-organisation and spontaneous orders are important and widespread in both nature and society, they rely on specific types of incentive alignment that ensure that most individuals have no reason to deviate from or disrupt the emergent order. Other payoff structures may not lead to optimal or satisfactory outcomes and additional factors may be necessary to reach a satisfactory outcome. One possibility is to rely on the enforcement measures of a third party. Another possibility is that the persistence of a satisfactory solution for a while may lead to a shift of preferences that favours its prolongation. These two possibilities are not mutually exclusive and one process could benefit from the other. The first process involves external enforcement and the second would be an example of systemically endogenous enforcement through reconstitutive downward causation of individual preferences (Hodgson, 2002a).

Normative issues are clearly raised at this point. Although all rules involve costs and benefits, there is a big difference between following a rule because it is convenient to do so, and following a rule because of a normative belief. Coordination rules are foremost examples of rules that are followed primarily because of convenience. Viktor Vanberg (1994, p. 65) has rightly pointed out that writers in the spontaneous order tradition – from Hume and Smith through Menger to Hayek – have failed to account adequately for the difference between coordination rules and rules involving normative constraints (legal or moral rules). Walter Schultz (2001, pp. 64–6) stressed a similar distinction in his powerful discussion of the problem of enforcement of social rules.

Until recently, as noted above, the problem of enforcement has been neglected in much of the 'new' institutionalist tradition. Some institutions are largely self-enforcing. But things are even more different with many other laws and institutions. Laws that restrict behaviour, where there are substantial, perceived net advantages to transgression, are the ones that require the most policing. Hence people frequently evade tax payments or break speed limits. Without some policing activity the law itself is likely to be infringed, debased and 'brought into disrepute.'

Accordingly, there are incentives to debase money. With potential quality variation, individual agents have an obvious incentive to use a less costly, poor quality or fake version of the medium of exchange. Given that traders cannot readily detect all variations, then forgeries and debasements are possible. If they are allowed to endure, then bad money will drive out the good. Money is not self-policing in the same way as language.[3]

Self-policing mechanisms can be undermined if there is the possibility of undetected variation from the norm and there is sufficient incentive to exert such variations. Language and money differ in this respect. The argument for enforcement by a third party such as the state is thus stronger in the case of money and some laws, than in the case of language.

Furthermore, the boundary between potentially self-policing and other institutional arrangements depends on perception, which in turn may depend on the cultural context. While self-organisation is an extremely important phenomenon in both nature and human society, it cannot account for all the peculiar features of human social organisation. To treat human society as closely analogous to the spontaneous emergence of order in a simple chemical system or a slime-mould is to belittle the reality of human agency. It would ignore the importance of reconstitutive downward causation on human agents, including the human capacities to prefigure, imitate and adopt the dispositions of their neighbours.

Some conclusions and implications

We are now in a position to draw the key threads of the argument together. Marxism belittles the role and place of law in modern society by treating it as an epiphenomenon of unspecified, underlying social relations. Individualism sees law as an expression of interactions between individuals. Its account of the emergence of institutions exaggerates the relative importance of coordination games, to the neglect of situations where legal rules do not emerge so readily through individual interactions.

To overcome these problems, two key propositions must be accepted. First, at least in a society subject to the rule of law, legal relations are an important part of 'underlying' social reality and not merely epiphenomenal. This does not mean that social reality is or can be entirely defined in legal terms, because legal rules are inevitably incomplete. But it does mean that law is part of the constitution and nature of social reality, and it governs specific human interactions such as commodity exchanges and contract enforcements. As Warren Samuels (1989, p. 1567) put it in an article reaching a similar conclusion: 'the law is a function of the economy, and the economy (especially its structure) is a function of law'.

Second, many important legal rules, enforcements and structures cannot emerge spontaneously through individual interactions. They require additional third party enforcement by the state or another strong institution. This means that many key institutions and legal relations, arguably including property and markets, exist as a result of a combination of spontaneous and statutory mechanisms. The existence of one institution has to be considered in relation to the others that help to support and sustain it. Institutions are generally and inevitably intertwined, and often provide essential mutual support for one another.

At least in countries where the rule of law prevails, laws are part of socio-economic reality and have real effects. In general, legal relations are not mere formalities, but are backed with the powers and sanctions of the state legal system. Laws set bounds on our behaviour, including the kind of contracts that may be concluded. The courts and police, even if they are used infrequently, can be used to enforce the fulfilment of contracts or to enforce the collection of damages for non-performance. These are clearly matters of power and control. Legal relations do not constitute the whole story, but they are nevertheless vital. The nature of legal relations is an important determining factor for socio-economic behaviour and outcomes.

The propositions in the preceding two paragraphs are explicit or implicit in writings of some 'old' institutional economists (Commons, 1924; Mitchell, 1937). In addition, however, similar views are expressed, with criticisms of some of the defects of the individualist account, by a number of authors working at least nominally within the tradition of the 'new' institutionalism (Knight, 1992; North, 1997; Sened, 1995, 1997). Perhaps their fullest development so far is in modern 'economic sociology' (Friedland and Sanders, 1985; Block, 1990; Campbell and Lindberg, 1990; Lie, 1997).

The argument here reinforces Karl Polanyi's (1944) view that a self-regulating market is unattainable and his conclusion that markets are inevitably intertwined with the state. But the argument here is different in some respects. Polanyi argued that the state had to intervene in the development of a market economy to avoid malfunctions and excesses. Polanyi (1944, p. 76) wrote: 'Administrators had to be constantly on the watch to ensure the free workings of the system ... Society protected itself against the perils inherent in a self-regulating market system.' The argument here does not negate these propositions but combines them with the additional and reinforcing insight that markets and exchange are in part *constituted* by legal relations and the state. The state is involved in the market not merely to ensure its functioning and restrain any potential havoc, but also to constitute its very existence. This underlines the enduring relevance and importance of Polanyi's writings for the understanding of the complex relationship between the market and the state, even the arguments present here are not identical to Polanyi's in every respect.

Acknowledgements

The author thanks the participants at the October 2002 CRIC Workshop in Manchester and at a seminar in the Erasmus Institute for Philosophy and Economics in Rotterdam, including Mark Blaug, Uskali Mäki, Stan Metcalfe and Jack Vromen, for comments on an earlier draft of this essay.

Notes

1 This is not the case with regard to the later works of North (1997) who, for example, emphasises the importance of third-party or state enforcement of some laws.

2 See Ostrom et al. (1994, p. 77) for a discussion of the way in which additional rules such as these may 'affect the benefits and costs assigned to actions and outcomes'.
3 See my discussion of Menger's theory of money in Hodgson (2001, Chapter 7).

References

Alchian, A. A. (1977), 'Some Implications of Recognition of Property Right Transaction Costs', in K. Brunner (ed.), *Economics and Social Institutions: Insights from the Conferences on Analysis and Ideology,* Boston, Martinus Nijhoff.

Axelrod, R. M. (1984), *The Evolution of Cooperation,* New York, Basic Books.

Binmore, K. (1998), Review of *Complexity and Cooperation* by Robert Axelrod, *Journal of Artificial Societies and Social Situations,* 1(1), available at http://jasss.soc.surrey.ac.uk/JASSS/1/1/review1.html.

Block, F. (1990), *Postindustrial Possibilities: A Critique of Economic Discourse,* Berkeley, University of California Press.

Campbell, J. L. and Lindberg, L. N. (1990), 'Property Rights and the Organization of Economic Activity by the State', *American Sociological Review,* 55(5), pp. 634–47.

Clay, K. (1997), 'Trade without Law: Private-order Institutions in Mexican California', *Journal of Law, Economics and Organization,* 13(1), pp. 202–31.

Commons, J. R. (1924), *Legal Foundations of Capitalism,* New York, Macmillan.

Durkheim, É. (1984), *The Division of Labour in Society,* translated from the French edition of 1893 by W. D. Halls, with an introduction by Lewis Coser, London, Macmillan.

Friedland, R. and Sanders, J. (1985), 'The Public Economy and Economic Growth in Western Market Economies', *American Sociological Review,* 50(4), pp. 421–37.

Greif, A. (1989), 'Reputations and Coalitions in Medieval Trade: Evidence on the Maghribi Traders', *Journal of Economic History,* 49(4), pp. 857–82.

Greif, A. (1993), 'Contract Enforceability and Economic Institutions in Early Trade: The Maghribi Traders' Coalition', *American Economic Review,* 83(3), pp. 525–48.

Greif, A. (1994), 'On the Political Foundations of the Late Medieval Commercial Revolution: Genoa During the Twelfth and Thirteenth Centuries', *Journal of Economic History,* 54(2), pp. 271–87.

Greif, A., Milgrom, P. and Weingast, B. R. (1994), 'Coordination, Commitment, and Enforcement: The Case of the Merchant Guild', *Journal of Political Economy,* 102(4), August, pp. 745–76. Reprinted in Knight, J. and Sened, I. (eds) (1995), *Explaining Social Institutions,* Ann Arbor, University of Michigan Press.

Heijdra, B. J., Lowenburg, A. D. and R. J. Mallick (1988), 'Marxism, Methodological Individualism, and the New Institutional Economics', *Journal of Institutional and Theoretical Economics,* 144(2), pp. 296–317.

Hodgson, G. M. (1984), *The Democratic Economy: A New Look at Planning, Markets and Power,* Harmondsworth, Penguin.

Hodgson, G. M. (1999), *Economics and Utopia: Why the Learning Economy is Not the End of History,* London and New York, Routledge.

Hodgson, G. M. (2001), *How Economics Forgot History: The Problem of Historical Specificity in Social Science*, London and New York, Routledge.
Hodgson, G. M. (2002a), 'Reconstitutive Downward Causation: Social Structure and the Development of Individual Agency', in E. Fullbrook (ed.), *Intersubjectivity in Economics: Agents and Structures*, London and New York, Routledge.
Hodgson, G. M. (2002b), 'The Evolution of Institutions: An Agenda for Future Theoretical Research', *Constitutional Political Economy*, 13(2), pp. 111–27.
Hodgson, G. M. (2003), 'The Hidden Persuaders: Institutions and Individuals in Economic Theory', *Cambridge Journal of Economics*, 27(2), pp. 159–75.
Ingham, G. (1996), 'Money Is a Social Relation', *Review of Social Economy*, 54(4), pp. 507–29.
Knight, J. (1992), *Institutions and Social Conflict*, Cambridge, Cambridge University Press.
Landa, J. (1994), *Trust, Ethnicity, and Identity: Beyond the New Institutional Economics of Ethnic Trading Networks, Contract Law, and Gift Exchange*, Ann Arbor, University of Michigan Press.
Lie, J. (1997), 'Sociology of Markets', *Annual Review of Sociology*, 23, pp. 341–60.
Marx, K. (1971), *A Contribution to the Critique of Political Economy*, translated from the German edition of 1859 by S. W. Ryazanskaya and edited with an introduction by M. Dobb, London, Lawrence and Wishart.
Marx, K. (1976), *Capital*, Vol. 1, translated by Ben Fowkes from the fourth German edition of 1890, Harmondsworth, Pelican.
Marx, K. and Engels, F. (1976), *Karl Marx and Frederick Engels, Collected Works*, Vol. 5, *Marx and Engels: 1845–47*, London, Lawrence and Wishart.
Mises, L. von (1949), *Human Action: A Treatise on Economics*, London, William Hodge.
Mitchell, W. C. (1937), *The Backward Art of Spending Money and Other Essays*, New York, McGraw-Hill.
North, D. C. (1991), 'Institutions', *Journal of Economic Perspectives*, 5(1), pp. 97–112.
North, D. C. (1997), 'Prologue', in John N. Drobak and John V. C. Nye (eds), *The Frontiers of the New Institutional Economics*, San Diego and London, Academic Press.
Ostrom, E., Gardner, R. and Walker, J. (1994), *Rules, Games, and Common-pool Resources*, Ann Arbor, University of Michigan Press.
Polanyi, K. (1944), *The Great Transformation: The Political and Economic Origins of Our Time*, New York, Rinehart.
Polanyi, K., Arensberg, C. M. and Pearson, H. W. (eds) (1957), *Trade and Market in the Early Empires*, Chicago, Henry Regnery.
Posner, R. A. (1980), 'A Theory of Primitive Society, with Special Reference to Law', *Journal of Law and Economics*, 23(1), pp. 1–53.
Quine, W. van Orman (1960), *Word and Object*, Cambridge, MA, Harvard University Press.
Samuels, W. J. (1989), 'The Legal-economic Nexus', *George Washington Law Review*, 57(6), pp. 1556–78.
Schotter, A. R. (1981), *The Economic Theory of Social Institutions*, Cambridge, Cambridge University Press.

Schultz, W. J. (2001), *The Moral Conditions of Economic Efficiency*, Cambridge and New York, Cambridge University Press.
Searle, J. R. (1995), *The Construction of Social Reality*, London, Allen Lane.
Sened, I. (1995), 'The Emergence of Individual Rights', in Jack Knight and Itai Sened (eds), *Explaining Social Institutions*, Ann Arbor, University of Michigan Press.
Sened, I. (1997), *The Political Institution of Private Property*, Cambridge, Cambridge University Press.
Sensat, J. (1988), 'Methodological Individualism and Marxism', *Economics and Philosophy*, 4, pp. 189–219.
Sugden, R. (1986), *The Economics of Rights, Co-operation and Welfare*, Oxford, Basil Blackwell.
Vanberg, V. J. (1994), *Rules and Choice in Economics*, London, Routledge.
Veblen, T. B. (1919), *The Place of Science in Modern Civilization and Other Essays*, New York, Huebsch.
Williamson, O. E. (1975), *Markets and Hierarchies: Analysis and Anti-Trust Implications: A Study in the Economics of Internal Organization*, New York, Free Press.
Williamson, O. E. (1983), 'Credible Commitments: Using Hostages to Support Exchange', *American Economic Review*, 74(3), pp. 519–40.
Wittgenstein, L. (1953), *Philosophical Investigations*, Oxford, Basil Blackwell.

5
Karl Polanyi and the instituted process of economic democratisation

Marguerite Mendell

> The scholar's endeavor must be, first to give clarity and precision to our concepts, so that we may be enabled to formulate the problems of livelihood in terms fitted as closely as possible to the actual features of the situation in which we operate; and second to widen the range of principles and policies at our disposal through a study of the shifting place of the economy in human society ... Accordingly, the theoretical task is to establish the study of man's livelihood on broad institutional and historical foundations. The method to be used is given by the interdependence of thought and experience. Terms and definitions constructed without reference to data are hollow, while a mere collecting of facts without a readjustment of our perspective is barren. To break this vicious circle, conceptual and empirical research must be carried pari passu. Our efforts shall be sustained by the awareness that there are no short cuts on this trial of inquiry. (Polanyi, 1977, p. liv)

Introduction

Karl Polanyi's concept of an 'instituted economic process' describes the paradoxical need for a social and political apparatus to install the nineteenth-century self-regulating market economy. It also describes other social systems, or sub-systems that structure economic activity to correspond with and reflect a variety of norms, patterns of integration – social, cultural, political. The richness of Polanyi is found in his historical analysis of economies governed under very different principles, economies that feature production, consumption, exchange, but are not coordinated by the market system. His foray into non-market societies (with extensive reference to the literature in economic anthropology) documents economic activity embedded in societal forms, an instituted economic process that can only be understood in its larger societal context. This is familiar to Polanyi scholars. What is perhaps less familiar and resonates with the objectives of this volume to examine processes of institutionalisation and de-institutionalisation, are earlier writings by Polanyi in which he addresses the process of social transformation through another lens. In these writings, many foundational questions are also raised that in today's context, are helpful in understanding socio-economic and institutional transformation. In particular, Polanyi's insistence on *agency*. As he would write much later in *The Livelihood of Man*:

> For the dogma of organic continuity must, in the last resort, weaken man's power of shaping his own history. Discounting the role of deliberate change in human institutions must enfeeble his reliance on the forces of the mind and spirit just as a mystic belief in the wisdom of unconscious growth must sap his confidence in his powers to re-embody the ideals of justice, law, and the freedom in his changing institutions. (Polanyi, 1977, p. liv)

In contrast to both the atomistic individual in neoclassical theory and the socially embedded individual underlying network analysis, Polanyi adopts the Aristotelian conceptualisation of the societalised individual. His foundational argument, influenced by Christian philosophy, is that each individual is social in essence. Among contemporary thinkers, Charles Taylor contributes most to our understanding of the societalised individual. It is our social, indeed, our dialogical nature that governs our lives as individuals, that determines how we identify ourselves in the context of and with others, as well as our membership in social groups (Polanyi, 1935; Taylor, 1989, 1991).[1] This is markedly distinct from the current instrumentalist approach to social capital and trust (Coleman, 1988; Putnam, 1995; Fukuyama, 1995). In Polanyi, the emphasis is on the constitutive elements that define us as social beings. The atomistic individual motivated by self-interest is a social artefact. 'Society is not something between men, nor over them, but is within them ... so that society as reality ... is inherent within the consciousness of each individual' (Polanyi-Levitt and Mendell, 1987, p. 24). Relationships are the 'key loci' of the self. This is a powerful conceptual tool with which to reject methodological individualism that denies the essence of individuals as socially constituted. Moreover, it does not slide into a collectivist approach that erases individuality.[2]

Individuals are also agents of social change; they are not passive actors constrained by their institutional settings. Today's reality increasingly confirms this as new institutional arrangements emerge and become part of a complex and interwoven institutional order that is increasingly fragile, despite pretences to the contrary. It features a great deal of experimentation 'with old and new forms of politico-economic rearrangement' that cannot easily be reduced to any simple notion of transition (Amin and Palen, 2001, p. 570). This is true whether we consider institutional change at local or national or, for that matter, international levels.

We have a rich legacy of institutional thought to draw upon with which Polanyi is associated, that addresses the processes of institutional change or transformation and considers the impact of institutions on patterns of behaviour and habit as well as the impact of individual action on institutions, thereby taking account of pressures on existing institutional arrangements from below, so to speak. Despite this literature, J. Rogers Hollingsworth, in an article on the implications of doing institutional analysis for the study of innovations, states that we do not really have a consensus within the social sciences on what we mean by institutions or by institutional analysis. Although we talk a great deal about institutional change, we can neither measure the pace of this change nor understand how new institutions emerge. 'One of the reasons for these shortcomings is that the social sciences are deficient in a theory of institutions. The building of new institutions and redressing the decline of some of the most important institutions of our societies are among the most important problems of our time' (Hollingsworth, 2000, pp. 598, 600).

Order, disorder and social innovation

Considering the morphology of adaptation and transformation, a given model centres empirically on a core of actors whose behaviour conforms most closely to it; outside it there are successive layers of increasingly variability, which protect and legitimate the core model, but are themselves more exposed to external pressures... Under external pressure for change, core actors may first be driven to a more fervent assertion of the model, because of the way they have become 'locked in' to particular modes of behaviour, while *peripheral actors are more likely to innovate and adapt. Over time, the pressure for change is then transmitted to the ever more exposed core* (Radice, 2000, p. 732).[3]

Societies are coordinated by many institutional arrangements and patterns of governance – by markets, hierarchies, networks, associations, communities, clans, the state – calling for 'configurative analysis' to describe the relationship between these institutional arrangements and the rules and norms that govern a society (Hollingsworth, 2000, p. 605). These arrangements intersect and constrain each other; they generate inter-institutional tensions that force change in modes of societal governance or regulation. This is rare in societies with little institutional diversity, such as the former Soviet Union. The greater the diversity in institutional arrangements within society, the greater its capacity to adapt to new circumstances, the greater the probability for institutional innovation. 'In sum, the robustness of institutions often depends on multiple and diverse principles and logics of actions, on the inconsistency of principles and procedures, on *patterned forms of disorder*' (*ibid.*, p. 613).[4] What Hollingsworth refers to as 'incoherence in governance' is destabilising in that it provokes ongoing change. It is this incoherence or instability that inspires social and institutional innovation. If we now consider agency, we may have the basis for a conceptual framework to understand institutional innovation as the product of complex, continuous and extensive interaction between individuals in different institutional settings, that both responds to and shapes the larger institutional context in which they reside.

For those engaged in dynamic social change occurring within civil society in a variety of institutional contexts and their uneven but visible impact on societal modes of coordination, this proposed analytical framework captures the processes of institutional change at local, regional, national and international levels. It reveals the incoherence within apparently stable governing institutions and opens the way for theorising the role of actors in disturbing established patterns of governance. This is a powerful tool as it goes far beyond the more common appeal to engage in a linear, bottom-up analysis to evaluate the impact of social groups, movements on public policy and institutional innovation. It forces *continuous* analysis of *continuous* change. Unlike technological innovation, itself a complex field, social and institutional innovation is more difficult to evaluate as it is an iterative and interactive process that challenges power relations embedded within institutional settings at all levels.

Hollingsworth's analysis of institutional innovation is extremely useful as current empirical research demonstrates that social innovation that is transmitted to a macro policy regime is, in fact, occurring within micro and meso settings or sub-systems of regulation that are challenging norms through successful practice. Even if their larger impact remains incremental, they are contributing to a process of institutional reconfiguration. His insistence on the need for more descriptive studies to document institutional complexity, resonates with Polanyi's proposed method to study 'man's livelihood' by combining 'conceptual and empirical research', by conceptualising lived realities.[5]

Our interest is in the impact of so-called civil society on policy or institutional innovation, on the pre-conditions that institutionalise, so to speak, those practices that are then transmitted across institutional sub-systems and vertically to macro or governing institutions. The innovation that results in instituted processes of economic democratisation, the focus of this paper, is rooted in civil society and is generating the tension that Hollingsworth claims is the source of innovation. Our focus is on the actors, on agency and their role in constructing institutional settings, or sub-systems that contribute to the diversity of institutional spaces that have multiplied in recent years. In particular, the social innovation associated with community or civil society based sub-systems that are institutionalised territorially (local and regional intermediary or meso institutional settings) and/or sectorally (regional, national and supra-national movements).

Our job is to document these diverse and often divergent experiences as they emerge and evolve in their respective societies and cultures. In so doing, we are constructing an analytical framework, a methodology that combines *thought and experience*, leaving behind the barren conceptual world of axiomatic reasoning for a more complex analysis of social systems and their economies (Polanyi, 1977). The institutional complexity of contemporary society, the co-existence of many sub-systems that often compete with or contradict the dominant order, challenge prevailing institutional structures. Their increased visibility and impact on patterns of coordination strongly suggests that 'disorder within order' (Amin, 2001, p. 567) or 'patterned forms of disorder' (Hollingsworth, 2000, p. 613) more accurately describe contemporary reality. As these sub-systems become more numerous, complex and effective, we follow Polanyi's guidance and simultaneously describe and conceptualise this institutional complexity. And we recall Polanyi's emphasis on agency, of the capacity of social actors to construct, modify and transform their institutions.

Deconstructing Polanyi

In re-reading Polanyi, especially his writings in economic anthropology and economic history, one returns to the heated debates between so-called formalists and substantivists he inspired in the 1960s, creating two rival schools of thought. In these writings, Polanyi confirmed the uniqueness of nineteenth-century liberalism. The market system is one of many possible institutional forms. Markets had existed throughout history as 'accessories of economic life'; the economy was always 'submerged in social relationships'. His search for a comparative economics led him to study the social arrangements that distinguish societies, to discover 'the place of the economy in society', thereby abandoning the artificial identification of the economy with its market form. In 1947, he wrote that the student of social anthropology is well equipped to understand the reality of society and to resist the universal application of economic determinism to all societies.

Polanyi's critique of market liberalism is well known and increasingly adopted within mainstream thinking.[6] Ideas do eventually have to catch up with reality. What is less often referred to are the principles that underlie his critique – the foundational principles that challenge both utilitarian and collectivist views of individuals. Polanyi's writings both before and after the publication of *The Great Transformation* provide the basis for a methodology that we can only begin to explore. These writings, in a sense, foreground the powerful analysis and critique of market society in *The Great Transformation*, of systemic breakdown, as the separation of the economy from society calls for continuous intervention to ensure the survival of the system, and for what we may call instituted sub-systems or 'liberatory alternatives' that are the result of a different conceptualisation of humanity (Harvey, 2000, p. 186). These are alternatives that, for the time being, exist within the dominant system but are forcing change, however uneven this may be. Their emergence or visibility (many have existed for a long time) is now being documented extensively around the world.[7] The conceptual work remains to be done. But for this, we need to join those who are calling for a broader interdisciplinarity. With few exceptions, those theorists who refer to themselves as heterodox economists have not reached out sufficiently to philosophy, epistemology and feminist studies.[8]

Polanyi provides important guideposts for such a methodology. Moreover, to Polanyi's insistence on the need for conceptual and empirical work, we must add strategy. The gathering of experiences that are contesting the dominant paradigm through lived realities is itself a strategy for change in different settings. While differences distinguish experiences from each other, they share the capacity to build alternatives within a larger institutional setting and force change when reality is increasingly in conflict with theory and policy. Polanyi's analysis also helps to understand why barriers to change are erected, but as Hugo Radice (2000) states, the contrast between innovative practices by 'peripheral actors' and the tenacious grip on a model that corresponds less and less with reality and reveals the intransigence of its advocates, eventually gives way, even if a coherent new model is yet to be invented, let alone applied.

Instituted processes of economic democratisation

How do institutional arrangements emerge, interact with each other? How do they survive within the larger society? What gives rise to this institutional hybridity in the first place? We know that interaction between these various institutional settings is key to larger social innovation and transformation. Do the same conditions hold within each of these individual institutional settings, that is, the need for interaction between social actors committed to designing new institutional spaces? The literature extends from those such as Hollingsworth who are particularly interested in innovation, to those who address the question more politically to consider the design of democratic participatory institutions that exist within a larger institutional configuration but challenge its norms through different structures of governance and practice (Fung and Wright, 2001), to those who examine spatial institutional arrangements from the perspective of learning environments and sites for territorial transformation that call into question market dominated strategies (Harvey, 2000; Stohr, 2000; Torjman and Leviten-Reid, 2003a). While the impact of these institutional arrangements on larger institutional change varies, their increasing visibility and success contributes to growing pressure for broader institutional change. How is this transmitted? What are the processes of transmission and transformation at each level? As we try to answer complex questions such as this, we discover quickly that a binary view of the world is not helpful. Systemic breakdown does not reveal the institutional complexity and processes of adaptation and transformation of contemporary society.[9]

Karl Polanyi's writings on economic democracy, his proposal for a functional democracy (functional socialism), influenced by the guild socialism of G. D. H. Cole, the writings of Robert Owen, and especially those of Otto Bauer and the experience of 'Red Vienna' (1917–34), and his writings on education, contribute towards a conceptualisation of contemporary processes of institutionalisation, in particular, to what I have called *instituted processes of economic democratisation*.

Polanyi provides a framework, however incomplete, that allows us to explore how he envisaged a transformation to a functional democracy might come about. The seeds were there. Vienna had constructed a municipal socialism that was participatory, inclusive and democratic. In response to Ludwig von Mises who insisted that a socialist economy was impossible, Polanyi argued that a democratic associative model of socialism was indeed feasible and, contrary to Von Mises, that a system of prices and a well functioning economy could be built on principles other than the free market. I recall this socialist pricing debate briefly because of its contemporary resonance (Mendell, 1990). Today, these writings by Polanyi provide an important historical reference for the current references to associational democracy or democratic associationalism that try to capture many alternative institutional arrangements.[10] Community based or locally organised socio-economic initiatives are developing viable organisational forms with functioning economies that challenge the prevailing model through practice. Like the many contemporary writers who are conceptualising these democratic sub-systems of regulation or parallel systems of socio-economic organisation, that exist and co-exist within a larger institutional context and in sharp contradiction with the dominant paradigm, Polanyi was engaged in debates to dispel the impossibility of socialism thesis and in conceptualising an alternative grounded in the lived reality of socialist Vienna.

In his proposal for a functional democracy that was dynamic and interactive, Polanyi designed an institutional arrangement of associations of producers and consumers and an overarching 'kommune', a citizens assembly of sorts, to work in the collective interest. For this functional democracy to succeed, it required both the commitment to the collective well-being as well as the 'effective performance of each individual within his particular occupation and function'. This, however, is only possible if each individual is conscious of his particular function.

Consciousness of particular economic functions requires, as its precondition, an overview and collective comprehension of all the elements of the economy. Bauer is absolutely correct in his insistence that the educational work to be done is the problem of social organization ... consciousness without context, without specific circumstances, without – in the case of a collectivity – Ubersicht (overview) is an impossibility (Polanyi, 1922).

Polanyi emphasized the need to study the processes of transformation in which people participate and how these processes respond to needs. He referred to this as the 'inner-overview' or democratic surveillance *ubersichtleitung* – from the inside out – in which our lives and our lived experiences are foundational. Associations, trade unions, can provide this information, as civil society organisations (social movements, community groups) are well placed to do so. This data is essential to an 'overview' *ubersichtsproblem* of the economy – the macro picture. The link between the micro and the macro is provided by associations. This resonates with the emergent and hybrid institutional sub-systems that, in many cases, reconfigure relations between the private, public and community sectors, often in the form of partnerships. And with the key role that social groups are playing in constructing a body of knowledge in which people are the agents of socio-economic organisation and transformation. Today we speak of capacity building, empowerment, learning environments and so on. While one has to carefully evaluate how these concepts are being applied, I believe that they help to understand dynamic processes of institutional change; they do matter. Polanyi's emphasis on collective learning provides us with a very important strategic and transformative tool. And his insistence that the laws of the economy can be negotiated applies to market liberalism as well in which laws of the economy are negotiated to serve the imperatives of the market economy.

Democracy and social learning

In an article on the international crisis, written in 1933, Polanyi wrote that a reconstituted democracy requires an active citizenry; in an alienating environment, this can only occur through social learning. 'Knowledge' of the situation is both necessary and sufficient to dispel the myth of inevitability and powerlessness. 'Knowledge' of the prevailing political and economic environment and the realisation that one can resist, mobilises individual and collective action. This requires institutional innovation. In Polanyi's words, 'the more richly, deeply and diversely the institutions of democracy are cultivated, the more realistic it is to devolve responsibility on the individual' (Polanyi, 1933).

The market as an instituted process relies on a social construction of knowledge that reinforces the prevailing orthodoxy through text, through interpretation, through language, through the media and the formation of public opinion. Polanyi argued passionately for curriculum reform and universal access to education. In the 1940s, he participated in the debates on educational reform in the UK, on socialist education within the labour movement, and on adult education. He spoke of the need to develop the intellectual and cultural equipment of the working class to enable it to transform society, to construct a body of valid knowledge that denies the inevitability of a class society and the impossibility of democratic planning. This required a radical reorganisation of knowledge to reflect the reality of working-class experience. This is very close to the critical and vital work of feminist scholars and their legitimation of everyday experience as their corpus of basic knowledge and as a mobilising force for women in transforming the lives of both men and women.

Lived reality challenges the dominant paradigm. Equipped with this knowledge, 'the individual is himself, economically as well as epistemologically, a different individual'.[11] But let's have a look at different ways in which education or knowledge construction can be seen. Geoffrey Hodgson writes that 'learning takes place through and within social structures and... involves adaptation to new circumstances and ultimately to the reconstitution of individuals' such that, 'institutions and cultures play a vital role in establishing the concepts and norms of the learning process' (Hodgson, 2002, pp. 176–7). Polanyi examines the nature of those institutions and cultures and whether people can recognise themselves in the learning process. If they cannot, they are disempowered and indeed, disengaged. Once again the experience of Red Vienna and its commitment to culture, social issues and education, played a critical role in his analysis, having seen the powerful impact of a socially situated educational experience.

In Vienna, 'the leading idea was to create a new environment for human life by institutional means at the center of which was school reform, rooting the child's mind in its cultural setting'. The social democrats took this further to transform citizens into a 'socialized humanity' through a 'politics of pedagogy' (Mendell, 1994). The objective was to transform the 'outlook' of the working class. Education, the reappropriation of knowledge was critical for an emancipatory politics. Or in the words of Raymond Williams (1989), it is necessary to mobilise imaginations; people need to believe that change is possible.[12] We need to construct 'discursive regimes' – systems of knowledge and ways of thinking to define a different kind of imaginary and different modes of action that reflect our daily lives and the world in which we live (Harvey, 2000, p. 214). We read this and think of course, of popular education and the important work of Paolo Freire and the politics of pedagogy. But as Veblen insisted, this also applies to technological change that requires a 'change in how people think'. It is not enough to embed knowledge in those implementing technological change; the 'acquisition and transmission of knowledge is a social process' (McCormick, 2002, p. 274). Today, knowledge as a social process underlies the growing references to 'situated knowledge', to learning environments that describe socio-economic innovation in communities, localities, regions. These innovations are the outgrowth of a collective learning process as individuals and groups engage in successful strategies to transform their economies (Torjman and Leviten-Reid, 2003b).

Most of these recent experiences emerged in response to economic restructuring in the 1980s, and to a critique of a clientelist approach of the welfare state levelled by many progressive groups, though some have a longer history. As these experiences become more numerous and more visible today, they appear less as fragments and more as institutional subsystems that are the result of negotiation, collaboration and partnerships between stakeholders – private, public and popular or social movements. Social entrepreneurship, collective ownership and social investment compete effectively with market based structures of private ownership and individual profit. These initiatives are occurring within new hybrid institutional settings, often at the meso level. They are creating horizontal linkages between different social actors and the state and vertical sectoral linkages. They are locally or regionally based; they may be represented by larger associative networks that negotiate on their behalf with different levels of government. These initiatives depend on co-evolution, a combination of learning and resilience on the part of those involved (Paquet, 1999). But the foundation for these initiatives rests with local actors, who are transforming their communities by reclaiming knowledge, by denying the narratives of inevitability through practice. The result is a mix of political, social and economic mechanisms that vary from community to community and between countries. What some refer to as an innovative learning process is, in fact, a radical cognitive project, out of which a new conceptual discourse based in action is emerging, forcing the state to react, to participate and, in many cases, to itself engage in institutional innovation. These new institutional arrangements are reconfiguring social relations and are having an impact on the larger agenda, on transforming regimes of governance.

For Polanyi, working-class education was about more than access, though this was certainly critical in the debates in which he took part in the 1940s. A working-class education was essential for capacity building, for mobilisation, for social transformation. Today, 'citizens and community have in associative forms the process of production and management as well as a field for democratic learning and experimentation, a mechanism of autonomy in the face of market alienation and bureaucratic power of the state' (Carpi, 1997, p. 265). The institutional settings that consolidate these initiatives become strategic learning environments as they bring together actors previously situated in hierarchical institutional arrangements.

I would like to take this further and suggest that today, there is a *process* or, rather, there are *processes of economic democratisation* underway that are re-embedding the economy in social contexts and that these are taking many forms; community and local economic development, the social economy, industrial districts, new instruments of capital accumulation, participatory budgets, to name a few, with demonstrated socio-economic objectives. One would have previously considered these as a catalogue of counter-movements in response to the (predictable) failure of the neo-liberal agenda. While this is certainly true, they are also demonstrating the importance of *process* as they emerge and evolve. This is generating debate among political scientists with growing reference to deliberative democracy to describe the impact of these initiatives on institutional innovation.

An interesting challenge by Chantal Mouffe questions deliberative democracy as an appropriate theory of democracy since its ultimate goal is to resolve crisis and achieve consensus, which she says, is not the essence of democracy. For Mouffe, agonistic democracy better captures this environment and reflects the dynamic tensions and negotiations that define and enrich democracy (Mouffe, 2000). These are important conceptual debates that bring us closer to understanding how systemic change occurs, at the micro, meso and macro level. The actors are, in a very real sense, writing the script. Within the reality of society, the many experiences occurring in the north and in the south challenge any notion of institutional isomorphism or inertia as institutions are forced to react, however slowly, however incrementally. Indeed, these experiences occur within a larger institutional setting that maintains its grip on the economy. That said, processes of change originating in civil society, are influencing individual and collective behaviour and institutional transformation. What may appear as disaggregated double movements spread over time and space or as differentiated, isolated and marginalised socio-economic innovations, are, in fact, located within new and intersecting institutional sub-systems. They demonstrate, in Polanyi's words, 'the role of deliberate change in human institutions' of the 'freedom to change institutions' (Polanyi, 1977).

These processes of change are forms of resistance that move beyond claims for resources and political space, beyond a politics of contestation to negotiating new social arrangements within a plurality of institutions that intersect and overlap and in so doing, increasingly blur the boundaries between civil society and governing institution.

Notes

1 John Dewey also began with 'sociable individuals'. Today, there is a great deal of interest in Dewey's 'deliberative democracy'. His notion of the 'public' must, however, not only be understood as functional, as people coming together to reduce the 'burden of their separate actions' [sic] and to engage in 'collective self-regulation' but as foundational in his recognition of the 'unbreakable distinction between individuals and society' (Sabel, 1997, p. 182).
2 Philosophers, theologians and more recently, feminist scholars, address this in ways that economists and other social scientists do not. Julie Nelson, in her book, *Feminism, Objectivity and Economics* emphasizes that 'connection and relation do not necessarily imply the dissolving of individual identity' and the need for 'the reconfiguration of selfhood as including both individuality and connectedness or relatedness'. The 'feminist approach to economics' she is proposing 'is by no means only 'more sociological' than current economics, if what is meant by that is a turn to analysis assuming that agency lies entirely outside the individual' (Nelson, 1996, p. 33–4).
3 Emphasis, M. Mendell. Radice (2000) reinforces our argument that 'state centered analysis tends to beg the question of what agencies in society shape the agenda of the state'. He concludes that institutional variation should be approached via historical political economy. Only this way can we analyse, to borrow from Polanyi, 'the shifting place of the economy in human society' as institutional variation does imply a variegated set of relationships between economy and society.
4 Emphasis, M. Mendell.

5 In an article published in 1997, J. Rogers Hollingsworth and Robert Boyer provide an extremely useful portrait of the many 'modes of governance' within various levels of society and how institutional arrangements that were previously 'congruent at national levels are now more dispersed at multiple spatial levels'. They are increasingly 'nested' in regimes at regional, national, continental and international levels. In Hollingsworth's article written in 2000, he examines the institutional contexts themselves to evaluate their potential for innovation. By taking his analysis further to explore the role of actors in this changing institutional environment, we may be able to answer the question Hollingsworth and Boyer raised earlier in 1997. Does this institutional complexity; the 'nestedness' to which they refer, affect our capacity to govern ourselves democratically? In other words, how does democracy express itself in this complex environment? (Hollingsworth and Boyer, 1997, pp. 470–7). Similar questions are being raised by those attempting to conceptualise the increasing political role played by social movements that are not only spatially dispersed, but are often in contradiction with each other. How they 'displace contradictions' and work together to transform both their traditional 'fixed positions' and their impact on policy regimes is another way of exploring the issues with which we are concerned (Hardt, 2002, p. 117).
6 The Karl Polanyi Institute of Political Economy, located at Concordia University in Montreal is currently researching the web for references to Polanyi since 1989. There are approximately 25,000 references in this period alone. A similar search will be conducted for the 1980s. It is not surprising that there was a surge of interest after 1989.
7 Some experiences, such as the participatory budget in Port Allegre or the Grameen Bank in Bangladesh are well known. These are often showcased to demonstrate the capacity of civil society to successfully initiate alternative socio-economic strategies and institutions. The experiences and initiatives are so numerous that many analysts increasingly refer to the emergence of a parallel economy. Others speak of a citizens economy. Still others continue to maintain that these experiences remain on the margins. Clearly, we disagree. Whether we address the growing social investment movement worldwide and its international networks, individual experiences such as Mondragon in Spain, the social economy and its supporting institutional context in the North and in the South, as well as new instruments, tools and practices such as fair trade, while these are, in many cases, fragmented and differentiated, they are increasingly networked internationally are influencing policy at national and supranational levels, the European Union, for example. Many of these experiences emerged in the South; many of these have inspired alternative strategies in the North.
8 Feminist economists are contributing to this work. See for example Marianne A. Ferber and Julie Nelson (1993).
9 Jane Tooke, in an interesting article on community involvement, contributes to this argument from a different and very useful perspective. She explores transformative politics within 'spaces for community involvement' and concludes that the capacity for community organisations to challenge power relations is demonstrated in their ability to simultaneously acquiesce and rebel. While they must comply with regulations, norms, etc. they have the ability, through practice, to transform these. Drawing on Foucault, Tooke suggests

that 'governmental power is an "open and strategic game" rather than simply a question of imposing laws'. This is another way of saying that within institutional contexts or sub-systems, innovation is possible. Our question is when and how this gets transmitted to coordinating institutions (Tooke, 2003, p. 234).
10 See Cohen and Joel Rogers (1995) and Amin (1996).
11 See Vickers (1994), quoted in Hodgson (2002, p. 177).
12 Raymond Williams, *Resources of Hope*, quoted in David Harvey (2000, p. 17).

References

Amin, A. (1996), 'Beyond Associative Democracy', *New Political Economy*, 1(3), pp. 309-33.
Amin, A. and Palan, R. (2001), 'Towards a Non-rationalist Political Economy', *Review of International Political Economy*, 8(4), pp. 559-77.
Carpi, T. (1997), 'The Prospects for the Social Economy in a Changing World', *Annals of Public and Cooperative Economics*, CIRIEC International, 68(2), pp. 247-80.
Cohen, J. and Rogers, J. (eds) (1995), *Associations and Democracy*, New York, Verson.
Coleman, J. (1988), 'Social Capital in the Creation of Human Capital', *American Journal of Sociology*, 94, pp. S95-S120.
Ferber, M. A. and Nelson, J. (eds) (1993), *Beyond Economic Man: Feminist Theory and Economics*, Chicago, University of Chicago Press.
Fukuyama, F. (1995), *Trust: The Social Virtues and the Creation of Prosperity*, London, Hamish Hamilton.
Fung, A. and Wright, E. O. (2001), 'Deepening Democracy: Innovations in Empowered Participatory Governance', *Politics & Society*, 29(1), pp. 5-41.
Fulbrook, E. (ed.) (2002), *Intersubjectivity in Economics: Agents and Structures*, London, Routledge.
Hardt, M. (2002), 'Today's Bandung?', *New Left Review*, 14 (second series), pp. 112-18.
Harvey, D. (1996), *Justice, Nature and the Geography of Difference*, Oxford, Basil Blackwell.
Harvey, D. (2000), *Spaces of Hope*, Berkeley, University of California Press.
Hodgson, G. (2001), *How Economics Forgot History*, London, Routledge.
Hodgson, G. (2002), 'Reconstitutive Downward Causation: Social Structure and the Development of Individual Agency', in Edward Fulbrook (ed.), *Intersubjectivity in Economics: Agents and Structures*, London, Routledge.
Hollingsworth, J. R. (2000), 'Doing Institutional Analysis: Implications for the Study of Innovations', *Review of International Political Economy*, 7(4), pp. 595-644.
Hollingsworth, J. R. and Boyer, R. (1997), 'From National Embededdness to Spatial and Institutional Nestedness', in *Contemporary Capitalism: The Embeddedness of Institutions*, Cambridge, Cambridge University Press.
Hollingsworth, J. R. and Boyer, R. (eds) (1997), *Contemporary Capitalism: The Embeddedness of Institutions*, Cambridge, Cambridge University Press.

McCormick, K. (2002), 'Veblen and the New Growth Theory: Community as the Source of Capital's Productivity', *Review of Social Economy*, 60(2), pp. 263–77.
McRobbie, K. (ed.) (1994), *Humanity, Society and Commitment*, Montreal, Black Rose Books.
Mendell, M. (1990), 'Karl Polanyi and Feasible Socialism', in Kari Polanyi-Levitt (ed.), *The Life and Work of Karl Polanyi*, Montreal, Black Rose Books.
Mendell, M. (1994), 'Karl Polanyi and Socialist Education', in Kenneth McRobbie (ed.), *Humanity, Society and Commitment*, Montreal, Black Rose Books.
Mouffe, C. (2000), *The Democratic Paradox*, London, Verso.
Nelson, J. (1996), *Feminism, Objectivity and Economics*, London, Routledge.
Paquet, G. (1999), *Governance through Social Learning*, Ottawa, University of Ottawa Press.
Polanyi, K. (1922a), 'The Functionalist Theory of Society and the Problem of Socialist Economic Calculability'. Translation from German by Kari Polanyi-Levitt of 'Die Funktionelle Theorie der Gesellschaft und das Problem der Sozialistichen Rechnungslegung', *Archiv fur Sozialwissenschaft und Sozialpolitik*, 52(1), pp. 218–28.
Polanyi, K. (1922b), 'Some Reflections concerning Our Theory and Practice'. Translation from German by Kari Polanyi-Levitt of 'Neue Erwangen zu unserer Theorie und Praxis', *Der Kampf*, January, pp. 18–24.
Polanyi, K. (1933), The Mechanisms of the World Economic Crisis'. Translation from German by Kari Polanyi-Levitt of 'Der Mechanismus der Weltwirtschaftskrise', *Der Oesterreicische kswirt*, 25.
Polanyi, K. (1935), 'The Essence of Fascism', in J. Lewis, K. Polanyi and D. K. Kitchin (eds), *Christianity and Social Revolution*, London, Victor Gollancz.
Polanyi, K. (1977), *The Livelihood of Man*, ed. Harry Pearson, New York, Academic Press.
Polanyi-Levitt, K. and Mendell, M. (1987), 'Karl Polanyi: His Life and Times', *Studies in Political Economy*, spring, pp. 7–39.
Putnam, R. D. (1995), 'Bowling Alone: America's Declining Social Capital', *Journal of Democracy*, 6(1), pp. 65–78.
Rabinbach, A. (1983), *The Crisis of Austrian Socialism: From Red Vienna to Civil War, 1827–1934*, Chicago, University of Chicago Press.
Radice, H. (2000), 'Globalization and National Capitalism: Theorizing Convergence and Differentiation', *Review of International Political Economy*, 7(4), pp. 719–42.
Sabel, C. (1997), 'Constitutional Orders and Trust Building and Response to Change', in J. R. Hollingsworth and R. Boyer (eds), *Contemporary Capitalism: The Embeddedness of Institutions*, Cambridge, Cambridge University Press.
Stohr, W. B. (2000), 'Changing Approaches to Local Restructuring and Development'. Paper presented for the International Symposium, 'Industrial Reconversion: Initiatives Implemented by Actors in Civil Society', OECD, Montreal.
Stohr, W. B., Edralin, J. S. and Mani, D. (eds) (2001), *New Regional Development Paradigms*, Vol. 3: *Decentralization, Governance and the New Planning for Local-level Development*, Westport, Greenwood Press.
Taylor, C. (1989), *Sources of the Self: The Making of the Modern Identity*, Cambridge, MA, Harvard University Press.

Taylor, C. (1991), *The Malaise of Modernity*, Concord, Anansi.
Tooke, J. (2003), 'Spaces for Community Investment: Process for Disciplining and Appropriation', *Space and Polity*, 7(3), pp. 233–46.
Torjman, S. and Leviten-Reid, E. (2003a), *Community Renewal*, Ottawa, Caledon Institute of Social Policy.
Torjman, S. and Leviten-Reid, E. (2003b), *Innovation and CED: What They Can Learn from Each Other*, Ottawa, Caledon Institute of Social Policy.
Vickers, D. (1994), *Economics and the Antagonism of Time: Time, Uncertainty and Choice in Economic Theory*, Ann Arbor, University of Michigan Press.
Williams, R. (1989), *Resources of Hope: Culture, Democracy, Socialism*, London, New York, Verso Press.

Reinstituting the economic process: (re)embedding the economy in society and nature[1]

Fikret Adaman, Pat Devine and Begum Ozkaynak

> The study of the shifting place occupied by the economy in society is therefore no other than the study of the manner in which the economic process is instituted at different times and places. (Polanyi, 1957, p. 250)

> ... the control of the economic system by the market is of overwhelming consequence to the whole organization of society: it means no less than the running of society as an adjunct to the market. Instead of economy being embedded in social relations, social relations are embedded in the economic system. The vital importance of the economic factor to the existence of society precludes any other result. For once the economic system is organized in separate institutions, based on specific motives and conferring a special status, society must be shaped in such a manner as to allow that system to function according to its own laws. This is the meaning of the familiar assertion that a market economy can function only in a market society. (Polanyi, 1944/2001, p. 60)

> The choice between capitalism and socialism, for instance, refers to two different ways of instituting modern technology in the process of production. (Polanyi, 1957, p. 249)

Introduction

Polanyi's analytic and historical vision, as set out in *The Great Transformation*, is summarised at the very beginning of his major work:

> Our thesis is that the idea of a self-adjusting market implied a stark utopia. Such an institution could not exist for any length of time without annihilating the human and natural substance of society; it would have physically destroyed man and transformed his surroundings into a wilderness. Inevitably, society took measures to protect itself, but whatever measures it took impaired the self-regulation of the market, disorganized industrial life, and thus endangered society in yet another way. (1944/2001, pp. 3–4)

Thus, Polanyi argued that the project of creating a fully self-regulating market was utopian, in the sense of impossible. However, movement towards this utopia, the ever greater but never completed process of disembedding the economy from both society and nature, creates growing dislocations and tensions which call forth a counter-movement. This double movement may be conceptualised as successive changes in the way in which the economic process is instituted. One way of thinking about this, after the initial institution of the capitalist market economy as a separate system with its own laws of motion, is in terms of successive cycles of regulation and deregulation. The highest point so far in the attempt to assert some degree of social control over the economy was the post-1945 golden age of welfare state Keynesianism. However, the prolonged period of relatively full employment caused the capitalist market economy to seize up, particularly the markets for what Polanyi called the 'fictitious commodities', labour and money, resulting in accelerating inflation and falling profits.[2] The result was the epoch of neo-liberal deregulation and privatisation, with the control of inflation replacing the maintenance of full employment as the principal policy objective together with the drive to extend market principles to ever wider spheres of human activity and its interaction with non-human nature. It may be that the rise of the anti-capitalist, anti-globalisation movement heralds the beginning of a new era of regulation, this time with a more global dimension, in order to deal with the increasingly acutely felt social injustices and the ominous ecological threats facing society at the start of the twenty-first century.

The focus of the paper is on the meaning of embeddedness, the ways in which the economy was reinstituted during both the Great Transformation and the subsequent counter-movements, and alternative approaches to further reinstituting the economy in ways that (re)embed it more firmly in society and nature. It is argued that prior to the creation of the capitalist market the economy was organically embedded in society and nature. However, the creation of separate economic institutions, the institution of the economic process as a distinct system with its own laws of motion, severed these organic links and the economy came to dominate both society and nature. Here, however, the symmetry between society and nature ends. Society has the capacity for conscious, purposeful action; nature does not. For the economy to be reinstituted in ways that create a sustainable organic relationship with nature, it must first be reinstituted in ways that bring it under social control.

Polanyi coined the term 'fictitious commodity' to express the commodification of labour, land and money in a self-regulating market system. He argued that while the first movement, towards instituting labour, land and money markets, was the result of deliberate action by the state, historically the counter-movement against economic liberalism was largely piecemeal and spontaneous: '*Laissez-faire* was planned; planning was not' (1944/2001, p. 147). He also called for social resistance against the market mentality and, looking to the future, in his plea for re-embedding the economy in society and nature argued for coordinated social intervention, through participatory and democratic means, to deal with the fictitious commodities.

This chapter offers a possible model for (re)embedding the economy in both society and nature. It first discusses the relationship between institutedness and embeddedness. It then critically reviews the approaches taken by existing economic schools of thought and models to the conceptualisation of the relationship between economic activity and nature and the operationalisation of policy. This covers the capitalist free-market model (with reference to the Coasian approach of assigning property rights to nature), the regulated capitalist market approach (distinguishing between neoclassical environmental economics and ecological economics), the centralised socialist model, and the market socialist approach. Following this critical review, the chapter then proposes a 'participatory planning' approach as a possible alternative model of societal organisation which institutes the economy in a way that embeds it in both society and nature. The model develops a set of social relations and institutions through which civil society exercises control over both the state and the economy and is thus able to mediate the relationship between the economy and nature directly. This marks a qualitative break with approaches that rely on the coercive power of either the state or market forces, which both operate with inherently unpredictable and unintended consequences. The chapter concludes by suggesting that participatory planning provides a productive framework for operationalising the argument of Polanyi on the need for economic activity to be (re)embedded in society and nature.

Institutedness and embeddedness

Polanyi's basic thesis may be summarised as follows. The economy is 'an instituted process of interaction between man and his environment' (1957, p. 248) which produces the means for satisfying human wants. Before the great transformation and the establishment of the capitalist market system there existed an organic relationship between economic activity and society. Markets often existed but they were not a self-regulating mechanism for the organisation of production. Economic activity was instituted as an inseparable, organic aspect of all other forms of social activity. It was inextricably and holistically embedded in society and nature.[3] The capitalist market system reinstitutes the economy as a separate and distinct sphere, with its own logic and laws of motion, disembedding it from society and nature by creating markets for labour, land and money. Varieties of capitalism may institute the economy in different ways, but what they all share is that economic activity is instituted separately from other aspects of human activity. However, disembedding can never be complete since laissez-faire economic liberalism undermines the conditions necessary for continuous capitalist reproduction and calls forth movements of resistance.

Society therefore seeks ways of (re)embedding the economy in society and nature by subjecting it to forms of social control, by continuously revising or reinstituting the ways in which markets, above all labour, land and money markets are instituted.

However, although the tension between the logic of the self-regulating market and society's attempts to protect itself from the consequences of that logic is ever present, society can never win as long as the economy remains instituted as a separate sphere of activity. Thus:

> For a century the dynamics of a modern society was [sic] governed by a double movement: the market expanded continuously but this movement was met by a countermovement checking the expansion in different directions. Vital though such a countermovement was for the protection of society, in the last analysis it was incompatible with the self-regulation of the market, and thus with the market system itself. (Polanyi, 1944/2001, p. 136)

Polanyi rejected the 'economistic fallacy' ... an artificial identification of the economy with its market form (1957, p. 270). Instead, he looked for alternative, non-capitalist, ways of instituting the economic process in order to reintegrate economic activity with all the other aspects of social life, to (re)embed it in society and nature. However, this cannot be done by seeking to recreate the organic integration of society, economy and nature along traditional lines, as was the case prior to the Great Transformation: *'The congenital weakness of nineteenth-century society was not that it was industrial but that it was a market society'* (1944/2001, p. 258, Polanyi's emphasis). He looks forward to the replacement of the capitalist market system by a system of democratic social control over the economy, premised on the abolition of labour, land and money markets but not necessarily product markets:

> Socialism is, essentially, the tendency inherent in an industrial civilization to transcend the self-regulating market by consciously subordinating it to a democratic society. It is the solution natural to industrial workers who see no reason why production should not be regulated directly and why markets should be more than a useful but subordinate trait in a free society ... it breaks with the attempt to make private money gains the general incentive to productive activities, and does not acknowledge the right of private individuals to dispose of the main instruments of production. (1944/2001, p. 242)

In future 'the market system will no longer be self-regulating, even in principle, since it will not comprise labour, land and money' (1944/2001, p. 259). However:

> the end of market society means in no way the absence of markets. These continue, in various fashions, to ensure the freedom of the consumer, to indicate the shifting of demand, to influence producers' income, and to serve as an instrument of accountancy, while ceasing altogether to be an organ of economic self-regulation. (1944/2001, p. 260)

Polanyi may have been optimistic about what comes naturally to industrial workers, and his proposals for instituting economic activity in a way that embeds it fully in society remain sketchy, but his brilliant insight into the fact that '[a] market economy can exist only in a market society' (1944/2001, p. 74) and his insistence that labour, land and money must be reinstituted on a non-market basis if the economy is to be fully reembedded in society have if anything a greater urgency today than when he first published them. Figures 6.1 and 6.2, based on Polanyi's work but going beyond it, are an

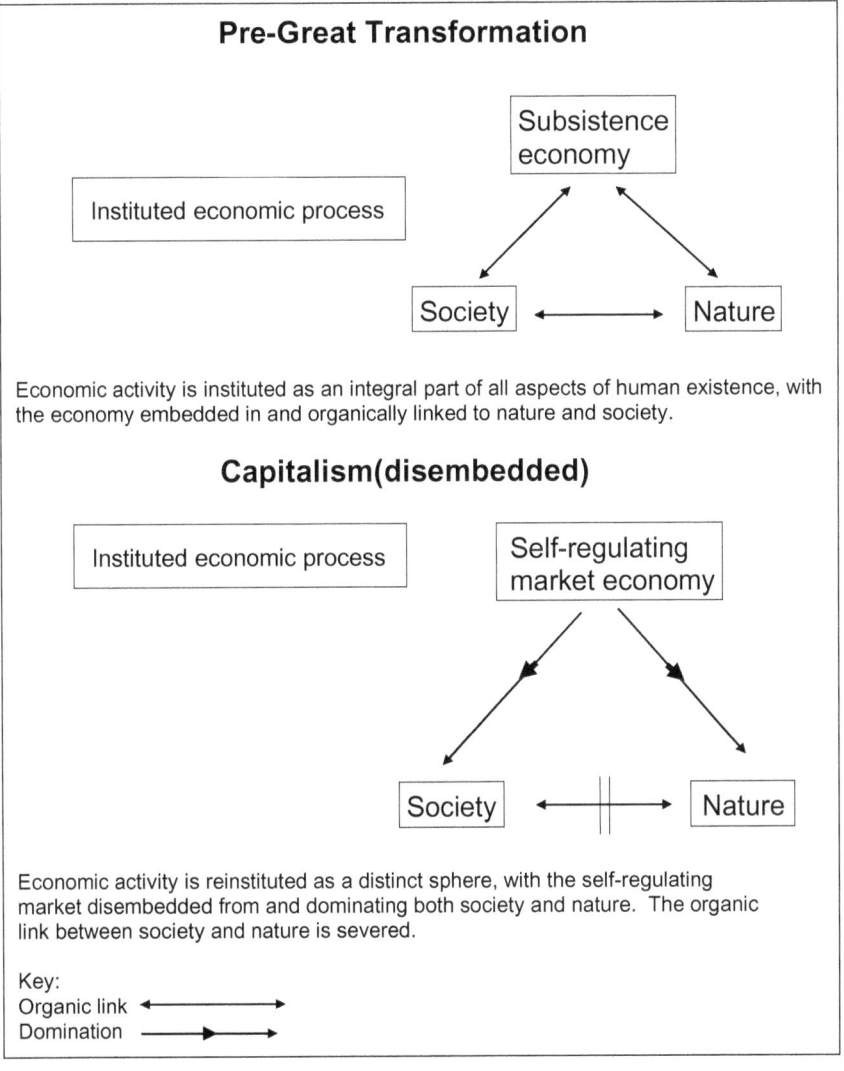

Figure 6.1 Historical Society

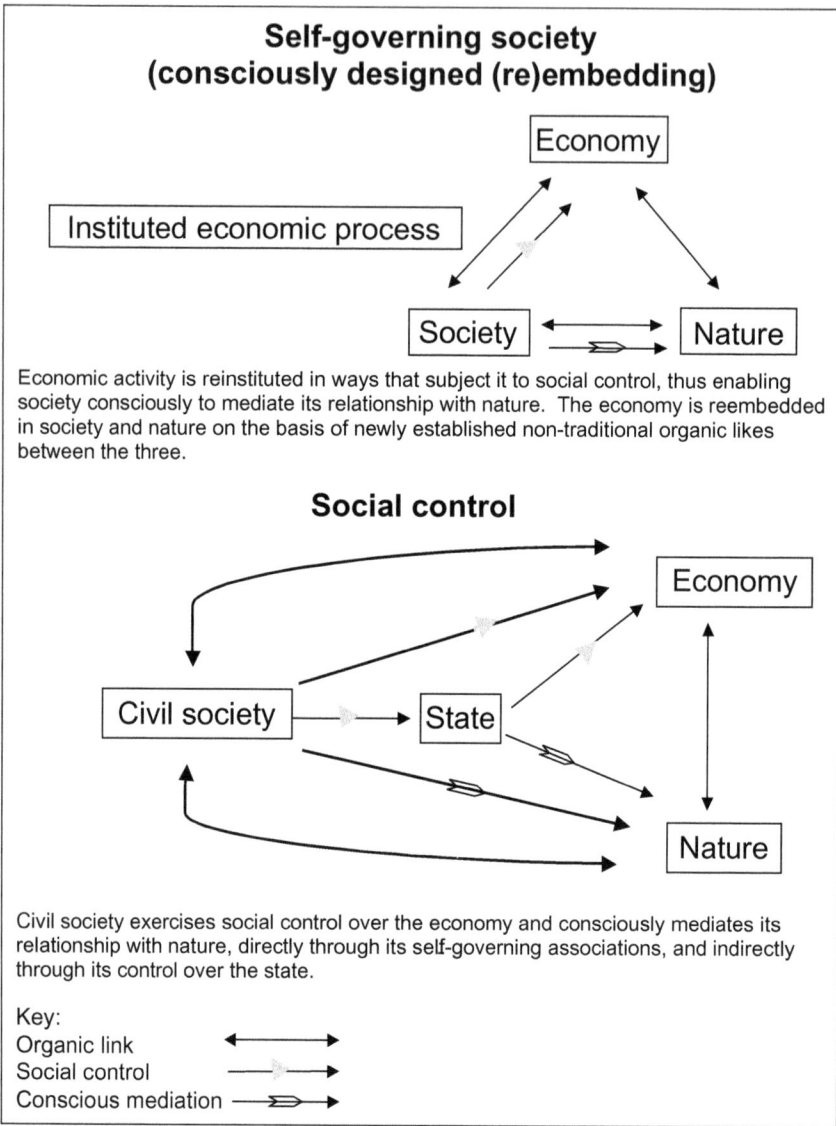

Figure 6.2 Visions of the future

attempt to provide a schematic framework for thinking about how this might be achieved.

This schematic framework provides the background for an evaluation of the approaches taken or implied by existing economic schools of thought to the relationship between nature and the economy. This is done by analysing the alternative ways in which the economic process is instituted and embedded in different models of both capitalist and socialist society. The paper then outlines a model of participatory planning as a possible way of realising Polanyi's objective of consciously instituting and embedding the economy in society and nature.

Capitalist solutions

We distinguish three approaches within the capitalist solution: free market; neoclassical interventionism; and ecological economics. The first two are based on the couplet of methodological individualism and market relations. They both see the adverse effects that economic activity has on nature, i.e., the overuse of natural resources and/or waste disposal above the ecosystem's assimilative capacity, as arising from the absence of a complete set of property rights and markets for the elements of nature that enter into the production process. Accordingly, individuals neither recognise the full benefits of 'environmental goods and services' nor bear the full cost of using them. The third approach, that of ecological economics, explicitly attempts to embed the economic system in the social system and the environment. However, in the final analysis it nevertheless accepts the premise of a capitalist market system.

The free market approach

The approach that is furthest away from that of Polanyi sees the solution to environmental problems in assigning ownership rights and establishing markets where they are lacking. This concept of the full commodification and marketisation of nature has been associated above all with Coase, who argued that if property rights to nature were clearly and fully defined then the interested parties would bargain over the use of environmental resources, thus resolving environmental problems within the self-regulating market system. Resources would therefore be used efficiently in the sense that their use would correspond to the preferences of their owners and potential users as mediated by the market. Taking this argument to its logical end would, of course, imply the assignment of property rights for such goods as genetic codes, seeds, the atmosphere, the oceans and even space.[4]

The Coasian framework is subject to a set of obvious drawbacks even in its own terms, that is, leaving aside the problems inherent in any market system. First, there is the question of the principle on the basis of which property rights should be assigned. One possibility is an equal per capita distribution across the global population. Another is an auction system designed to allocate rights to those who value them most, as measured by ability and willingness to pay. However, as the rich are able to pay more they will appear to place a higher value on environmental and ecological issues than do the poor, thus leading to social and geographical dumping. Second, transaction costs are likely to be high, not least because the individualist methodology on which the Coasian approach is based gives rise to problems of 'collective action'.

Interventionist approaches
Neoclassical environmental economics Neoclassical environmental economics, as a modified version of neoclassical theory, is the most developed theory in the literature concerned with environmental problems, explicitly addressing the interactions that exist between the economy and the environment. Within this framework, if a full set of property rights cannot be created, market failure can be corrected by regulation, either through 'command-and-control' intervention based on standards and quotas, or through 'incentive-based' mechanisms such as pollution taxes or emissions trading regimes.[5] In both approaches, the aim is to restore either 'efficiency', by internalising the 'externalities', or the 'optimal path', by maximising the 'present value' of the stream of net benefits obtained from using the resource now and in the future. Within this framework, the first approach provides firms with less flexibility than the second and, in theory, incentive-based mechanisms may ensure optimality at a lower cost than command-and-control mechanisms. Nevertheless, it is acknowledged that ease of implementation may at times require the use of standards and quotas.

A concrete example of the application of the neoclassical environmental economics approach is the proposed creation of a 'marketable permits' system in relation to natural resource use. Economic agents are given the use right to consume environmental resources according to some principle of distribution and are then allowed to sell any rights they own. Thus, a market is created in the right to consume resources as inputs or to pollute. Within an *a priori* determined overall level of resource use (as in the case of fisheries) or of emissions (as in the case of environmental pollution), permits are left to find their own price and the resource is used 'efficiently', in the sense that it is allocated according to the owners' preferences, given the initial distribution of use rights.

The neoclassical interventionist solution is contingent on measuring the value assigned by individuals to environmental goods and services in money terms. The aim is to weigh the costs and benefits of avoiding ecological damages. Where there are well-developed markets for environmental goods, the costs and benefits are calculated using market prices. Where there are no or incomplete markets, a body of techniques has been developed to simulate markets by estimating monetary valuations based on individual preferences. One of the most commonly used of such techniques is the so-called 'contingent valuation' method. This involves the creation of hypothetical markets in which people are asked how much they would be 'willing to pay' to preserve some areas in their unpolluted condition, or would be 'willing to accept' in compensation for allowing them to be polluted (Pearce and Turner, 1990).[6] Of course, this kind of calculation requires a method of discounting preferences in relation to the future and these preferences can only be those of the present generation. The preferences of *future* generations themselves for natural resource use can only be taken into account insofar as they are reflected in the preferences of *current* generations.[7] Once the actual and future costs and benefits associated with economic activities that impact on the environment have been calculated, in terms of the present generation's preferences, an optimality calculation is then undertaken, usually in the form of 'cost–benefit' and 'cost-effectiveness' analysis, with an *a priori* chosen rate of discount.

It should be remembered that in neoclassical environmental economics the economic system is seen as being composed of separate and autonomous individuals, seeking to satisfy preferences which are exogenously determined and ethically unchallengeable, and acting in a context of social institutions designed to discover these individual preferences and aggregate them. Given this, the neoclassical interventionist approach has been subject to the same kinds of criticism as the free market solution. First, the unequal bargaining position in the market of rich and poor has a critical impact on the valuations generated. A change in the initial distribution of ownership will have an effect on incomes, the pattern of demand, and the price vector, including of course the prices of environmental goods and services. Second, the analysis remains separate from other domains of social life, in the sense that the social, cultural and political status of the individual is reduced to that of a consumer/worker/resource owner. The isolated, private and non-changeable preference model, with its associated 'willingness to pay' techniques, is abstracted from any institutional context and hence is very misleading, especially in the case of environmental decisions of major importance. Social processes, the context within which choices are made, play a major role in defining and forming people's preferences in relation to the common good.[8] Attitude formation towards the common good involves people acting as citizens and requires an interaction with other people and an understanding of their interests. Third, in relation to the values derived in contingent valuation surveys, there is the problem of how to aggregate the values assigned to different environmental resources in order to get an overall value of the environment. Lastly, it is recognised that implementing interventionist mechanisms requires the existence of a social guardian/government and the assumption that the costs of any 'government failure' are less than those arising from the 'market failure' in question.

Thus, the first two capitalist solutions, the free-market and neoclassical interventionist approaches, far from responding to Polanyi's conceptualisation of the desired relationship between the economy and nature, seek to complete the institution of the very process of commodification and marketisation which led to his critique of the self-regulating market and the disembedded economy in the first place.

Ecological economics The newly developed approach of ecological economics differs from neoclassical environmental economics in three respects.[9] First, it adopts a co-evolutionary approach, recognising that economic activity has an impact on the ecosystem yet also depends on it. Human activity both shapes nature and is in turn shaped by it. Different ways of organising production and consumption affect nature differently, so that the way in which nature reacts back on economic activity also differs. Thus, more than one path-dependent evolutionary process is possible with very different consequences for sustainability.

Second, ecological economics draws on the laws of thermodynamics and the concept of entropy for insights into the types of interaction that exist between the economic and ecological systems. Key among these insights is that these interactions cannot be adequately characterised by seeking to reduce nature to a set of commodities which can then have a monetary value placed upon them. Rather, the flow of high level to low level energy, the use of renewable and non-renewable resources, and the use of nature as a sink for waste, need to be monitored each separately and in physical terms.

Third, it is recognised that many environmental and ecological problems are so acute that action is needed now, before there is time for further scientific research to reduce significantly the uncertainty associated with them. Indeed, the ecosystems involved are so complex that there is always likely to be uncertainty in relation to any proposed course of action. Ecological economics therefore argues that such decisions, if they are to carry legitimacy, must be taken through a procedurally democratic process based on deliberative institutions in which all those with an interest in the outcome participate. Such a decision-making process would make use of existing, usually contested, scientific knowledge, but the uncertainties associated with different courses of action would be weighed in terms of the values of those involved.

Ecological economics represents an important step forward in conceptualising how the economy might be re-embedded in both society and nature. It argues that ecological decisions cannot be properly addressed by treating nature as a fictitious commodity and that such decisions must be made by society, not left to the self-regulating market, or to experts seeking to correct for market failures when externalities not captured by market prices exist. It envisages society making these decisions through a *deliberative democratic process* involving all affected groups. Although ecological economics has focused exclusively on ecological issues (land), the approach it has arrived at is equally capable of being applied to the other fictitious commodities (labour and money). In all three cases, the operation of self-regulating market forces needs to be replaced by conscious social control and mediation.

However, although ecological economics is an advance, it assumes, explicitly or implicitly, that the procedural democracy it recommends would take place within the framework of the instituted capitalist market economy. It recognises the importance of the distribution of power and resource ownership, which neoclassical environmental economics does not, but in general ecological economics does not address the question of whether the much greater equality likely to be necessary for the effective operation of a procedural democracy that confers real legitimacy is compatible with capitalism.[10] Furthermore, there is a very real issue over whether a permanent twenty-first century counter-movement, this time at the global level to regulate the activities of the multinational corporations, is compatible with the continued functioning of the global capitalist market. As we have seen, Polanyi's view would have been that it is not, since checks imposed on the operation of the self-regulating market sooner or later cause it to seize up. This then leads to a consideration of possible socialist alternatives to capitalism as ways of re-embedding the economy in society and nature.

Socialist solutions

Centralised socialism

The Soviet experience in relation to environmental degradation was no better, possibly worse, than that of the advanced capitalist countries. The Soviet model of central planning sought to allocate society's resources directly to production for use in the satisfaction of human needs, with money playing a passive role. The economic process was instituted *sui generis*. Since the self-regulating market ceased to operate, the fictitious commodity character of labour, land and money no longer existed. However, the economy was not re-embedded in either society or nature.

This illustrates the difficulties that exist in thinking about how such re-embedding can be achieved. In the Soviet model, far from society controlling the economy and its interaction with nature, the political instance was dominant, with the ruling *nomenklatura* controlling the state, the economy and a fragmented, atomised and alienated society.

However, although no longer fictitious commodities, the situation of labour and land was not the same. The dominance of the political instance meant that the ruling group depended for its legitimacy on the revolutionary origins of the regime and its claim to represent the working class. This imposed limitations on the extent to which workers could be exploited and oppressed. The abolition of unemployment brought real gains in security and in the two decades to the mid-1970s there were also real improvements in social welfare and living standards. No such limitations existed on the exploitation and degradation of nature. Indeed, it could be argued that the productivist interpretation of Marxism that prevailed gave licence to the neglect of nature and even to a frontier society mentality seeking to conquer nature. Furthermore, the absence of political democracy meant that an independent environmental movement, acting as an advocate and pressure group for nature, could not develop to any significant extent.

In addition to the socio-political characteristics of the regime there were also more technical economic problems associated with the Soviet model of central planning. Even in the presence of political democracy, much knowledge relevant for efficient production cannot be transmitted to a central planning agency. So-called tacit knowledge, knowledge acquired through experience, through learning by doing, can only be effectively used by the individuals or groups who possess it. It follows that the efficient use of society's productive resources can to a large extent only be achieved through decentralised decision making. This is also true with respect to many environmental and ecological issues. While some key issues concerning the ecosystem have to be addressed at the global level, many issues arise in relation to local ecosystems and require local knowledge if they are to be effectively dealt with.

Theoretical models of centralised planning, or at least centralised algorithms for coordinating production decisions, have been developed using modern computing and information technology.[11] They assume that in the absence of exploitative and oppressive regimes problems of alienation and motivation can be overcome. In principle, environmental and ecological considerations could form part of the information on the basis of which decisions are made. However, these models are vulnerable to the problems associated with attempts to transmit tacit knowledge to a centre and they tend to view people as workers and consumers but not as citizens. It is difficult, therefore, to see how they could provide the institutional framework for re-embedding the economy in nature, which requires a deliberative democratic process in which people participate as citizens, not just as workers and consumers, and make use of their tacit knowledge.

Market socialism

The response of many socialists to the experience of the Soviet model and the perceived theoretical difficulties associated with centralised computer-based models has been to espouse some form of market socialism. There is now a wide spectrum of such models. At one pole are those that accept the general neoclassical framework and analyse the same issues, using the same techniques, the only difference being that private ownership is replaced by some form of state or worker cooperative ownership. At the other pole are models that situate the operation of the market in a set of institutions that encourage the exchange of information and seek to exercise some social control over the allocation of capital.[12]

Market socialist models in general do not explicitly discuss environmental and ecological concerns. The neoclassical market socialist models make no attempt to discuss the extent to which they are able to re-embed the economy in society, let alone in nature. However, the approach of neoclassical environmental economics is as applicable to neoclassical market socialist models as it is to the neoclassical analysis of capitalism and so, of course, are the drawbacks associated with this approach. In neoclassical market socialism the self-regulating market remains the principal coordinator of economic activity and labour, land and money remain fictitious commodities.

The situation is less clear cut in the case of those market socialist models that situate the market institutionally. Elson (1988) for example, refers to the socialisation of the market, transcending its private character but not abolishing it, rather than to market socialism. She proposes a set of interlocking institutions that alter the way in which the market process operates by making public the prices at which exchange takes place, facilitating the exchange of information about investment, and encouraging dialogue between producers and consumers over what is socially needed. Schweikart (1993) proposes an investment fund that is raised from taxation and allocated to regions on a per capita basis. Enterprises in the regions then bid for a share of the regional investment fund on the basis primarily of expected profitability but taking account also of other relevant criteria.

These institutionally based models are certainly an improvement on the neoclassical models. Although once again environmental and ecological concerns are not a central focus of the models, the rich institutional setting seems to allow for the embedding of such concerns in the decision-making process. However, the operation of market forces, the self-regulating market, remains a major determinant of the allocation of investment and in the end enterprises continue to act atomistically, with their interdependent decisions being co-ordinated *ex post* by the invisible hand rather than *ex ante* through a process of participatory planning. Furthermore, the efficiency allegedly associated with the market process is obtained, if at all, by creating losers as well as winners and so is likely to be incompatible with the values of equality and solidarity associated with the socialist vision. Finally, labour and land retain some of the character of fictitious commodities. Thus, even the most promising market socialist models seem unable to re-embed the economy in either society or nature.[13]

Participatory planning

Participatory planning is an approach that replaces the self-regulating market by a process of negotiation, thus avoiding the drawbacks of both centralised socialism and market socialism.[14] It envisages a self-governing society in which, rather than the state or the self-regulating market or some combination of the two coercing society, the diverse voluntary associations that make up civil society control both the state and the economy. Self-government may be defined as a situation in which those affected by a decision participate in making the decision, in proportion to the extent to which they are affected by it. The institutional form that this takes is that of social ownership, ownership by those who are affected. Thus, there will be different social owners, from local to global, depending on how widespread the consequences of the decision are, in line with the principle of subsidiarity.

The model is based on a distinction between market exchange and market forces. Market exchange involves the buying and selling of the output of existing productive capacity. The operation of market forces is the process through which the structure of productive capacity in a market economy is changed by investment and disinvestment. This involves the buying, hiring or borrowing of the fictitious commodities labour, land and money, as well, of course, of real commodities in the form of capital goods. The driving force behind this process is the decisions made by the owners of capital in pursuit of the highest expected rate of profit. However, these decisions are made atomistically, even though their outcome depends to a significant extent on the simultaneously made decisions of other capital owners. These interdependent decisions are coordinated after they have been implemented, in response to the pattern of profit and loss that results from their aggregate effect, as new decisions are made on the basis of what are now expected to be the most profitable areas for investment. This is the self-regulating market at work. The distinction between market exchange and market forces is essentially the same as Polanyi's distinction between the market and the market system, with markets for products clearly distinguished from markets for factors of production.

In the model of participatory planning, market exchange is retained but market forces are replaced by a process of negotiated coordination between the social owners at the relevant level – industry or sector, local, regional, national, international, global. Whereas the self-regulating market results in an outcome no one willed, oblivious of the human, social, environmental and ecological consequences of its operation, negotiated coordination enables those who are likely to be affected by the outcome to engage in a deliberative process of democratic decision making, which takes account not only of the need to use society's productive resources efficiently but also of the social and natural consequences of alternative courses of action. Thus, participatory planning through negotiated coordination based on social ownership is a form of reinstituting economic activity by transcending the separation of the economy from the rest of society. It provides an institutional framework for the social relations necessary to re-embed the economy in both society and nature.

Let us look at how this process might work at three different levels – macro/strategic, industry or sector, and firm. We can think of the macro/strategic level as being global, national or local, with those affected at each level taking a view of the sort of society they want to move towards, the balance between material and spiritual in the quality of life they aspire to, and the relationship they seek with nature. These decisions clearly have implications for the scale, type and location of productive activity, for energy and transport policy, and for the relationship between urban and rural areas. Through a multi-tiered network of democratic institutions people would participate in making, implementing, monitoring and revising the decisions that shape their lives.

The model envisages this process as having three dimensions or stages. First, voluntary associations formed around particular functions, interests or causes – the bedrock of self-government – would negotiate and cooperate with each other in the process of running the various aspects of social life close to people's daily existence – firms, producing goods and services, and public utilities or agencies, dealing with energy, transport, housing, health, care of young and old, education, culture and leisure. Second, these voluntary associations would come together at each level to draw up strategic plans based on negotiations over the priority to be given to their particular concerns. Third, representative assemblies at each level, elected on the basis of universal suffrage, would be the ultimate decision-making bodies with respect to human rights, the choice of strategic plan in the event of disagreement at the second stage, the (re)distribution of resources, the legislative and regulatory framework, and policies to promote environmental and ecological sustainability. Each dimension is necessary if the dangers of state bureaucracy, elective dictatorship and local autarky are to be avoided.

At the industry or sectoral level what is envisaged is an industry-wide negotiated coordination body responsible for investment decisions. It would consist of the social owners of the industry – the firms involved, the workers in the industry, major suppliers and users, the communities in which the industry is located, the relevant planning commission, environmental and equal opportunities groups, and any other group with a legitimate interest in the industry's activities. The social owners would negotiate a pattern of investment and disinvestment, coordinated in advance, that took into account information on the performance of the firms in the industry, expected future trends, and their own interests and values. Thus, resources would be reallocated as social needs and possibilities changed, but on the basis of the conscious choices of those affected rather than as a result of the operation of spontaneous market forces. Self-government through negotiated coordination would replace the self-regulating market.

Finally, at the firm level a different set of social owners would negotiate over general policy and strategic issues and would monitor the self-managing workforce. These social owners, those affected by the activities of the firm, would include its workers, supplying firms and customers, other firms in the industry, the industry-level negotiated coordination body, the community(ies) in which the firm is located, and again environmental and equal opportunities groups and any other groups with a legitimate interest. Firms would engage in market exchange, selling their output at a price that covered long-run costs, which would include both bought-in intermediate inputs and the cost of primary inputs. The latter – rental on the use of natural resources, wage rates, and rate of return on assets employed – would be determined in accordance with the social priorities arrived at through the process of macro/strategic decision making at the societal level outlined above, not by the operation of self-regulating markets. Thus, labour, land and money would cease to be fictitious commodities, society would control economic activity, and the economy would be re-embedded in both society and nature.

Conclusion

The chapter started by reviewing Polanyi's concepts of instituted economic process and embeddedness and the relationship between them. It then proposed a schematic framework for thinking about the way in which, by transcending the self-regulating market and decommodifying the fictitious commodities – labour, land and money, economic activity might be reinstituted and (re)embedded in both society and nature. This provided the background for an analysis of the different ways in which schools of economic thought and economic systems and models have addressed the impact of economic activity on nature. The capitalist free-market and neoclassical interventionist approaches to environmental and ecological issues are based on the project, diametrically opposed to that of Polanyi, of completing or simulating the full commodification and marketisation of nature. Ecological economics recognises the need for inclusive deliberative institutions if policy decisions that have to be made in conditions of inherently uncertain and contested knowledge are to be accepted as legitimate. However, it presupposes the continued existence of the self-regulating capitalist market and fails to address the institutional structure necessary for the process of deliberative democracy to be real rather than formal and co-optive.

Socialist economic systems and models have so far also failed to rise to Polanyi's implicit challenge. The centralised solution, even in its democratic form, is unable to take account of the tacit element in knowledge and the role of people as self-reflexive citizens, capable of learning and modifying their positions in the course of deliberatively democratic discursive processes. Market socialist models, although their authors are for the most part aware of the need for social regulation, nevertheless retain an atomised institutional ownership structure in which separately taken decisions are coordinated *ex post*. Thus, in so far as environmental and ecological issues are taken into account, this occurs either through the commodification and marketisation of nature, or through the establishment of institutions which work against the logic of self-regulating market forces, exhibiting in acute form the underlying and irreducible contradiction of interventionist capitalism or socialism.

The paper ended by arguing that a system of participatory democratic planning, based on negotiated coordination, provides the most developed and promising framework for reinstituting economic activity and embedding the economy in society, which it is argued is a necessary condition for embedding the economy in nature. It is not enough to continuously rework the insights of Polanyi into the problems caused by the self-regulating market. It is also necessary to develop models of the concrete ways in which the re-embedding of the economy in society and nature can be realised. We believe that the model of a self-governing society based on participatory planning is a contribution to this, but further work is needed to incorporate environmental and ecological concerns explicitly.

There is scope here for both theoretical and empirical research. At the theoretical level, much work is already underway discussing the modalities of participation – the institutional forms and procedures which facilitate participation, promote consensus, and recognise difference where consensus cannot be reached. At the empirical level, there is now the rich and rapidly growing experience of the current wave of global protests catalysed and linked by the global and continental social forums that have developed in recent years. These movements towards the creation of a global civil society all emphasise their participatory character, both as an end in itself and as a means of working towards the democratisation of power. They also frequently combine a focus on social justice with concern for environmental sustainability and a recognition of the connection between the two. Structured case studies of this experience would throw important light on the conditions for the emergence of such movements, the factors which determine their relative success or failure, and their potential or lack of potential for initiating more fundamental changes in the distribution of power in society. Although there is no shortage of research impinging on these questions, situating future work within Polanyi's concept of the 'double movement' and the need for economic activity to be reinstituted in the context of a self-governing society would impart a critical edge and contribute to the strengthening of the transformatory impetus of existing and future participatory social movements.

Notes

1 This chapter draws on our earlier work: see Adaman (1997); Adaman et al. (mimeo); Adaman and Ozkaynak (2002); Devine (mimeo); Ozkaynak (2000); and Ozkaynak et al. (2002). Earlier versions of the chapter were presented to the eighteenth Karl Polanyi International Conference, Mexico City, November 2001 and the CRIC Workshop on 'Polanyian Perspectives on Instituted Economic Processes, Development and Transformation', University of Manchester, October 2002. We should like to thank Bettina Lange, Elena Lieven, Eyup Ozveren and the participants in the above mentioned conference and workshop for helpful comments and suggestions.
2 For Polanyi, as for Marx, commodities are produced for sale in the market. Factors of production – labour (power), land and money – are not produced for sale and hence when traded in markets their commodity status is fictitious.

The institution of labour, land and money as (fictitious) commodities was for Polanyi the defining characteristic of the self-regulating market, just as for Marx the commodification of all inputs into the production process, most notably of course labour power, was the defining characteristic of the capitalist mode of production. They are, of course, the same thing.

3 'To separate labor from other activities of life and to subject it to the laws of the market was to annihilate all organic forms of existence and to replace them by a different type of organization, an atomised and individualistic one' (1944/2001, p. 171). '[I]t [the extension of the franchise to better-off workers] helped to overcome the obstacles presented by the surviving organic and traditional forms of life among the laboring people' (1944/2001, p. 181).

'Traditionally, land and labor are not separated; labor forms part of life, land remains part of nature, life and nature form an articulate whole. Land is thus tied up with the organizations of kinship, neighborhood, craft, and creed – with tribe and temple, village, guild, and church. One Big Market, on the other hand, is an arrangement of economic life which includes markets for the factors of production. Since these factors happen to be indistinguishable from the elements of human institutions, man and nature, it can readily be seen that market economy involves a society the institutions of which are subordinated to the requirements of the market mechanism. The proposition is as utopian in respect to land as it is in respect to labor. The economic function is but one of many vital functions of land. It invests man's life with stability; it is the site of his habitation; it is a condition of his physical safety; it is the landscape and the seasons' (1944/2001, p. 187).

4 See Coase (1960). For an example of the 'ultra-liberal' position, see Anderson and Leal (1991).
5 See Hahn and Stavins (1992); and Pearce and Turner (1990).
6 Among other methods, it is possible to mention 'replacement cost' and 'avoidance cost', in terms of supply, and 'hedonic pricing', and 'travel cost', in terms of demand. For further discussion see Pearce and Turner (1990); Turner (1993); and O'Connor and Spash (1999).
7 See Braden and Kolstad (1991).
8 See Vatn and Bromley (1995).
9 See Martinez-Alier et al. (1998); Munda (1997); Ozkaynak (2000); and Ozkaynak et al. (2002).
10 See O'Connor (1994).
11 See Albert and Hahnel (1991); and Cockshott and Cottrell (1993).
12 See Bardhan and Roemer (1992); Elson (1988); and Schweikart (1993).
13 For a more extended discussion of the issues raised in this section, see Adaman and Devine (1996, 1997).
14 See Devine (1988, 2002).

References

Adaman, F. (1997), 'The Political Economy of the Environment in Turkey', *New Perspectives on Turkey*, 17, pp. 129–50.

Adaman, F. and Devine, P. (1996), 'The Economic Calculation Debate: Lessons for Socialists', *Cambridge Journal of Economics*, 20(5), pp. 523–37.

Adaman, F. and Devine, P. (1997), 'On the Economic Theory of Socialism', *New Left Review*, 221, pp. 54–80.

Adaman, F. and Ozkaynak, B. (2002), 'The Economics–Environment Relationship: Some Critical Remarks on the Neoclassical, Institutional, and Marxist Approaches', *Studies in Political Economy*, 69, pp. 109–35.

Adaman, F., Gosen, S. and Zenginobuz, U. (2001), 'Power of the Markets and the Environment', mimeo, presentation to the fifth conference of the European Sociological Association, 28 August – 1 September, Helsinki.

Albert, M. and Hahnel, R. (1991), *The Political Economy of Participatory Economics*, Princeton, Princeton University Press.

Anderson, T. and Leal, D. (1991), *Free Market Environmentalism*, San Francisco, Pacific Research Institute for Public Policy.

Bardhan, P. and Roemer, J. (1992), 'Market Socialism: A Case for Rejuvenation', *Journal of Economic Perspectives*, 6(3), pp. 101–16.

Braden, J. and Kolstad, C. (eds) (1991), *Measuring the Demand for Environmental Quality*, Amsterdam, North Holland.

Coase, R. H. (1960), 'The Problem of Social Cost', *Journal of Law and Economics*, 3, October, pp. 1–44.

Cockshott, P. and Cottrell, A. (1993), *Towards a New Socialism*, Nottingham, Spokesman Books.

Devine, P. (1988), *Democracy and Economic Planning*, Cambridge, Polity Press.

Devine, P. (2002), 'Participatory Planning through Negotiated Coordination', *Science and Society*, 66(1), pp. 72–85.

Devine, P. (2003), 'Industrial Policy, Ecological Economics and Deliberative Democracy', paper presented to the European Society for Ecological Economics Conference, 'Frontiers 2: European Application of Ecological Economics', Tenerife, Canary Islands, 11–16 February.

Elson, D. (1988), 'Market Socialism or Socialization of the Market?', *New Left Review*, 172, pp. 3–44.

Hahn, W. and Stavins, R. (1992), 'Economic Incentives for Environmental Protection: Integrating Theory and Practice', *American Economic Review*, 82(2), pp. 464–8.

Martinez-Alier, J., Munda, G. and O'Neill, J. (1998), 'Weak Comparability of Values as a Foundation for Ecological Economics', *Ecological Economics*, 26(3), pp. 277–86.

Munda, G. (1997), 'Environmental Economics, Ecological Economics and the Concept of Sustainable Development', *Environmental Values*, 6(2), pp. 213–33.

O'Connor, M. (ed.) (1994), *Is Capitalism Sustainable? Political Economy and Politics of Ecology*, New York and London, Guilford Press.

O'Connor, M. and Spash, C. (eds) (1999), *Valuation and the Environment: Theory, Method and Practice*, Cheltenham, Edward Elgar.

Ozkaynak, B. (2000), 'Operationalising Sustainability', MPhil thesis, University of Manchester.

Ozkaynak, B., Devine, P. and Rigby, D. (2002), 'Whither Ecological Economics?', *International Journal of Environment and Pollution*, 18(4), pp. 317–35.

Pearce, D. and Turner, K. (1990), *Economics of Natural Resources and the Environment*, Hertfordshire, Harvester Wheatsheaf.

Polanyi, K. (1944/2001), *The Great Transformation*, Boston, Beacon Press.

Polanyi, K. (1957), 'The Economy as Instituted Process', Ch. 13 in K. Polanyi, C. Arensberg and H. Pearson (eds), *Trade and Market in the Early Empires*, Glencoe, IL, Free Press.

Schweikart, D. (1993), *Against Capitalism*, Cambridge, Cambridge University Press.

Turner, K. (1993), 'Sustainability: Principles and Practice', in Kerry Turner (ed.), *Sustainable Environmental Economics and Management: Principles and Practice*, London, Belhaven Press.

Vatn, A. and Bromley, D. (1995), 'Choices without Prices without Apologies', in D. Bromley (ed.), *Handbook of Environmental Economics*, Oxford, Basil Blackwell.

7

Moral philosophy and economic sociology: what MacIntyre learnt from Polanyi

Peter McMylor

Introduction

It is increasingly clear that the assumptive worlds that sustained a variety of sociological determinisms are, for many, no longer persuasive e.g. positivist, structuralist or Marxian. The return of the actor has been signalled in a number of ways (Touraine, 1988; Shceff, 1990) but not least in the revival of interest in ethics and morality within social thought (see especially Bauman, 1996; Tester, 1997). This has gone hand in hand with a preoccupation with the nature and trajectory of the self in modernity, most influentially in Anthony Giddens's work (Giddens, 1991). It has become clear that morality can no longer be regarded as primarily belonging to the arena of personal life, as it has conventionally been seen in much liberal thought, but is now being also understood as central to social practices and economic activity (Etzioni, 1988; Blau, 1993; Fukuyama, 1995) However, this understanding, true to the spirit of the owl of Minerva, appears at a time when many western societies see themselves as living on depleted moral resources, provoking rather feeble intellectual and social movements designed to reverse this process, often working under the studiedly vague term 'communitarianism' (Etzioni, 1995, 1997) Tempting though it might be in this context to follow up Nietzche's aphorism 'when you see something falling give it a shove', this should be resisted for there are good reasons for thinking that however thread-bare much of our contemporary moral rhetoric is, self-indulgent intellectual iconoclasm can only make things worse (see MacIntyre, 1981, especially Ch. 9; Rosen, 1987). This chapter takes for granted that the renewed discussion of morality in social science is not in general some form of ideological discourse, although it may be in certain situations, but rather an inescapable dimension of social practice once deterministic guarantees have disappeared from social thought. In this respect it shares some parallel concerns with Giddens's work on the self, referred to above, even at one point an apparent overlap of terminology in use of the concept of 'disembedding'. For Giddens the metaphor of 'disembedding' refers to the confluence of symbolic tokens, such as money, and expert systems of abstracted technical knowledge which pull away from local particularities. However the discussion below, although not entirely distant from this approach, focuses more narrowly on the connections, parallels and affinities between the transformations of moral discourse outlined by MacIntyre, and the patterns of changing economic and social organisation analysed by Polanyi, who, as Bernard Barber has shown, is the original source of the 'disembedding' metaphor (Barber, 1995).

Alasdair MacIntyre is probably the most influential moral philosopher in the English speaking world, since the early 1980s (MacIntyre, 1981, 1988) MacIntyre's key work is *After Virtue* (1981). Here, in a complex historical account of the transformation of moral concepts, he sets out the most cogent version of his view that the moral basis of liberal society has hopelessly fragmented. It is not, he suggests, that we are confused over particular moral questions, although we often are, but rather that we have lost the basis for understanding what a coherent moral argument is. This is because our moral vocabulary has lost the institutional framework, especially in the form of educational institutions, which contained shared and inherited forms of enquiry and understanding which provided it with meaning and persuasiveness. MacIntyre sets this out well in his London Education lectures (MacIntyre, 1987). But with moral vocabulary torn from its original context, we are left with only fragments of a once meaningful moral scheme. The fragments are still used as reference points, so people continue to act as if there remained an overarching moral framework within which to relate to one another. In practice, MacIntyre suggests, we have a tendency to appeal to the parts of moral discourse that suits us.

MacIntyre work should be of particular interest to sociologists because its accounts of the debates in moral philosophy, as in all his previous work, are very carefully situated within their social and historical context. What seems to have escaped any detailed attention within sociology is the way in which MacIntyre's account of moral change is explicitly dependent upon the work of the social scientist, Karl Polanyi, especially his most important work, *The Great Transformation* (Polanyi, 1944). This is a time when Polanyi's work is undergoing a revival of interest within sociology, especially within the field of economic sociology (Swedberg, 1987; Smelser and Swedberg, 1994). I intend to argue that this connection between MacIntyre's account of moral change and Polanyi's account of the social context of economic change and activity, requires some sustained attention from social scientists, both for what they reveal about the substance of the historical and social processes as well as of the conceptualisations required to grasp them.

MacIntyre, Polanyi and the moral perspective

Before looking at the detail of their substantive affinities it is necessary to refer at least briefly to aspects of their respective biographies to reveal the intellectual ground for their affinities. It should, perhaps, come as no surprise in regard to authors of bodies of work in which morality and moral criticism are so inextricably tied to social analysis that their views on the nature of the great religious, political and social forces of their age are vital for understanding their intellectual development. In particular, much can be learnt about these thinkers' social analysis and their compatibility with each other from their responses to both Marxism and Christianity.

If we turn to Polanyi first, we should note the formative role of his social background. His outlook was shaped in Central European, specifically a Hungarian context. Karl Polanyi was born in Vienna in 1886 but largely brought up in Budapest (Congdon, 1976; Polanyi-Levitt and Mendell, 1987). His family were Hungarian Jews who converted to Protestant Christianity. Congdon describes the experience of Polanyi, part of this young pre-war generation of intellectuals in Austro-Hungary, as being part of a counter-culture that called for a progressivist orientated moral and political reform of Hungarian society and found its clearest institutional embodiment in the famous Galileo Circle. This group which included such future luminaries as the sociologist Karl Mannheim, sought a non-revolutionary liberal minded socialist future (Kettler et al., 1984). Polanyi summed up its view in his presidential address to the society, where he said, 'We do not dream of bloody struggles and triumphant battles. Our genuine hope is that our generation will be different from the previous one by showing greater commitment to social justice' (Kadarkay, 1991, p. 61).

Polanyi's character and sensibility seems to have fitted perfectly with this rather high-minded group, for he appears to have inherited from his family a fiercely independent moral outlook. His future wife was to describe him in relation to the unhappiness that practising as a lawyer caused him, especially when the needs of the poor were ignored, 'Not only was he a man who could not lie, but also one who discovered his true calling ... in the articulation of unpleasant truths' (Congdon, 1976, pp. 173–4). Already before the catastrophe of World War I, Polanyi was strongly opposed to theories, which he believed included Marxism, that seem to view human progress as an automatic process guaranteed by abstract laws of social development. He bitterly opposed any system of thought that minimised the role of individual moral responsibility and choice.

Like many intellectuals in Central Europe at this time he was attracted by the clear and powerful ethical messages of the great Russian novelists especially in his case, Tolstoy (Litvan, 1991). No doubt in general Polanyi can be seen as part of a wider reaction against scientism and positivism that began to emerge in the last decade of the nineteenth century in European thought (see Janik and Toulmin, 1973) but for him as for many others it was the experience of fighting in the world war that crystallised the significance of ethics in human life. It is in the early 1920s, as he worked in workers' education, that he produces some substantial discussions of ethical matters in relationship to social science.

The fruit of Polanyi's thought at this time were two lengthy works, known as 'Behemoth', and 'Uber Die Freiheit', so far unpublished, but, according to Gregory Baum, who has produced the most substantial discussion of Polanyi's ethical thought, they formed the foundation of his later theoretical and ethical thinking (Baum, 1996). These papers are a plea for the ethical foundation of all human knowledge. Their immediate target is the positivistic climate of Austria both in terms of the Marxism of Austrian Social Democracy and its liberal economic opponents. Central to this is Polanyi's concept of 'Lebensweg', which means in Baum's explanation, 'the first thing we know is . . . the experience of being engaged in the day to day ethical tasks of living: how to relate ourselves to those dear to us . . . how to respond to the culture in which we live, how to assume an appropriate self critical attitude towards ourselves' (Baum, 1996, p. 22). Unsurprisingly, Baum characterises Polanyi as seeing humans as 'beings of conscience'. This emphasis on conscience and the lived experience of moral formation led him to oppose the Soviet-style command economy as an option not simply because of its inefficiency, but also because it constrained human choice, including ethical choices (Polanyi-Levitt and Mendell, 1987, p. 11).

It would be hard not to notice the presence here of a partially secularised Christian conscience, or the affinity with Max Weber's ethic of responsibility, itself also rooted in Protestant Christianity. As his friend Abraham Rotstein put it, 'in Karl's perspective, man has a soul to lose and if he takes a false step, if he violates the convictions of his own conscience, if he goes awry in what he fundamentally stands for, he may (in a inner sense) 'go to Hell' ' (Rotstein, 1994, p. 138). From this starting point we should not be surprised to see that in these writings Polanyi begins to unfavourably compare the tradition of Marxist socialism with the ethically self conscious tradition that developed from Robert Owen and then later in Guild Socialism in Britain

Once he is forced to emigrate to Britain we find that Polanyi starts to work in workers education again and finds his closest intellectual allies among the Christian left that had emerged a few years earlier. Now Polanyi develops his strongest claims for the significance of the Christian ethic for modern societies in his essay 'The Essence of Fascism' (Polanyi, 1936). Here, he argues that fascism must seek to destroy both the Workers Movement and the Christian churches as a locus of moral respect for the individual in society. However far Christianity has departed from its ethical core, it nonetheless he argues provides the moral drive in western society for transcending the present society, as he put it:

> The Christian idea of society is that it is a relationship of persons. Everything else follows logically from this . . . That its assertions and propositions are more startling than anything which Radicals of the left have ever produced ought, however, not to surprise us. Revolutionary Socialism is but a different formulation and a stricter interpretation of truths generally accepted in Western Europe for almost two thousand years. (Polanyi, 1936, pp. 370–1)

It is doubtful that this rather ahistorical statement could be completely defended, nonetheless it is clear that in the depths of a the greatest economic and political crisis in the west of the twentieth century, Polanyi found inspiration for his historically informed critique of nature of the market order in Christianity.

If we turn to MacIntyre, his relationship to, and understanding of, the connection between Marxism and Christianity is more complex than in the case of Polanyi, indeed I have dealt with the matter at some length elsewhere (see McMylor, 1994). But at least in the MacIntyre case the relationship has been overtly discussed in his published corpus of work. The essential feature to note about MacIntyre is that he began his career and has ended it, at least to this point, as a Christian moral philosopher. This does not mean there has been no development in this intervening period, very far from it, as the twists and turns of his development cast a great deal of light on a large number of our current problems (see especially, MacIntyre, 1981). Nor even more emphatically should the title Christian moral philosopher be seen as reductive pigeon-holing classification, that it all so often is (see Milbank, 1990; and Voegelin, 1975, for why that should be). What it should sensitise us to is the fundamental conditioning, but not determining factor, behind the whole enterprise of MacIntyre's moral philosophy. MacIntyre sought not to resolve the antinomies of modern secular liberalism, as so much Anglo-Saxon moral and political philosophy does (see Grey, 1995, especially Chs 1 and 2), but to assess the shape of moral life that resulted from the loss of the perspectives and understandings of Christianity.

MacIntyre's first book was, *Marxism: An Interpretation* (1953) and was very much a philosophically informed theologians account of the subject. He wrote because he saw Marxism as the main alternative framework of thought to Christianity in the modern world and moreover a philosophy which had religious roots in the Christianity it was so critical of. What MacIntyre finds most interesting about Marxism are the elements that it receives from Christianity and deploys in a critical or even prophetic way in relationship to capitalist society. At the heart of his argument is the view that it is Marxism's religious roots that gives it a good deal of its vision and understanding of the good life of peace and reconciliation at the end of history, mediated often by Hegel, through concepts like alienation and estrangement (see MacIntyre, 1968; McMylor, 1994, Ch. 1; Lash, 1981).

MacIntyre, as is well known, abandons Christianity at first for Marxism and then by the time of his revised book, Marxism and Christianity in 1968 (MacIntyre, 1968), for a position that was distant from both positions. He has been able to state the following about his position at this time:

> Whereas in 1953 I had doubtless naively supposed it possible to be both in some significant way both a Christian and a Marxist, I was by 1968 able to

be neither, while acknowledging in both standpoints a set of truths with which I did not know how to come to terms with. (MacIntyre, 1995, p. xix)

What the critical truths of these two standpoints revealed were their common rejection of the privatised and arbitrary nature of moral judgement within modern liberalism. This arbitrariness had emerged out of a secularisation process that ironically eroded not only Christianity but also, later Marxism itself, by basing morality on abstract moral principles that could no longer be grounded in a teleology of divine law or human nature realised in history.

Within this framework it should come as no surprise that MacIntyre understands the nature of Marx's social theory in such a way as to be at variance with orthodox (Stalinist) accounts centred on the base/superstructure metaphor and is able to highlight the central place of moral practices within this reading. There could be no rigid distinction between the economic base of a society and the cultural and political superstructures which apparently arose out of it. There could be no question of using an implicitly utilitarian argument in which political dictatorship and military force could in some way construct the material foundations of socialism. Writing in 1958, whilst still describing himself as a Marxist, he states:

> the economic basis of society is not its tools, but the people co-operating using these particular tools in the manner necessary to their use, and the superstructure consists of the social consciousness moulded by and the shape of this co-operation. To understand this is to repudiate the ends-means morality for there is no question of creating the economic base as a means to the socialist superstructure. Creating the basis, you create the superstructure. There are not two activities but one. (MacIntyre, 1958–1959, p. 98)

Human co-operation, defined in such a way, meant that morality was an inescapable element in the nature of the social order. He later understands Aristotelian concepts of morality as the best theory for grasping this process, and one that he sees Marx, as well as much of the Catholic tradition, indebted to it (MacIntyre, 1994, 1995). Whatever MacIntyre's intellectual moves, for him, morality was never to be sacrificed to any scientism, but seen as an irreducible component of social practice. It is in this position that lies the crucial connection between MacIntyre's work and Polanyi's. Because MacIntyre viewed Marxism as having a moral dimension, he can see Polanyi's work, at least from the perspective of the 1990s, as a legitimate development of Marx's thought (MacIntyre, 1995, p. xviii).

How then in practice does the historical and social account of moral transformation presented by MacIntyre find support in Polanyi's work?

Markets and moral orders

MacIntyre's philosophical and sociological theory, presupposes a particular history. It is rooted in the significance attached to the development of a liberal capitalist market order out of a feudal society. For MacIntyre feudal society, whatever its distinctive features, shared enough in common with other non-capitalist, pre-industrial cultures (e.g. the classical world or the Arab Empire) to make the emergence of a capitalist market society, a quite distinct social form. Clearly there is a necessarily totalistic element in MacIntyre's account of these changes, for it is, in part, dependent upon connecting, in a relatively loose non-deterministic manner, economic, political and cultural changes. And it is here that we get a sense of what it is about Polanyi's analysis that MacIntyre likes. MacIntyre makes the whole issue clear when he states:

> my preference for Polanyi's type of narrative is that it avoids the methodological mistakes which all three (Marxist, Neo Marxist, Weberian) make most notably the error of supposing that we can identify economic or social factors independently from ideological or theoretical factors in such a way as to produce causal explanations of a cogent kind. My thesis is not that we cannot distinguish economic or social items from ideological or theoretical items; there is indeed more than one way of marking such a distinction. But when we try to understand the narratives of historical change in terms of any one of these sets of distinctions, the causal explanations which they yield are generally implausible. It is only when we understand and categorise the social and economic phenomena in such a way as to recognise that agents' and participants' under-standing of social and economic activity is integral to and partially constitutive of the characteristics of such activities that we provide characterisations which enable us to write rationally defensible explanatory narratives. Karl Polanyi's was just such a narration. (MacIntyre, 1984, pp. 253–4)

This can leave us in no doubt as to the integral connectedness of economic and social, cultural and theoretical phenomena in MacIntyre's thought. In a later work, *Whose Justice, Which Rationality* (1988), MacIntyre cites sympathetically the paper on Polanyi's method by Block and Somers (1984), in which the anti-economistic yet totalistic dimension of Polanyi's work is emphasised.

What emerges quite centrally in Polany's work is a complete absence of any modernist condescension towards past societies. He, like MacIntyre, wishes to understand past societies on their own terms and wishes to learn something from them about our own situation. Polanyi sought to oppose ideas, popular with some economists and economic anthropologists, that aimed at a unified economic theory which could cover all human societies, past and present. Polanyi's contention is that those who have attempted to uncover an overall economic science have imposed concepts derived from their understanding of market economies onto non-market ones. In this process, he maintains that they have seen past societies as filled with acquisitive individualists and thereby supporting the theory of human nature held by Adam Smith and his followers.

Polanyi sets out his basic theoretical orientation both in *The Great Transformation* (1944) and in a lengthy essay 'The Economy as Instituted

Process' (Polanyi, 1971a). Here, he makes the very Weberian distinction between 'substantive' and 'formal' economies. He argues that:

> the substantive meaning of economic derives from man's dependence for his living, upon nature and his fellows. It refers to the interchange with his natural and social environment, in so far as this results in supplying him with the means of material want – satisfaction. (Polanyi, 1971a, p. 139)

In essence this definition is close to what Marx means by the concept of 'use value'. Whilst the formal meaning of economic derives from the logical character of the means–ends relationship as apparent in such words as 'economical' or 'economising'. It refers to a definite situation of choice, namely that between the different uses of means induced by an insufficiency of those means. (Polanyi, 1971a, pp. 139–40)

Clearly Polanyi believes the formal definition is readily applicable to the capitalist industrial societies of the west, and that to apply its terms of reference to earlier pre-market societies can only cause grave distortion. Indeed, he goes so far as to argue that:

> The two root meanings of economic, the substantive and the formal have nothing in common. The latter derives from logic, the former from fact. The formal meaning implies a set of rules referring to choice between the alternative uses of insufficient means. The substantive meaning implies neither choice nor insufficiency of means: man's livelihood may or may not involve the necessity of choice and, if choice there be, it need not be induced by the limiting effect of a 'scarcity' of the means; indeed some the most important physical and social conditions of livelihood such as the availability of air and water or a loving mother's devotion to her infant are not as a rule so limiting. (Polanyi, 1971a, p. 140)

It is not surprising therefore that Polanyi's work has been an important influence on those who have sort to understand the so called shadow, or, black economy in a variety of societies (see Shanin, 1988).

It is clear from Polanyi's comments that what he terms the empirical or substantive economy must in some sense exist everywhere. The crucial difference between market and non or pre-market societies is that in these latter societies the economy is 'embedded' within the overall society, whilst in the former it is not. What does this embeddedness consist of? Principally Polanyi is referring to a wide range of non-economic institutions such as those of kinship, religion, political/state forms, that provide the context within which economic functions proper are performed. The consequence is that the goals or ends of economic activity are to a considerable degree shaped by these non-economic institutions and values, and it is almost never left simply to small groups or individuals to pursue their own material self-interest. Polanyi's view also has in its favour the fact that it is not based upon a static view of human nature. For he argues, in a whole variety of societies, tribal ones, small hunting or fishing communities, and even in great empires such as those societies at one time referred to as 'oriental despotism':

> Neither the process of production nor that of distributions linked to specific economic interests attached to the possession of goods, but every single step in that process is geared to a number of social interests which eventually ensure that the required step be taken. (Polanyi, 1957, p. 46)

Are such views based on romantic notions of primitivism and altruism? No. For, as Polanyi argues in the case of a tribal society it is unlikely that most of the time an individual's absolute interest in survival will be put in question, because the community keeps all of its members from starving, unless there is a disaster that threatens all of them. However, for this support to operate, the maintenance of social ties is quite crucial:

> Firstly because by disregarding the accepted code of honour, or generosity, the individual cuts himself off from the community ... second because in the long run, all social obligations are reciprocal, and their fulfilment serves also the individual's give-and-take interests best. (Polanyi, 1957, p. 46)

Polanyi goes on to suggest that the nature of these social relationships may be such that there is pressure:

> on the individual to eliminate economic self-interest from his consciousness to the point of making him unable, in many cases (but by no means all), even to comprehend the implications of his own actions in terms of such an interest. (Polanyi, 1957, p. 46)

So in non-market societies the human economy is enmeshed firmly in a variety of institutions both economic and non-economic, and this means that: 'religion and government may be as important for the structure and functioning of the economy as monetary institutions or the availability of tools and machines themselves that lighten the toil of labour' (Polanyi, 1971a, p. 148). Crucially, therefore, an analysis of the changes of the role of the economy in society turns out to be: 'no other than the study of the manner in which the economic process is instituted at different times and places' (Polanyi, 1971a, p. 148)

Clearly then at the abstract level, the corollary of this notion of non-market societies being enmeshed economies within other dominating frameworks, is that in market societies the economy with a capital 'E' is no longer so embedded. The market means that there is in some sense, a differentiation of economic activity into a separate institutional sphere, no longer regulated by norms that have their origin elsewhere. The individual economic agent is free to pursue economic self-interest, without 'non-economic' hindrance. Not that for Polanyi and MacIntyre, culture and tradition could be just wished away; neither believed that a pure capitalist market is possible. However they both assert that there is a radically distinctive quality to liberal capitalist societies that mark them out from any other. Polanyi is at pains to stress the radical novelty of the market order of nineteenth-century capitalism compared with any other society from virtually any period:

> Whether we turn to ancient city-state, despotic empire, feudalism, thirteenth-century urban life, sixteenth-century mercantile regime or eighteenth-century regulationism – invariably economic system is found to be merged in the social. Incentives spring from a large variety of sources, such as custom and tradition, public duty and private commitment, religious observance and political allegiance, judicial obligation and administrative regulation as established by prince, municipality or guild. (Polanyi, 1971b, p. 66)

It is worth noting that Polanyi does not deny that markets existed in many of these societies, rather his main contention is that isolated markets did not link up into an economy that made the rest of society, a kind of appendage to it.

We are now in a position to understand MacIntyre's stated dependence on Polanyi historical account in *The Great Transformation*. In the first place as we have seen, MacIntyre believes this account is important for the narrative of *After Virtue* because it avoids common methodological errors, but yet treats the transformation as a total process. But MacIntyre's preference runs much deeper than this. In essence this is because of their shared commitment to an overt discourse of moral assessment that bases itself on criteria that fall outside that of a liberal contractual culture Polanyi's account carries a strong moral charge, which emphasises the novelty and immorality of the transformation of human labour and the natural world into commodities. It is also characteristic of Polanyi's analysis that the similarities between different pre-modern societies are emphasised, in contrast to that of the modern, as in the last quotation. We can compare this with the following, from MacIntyre:

> the modern world in everything that makes it peculiarly modern is a society of strangers, that is, a society where the bonds of mutual utility and of appeals to rights have replaced older conceptions of friendship which pre-suppose an allegiance to the virtues. (MacIntyre,1983, p. 465)

Both MacIntyre and Polanyi are involved in locating what is specifically new within modern western societies. In Polanyi's case he does not for a moment deny the enormous variety of institutional and economic forms present within the very different types of society that he lists, but he does insist, that for all their differences there are some core elements of similarity, i.e. the embeddedness of the economic within the social. This is precisely the structure of argument employed by MacIntyre. In order to be able to locate and illustrate, the unique aspects of the modern, MacIntyre must be able to extract, for purposes of comparison, elements of similarity from beneath the apparent diversity of moral concepts – in pre-modern societies. His task is perhaps more difficult than Polanyi's, but they possess a unity of purpose nonetheless.

MacIntyre examines the role of the virtues in Homer, Aristotle, the New Testament and then for further comparison two more recent figures, Benjamin Franklin and Jane Austen. They would appear, at least at first, to have very different notions of the virtues, suggesting perhaps, that they differ as much amongst themselves as they do from our culture. The problem seems to become worse when one considers the enormous variety of social and cultural contexts that they inhabited. It is quite explicable in cultural terms that Homer saw the warrior as the model of human excellence and achievement, whilst Aristotle in the changed context of a fairly stable Athenian city-state, saw goodness and virtue embodied in the Athenian gentleman.

MacIntyre points out that in the case of Aristotle:

> certain virtues are only available to those of great riches and high social status, there are virtues which are unavailable to the poor man, even if he is a free man. And those virtues are on Aristotle's view ones central to human life; magnanimity... (MacIntyre, 1981, p. 17)

No greater contrast could be found than in the New Testament, for here are virtues that find no place in Aristotle's thought, such as faith and hope, but there is also praise for something Aristotle would probably have seen as a vice, humility – the corresponding vice to his virtue of magnanimity, as he understood it. Aristotle's social priorities are reversed in the New Testament, as slaves seem to have more chance of achieving virtue than rich men.

The situation is no easier when we move to later figures like Jane Austen and Benjamin Franklin. For MacIntyre argues that in Austen we find an immediate contrast with Aristotle, for where he sees a virtue in 'agreeableness' she sees only the artificial simulation of a genuine virtue she calls 'amiability'. The difference lies in the latter's Christianity, as she attaches importance to the need for some real feeling to be involved. The case of Franklin is different again: 'Franklin includes virtues which are new to our consideration such as cleanliness, silence and industry; he clearly considers the drive to acquire, itself a part of virtue, whereas for most ancient Greeks this is the vice of pleonexia' (MacIntyre, 1981, p. 171). Franklin is a complicating case for MacIntyre, as we'll see below, because of his relation to, and proximity with the modern market order. He is, nonetheless, important because there are few clearer examples from his period of the systematic redefining and reordering of older conceptions of the virtues (see Weber's discussion 1976, pp. 51–6).

The differences, therefore, are numerous, and there seems little common ground. However, so far we've looked at particular virtues and changed definitions, but what of the underlying structure of argument in the placing of virtues in their various social contexts. We will see that at this deeper level similarities emerge.

To elucidate the underlying structure of virtues, we can follow MacIntyre's definitions of his five cases. In Homer, a virtue is a quality which enables someone to do exactly what it is that their social role requires of them. So that, 'the concept of what anyone filling such-and-such a role ought to do is prior to the concept of a virtue; the latter concept has application only via the former (MacIntyre, 1981, pp. 171-2).

In Aristotle, despite some virtues only being possible for certain kinds of people, his basic notion of human virtue follows his general understanding of metaphysics, virtue attaches to the nature of man's being as such. It is the telos of humanity as a natural kind species which decides what behaviour counts as a virtue. But in the New Testament, although its virtues are different from Aristotle's, nonetheless, as MacIntyre argues: 'A virtue is, as with Aristotle a quality, the exercise of which leads to the achievement of the human telos. The good for man is, of course, a supernatural and not only a natural, but supernature redeems and completes nature, (MacIntyre, 1981, p. 172).

We can add to this, that for MacIntyre's argument there is another extremely important similarity between the Christian and Aristotelian conception of the virtues; that is that for both, the relationship between means and ends is an internal one, and not external. What is meant by this is, that the means by which the end is achieved are inseparably connected, so that the very process of movement and development, partly constitutes what it is to achieve the end itself.

It is precisely this internal relationship between means and ends that Polanyi describes in his location of the role of the economy in pre-modern societies. Naturally, it is this deep parallel between the role of virtues in Aristotle and in the New Testament, that allows Aquinas to make his famous synthesis between the two. But MacIntyre argues for a deeper parallel between these two and the type of outlook represented by Homer. For both Aristotle and the New Testament, the concept of 'good life for man' comes prior to any particular virtue or hierarchy of virtues, so in Homer the concept of a person's social role was prior to any notion of a virtue.

In regard to Austen, MacIntyre (echoing C. S. Lewis, 1954 and Gilbert Ryle, 1971) is able to subsume her also within the Christian and Aristotelian traditions, the latter he suggests, she probably gained from reading Shaftsbury (MacIntyre, 1981, p. 172). The case of Franklin is more complex but interesting. MacIntyre's account is too brief here and requires supplementing. Franklin, in his understanding of the virtues, shares Aristotle's teleology, but his reasons are utilitarian ones. For MacIntyre this means that his conception of means-ends relationships is external rather than internal, i.e. governed by utility:

> The end to which the cultivation of the virtues ministers is happiness, but happiness understood as success, prosperity in Philadelphia and ultimately in Heaven. The virtues are to be useful and Franklin's account continuously stresses utility as a criterion in individual cases: 'make no expense but to do good to others or yourself. Avoid trifling conversation'. (MacIntyre, 1981, p. 173)

These are typical of Franklin's ideas of the virtues along with punctuality, industry, frugality plus many others, but always for utilitarian ends.

On the face of it, Franklin's utilitarianism may seem to pose problems for the argument so far developed. For utilitarianism features in *After Virtue*, and in much else of MacIntyre's work, as a paradigm viewpoint of modernity, which prioritises the pursuit of external goods and is hence, ideally compatible with a rationalistic market order of society. For such a viewpoint the simulation of virtues would be quite sufficient to get what one wants, e.g. a hard-working reputation, for credit worthiness. But if this is true how can it be that Franklin has a teleological vision of the virtues?

The answer to this lies in Franklin's location as a transitional figure between two radically different cultures. His apparently pragmatic utilitarianism is in fact sustained by something far more fundamental, for as Weber puts it after noting the potential hypocrisy of Franklin's position:

> The circumstances that he ascribes his recognition of the utility of virtue to a divine revelation which was intended to lead him in the path of righteousness, shows that something more than mere garnishing for purely egocentric motives is involved. (Weber, 1976, p. 53)

In effect, Franklin illustrates well the argument made by a number of social theorists concerning the dependence of capitalist societies on cultural boundary conditions that cannot be renewed by themselves (Habermas, 1976; Hirsch, 1976; Bell, 1996).

Franklin's teleological view of the virtues is therefore sustained by a key element in the tradition which saw the virtues as a system of internal goods leading to determinate ends, to which behaviour was subordinated. As is well known later utilitarians such as Mill, were to remove this underpinning from their theory and replace it initially with a calculus of pleasure and pain and later with notions of want satisfaction.

In summary, MacIntyre argues that we have three conceptions of the virtues here: Firstly, that a virtue is what enables an individual to carry out his/her role, this is the view present in Homer; secondly, a virtue is a human quality that allows an individual to move towards achieving a specific human telos, which can be supernatural or natural, the position of Aristotle, the New Testament authors, Aquinas and Jane Austen; thirdly, a virtue is a quality which has 'utility' in achieving earthly and heavenly success, held by Benjamin Franklin.

Is there, then, within these three forms, some core concept or shared conception of the virtues? There is enough here for a least a provisional judgement. It should be noticed that one aspect of the virtues has emerged with some clarity. It seems to be the case that for the concept of virtues to operate at all in a society: 'it always requires for its application the acceptance of some prior account of certain features of social and moral life, in terms of which it (virtue) has to be defined and explained' (MacIntyre, 1981, p. 174). This means that in Homer virtue is secondary to and dependent upon a clear concept of social role. In Aristotle and related accounts, it depends on what the 'good life for man as the telos of human action' is defined as. In Franklin, it is dependent upon some specified notion of utility. For each of these writers prior agreement on crucial aspects of social and moral life cannot be merely theoretical, it must have some material embodiment conceptions to have any purchase at all. The obvious examples are the role of the Polis in Aristotle's thought – perhaps we should say more accurately that the Polis makes Aristotle's thought possible – like the role of the church for New Testament writers.

This is the heart of the matter. The very diversity of these writers and the cultures they in part represent all, nevertheless, imply and demand some definite institutionalisation for their conception of the virtues to operate. Jane Austen requires a type of Agrarian capitalism – albeit a not entirely marketised society – with a country house and a certain form of the institution of marriage for her Christian Aristotelianism. This is the deep structure of similarity that unites these writers even in their diversity and most importantly what distinguishes them most profoundly from modern liberal individualistic thought. It can make no assumption about social context, except to say no way of life must have institutional precedence over others.

Conclusion

The parallel and connection between MacIntyre and Polanyi is now clear: for Polanyi the wide diversity of pre-market economic forms all require embedding within some wider set of social relations to avoid economics being a narrow means–ends relationship of self-interest; so with MacIntyre's account, for in order for virtue to be exercised, or even understood, there must be criteria embodied in some shared account of our own context. When that shared account collapses, then the moral self is as disembedded as economic relations are in the market place.

Further we can see that a market order is one in which the unencumbered self feels most at home. In this sense conservative free-market advocates may well have been correct and prescient in the 1970s to make a pitch for the apparently left-wing romantic individualists of the 1960s generation (Brittan, 1973). There were deeper affinities between them than their self-assigned political labels would allow for. Correspondingly social democrats and socialists, committed to a politics of redistribution and social welfare, may well have misunderstood the cultural dynamics within market-based societies, with consequences today that are all too clear. This is not to suggest that social democrats and socialists simply neglected the significance of ethical considerations for their politics but rather that they failed to grasp that particular social contexts and institutional forms make some ethical commitments seem right and plausible but tend to exclude others from the self-understanding of social actors. The forms that social welfare, public ownership or redistributive taxation take or could have taken are no doubt crucial for shaping the narrowness or the breadth of a social actors sense of self-interest and moral responsibility.

Acknowledgements

The comments of participants at the Polanyian Perspectives on Instituted Economic Processes, Development and Transformation workshop held at the University of Manchester, October 2002 are gratefully acknowledged. Of course all errors and omissions remain my own.

References

Barber, B. (1995), 'All Economies Are "Embedded": The Career of a Concept, and Beyond', *Social Research*, 62(2), pp. 387–413.
Baum, G. (1996), *Karl Polanyi: On Ethics and Politics*, Montreal, McGill–Queen's University Press.
Bauman, Z. (1996), *Postmodern Ethics*, Oxford, Basil Blackwell.
Bell, D. (1996), *The Cultural Contradictions of Capitalism*, New York, Basic Books.
Block, F. and Somers, M. (1984), 'Beyond the Economistic Fallacy: The Holistic Social Science of Karl Polanyi', in T. Skopal (ed.), *Vision and Method in Historical Sociology*, Cambridge, Cambridge University Press.
Blau, J. R. (1993), *Social Contracts and Economic Markets*, New York, Plenum Press.
Brittan, S. (1973), *Capitalism and the Permissive Society*, London, Macmillan.
Congdon, L. (1976), 'Karl Polanyi in Hungary 1900–1919', *Journal of Contemporary History*, 11(1), pp. 167–83.
Etzioni, A. (1988), *The Moral Dimension: Towards a New Economics*, New York, Free Press.
Etzioni, A. (1995), *The Spirit of Community: Rights, Responsibility and the Communitarian Agenda*, London, Fontana.
Etzioni, A. (1997), *The New Golden Rule: Community and Morality in a Democratic Society*, London, Profile Books.
Fukuyama, F. (1995), *Trust: The Social Virtues and the Creation of Prosperity*, London, Hamish Hamilton.
Giddens, A. (1991), *Modernity and Self-identity: Self and Society in the Late Modern Age*, Cambridge, Polity.
Grey, J. (1995), *Enlightenment's Wake: Politics and Culture at the Close of the Modern Age*, London, Routledge.
Habermas, J. (1976), *The Legitimation Crisis*, London, Heinemann.
Hirsch, F. (1976), *The Social Limits of Growth*, Cambridge, MA, Harvard University Press.
Hughes, H. S. (1974), *Consciousness and Society: The Reorientation of European Thought*, London, Paladin.
Janik, A. J. and Toulmin, S. (1980), *Wittgenstein's Vienna*, New York, Simon & Schuster.
Kadarkay, A. (1991), *Georg Lukacs: Life, Thought and Politics*, Oxford, Basil Blackwell.

Kettler, D., Meja, V. and Shehr, N. (1984), *Karl Mannheim*, London, Tavistock.
Lash, N. (1981), *A Mattter of Hope: A Theologian's Reflections on the Thought of Karl Marx*, London, Darton, Longman and Todd.
Lewis, C. S. (1954), 'A Note on Jane Austen', *Essays in Criticism*, Part IV, October.
Litvan, G. (1991), 'Democratic and Socialist Values in Karl Polanyi's Thought', in M. Mendell and D. Salee (eds), *The Legacy of Karl Polanyi*, New York, St Martin's Press.
MacIntyre, A. (1953), *Marxism: An Interpretation*, London, SCM Press.
MacIntyre, A. (1968), *Marxism and Christianity*, London, Duckworth.
MacIntyre, A. (1958–59), 'Notes from the Moral Wilderness I & II', *New Reasoner*, 7, pp. 90–100.
MacIntyre, A. (1981), *After Virtue: A study in Moral Theory*, London, Duckworth.
MacIntyre, A. (1983), 'Moral Rationality and Tradition and Aristotle: A Reply to Onora O'Neill, Raimond Gaita and Stephen R. L. Clark', *Inquiry*, 26(4), pp. 447–66.
MacIntyre, A. (1988), *Whose Justice, Which Rationality*, London, Duckworth.
MacIntyre, A. (1984), 'After Virtue and Marxism: A Response to Wartofsky', *Inquiry*, 27(2–3), pp. 251–4.
MacIntyre, A. (1987), 'The Idea of an Educated Public', in G. Haydon (ed.), *Education and Values*, London, London University, Institute of Education.
MacIntyre, A. (1994), 'The Theses on Feuerbach: A Road Not Taken', in C. C. Gould and R. S. Cohen (eds), *Artifacts, Representations and Social Practice*, Deventer, Kluwer.
MacIntyre, A. (1995), *Introduction to Reissued, Marxism and Christianity*, London, Duckworth.
McMylor, P. (1994), *Alasdair MacIntyre: Critic of Modernity*, London, Routledge.
Milbank, J. (1990), *Theology and Social Theory: A Critique of Secular Reason*, Oxford, Basil Blackwell.
Polanyi, K. (1936), 'The Essence of Fascism', in K. Polanyi, J. Lewis and D. Kitchin (eds), *Christianity and the Social Revolution*, New York, Charles Scribner's Sons.
Polanyi, K. (1944/1957), *The Great Transformation*, Boston, Beacon Press.
Polanyi, K. (1971a), 'The Economy as an Instituted Process', in G. Dalton (ed.), *Primitive, Archaic and Modern Economics: Essays of Karl Polanyi*, Boston, Beacon Press.
Polanyi, K. (1971b), 'The Obsolete Market Mentality', in G. Dalton (ed.), *Primitive, Archaic and Modern Economics: Essays of Karl Polanyi*, Boston, Beacon Press.
Polanyi-Levitt, K. and Mendell, M. (1987), 'Karl Polanyi: His Life and Times', *Studies in Political Economy*, 22, pp. 7–39.
Rosen, S. (1987), *Hermeneutics as Politics*, Oxford, Oxford University Press.
Rotstein, A. (1994), 'Weekend Notes: Conversations with Karl Polanyi', in K. McRobbie (ed.), *Humanity, Society and Commitment: On Karl Polanyi*, Montreal, Black Rose Books.
Ryle, G. (1971), *Collected Papers*, London, Hutchinson.

Scheff, T. (1990), *Micro Sociology: Discourse, Emotion and Social Structure*, Chicago, Chicago University Press.
Seligman, A. (1997), *The Problem of Trust*, Princeton, Princeton University Press.
Shanin, T. (1988), 'Expolary Economies: A Political Economy of Margins, Agenda for the Study of Modes of Non-Incorporation as Parallel Forms of Social Economy', *Journal of Historical Sociology*, 1(1).
Smelser, N. J. and Swedberg, R. (eds) (1994), *Handbook of Economic Sociology*, Princeton, Princeton University Press.
Swedberg, R. (1987), 'Economic Sociology', *Current Sociology*, 35(1), pp. 1–221.
Tester, K. (1997), *Moral Culture*, London, Sage.
Touraine, A. (1988), *The Return of the Actor*, Minnesota, University of Minnesota Press.
Voegelin, E. (1975), *From Enlightenment to Revolution*, North Carolina, Duke University Press.
Weber, M. (1976), *The Protestant Ethic and the Spirit of Capitalism*, London, Allen & Unwin.

Part II
New directions

8

Issues for a neo-Polanyian research agenda in economic sociology

Sally Randles

Introduction: Polanyi-given, Polanyi-inspired

'Polanyi-scholarship' encompasses a number of very diverse positions and projects. Stylistically, these may be categorised into two quite different (though not mutually exclusive) groupings. A first group might be defined as those who work within a 'Polanyi-*given*' frame. They comprise at least three sub-groups: those intent on interpreting the Polanyi texts, as they stand and without any human contextualisation in terms of understanding the life, times, and society of the author (a distinctly non-anthropological approach); those who prefer to contextualise the Polanyi texts within a broader understanding of Polanyi's concerns and normative position, informed essentially and inevitably by a historical appreciation of the author's life and times; and finally those critical of Polanyi who, on evaluating his concepts find them to be either fatally flawed (extreme critics) or at least in need of some modification (sympathisers) before they can be utilised by contemporary scholars as either an adequate or appropriate lens through which to analyse contemporary real world phenomena and relations.

A second group of scholars use Polanyi quite differently. These might be stylised as *Polanyi-inspired* writers engaged in theoretical *development* and empirical analyses. Among them we can distinguish at least two sub-groups: the first takes an empirical focus. They are inspired by the view that Polanyian insights, worked out over a period of some thirty years of the twentieth century, appear to provide such a high degree of relevance and application to problems facing the world today. This being the case even when many contemporary spatially temporally contingent situations were not empirically available to Polanyi himself. Some examples would be: an assessment of the power and reach of transnational corporations, attention to the new and enlarged agenda of environmental protection, and concerns about the unprecedented free flow of international capital and its consequences.

The second sub-group of *Polanyi-inspired* authors takes key notions from Polanyi's work, and either uses them as a taken-for-granted entry point to their own analysis and position, or as a deeper and more considered point of entry in developing a particular line of theoretical and conceptual thought. This approach is sympathetic, in general terms, to the Polanyi original, but in fact moves the Polanyi conceptual frames a long way from their origins. Examples might be: the notion of labour as a fictitious commodity for which the term 'market' cannot and/or should not be applied; the notion of 'embeddedness' and the perennial question of the relationship between economy and society; the notion of an ontological, dynamic, action-response (double) movement between regulation and markets; and the notion of economy as instituted process.

Of course these categorisations of project and position are schematic and are suggested here for illustrative purposes only. They are little more than 'tendencies' noticed in the secondary Polanyi literature, appropriations, and ongoing research agendas. They are neither discrete nor cast in stone. They demonstrate the range of ways that contemporary scholars have appropriated Polanyi and serve as an entry point to our questions regarding the Polanyi legacy and the scope and possibilities of neo-Polanyian scholarship. Indeed the position taken in this paper is a mix of contextualisation of the Polanyi texts within an appreciation of the man and his life (Polanyi-*given*); sympathetic critique (Polanyi-*given*); and scope for theoretical and empirical development (Polanyi-*inspired*).

The chapter is in four sections. First, it suggests the beginnings of a response to the question of the 'deafening silence from England'. Second, it provides a broad introductory appreciation of the main normative, theoretical and methodological themes in Polanyi's work, at the same time considering how contemporary authors have appropriated these themes. Third, it attempts to balance a celebration of Polanyi's scholarship with critical distance and appraisal. Fourth, it raises some issues and questions as a necessary precursor to deciding on the merits or otherwise of a potentially longer term endeavour: that of defining and developing a *neo*-Polanyian approach to the study of competition and innovation within economic sociology.

From England there was silence...

> As for England, where *The Great Transformation* was conceived, Polanyi's work has been greeted with a deafening silence. Strange and yet to be explained. (Polanyi-Levitt, 1990b, p. 6)

In order to shed light on why Karl Polanyi was unable[1] to penetrate the closed world of English academia, during the inter-war and post-World War II period, we must first consider his formative years in Budapest and his escape from the rising tide of German fascism. Of Hungarian-Russian descent Polanyi, was born in Vienna in 1886. His Jewish middle-class upbringing combined the parentage of a rising entrepreneur-engineer father and influences from his mother's (Cecile Wohl) historian rabbi father. As a result of Cecile's intellectual charm and natural social abilities the Polanyi home was to become a welcoming meeting place of the Budapest intelligentsia. The mother (and the young Karl) found themselves at the centre of this circle. Third child in a family of six, the daily life of the young Polanyi as part of Budapest's urban bourgeoisie was at first very comfortable, in material terms, if frugal and highly disciplined, a life of 'high principles and lofty education' (Polanyi-Levitt, Polanyi, 2000, p. 304). So frugal in fact was their father's household that when his rail-construction business collapsed (Karl was only fourteen years old), little changed outwardly in terms of the family's daily regime and lives, even though the family were reduced to a poverty which was 'instant and complete' (*ibid.*, p. 304). Already academically inclined, the young Karl was required to help support the family through his teenage years by tutoring. When Karl was 19, his father died, shattering the family. Responsibility for the economic well-being of the younger siblings fell squarely onto the shoulders of Karl and his elder brothers.

A law graduate, Polanyi turned his back on this profession, preferring the less lucrative life of economic historian and social commentator. His politics could not easily be pigeon-holed even at this early stage. He was about 22 when he abandoned the Marxist views he had previously held and he later became a most outspoken critic of the rising communist movement in Hungary, attacking with a vengeance the idea of a 'dictatorship of the proletariat' (Polanyi-Levitt, 2000, p. 309). His founding role and long-support of the Galileo Circle in Budapest perhaps best represents his most enduring normative and ideological position, and within this we can see the origins of a belief system which was later to infuse his policy prescriptions as well as his theoretical base. The circle converged around the vision:

> to mobilise against clericalism and corruption; against the privileged, and against bureaucracy, – against that ever present and pervasive morass in this semi-feudal country. (Polanyi-Levitt, 2000, p. 307)

Polanyi was noted for being outspoken and for his rhetorical polemical style. Much later, his advocate and supporter George Dalton noted that the words of this powerful orator did not always translate easily into print:

> what was forceful, lucid and articulate in the lecture hall sometimes became hyperbole and polemic in print. A friend sympathetic to his work describes Polanyi's writing style as a stiletto set in the far end of a battering ram. (Dalton, 1968, p. x)

A ten-year period of sadness and frustration took their toll on Polanyi in his thirties (Polanyi, 1925). This was followed by a period working as an economics correspondent[2] with a leading Austrian financial and economics newspaper from 1924 to 1934.[3] Like many others fleeing the rising tide of German fascism he moved to England in 1934 where he lectured at a variety of institutions across London and the south east of England, on behalf of the Workers Educational Association (WEA) until his departure for Bennington College, USA in 1940.[4] It was during his years tutoring for the WEA that he observed first hand working-class life in England and the charred English landscapes, legacy of the industrial revolution. During this time he also engaged in intensive study of English economic and social history. Together, these observations and the lecture notes from his WEA courses were to form the basis of *The Great Transformation*. He did not secure a permanent position at any of the more élite English Universities. Indeed it was not England but America which offered Polanyi his first full-time academic appointment. This did not come until 1947 when at the age of 61 years he was appointed Visiting Professor of Economics at Columbia University teaching General Economic History and researching the *origins of institutions*. In the meantime, *The Great Transformation* published in English in 1944, fell on deaf, unappreciative, ears in England.

Polanyi had therefore arrived in England, a central-European émigré escaping political persecution and holding few assets in terms of contacts and status-enhancing qualifications from a well-regarded university. It was perhaps unsurprising if regrettable that he found it difficult to break into the closed world of the English academic establishment. However, whilst contributory, this account is, so far, insufficient to explain[5] why Polanyi's life-work did not find an audience in England, either immediately or for many years, despite being acclaimed in the US and around the world from Central and Mediterranean Europe to Japan and South America.

The guiding political principles that characterised Polanyi's later writing were visible in his Budapest/Galileo Circle days. He emphasised the values of individual freedom, an 'open society' and above all cultural pluralism. Herein we see a privileging of the 'local' and localised decision making over any form of central planning. Translated into a politico-economic 'ideal-type' Polanyi advocated a form of 'Guild Socialism' during the 1920s. Akin to the modern-day worker co-operative, this model placed faith in the locally negotiated economy, wherein productive sector-based groups would negotiate, through the representation of the interests of labour, production, consumers and civic society, levels of output and prices. In so doing, according to Polanyi, socially 'fair' compromises on decisions of price would be reached. Such a position clearly brought him into direct conflict with the Austrian School, especially Mises and his student Hayek.[6] Both were hostile to market intervention of any kind and considered guild-socialism a totally unfeasible model of socialist-accounting (Rosner, 1990). Moreover the Polanyi model stood in theoretical and normative opposition to their own attachment to individual freedom brought about through a very different route – by the 'freeing' of markets to their most unregulated form. Normatively and in terms of policy prescription the Mises/Hayekian branch of Austrian economics advocated incentivising (the assumed) universal and naturally calculative economic agent to raise his [sic] personal material wealth by finding and engaging in optimally efficient productive activity.[7] As early as the 1920s, the Mises/Hayek accounts found support among certain sections of the English economic establishment and Hayek was brought from Vienna to the London School of Economics by Lionel Robbins to counter the developing doctrines of Keynes in Cambridge (Polanyi-Levitt, 2000, p. 4).

And yet it was not laissez-faire but Keynsianism that temporarily held sway over the policy and ideological stage in England, emerging to dominate post-war economic policy. Demand-management and the heady early days of the English welfare state were in the ascendancy and admired across Europe. Hayek's book on the other hand, whilst it was met with disbelief in the New Deal atmosphere of the US, *did* receive some support in England (Polanyi-Levitt, 2000), seemingly suiting an agenda of legitimate opposition to the Keynesian revolution.

So it seems that Polanyi's absence of status-enhancing qualifications from a well-regarded university, lack of social connections with the English academic establishment, and very different methodological-disciplinary bases[8] to those which dominated the teaching (and reading lists) of English academia for several decades post-World War II; together with his opposition to the laissez-faire economists (from Smith, Ricardo and Walrus to Mises and Hayek) would have made it near impossible for Polanyi to find a readership, intellectual home, and people of like-minded endeavour in England. And this was a position which was evidently sustained for many decades after *The Great Transformation* was published in English in 1944.

Herein lies a contribution to the quest for an explanation for Polanyi-Levitt's assertion that *The Great Transformation* was met with a deafening silence in England. The book (alongside Polanyi's own potential career path) appears to have fallen between a rock and a hard place, traced along a number of ideological, intellectual, methodological and academic/establishment dimensions. As a result, unfortunately, Polanyi was disadvantaged from the outset in any quest to secure a constituency of readers in England.

And so for many years *The Great Transformation* remained largely invisible to the eyes of the English academic establishment and its students. By contrast since the 1980s, Polanyi's work has become more visible and increasingly more fashionable on both sides of the Atlantic. In England this can partly be attributed to a shift towards pluralist, multi-disciplinary approaches in higher-education (consistent with Polanyian method, combining economics, political economy, sociology, history and geography in various ways). Partly it can be attributed to major empirical structural shifts in international political economy dating from the collapse of Bretton Woods in 1973, where cascades of events and their transformational consequences invoke Polanyian analysis (Helleiner, 2000). In the next section I turn to the task of identifying who has been using Polanyi, why, how, and why now. However, I go on to situate this within a more critical appreciation of Polanyi's whole system of conceptual and theoretical ideas.

An overview of Polanyian concepts and methodology: the view from his supporters

The Great Transformation had a very different objective and orientation to Polanyi's later works. Written primarily as a historical text, it sought to articulate and explain why a 'hundred years peace' (from 1815 to 1914) itself a phenomenon unheard of in the annals of Western civilisation, was succeeded by equally spectacular and unprecedented economic and social collapse, international in character and deeply pervasive in mode. He found his explanation within the very institutions which had underpinned and propagated the era of peace and prosperity. The four institutions upon which he believed nineteenth-century civilisation rested, were:

1 the balance-of-power system which for a century had held at bay the warring tendencies of the Great Powers;
2 the international gold standard which represented a unique (and it turned out, temporary) organisation of the world economy;
3 the liberal state; and
4 the self-regulating market which produced an unheard of (aggregate level) of material welfare.

Of the four, it is his conceptualisation and evaluation of (4) which is of most concern for this chapter. His analysis of an integrative institutional framework that necessarily surrounds and facilitates the self-regulating market provides the conceptual basis from which he later theorised the economy as *instituted process*. Indeed, Polanyi's writing becomes increasingly antagonistic and pessimistic towards the market as mode of allocation as his writings progress, and he refers in *Our Obsolete Market Mentality* (Polanyi, 1947) to *the market trauma* and a *dark undertone of concern* (*ibid.*, p. 110). He comes to couple 'liberal capitalism', with a particular form of laissez-faire market organisation. He insists that both are non-universal temporally spatially contingent modes of economic integration, and historically situates their rise to the status of taken-for-granted *dominant* mode of economic integration in the last two centuries of western capitalism, with its institutional origins in nineteenth-century England. He ultimately links both to the ensuing socio-economic collapse which entrained two world wars.

This empirical account provides support to Polanyi's lifelong normative critique of self-regulating markets. However, in terms of theory building, it was not then but much later, indeed 13 years later that his theory of the economy as instituted process emerged. Armed with a new fascination for anthropological perspectives, a research programme on the origin of institutions, and a circle of eager students and research assistants, Polanyi developed his main thesis (Polanyi, 1957). This is the closest the writer comes to a 'general' economic theory. Integral to his position however is attention to the contingent specificity of socio-economic empirical worlds, the methodological implication of which is a preference for comparative method – both historical and geographical – and a systematic rejection of Western ethno-centricity.

Polanyi's notion of 'economy as instituted process' brings to the fore the essential feature of institutional variety and was supported by a research programme into the myriad ways societies provision for themselves and devise modes of economic integration. A key outcome of the programme was to require that economists cease to privilege market exchange as the sole or central economic institution, but rather pay attention to empirical variety in the ways econom(ies) situate within societ(ies).

Polanyi (1957) begins with a methodological critique of many of the foundational tenets of mainstream neoclassical economics, a critique which has been played out more or less consistently, particularly by writers labelling their disciplinary perspective New Economic Sociology (NES) ever since.[9] Polanyi in many ways pre-empted this debate by distinguishing the 'substantive economic' which he applauded, from the 'formal economic' which he critically challenged. The former he equates with real-world empirics 'the fount of the substantive concept is the empirical economy' (*ibid.*, p. 248). It relates to 'the place occupied by economic life in society' (Polanyi et al., 1957b, p. v) where economy has to do with the creation, accumulation and distribution of *material wealth*. This methodological concern to trace and critically comment upon the social and economic consequences arising from *real* flows and concentrations of material wealth is a simple point, but one which, arguably, is often notable for its omission from *new* economic sociology (a point to which we return later). The 'substantive economic' he finds to be contingent on particular societal forms where social process is described as:

> a tissue of relationships between man as a biological entity and the unique structure of symbols and techniques that results in maintaining his existence. (Polanyi et al., 1957b, p. 239)

By contrast, he finds many of the assumptions of the 'formal meaning of economic' wanting.[10] In order to illustrate the flaws in these assumptions, he takes the three institutions of trade, money, and the (price-setting) market to demonstrate how each is far from universal, but on the contrary is found to be socially constructed and socially contingent when inductively investigated. He says: '[t]he economy, then, is an instituted process' (Polanyi, 1957, p. 248).

This requires that both 'process' and 'instituted' be defined. By 'process' he means the 'motion' through which changes in location, or in appropriation, or both occur. Motion may take the form of *circulation* which he describes as the appropriative movement resulting from (economic) *transactions* (of the market). Alternatively, motion can be brought about by administration (allocation decisions consciously made) which he describes as the appropriative movement resulting from *dispositions*.

In Polanyi's discussion of 'instituted' the analytical framework moves far away from the mechanistic, a-social, free-wheeling, ever-changing world of the Austrian School which centralises 'knowledge' as the dynamo of change and transformation. By contrast, Polanyi considers the *instituted* process to find some fixity and incentivised form, depending on the socially contextualised conditions from where the *process* springs:

> in the absence of any indications of the societal conditions from which the motives of the individuals spring, there would be little, if anything, to sustain the interdependence of the movements and their recurrence on which the unity and the stability of process depends. (*ibid.*, p. 249)

He continues:

> The instituting of the economic process vests that process with unity and stability; it produces a structure with a definite function in society, thus adding significance to its history; it centres interest on values, motives and policy. Unity and stability, structure and function, history and policy spell out operationally the content of our assertion that the human economy is an instituted process. (*ibid.*, p. 250)

Polanyi illustrates and develops this analysis by describing what in his opinion are the three (primary) institutions of economic integration, namely reciprocity, redistribution and exchange. He notes the role each plays in producing characteristic variants of *integrated* economic system. For example (but only by way of example) he describes a system integrated by price-making markets. His analysis involves searching for a small number of explanatory factors which provide pattern and therefore an underpinning stable architecture to the institutionalisation of socio-economic relations. An example is the institution of *mutuality*. He observes, importantly, many alternatives to price-making markets, such as mutual gift giving and sharing, operating outside the *quid pro quo* of the contractually enforceable price-making market.

Polanyi further wishes to distinguish ad-hoc acts of exchange from the type of repeated exchanges which are necessary for instituted price making systems:

> Acts of exchange on the personal level produce prices only if they occur under a system of price-making markets, an institutional set up which is nowhere created by mere random acts of exchange. (*ibid.*, p. 251)

Specifically on market allocation systems, he in some senses previews the economic sociologists who were to follow him some thirty years later, by insisting on the diversity and contingency of real-world market institutions. This he believes to be a point of fact which became obscured in the name of the supply–demand–price mechanistic models of the 'formal economic'.

Since the 1980s, a large number of writers (including English writers) have found favour with Polanyi. Their reasons have been quite diverse. However, we do see a common temporal start-point, in a concern to uncover the implications for world political economy of the *crisis* of the Keynsian Welfare State, interpreted as the result of a contagion of world forces and events. The two oil crises in the 1970s, technological maturity of the sectors which underpinned post-world war reconstruction, the breakdown of a system of international regulation of capital markets embodied in the Bretton Woods agreement, itself rejected by America in the early 1970s, and the ensuing abolition of international exchange controls which swept successively across western economies from 1974 onwards all contributed to the crisis.

In its place, Western economies were complicit in instituting a return to overt and extreme laissez-faire policies, beginning with the election of Margaret Thatcher and the Conservative administration in the UK in 1979 and driven by the Thatcher–Reagan alliance which endured through much of the 1980s. Nations engaged in a 'race to the bottom' (Peck and Tickell, 1996) of competitive policy responses, with markets becoming increasingly de-regulated and corporate functions becoming increasingly more mobile in an international search for the best (often cheapest and most-deregulated) terms for securing labour, land and capital, encouraging the de-territorialisation of parts of productive system (Storper, 1997a, 1997b). Across Europe, such policies crept into non-obvious arenas such as the political economy and governance of cities (Randles, 2000). So, around the notion of heightened international competition there converged a range of internally coherent national and international policies based on the deregulation of capital, product, and labour markets.[11] And to varying degrees in different countries, a move to provide through the private-sector products and services previously delivered by agencies of the state.[12]

Clearly, this international mood was ripe for a critical counter-analysis by international political economy scholars using the writing of Karl Polanyi (1944, 1957) to posit a subsequent 'Great Transformation' occurring 1920–90. Polanyi's main works (Polanyi, 1944, 1957) therefore became newly relevant in at least seven respects.

First, parallels have been drawn between the laissez-faire premised 'hundred years peace' of 1815–1914 and the renewed Thatcher–Reagan sponsored utopian belief in market-allocation mechanisms. Second, commentators of the institutions and regulation of international capital markets have drawn attention to the tendencies of these institutions to transform in a series of 'unplanned' (but politically motivated) ways.[13] At the same time these authors draw attention to the sequence of offensive and counter-offensive policies aimed at, in-turn, liberating and regulating volatile international capital and goods flows, reminiscent of Polanyi's 'double movement' where free markets are inevitably and 'naturally' followed by pre-meditated regulatory response.

So, the emergence of a 'casino' world (Strange 1986) of liberated international markets for capital, resonates with Polanyi's account of the collapse of the Gold Standard and a sense of *déjà-vu* prevails among contemporary scholars of international finance regimes (Helleiner 2000).[14] We witness new strains upon the contemporary international financial system, with its tendencies to tip whole regions into financial crises, such as that experienced by East Asia and Latin America in the late 1990s. These events which have led critics to invoke Polanyi, in order to theorise the inherent instabilities of current deregulated markets for international capital. Commentators further note that the now international scope of currency and finance markets further exaggerate their volatility compared to the antecedents of Polanyi's analysis (Block 2000).

Third, critics of markets invoke Polanyi in their projects to stress the social consequences of 'disembedded'[15] economies (e.g. Bourdieu, 2000). Fourth and related to the third, quite radical anti-globalisation, anti-market, and anti-capitalist social movements and political causes can now be found converging on Polanyi's opposition to 'planetary interdependence'. Mobilisation projects such as these can be found appropriating the Polanyi name to provide academic and historical legitimacy in support of the anti-globalisation cause, coupled with an emphasis on local citizen empowerment, personal freedom and cultural pluralism.

Fifth, the dangers associated with the transfer of deregulated market policies out of context into economies in transition (Kregel, 2000; Müller, 2000; Konstantinove, 2000) and in development (Amin, 2000; Hart, 2001) are noted by another group of neo-Polanyians. Sixth, like many others the English economic geographer Jamie Peck (Peck 1994) takes Polanyi's description of labour as a fictitious commodity as an entry point to critique (mainstream economic) labour market theory and policy prescriptions which presuppose or promote the notion of labour as commodif*iable* units (Peck 1994; Zukin and DiMaggio, 1990), in some cases taking a more overt Polanyian lead by developing in their place a theoretical lens viewing labour economies as instituted (Moncel, 2002).

Seventh, and perhaps more relevant to this chapter, others, such as the English institutionalist Hodgson (1988, 1994), invoke Polanyi as an entry point to a view that markets be theorised as socially constructed institutions comprising normalised, routinised, and habitually reproductive or repeatable exchange events. In the broadest possible sense, this means not only that markets themselves exhibit a myriad different institutional forms (Boyer, 1997; Swedberg, 1996) which escape economistic attempts to reduce the variety of markets to a single '*the* market' mode of exchange. But more particularly it stresses from Polanyi's perspective that market-based exchange must be located alongside (a number of) alternative (non-market) modes of co-ordinating the provisioning, distribution and consumption of goods and services. These, societies – ancient and contemporary – have developed to provide for themselves in highly contextualised material, 'spiritual' and meaningful (in the sense of encultured) ways.

Yet arguably, all of the above still fall prey to the charge of an overly fragmented (and fragmenting) secondary appropriation of Polanyi. Nowadays Polanyi's name is often used as a fashionable 'label' or convenient point of entry into an argument which thenceforth bears little resemblance, and offers little analysis – supportive, critical or otherwise – of the 'totality' of Polanyi's writing. Perhaps this is what concerns Polanyi-Levitt when she refers to the potential abuse of the Polanyi legacy. As at the temporal juncture of 1990, she describes Polanyi's writing as never having been fashionable (presumably among a 'mainstream') and therefore paradoxically steering clear of tendencies to lose its power through over-use (dilution or misappropriation?) and obsolescence (Polanyi-Levitt, 1990a, p. 1).

Indeed this insightful comment is probably still true of the situation in England. In spite of the many in-passing references and usage of Polanyian themes by English and other scholars, there remain on University shelves[16] a notable absence of thorough secondary analyses of the man, his life and his work.[17] This when compared to other economist/sociologist 'forefathers' such as Smith, Weber, Durkheim, Schumpeter, Hayek, Keynes and others. Polanyian perspectives, as they have become more fashionable, even fetished, have arguably fallen foul of a tendency for their selective and rather atomistic appropriation. As Berthoud (1990) points out, secondary academic scholarship sourcing Polanyi exhibits an overly reductionist and selective mode, homing in on one isolated part of the Polanyian framework whilst conveniently leaving aside the rest. So, he argues:

> his contribution is reduced to two well-known aspects: the three principles of integration – reciprocity, redistribution and exchange; and the three institutions of trade, money, and market. (*ibid.*, p. 171)

Moreover as he observes, specialists derive from Polanyi's work what they see as appropriate to their own pre-occupation. Thus, the notion of redistribution is widely debated among historians interested in the 'archaic' state; the idea of reciprocity is similarly discussed by anthropologists working on kinship-based societies, whereas sociologists and economists researching present-day societies are concerned with 'exchange'. Berthoud believes that such a fragmentation is responsible for producing in the secondary literature two Polanyis: one considered a theoretician of primitive and archaic societies, the second, a radical critic of our economic modernity.

Berthoud bemoans this situation and continues:

> Nothing could be more detrimental to a genuine comprehension of Polanyi's work which must be understood as a whole, within the same comparative approach. More precisely, there are in Polanyi's writing three connected domains of reflection: general theory, history, and policy. The first is equated with the search for universal and general concepts in order to compare economies within societies; the second is identified with the study of specific historical periods and societies; the third addresses the most crucial problems faced by humanity, on the basis of the first two domains of reflection.
> (*ibid.*, p. 171)

So, in this chapter it is proposed that in order to progress the *development* of *Polanyi-inspired* theory of *economy as instituted process* – as opposed to the uncritical appropriation of Polanyi's base writing – we need a holistic appreciation of the life and times of the man, his general theory, his commitment to comparative method, and at least an appreciation of the ideology which led him to the general theory of which we are now very familiar. Furthermore, at least a cursory awareness of the policy direction and sentiment which Polanyi's normative position leads us to, almost of necessity, is required by those taking his work as a serious reference point. Contributing to a contextualised backdrop of this kind has been the aim of the first half of this chapter.

I raise in a very preliminary way, some ideas concerning the scope to develop Polanyi's framework according to a very particular agenda of broadening our understandings of contemporary contexts of exchange, markets, competition and innovation, beyond that which exists currently in economics, sociology, or indeed new economic sociology (NES) with its apparent closure around the dominant networks-and-embeddedness paradigm (Peck, 2005). Furthermore that section will continue our theoretical exploration and development of the Polanyian idea of economy as instituted process, as a way of progressing this much broader agenda. It could be argued of course that such an approach immediately falls prey to the trap of disciplinary and theoretical reductionism asserted by Berthoud above. A response would be that by fleshing out and under-girding the use of Polanyian insights, via a contextualised, more complete and holistic understanding of the life and work of Polanyi, Berthoud's charge is, at least in part, countered.

Before turning to this task, however, it seems clear that no thorough or balanced appreciation of any scholars work can be achieved without space for critical appraisal. The next section will therefore raise a number of questions about some of Polanyi's concepts.

Some critics and critiques of Polanyi's scholarship

This section is organised around five headings: (1) Polanyi's own Great Contradiction: the ontology or otherwise of self-regulating markets;

(2) the arrow of causality in Polanyi's 'double movement' of the emergence of markets, and their regulation; (3) the problematic notion of embeddedness; (4) Polanyi's own version of institutional reductionism; and (5) change, dynamics, and theorising processes of instituting: from institutional origins to instituted economies, but what mechanisms thereafter?

1 Polanyi's own great contradiction: the ontology or otherwise of self-regulating markets

Despite the wide and growing invocation of Polanyi by contemporary scholars outlined above, some of them (though by no means all), have yet to articulate, confront or explain some deep contradictions in Polanyi's own writing. This remains a project for the writing. For example, there is it seems a 'great contradiction' at the heart of Polanyi's writings on the 'self-regulated market'. Somewhere during the 13 intervening years between the publication of *The Great Transformation* (1944) and *The Economy as Instituted Process* (1957) Polanyi's own interpretation of the self-regulated market seems to have changed. That is, in the former, he sees the self-regulated market as ontologically possible, and says *this* particular and very real institutional form contributed to the underpinning of the hundred years peace, albeit it ultimately damaged the cohesion of the very societies it reproduced, in economic terms. In the latter he clearly believes that *all* markets are *instituted* in some way or another such that the 'unregulated' market never finds ontological reality, it is no more than an ideology, a utopian dream. The latter, in fact, is the position that recent supporters of Polanyi, such as Hodgson (1988) and Peck (1994) have taken as their starting point, and the contradiction is overlooked.

Swedberg and Granovetter make a similar point:

> Although in many places he [Polanyi] argued that the nineteenth century ushered in an utterly new type of society, dominated by the 'self-regulating market' he also made the (incompatible) argument that such a situation was never really possible except as an ideological construct or rhetorical device because society had to immediately intervene to prevent such an awful outcome. Both positions can be found in his first major work 'the Great Transformation'. (Swedberg and Granovetter, 1992, p. 22, note)

In fact, Polanyi himself decided at one point (in 1941) that, contrary to the complete and comprehensive anti-market sentiment expressed in *Our Obsolete Market Mentality* (Polanyi, 1947) that it was not all markets *per se* that he was opposed to, (indeed he ascribed some benefits to society of market-based exchange) but a particular expression of market, the 'self-regulating' market. But he has his own usage of this term. Not to be confused with the atomised abstractions of classical economics, the Polanyian view of the self-regulated market appears to be one which is regulated endogenously primarily by the sellers operating within it. The alternative to this, the 'regulated' market therefore refers to markets where society attempts or succeeds in 'externally' taming markets, i.e. through premeditated action taken by a wider set of interests mediated through institutions intent on achieving control over the otherwise 'unregulated' market:

> As early as 1931 I saw the main problem in a reform of the market system which would maintain money and its function of (a) safeguarding the consumer's freedom of choice; (b) ensuring an exact calculation of costs, and (c) serving as an indicator of a consumer's preferences by way of a regulated market system. Such a solution would be based on the conviction that only a self-regulating market system has proved unworkable, not, however, the market as such. (Polanyi, 1941, cited in Mendell, 1990, p. 75)

Whichever way we look at it, however, there remain inconsistencies (or more correctly position shifts) if we consider the totality of Polanyi's writing on the ontology and merits or otherwise of the self-regulating market.

2 The arrow of causality in Polanyi's 'double movement' of markets and regulation

Polanyi asserted that there exists a universal tendency for societies to self-protect against 'unregulated' market exchange. This he views as automatic societal defence against the perceived dangers of self-regulating market. These dangers are manifested as reduced social cohesion, security, unity (sense of belonging), and moral degeneration concomitant with the elevation of personal material wealth. This protective reaction, he theorised, could be manifested institutionally in a number of ways, but they had in common their origins as a *response and consequence* of the rise to dominance of the self-regulating market which historically/spatially found its most extreme expression in nineteenth-century England. And, he claimed, certain groups within society would lead an opposition to these dangers by bringing about the regulation of the market (through legislation, pressure from consumer movements, even extreme forms of political mobilisation such as the rise of fascism).

However, a range of alternative positions borrowing superficially from Polanyi's 'double movement' can be envisaged. Sometimes, the 'double movement' is evoked to analyse the emergence and instituting of (state-sponsored) market-regulation, seen as arriving, in temporal terms, one step behind the emergence of a market. The arrow of causality would be from the market, to regulation, and, arguably, this is the case-type from which Polanyi generalised his 'double movement'. Other accounts however would stress the simultaneous co-construction of markets and (self) regulation whereby (primarily sellers) engage in pre-meditated strategic attempts to construct and shape markets according to a particular vision, through the imposition of standards, restricted access, and other devices. Regulation, according to this account becomes *endogenous to* the market construction process, therefore something that cannot be analysed as an 'externality' as classical economists would have it.[18] The arrow of causality in this case would be absent (it is more a co-evolutionary process) or pointing both ways (an iterative process). A third variant would require the causal arrow to point *from* regulation *to* market construction. This would be the case where legislation produces 'demand-pull'. We could take the case of a regulation-induced 'pull' on markets for environmental technologies and services for example (Randles and Tether, 2002). Alternatively, an embryonic (small) group of practitioners/service providers may consciously establish codes of conduct to regulate *their own practices*, even to restrict access to the occupation and maintain their status as 'experts' in a field. In so doing they may (as an intended or unintended consequence) raise levels of confidence and trust among users/buyers of the service thus incentivising and shaping market construction and growth. (For example in the early stages of the development of 'markets for market research' in Britain, see Randles et al., 2002).

It appears therefore that although Polanyi's 'double movement' provides a useful entry point to the question of markets and regulation, the action–response nature of the market/regulation dynamic relation becomes a question requiring ontological clarification. This question is taken up in Chapter 13 of this collection.

3 The problematic notion of embeddedness

The notion of 'embeddedness' is receiving renewed critical interest particularly from both English sociologists (for example Sayer, 2002) from American new economic sociology (for example, Krippner, 2001) and from economic geography (Peck 2005). This debate is too multi-faceted to enter into in detail here. However it does raise interesting questions about Polanyi's original notion of embeddedness, whilst at the same time accrediting him as the originator of a concept which has received much analytical attention since, particularly after Granovetter re-introduced – and indeed completely re-worked the concept - in his seminal paper (Granovetter, 1985).

Polanyi brought us the idea that man's [sic] economy is, *as a rule*, embedded in his social relations. He then brought us the idea that as market exchange came to represent the dominant institution of economic integration, this had the effect of 'disembedding' economy from its social roots. Here, Polanyi primarily takes economy to mean the modes of societal provisioning for material objects and services. However sociologists and economic and cultural anthropologists would insist on widening this notion of economy considerably. They would include the many interdependent facets connecting the means by which the accumulation and distribution of economic (material) resources is enabled; to societal survival, which encompasses the systems of meanings and mechanisms which underpin and enable societal reproduction (Bourdieu, 2000).

The latter interpretation lies at the heart of the problem of 'embeddedness', which in any case (according to Sayer, 2002) is far too cosy a term, hinting at a benign humanist phenomenology, and one which almost invariably leads us blindly towards sociological determinism. It further suggests one domain 'the social' encircling and materially 'producing' the other: the 'economic' whilst its more recent derivative, the notion of 'double embeddedness' suggests an ontologically impossible situation whereby the 'social' embeds (surrounds) the economic whilst at the same time the economic embeds (surrounds) the social. Whereas, the rich anthropological and ethnographic record suggests that a rich intertwining of the social and economic domains exists.[19]

In fact, secondary sourcing of the notion of embeddedness referring to Granovetter (1985) often misrepresents his 1985 paper. Referenced to redress overly technological or economic accounts, the secondary quoting of Granovetter (1985) simply to point out that 'the social is, after all, important' often misses the point of his critique of Polanyi's notion of embeddedness. His critique comes from several directions. First he (and others) have shown that the supposed structural shift from non-market to market-dominated economic integration, coincident with a shift from an 'embedded' to a 'disembedded' economy is exaggerated. For example, Granovetter's contemporary study of job-search activities showed how individuals use their personal networks to find employment (Granovetter, 1974). This, and a whole literature of similar studies, suggest that in the contemporary Western market-organised societies, man's economy remains firmly rooted within socialised networks and structures, and that notions of the 'disembedded' or 'anonymous' economy are overplayed. However, as a further twist and counter-argument to Granovetter's (re-worked) usage and deployment of the term embeddedness, loyal Polanyists[20] rightly point out that Polanyi's notion was always positioned at a much higher, and more general level of abstraction that the 'middle-level' theory that concerns Granovetter and colleagues (see Granovetter, 2002, for a discussion of the middle-level theoretic project of this group within the American NES school). Polanyi was concerned not with the networks of connections between *particular individuals*, but with 'the organisation of the economic system as a whole ... economic systems as such are the object of analysis' (Cangiani, Ch. 2 in this collection).

Further anthropologists and economic historians argue that (some) ancient societies were motivated and organised around the object of material accumulation and personal gain, without reference to a notion of wider societal well-being, such that Polanyi's belief in a universally more socially cohesive 'pre-market' economy may be equally idealised.

Indeed, Dalton (1968, p. xiii) describes as 'ethnic nostalgia' the tendency to suggest that primitive (non-market organised) societies *necessarily* provide a higher level of material and/or psychological security than do their market-based counterparts. Occasionally, in Polanyi's romanticising of primitive and archaic societies (as well as in his early commitments to Guild Socialism) we find Polanyi's own version of pre-market or non-market utopia. In these, models – selectively taken from history or as in the case of Guild Socialism set up as an ideal-type – we are presented with strangely a-political worlds, depleted of competitive struggle, or struggle over economic resources, or devoid of strategies of subjugation or intentional or unintentional strategic social stratification. One of the strangest and deepest ambiguities in Polanyi's writing, therefore, is this apparent defaulting to a perversely a-political, political economy.

4 Polanyi's own version of institutional reductionism

It could be argued that the tradition of American Anthropology and Ethnography provides a most enduring and loyal heartland of appreciative Polanyian scholars. Here, Polanyi was not 'lost' and then 're-found'. Rather, he was never lost. Moreover his work was recognised and respected by the discipline's establishment. For example, the year after Polanyi died, in 1965, the American Ethnological Society dedicated their conference and post-conference proceedings to the memory of Karl Polanyi (Helm et al., 1965). Polanyi is credited with contributing much to economic anthropology: first, in his methodological commitment to detailed comparative economy; and, second, in his efforts to lay down a general theory of economy which combines in its framework (institutionalist) economics, society and culture. The latter is an important point and represents an acknowledged contribution to a discipline often criticised for producing long, winding, descriptive accounts but little by way of theory which can provide some guiding principles and theoretical cohesion to frame these accounts (Dalton, 1965).

Yet also from this heartland we find some critical voices. The main charge is that of institutional reductionism and closure. Polanyi theorises that societal modes of economic integration can find *only* three *main* expressions: reciprocity, redistribution and exchange. The important contribution of Polanyi's work in terms of balancing economic accounts which foreground 'market exchange', and render alternatives such as reciprocity and redistribution at best a minor irrelevance, at worst invisible, still stands in his favour. However anthropologists are used to studying the economies of societies in all their rich hues and colours, and here the opposite charge can be made. That is that Polanyi's account fails to pay sufficient attention either to integrative forms outside these three possibilities, or to the possibilities for two or more of the three integrative forms to co-exist, indeed to co-exist in a mutually supportive way. Further it could be argued that the Polanyi account fails to acknowledge the variety which exists *within* each of the three headings. Sahlins, for example provides a rich typology of different kinds of *reciprocity*. Within his typology we see a wide range of types of relations between 'givers' and 'receivers'; different degrees of symmetry versus asymmetry in these relations; and consequently widely divergent power plays associated with each expression of reciprocity (Sahlins, 1965). Comparing this to Polanyi's triad scheme, we can suggest that reciprocity does not necessarily or always represent a more benign, co-operative, or mutual form of integration than either (market) exchange or redistribution.[21]

5 Change, dynamics, and theorising processes of instituting: from institutional origins to instituted economies, but what mechanisms thereafter?
In the phrase 'instituted process' Polanyi immediately provides us with an interesting juxtaposition of fixity and flux.[22] Through the use of the term 'instituted', he insists we emphasise the normalisation of daily life, and the normalisation of behaviours, practices and meanings through which individuals impart or understand a sense of 'belonging' in a structured, stable and cohesively systemic[23] way. The term 'instituted' has an interconnected, interdependent and above all static quality. Whilst at the same time through the use of 'process' he captures the point that flows and movements (of goods and services, of people and ideas) contribute to the structuring of this stability. The term *instituted process* therefore gives scope both for institutional inertia and for change. However whilst there may be *scope* for change, it does not necessarily follow that change will occur. There may be no appetite for change from groups with the power or capability to affect change. Change may not be desired, may not be desired by all groups, may not find successful expression (though not for want of trying), or may not even be reflexively thought of as an option or expression of conscious collective desire. Arguably, this juxtaposition of fixity and flux is one of the most powerful ideas that we can appreciate in Polanyi's writing, and which has interesting scope for developing in the study of competition and innovation.

Yet Polanyi's theory does not actually take us this far. Much of this is implied or developed. It is Polanyi *inspired* rather than Polanyi *given*. In fact, arguably, the Polanyi-theoretical framework (Polanyi, 1957) offers at best a canvas for mapping out *comparative statics* – of an economic system exhibiting one 'instituted' expression, and then (some time later) re-emerging in a transformed form of 'institutedness' or, as a result of different histories, recognising the likelihood that one coherent economic society will exhibit a very different form of 'institutedness' to another.

The point is that a larger question remains. There does not appear to be, *within* Polanyi's framework an explicit mechanism for institutional change, since competitive struggle and innovation do not (paradoxically given our interest both in Polanyi, and in the study of innovation and competition) feature in the Polanyian frame at all. What we might need to add, using Polanyi as an essential start-point, is a mechanism for subsequent tensions and struggles which potentially or in actuality produce a *re-instituting* of whatever arena of substantive study we are interested in. Further our *developed* analysis would need to explicitly provide for this re-instituting to occur at a *range of temporal-spatial scales*, more than likely bringing groups of vested interest into competitive confrontation with each other (or alternatively mutual accommodation of each other).[24]

The above discussion brings us logically to a point of reflecting upon the potential merits and constituent parts of a *neo*-Polanyian approach to the study of exchange, competition and innovation in Economic Sociology.

Issues for a neo-Polanyian approach to the study of exchange, competition and innovation as instituted processes

As we have noted, Polanyi insisted that we view markets as no more, or less, than one *particular* form of economic integration. We must refuse to become blinded to other historically evidenced alternative or complementary modes of integration, for example in his particular analysis, the integrative institutions of reciprocity and redistribution. This raises subsequent questions and new avenues of theoretical development (see Harvey and Randles, 2002) and empirical research (see below) aimed at identifying the *origins*, empirical *saliency* and subsequent *roles* that different (market and non-market) institutions of exchange play in integrating and enabling the maintenance, reproduction and transformation of *interdependent* systems of exchange in economies.

Elsewhere (Harvey, 1999, 2002; Harvey et al., 2002; Randles 2002a, 2002b; Harvey and Randles, 2002) we have drawn on Polanyi's concept of *the economy as instituted process* to theorise the structures, linkages, relations and competitive and other transformative processes which surround and produce particular expressions of the organisation of exchange. This adheres to Polanyi's insistence on substantive method, both comparative-historical and comparative-spatial, and traces change in the nature and over-riding governing logics of various forms of instituted exchange. Empirical contexts to date have been diverse. For example investigating the rise to dominance of the supermarket in the retailing of English food and household goods (Harvey, 1999, 2002); exploring transformations of nature, society and economy viewed through the object of the 'humble' tomato (Harvey et al., 2002); analysing the politico-economic instituted and multi-scalar construction of the 'urban' in a comparative Lyon/Manchester setting (Randles, 2000; Randles and Dicken, 2004). Finally looking at the ways in which practices of inter-corporate non-market reciprocal or 'negotiated swaps' for drugs in development, exist alongside and materially influence markets for end-user drugs, inter-corporate markets for drugs in development, and markets for 'corporate control' (Randles, 2002b; Allen et al., 2002; this collection, Ch. 13). This latter analysis revealed a multiplex of instituted exchanges producing a *complex* (open, non-linear and *potentially* transforming) *interdependent system* of market and non-market exchange, the totality of which must be appreciated in order to better understand the *instituted* nature and pressures determining (from behind the scenes)[25] the phenomenon of mergers and acquisitions in pharmaceuticals.

Common to these empirical cases is the grounding of theory in highly specific geopolitical contexts. From this start-point, the substantive study of production-distribution-consumption practices, processes and their instituted settings can be observed and documented (Harvey et al., 2001). Comparative analysis and the combining of both inductive and deductive method is a feature.

Paradoxically, Polanyi says very little about competition.[26] And about innovation, as far as I can see, he says nothing at all. Rather a strange entry point for scholars of competition and innovation then? Yet, as this chapter and others have begun to suggest, it is precisely because the Polanyi frame (indeed the wider scholarship of economic anthropology) has been so little used by those studying innovation and competition that testing the application of key concepts from Polanyi in this area is so new, interesting, and potentially fruitful.

One key to unlocking how Polanyian insights can be useful to the study of competition and innovation is via his methodological emphasis on substantive, holistic and comparative method. And connecting Polanyi's commitment to holistic comparative study of societies to the notion of fixity and flux explicit in the term 'instituted process' we are provided with a fascinating link to the study of innovation and competition. Linked also to both is the very thorny question of *boundaries*. Inductive method is less seduced by the need to 'fix' boundaries ahead of empirical testing than is deductive reasoning. For this reason, Polanyi's empirics (and anthropology more generally) can give us fascinating insights into (knowledge, institutional, instituted, or scalar) boundaries under construction, and boundaries undergoing transformation.

We could think of a number of examples of significance to contemporary transformation where taking boundaries as the *object* of analysis can further our theoretical and empirical appreciation of competition, innovation, exchange and processes of transformation. That is, studying boundaries *per se*, how they come to be set, how they come to be changed, and the instituting and re-instituting of boundaries in a particular context.

We could think of the 'boundaries' – and interdependencies between:

1. economic and non-economic *(or underlying)* competition;
2. production, distribution and consumption;
3. market and non-market forms of provision, consumption and exchange;
4. public/collective provision and private/corporate provision (and other institutions of organised provision such as charities, co-operatives).

The study of competition and innovation, in this particular scheme would therefore equate to the study of how boundaries change or become re-thought. This may come about by the pre-meditated and strategic actions of actors or groups representing a particular set of interests; or it may be an unintended consequence of social change. An example would be the shift from extended family households, to nuclear family households, to 'micro' or single-person households, with their consequential impacts on lifestyle, consumption, and spending patterns.

To recap in summary, a rich multi-method institutionalist oriented substantive research programme is envisaged which reveals, in any particular contingent case, how the economic potentially constructs (normalises) the structured and relational meanings of social worlds. Inseparable and of equal importance is the need to understand how instituted, socio-political worlds of very particular spatial-temporal (and multi-scalar) expression give rise to and influence in powerful ways, the appropriation and distribution of economic resources. Such an over-arching research programme can be checked and underpinned empirically. This will enable ongoing theoretical development which interprets competitive processes and innovation as comprising instituted variety entraining social and economic consequences which must be identified in general terms as well as contingent detail, providing a far richer contextual and contingent framework, and basis for critique, than current theories of innovation and competition have been able to provide.

Acknowledgements

I would like to thank Mark Harvey for stimulating an interest in Polanyi, a curiosity about the man behind the notion of economy as instituted process and for useful comments on an earlier draft. I also extend warm thanks and appreciation to Kari Polanyi-Levitt for her helpful comments in the course of several fascinating discussions. Thanks also to Ronnie Ramlogan for organising the CRIC workshop 'Polanyian Perspectives on Instituted Economic Process, Development and Transformation', where an earlier version of this paper was presented and for his helpful comments on subsequent drafts. This work was funded by the UK Economic and Social Research Council via the mainstream programme of the Centre for Research on Innovation and Competition, University of Manchester. All errors are the responsibility of the author.

Notes

1 Though in reality, it seems he never really tried, believing such an endeavour could not be fruitful (in conversation with Kari Polanyi-Levitt, September–October, 2002).
2 He rose to the position of Foreign Editor by 1934 (McRobbie and Polanyi Levitt, 2000b), introductory photoscapes.
3 Der Oesterreichische Volswirt.
4 McRobbie and Polanyi-Levitt (2000b, p. ix) and in conversation with Kari Polanyi-Levitt, September–October 2002.
5 His brother, Michael, after all forged a long and successful career including a position at the University of Manchester, England. But recall that Michael Polanyi's background was initially in the physical sciences, from where he moved on to make his name articulating theories of the nature and development

of knowledge – a very different (positivist) epistemology and methodology to that advocated by Karl, and a very different route and career plan to that desired by Karl.

6 Polanyi considered Friedrich Hayek an intellectual adversary in just about every way. Indeed the account of how Polanyi's *The Great Transformation* and Hayek's *The Road to Serfdom*, both published in 1944, offered polar-opposites in terms of theoretical explanation of the rise of German fascism and the appropriate policy responses, provides a natural entry point for much of the secondary Polanyi literature (Dalton, 1968; Stanfield, 1986; Polanyi-Levitt, 1990c, 2000). Polanyi saw the rise of fascism as undesirable but nevertheless theoretically explained in terms of the 'double movement' of society's defensive response to the unregulated market and the social dislocation it entrains – of society attempting to wrest control back from the destructive forces of laissez-faire economic policy. Hayek, on the other hand, believed that fascism fed off disillusionment and economic regulation. This, he asserted, could only be overcome via a rise in economic growth brought about through the liberalised market.

7 This complement to Adam Smith's view of humankind possessing a universal propensity to 'truck and barter' (Smith, 1776) which Polanyi strongly refuted (Polanyi, 1944) equally brought him into direct conflict with proponents of laissez-faire.

8 As we can remind ourselves, Polanyi advocated substantive empirical research over formal-theoretic modelling. He was a broad institutionalist at a time when institutionalism was not in vogue in England. And he advocated the use of (social and economic) history over thought-experiment and abstract economic modelling as methods to underpin economic theory.

9 Compare Hirsch et al. (1987); Zukin and DiMaggio (1990); Swedberg (1996, p. x); Zelizer (1996 [1988]).

10 Including the premise of scarcity against which rational economic man is hypothesised to make choices in order to maximise or otherwise follow a set of pre-determined rules leading to 'economising' or optimal outcomes.

11 Accompanied by the underlying assumption that labour, capital and product/service markets are ontologically 'the same' at their core – a view which of course Polanyi disputed.

12 These events are of course well documented and analysed by contemporary political economy; see, for example, Harvey (1989); Helleiner (1994); Stubbs and Underhill (1994); Jessop (1996).

13 See Helleiner, 1994 on the establishment and subsequent collapse of Bretton Woods.

14 Albeit Helleiner (2000) is at pains to point out the differences between contemporary and nineteenth-century regimes of international finance trading.

15 See the discussion of the (contested) embeddedness term.

16 Speaking in particular of the University of Manchester.

17 With notable exceptions, such as Stanfield (1986).

18 See also Hodgson in this collection (Chapter 4) who writes from this perspective.

19 Polanyi places economy *within* society as an ontologically inseparable part of it. But, he decides that analytical abstraction of economy from society is a legitimate device for analysing the distinctively economic. Chapter 9 in this

collection looks at the Polanyian view of the relationship between economy and society in more detail.
20 In this collection, Chapter 2.
21 See also Bourdieu (2000) on the less benign face of gift giving.
22 For a contemporary discussion of fixity and flux – together with its implications for conceptualising the construction of scale – see Brenner (1998, 2000) whose writing is inspired by Henri Lefebvre.
23 Here I do not mean systems in the sense of mechanical input–output, deterministic, or 'closed' ways, but rather in terms of interconnected and interdependent systems of meanings and relations, and all those interdependent flows and circuits of capital, labour, goods and ideas occurring over (multi-scalar) space, which provides a universal feature of all economies, though manifested differently in different contingent contexts.
24 Anthropological/ethnographic studies often unintentionally reveal examples of such a re-instituting process, including shifts from non-market to market economic allocation systems. For example Helm (1965) describes how kin-ties which determined the allocation of economic resources of the indigenous Dogrib ethnic groups of northern Canada, gradually shifted to assimilate Euro-Canadian institutions introduced at ports of trade with the arrival of the Hudson Bay Company. This was closely linked to the assimilation of the traders, and their trading practices, into the tribes' existing normalised practices and institutions governing notions of leadership and redistribution, and key to this transformation was the labelling and adoption of a new (foreign) persona into their midst 'the trading chief'.
25 Discussed in more detail in Harvey and Randles (2002).
26 Further than linking the tendency for (formal) economics to pay particular and concentrated attention to the analysis and articulation of 'economic competition' with the same deep enduring normative belief in, and perceived universality of, price-making markets. He suggests that competition is a characteristic of some market institutions, such as price-making markets and auctions (Polanyi, 1957, p. 267).

References

Allen, P. M., Ramlogan, R. and Randles, S. (2002), 'Complex Systems and the Merger Process', *Technology Analysis and Strategic Management*, 14(3), pp. 315–30.

Amin, S. (2000), 'Conditions for Re-launching Development', in K. McRobbie and K. Polanyi-Levitt (eds), *Karl Polanyi in Vienna: The Contemporary Significance of the Great Transformation*, Montreal, Black Rose Books.

Baker, W. E. (1984), 'The Social Structure of a National Securities Market', *American Journal of Sociology*, 89(4), pp. 775–811 (and Ch. 19 in R. Swedberg (ed.), *Economic Sociology*, Cheltenham, Edward Elgar).

Berthoud, G. (1990), 'Toward a Comparative Approach: The Contribution of Karl Polanyi', in K. Polanyi-Levitt (ed.), *The Life and Work of Karl Polanyi: A Celebration*, Montreal, Black Rose Books.

Block, F. (2000), 'The Case for Control Over Cross-Border Capital Flows', in K. McRobbie and K. Polanyi-Levitt (eds), *Karl Polanyi in Vienna: The*

Contemporary Significance of the Great Transformation, Montreal, Black Rose Books.

Bognar, J. (1990), 'Opening Address', in K. Polanyi-Levitt (ed.), *The Life and Work of Karl Polanyi: A Celebration*, Montreal, Black Rose Books.

Bourdieu, P. (2000), *Les Structures sociales de l'economie*, Paris, Editions du Seuil.

Boyer, R. (1997), 'The Variety and Unequal Performance of Really Existing Markets: Farewell to Doctor Pangloss?', in J. Hollingsworth and R. Boyer (eds), *Contemporary Capitalism: The Embeddedness of Institutions*, Cambridge, Cambridge University Press.

Brenner, N. (1998), 'Between Fixity and Motion: Accumulation, Territorial Organisation and the Historical Geography of Spatial Scales', *Environment and Planning D: Society and Space*, 16(4), pp. 459–81.

Brenner, N. (2000), 'The Urban Question as a Scale Question: Reflections on Henri Lefebvre, Urban Theory and the Politics of Scale', *International Journal of Urban and Regional Research*, 24(2), pp. 361–78.

Dalton, G. (1965), 'Primitive, Archaic, and Modern Economies: Karl Polanyi's Contribution to Economic Anthropology and Comparative Economy', in J. Helm, P. Bohannan and M. D. Sahlins (eds), *Essays in Economic Anthropology: Proceedings of the 1965 Annual Spring Meeting of the American Ethnological Society*, Washington, Washington University Press.

Dalton, G. (ed.) (1968), *Primitive, Archaic and Modern Economics: Essays of Karl Polanyi*, New York, Anchor Books.

Dalton, G. (1990), 'Writings that Clarify Theoretical Disputes Over Karl Polanyi's Work', in K. Polanyi-Levitt (ed.), *The Life and Work of Karl Polanyi: A Celebration*, Montreal, Black Rose Books.

DiMaggio, P. (1994), 'Culture and Economy', in J. Smelser and R. Swedberg (eds), *The Handbook of Economic Sociology*, Princeton, Princeton University Press.

Fine, B (2001), 'The Cluttered Landscape of Consumption: An Economists Gaze', mimeo, School of Oriental and African Studies, University of London.

Fourie, F. C. (1991), 'The Nature of the Market: A Structural Analysis', in G. M. Hodgson and E. Screpanti (eds), *Rethinking Economics: Markets, Technology and Economic Evolution*, Aldershot, Edward Elgar.

Frenzen, J., Hirsch, P. M. and Zerrillo, P. C. (1994), 'Consumption, Preferences and Changing Lifestyles', in J. Smelser and R. Swedberg (eds), *The Handbook of Economic Sociology*, Princeton, Princeton University Press.

Granovetter, M. (1974), *Getting a Job: A Study of Contact and Careers*, Cambridge, MA, Harvard University Press.

Granovetter, M. (1985), 'Economic Action and Social Structure: The Problem of Embeddedness', *American Journal of Sociology*, 91(3), pp. 481–510.

Granovetter, M. (1992), 'Economic Institutions as Social Constructions: A Framework for Analysis', *Acta Sociologica*, 35(1), pp. 3–11 (also Ch. 14 in R. Swedberg (ed.) (1996), *Economic Sociology*, Cheltenham, Edward Elgar).

Granovetter, M. (1994), 'Business Groups', in J. Smelser and R. Swedberg (eds), *The Handbook of Economic Sociology*, Princeton, Princeton University Press.

Granovetter, M. (2002), 'A Theoretical Agenda for Economic Sociology', in M. Guillen, R. Collins, P. England and M. Meyer (eds), *The New Economic*

Sociology: Developments in an Emerging Field, New York, Russell Sage Foundation.
Granovetter, M. and Swedberg, R. (eds) (1992), *The Sociology of Economic Life*, Boulder, Westview Press.
Hart, G. (2001), 'Development Critiques in the 1990s: Culs de Sacs and Promising Paths', *Progress in Human Geography*, 25(4), pp. 649–58.
Harvey, M. (1999*)*, 'Innovation and Competition in UK Supermarkets', *CRIC Briefing Paper*, no. 3, ESRC Centre for Research on Innovation and Competition, University of Manchester.
Harvey, M. (2002), 'Competition as Instituted Economic Process', in S. Metcalfe and A. Warde (eds), *Market Relations and the Competitive Process*, Manchester, Manchester University Press.
Harvey, M. and Quilley, S. (1997), 'Varieties of Capitalism: Embeddedness and the "Logic" of the Market', paper presented to the joint CRIC/Geography Seminar 'Cultures of Innovation', University of Manchester, 11 June.
Harvey, M. and Randles, S. (2002), 'Market exchanges and "instituted economic process": an analytical perspective', *Revue d'Economie Industrielle*, 101(4), pp. 11–30.
Harvey, M., Beynon, H. and Quilley, S. (2002), 'Processes of Variation: How Capitalism Appropriated the Tomato', in M. Harvey, H. Beynon and S. Quilley (eds), *Capitalism or Capitalisms? Approaches to Varieties of Capitalism*, Manchester, Manchester University Press.
Harvey, M., McMeekin, A., Randles, S., Southerton, D., Tether, B. and Wade, A. (2001), 'Between Demand and Consumption: A Framework for Research', *CRIC Discussion Paper*, no. 40, University of Manchester.
Helleiner, E. (1994), 'From Bretton Woods to Global Finance: A World Turned Upside Down', in R. Stubbs and G. R. D. Underhill (eds), *Political Economy and the Changing Global Order*, Hampshire, Palgrave.
Helleiner, E. (2000), 'Globalisation and Haute Finance – Déjà Vu?', in K. McRobbie and K. Polanyi-Levitt (eds), *Karl Polanyi in Vienna: The Contemporary Significance of the Great Transformation*, Montreal, Black Rose Books.
Helm, J. (1965), 'Patterns of Allocation among the Arctic Drainage Dene', in J. Helm (ed.), P. Bohannan and M. D. Sahlins (co-eds), *Essays in Economic Anthropology: Proceedings of the 1965 Annual Spring Meeting of the American Ethnological Society*, Washington, Washington University Press.
Helm J., Bohannan, P. and Sahlins, M. D. (eds) (1965), *Essays in Economic Anthropology: Proceedings of the 1965 Annual Spring Meeting of the American Ethnological Society*, Washington, Washington University Press.
Hirsch, P., Michaels, S. and Friedman, R. (1987), 'Dirty Hands versus Clean Models: Is Sociology in Danger of being Seduced by Economics?', *Theory and Society*, 16(3), pp. 317–36 (also Ch. 15 in R. Swedberg (ed.), *Economic Sociology*, Cheltenham, Edward Elgar).
Hirsch, P., Michaels, S. and Friedman, R. (1990), 'Clean Models vs. Dirty Hands: Why Economics is Different from Sociology', Ch. 2 in S. Zukin and P. Dimaggio (eds), *Structures of Capital: The Social Organisation of the Economy*, Cambridge, Cambridge University Press.
Hodgson, G. M. (1988), *Economics and Institutions: A Manifesto for a Modern Institutional Economics*, Cambridge, Polity Press.

Hodgson, G. M. (1993), *Economics and Evolution: Bringing Life Back into Economics,* Cambridge, Polity Press.
Hodgson, G. M. (1994), 'The Return of Institutional Economics', Ch. 3 in J. Smelser and R. Swedberg (eds), *The Handbook of Economic Sociology,* Princeton, Princeton University Press.
Hodgson, G. M. (1995), *Economics and Biology,* Aldershot, Edward Elgar.
Hodgson, G. M. (1999), *Economics and Utopia: Why the Learning Economy Is Not the End of History,* London and New York, Routledge.
Hodgson, G. M. and Screpanti, E. (1991), *Rethinking Economics: Markets, Technology and Economic Evolution,* Aldershot, Edward Elgar.
Hopkins, T. K. (1957), 'Sociology and the Substantive View of the Economy', Ch. 14 in K. Polanyi, C. M. Arensberg and H. W. Pearson (eds), *Trade and Market in the Early Empires,* New York, Free Press.
Hunt, R. (1965), 'The Development Cycle of the Family Business in Rural Mexico', in J. Helm, P. Bohannan and M. D. Sahlins (eds), *Essays in Economic Anthropology: Proceedings of the 1965 Annual Spring Meeting of the American Ethnological Society,* Washington, Washington University Press.
Jessop, B. (1996), 'Post-Fordism and the State', in A. Amin (ed.), *Post-Fordism: A Reader,* Cambridge, MA, Basil Blackwell.
Kirman, A. (1999), 'Aggregate Activity and Economic Organisation', *Revue europèenne des sciences sociales,* 37(13), pp. 189–230.
Konstantinov, Y. (2000), 'Survival Strategies in Post-1989 Bulgaria', in K. McRobbie and K. Polanyi-Levitt (eds), *Karl Polanyi in Vienna: The Contemporary Significance of the Great Transformation,* Montreal, Black Rose Books.
Kregel, J. A. (2000), 'On the Implications of (Mis) Understanding Markets in Transition Countries', in K. McRobbie and K. Polanyi-Levitt (eds), *Karl Polanyi in Vienna: The Contemporary Significance of the Great Transformation,* Montreal, Black Rose Books.
Krippner, G. (2001), *The Elusive Market: Embeddedness and the Paradigm of Economic Sociology,* paper presented to the Polanyi conference, University of California at Davis, 12–14 April, redrafted July 2001.
Mason, E. (1939), 'Price and Production Policies of Large-scale Enterprises', *American Economic Review,* 29, pp. 61–74.
McRobbie, K. and Polanyi-Levitt, K. (eds) (2000a), *Karl Polanyi in Vienna: The Contemporary Significance of the Great Transformation,* Montreal, Black Rose Books.
McRobbie, K. and Polanyi-Levitt, K. (eds) (2000b), 'Introduction', in K. McRobbie and K. Polanyi-Levitt (eds), *Karl Polanyi in Vienna: The Contemporary Significance of the Great Transformation,* Montreal, Black Rose Books.
Mendell, M. (1990), 'Karl Polanyi and Feasible Socialism', in K. Polanyi-Levitt (ed.), *The Life and Work of Karl Polanyi: A Celebration,* Montreal, Black Rose Books.
Mizruchi, M. S. and Brewster-Stearns, L. (1994), 'Money, Banking and Financial Markets', in J. Smelser and R. Swedberg (eds), *The Handbook of Economic Sociology,* Princeton, Princeton University Press.
Moncel, N. (2002), *Labour Markets as Instituted Economic Process,* paper presented at the CRIC workshop Polanyian Perspectives on Instituted Economic Processes, Development and Transformation 23–5 October, Manchester.

Moss, T. (2001), 'Reshaping Infrastructure Systems to Meet Changing Resource Use Patterns: The Case of Derelict Land', presentation to the ESF Summer School Consumption, 'Everyday Life and Sustainability', 17–23 July, University of Lancaster.

Muller, B. (2000), 'From Planned Economy to Market Economy in the Former East Berlin', in K. McRobbie and K. Polanyi-Levitt (eds), *Karl Polanyi in Vienna: The Contemporary Significance of the Great Transformation*, Montreal, Black Rose Books.

North, D. C. (1996), 'Markets and Other Allocation Systems in History: The Challenge of Karl Polanyi', Ch. 9 in R. Swedberg (ed.), *Economic Sociology*, Cheltenham, Edward Elgar.

North, D. C. and Weingast, B. R. (1996), 'The Evolution of Modern Institutions of Growth', in L. J. Alston, T. Eggertsson and D. North (eds), *Empirical Studies in Institutional Change*, Melbourne, Cambridge University Press.

Peck, J. (1994), 'Regulating Labour: The Social Regulation and Reproduction of Local Labour Markets', Ch. 7 in A. Amin and N. Thrift (eds), *Globalization, Institutions, and Regional Development in Europe*, Oxford, Oxford University Press.

Peck, J. (2005), 'Economic Sociologies in Space', *Economic Geography*, 81(2), pp. 129–75.

Peck J. and Tickell, A. (1996), 'Searching for a New Institutional Fix: The After-Fordist Crisis and Global-Local Disorder', in A. Amin (ed.), *Post-Fordism: A Reader*, Oxford, Basil Blackwell.

Parsons, T. (1979), 'The Symbolic Environment of Modern Economies', *Social Research*, 46, autumn, pp. 436–53.

Polanyi, I. D. (2000), 'I first met Karl Polanyi in 1920 . . .', in K. McRobbie and K. Polanyi-Levitt (eds), *Karl Polanyi in Vienna: The Contemporary Significance of the Great Transformation*, Montreal, Black Rose Books.

Polanyi, K. (1925), 'Letter to a Friend, 1925', in K. McRobbie and K. Polanyi-Levitt (eds), *Karl Polanyi in Vienna: The Contemporary Significance of the Great Transformation*, Montreal, Black Rose Books.

Polanyi, K. (1944), *The Great Transformation*, Boston, Beacon Press.

Polanyi, K. (1947), 'Our Obsolete Market Mentality', *Commentary*, 3, February, pp. 109–17 (also Ch. 8 in R. Swedberg (ed.), *Economic Sociology*, Cheltenham, Edward Elgar).

Polanyi, K. (1957), 'The Economy as Instituted Process', Ch. 13 in K. Polanyi, C. M. Arensberg and H. W. Pearson (eds), *Trade and Market in the Early Empires*, New York, Free Press.

Polanyi, K., Arensberg, C. M. and Pearson, H. W. (eds) (1957a), 'The Place of Economies in Societies', Ch. 12 in K. Polanyi, C. M. Arensberg and H. W. Pearson (eds), *Trade and Market in the Early Empires*, New York, Free Press.

Polanyi, K., Arensberg, C. M. and Pearson, H. W. (eds) (1957b), *Trade and Market in the Early Empires*, New York, Free Press.

Polanyi-Levitt, K. (ed.) (1990a), *The Life and Work of Karl Polanyi: A Celebration*, Montreal, Black Rose Books.

Polanyi-Levitt, K. (1990b), 'Introduction', in K. Polanyi-Levitt (ed.), *The Life and Work of Karl Polanyi: A Celebration*, Montreal, Black Rose Books.

Polanyi-Levitt, K. (1990c), 'The Origins and Significance of The Great Transformation', in K. Polanyi-Levitt (ed.), *The Life and Work of Karl Polanyi: A Celebration*, Montreal, Black Rose Books.

Polanyi-Levitt, K. (2000), 'The Great Transformation: From the 1920s to the 1990s', in K. McRobbie and K. Polanyi-Levitt (eds), *Karl Polanyi in Vienna: The Contemporary Significance of the Great Transformation*, Montreal, Black Rose Books.

Polanyi-Levitt, K. and Mendell, M. (1987), 'Karl Polanyi: His Life and Times', *Studies in Political Economy*, 22, spring, pp. 7–39 (also Ch. 10 in R. Swedberg (ed.), *Economic Sociology*, Cheltenham, Edward Elgar).

Powell, W. W. and Smith D. (1994), 'Networks and Economic Life', Ch. 15 in J. Smelser and R. Swedberg (eds), *The Handbook of Economic Sociology*, Princeton, Princeton University Press.

Randles, S. (2000), 'Cities in Evolutionary Perspective: Diversity, Reflexivity, Scale and the Making of Economic Society in Manchester and Lyon', a thesis submitted to the University of Manchester for the degree of doctor of philosophy in the Faculty of Arts, School of Geography, University of Manchester.

Randles, S. (2002a), 'On Economic Sociology, Competition and Markets', *CRIC Discussion Paper*, no. 53, ESRC Centre for Research on Innovation and Competition, University of Manchester.

Randles, S. (2002b), 'Complexity Applied: The Merger That Made GlaxoSmithKline', *Technology Analysis and Strategic Management*, 14(3), pp. 331–54.

Randles, S. and Tether, B. (2002), 'Services, Scale, and Structures of Internationalisation: Northwest England's Environmental Technologies Firms', in M. Miozzo and I. Miles (eds), *Internationalisation, Technology and Services*, Cheltenham, Edward Elgar.

Randles, S. and Dicken, P. (2004), 'Scale and the Instituted Construction of the Urban: Contrasting the Cases of Manchester and Lyon', *Environment and Planning A*, 36, pp. 2011–32.

Randles, S., McMeekin, A. and Warde, A. (2002) 'The Making of a "Kiss": the Professionalisation and Industrialisation of Market Research', paper presented at the 12th International Conference of RESER, Services and Innovation, 26–7 September, Manchester.

Rosner, P. (1990), 'Karl Polanyi on Socialist Accounting', in K. Polanyi-Levitt (ed.), *The Life and Work of Karl Polanyi: A Celebration*, Montreal, Black Rose Books.

Sahlins, M. D. (1965), 'Exchange-value and the Diplomacy of Primitive Trade', in J. Helm, P. Bohannan and M. D. Sahlins (eds), *Essays in Economic Anthropology: Proceedings of the 1965 Annual Spring Meeting of the American Ethnological Society*, Washington, Washington University Press.

Sarkany, M. (1990), 'Karl Polanyi's Contribution to Economic Anthropology', in K. Polanyi-Levitt (ed.), *The Life and Work of Karl Polanyi: A Celebration*, Montreal, Black Rose Books.

Sayer, A. (1984), *Method in Social Sciences: A Realist Approach*, London, Hutchinson.

Sayer, A. (2002), 'Markets, Embeddedness and Trust; Problems of Polysemy and Idealism', in S. Metcalfe and A. Warde (eds), *Market Relations and the Competitive Process*, Manchester, Manchester University Press.

Smelser, J. and Swedberg, R. (eds) (1994a), *The Handbook of Economic Sociology*, Princeton, Princeton University Press.

Smelser, J. and Swedberg, R. (1994b), 'The Sociological Perspective on the Economy', Ch. 1 in J. Smelser and R. Swedberg (eds), *The Handbook of Economic Sociology*, Princeton, Princeton University Press.

Smith, A. (1776), *An Inquiry into the Nature and Causes of the Wealth of Nations*, Cannan Edition, New York, Wealth of Nations Library, 1994.
Stanfield, J. R. (1986), *The Economic Thought of Karl Polanyi: Lives and Livelihood*, Basingstoke, Macmillan.
Stanfield, J. R. (1990), 'Karl Polanyi and Contemporary Economic Thought', in K. Polanyi-Levitt (ed.), *The Life and Work of Karl Polanyi: A Celebration*, Montreal, Black Rose Books.
Storper, M. (1997a), 'Regional Economies as Relational Assets', in R. Lee and J. Wills (eds), *Geographies of Economies*, London and New York, Arnold.
Storper, M. (1997b), *The Regional World: Territorial Development in a Global Economy*, New York, Guilford.
Strange, S. (1986), *Casino Capitalism*, Oxford, Blackwell.
Stubbs, R. and Underhill, G. R. D. (eds) (1994), *Political Economy and the Changing Global Order*, Hampshire, Palgrave.
Swedberg, R. (1989), 'Joseph A. Schumpeter and the Tradition of Economic Sociology', *Journal of Institutional and Theoretical Economics*, 145(3), pp. 508–24 (also Ch. 7 in R. Swedberg (ed.), *Economic Sociology*, Cheltenham, Edward Elgar).
Swedberg, R. (1990), *Economics and Sociology: Redefining Their Boundaries: Conversations with economists and sociologists*, Princeton, Princeton University Press.
Swedberg, R. (1991a), *Joseph A. Schumpeter: His Life and Work*, Cambridge, Polity Press.
Swedberg, R. (1991b), 'Major Traditions of Economic Sociology', *Annual Review of Sociology*, 17, pp. 251–76 (also Ch. 1 in R. Swedberg (ed.), *Economic Sociology*, Cheltenham, Edward Elgar).
Swedberg, R. (1994), 'Markets as Social Structures', Ch. 11 in J. Smelser and R. Swedberg (eds), *The Handbook of Economic Sociology*, Princeton, Princeton University Press.
Swedberg, R. (ed.) (1996), *Economic Sociology*, Cheltenham, Edward Elgar.
Swedberg, R. and Granovetter, M. (1992), 'Introduction', in M. Granovetter and R. Swedberg (eds), *The Sociology of Economic Life*, Boulder, Westview Press.
Swedberg, R., Himmelstrand, U. and Brulin, G. (1990), 'The Paradigm of Economic Sociology', Ch. 3 in S. Zukin and P. Dimaggio (eds), *Structures of Capital: The Social Organisation of the Economy*, Cambridge, Cambridge University Press.
Tonkiss, F. (2000), 'Markets and Networks: The Case of the Cultural Industries', paper presented to the Research Symposium on Market Relations and Competition, 4–5 May, ESRC Centre for Research on Innovation and Competition, University of Manchester.
Vezer, E. (1990), 'The Polanyi Family', in K. Polanyi-Levitt (ed.), *The Life and Work of Karl Polanyi: A Celebration*, Montreal, Black Rose Books.
Vliet, B. V. and Chappells, H. (2001), 'Systems of Provision and Sustainable Consumption: The Differentiation of Energy, Water and Waste Services', paper presented to the ESF Summer School Consumption, Everyday Life and Sustainability, 17–23 July, University of Lancaster.
Warde, A., Harvey, M., McMeekin, A., Randles, S., Southerton, D. and Tether, B. (2001), 'Economic Integration and Practical Consumption: Some Theoretical Considerations', paper presented to the European Sociological Association

Conference, session of the Research Networks on Economic Sociology and Sociology of Consumption.

White, H. (1981), 'Where Do Markets Come From?', *American Journal of Sociology*, 87(3), pp. 517–47 (also Ch. 20 in R. Swedberg (ed.), *Economic Sociology*, Cheltenham, Edward Elgar).

Zelizer, V. (1988), 'Beyond the Polemics on the Market: Establishing a Theoretical and Empirical Agenda', *Sociological Forum*, 3(4), pp. 614–34 (also Ch. 16 in R. Swedberg (ed.), *Economic Sociology*, Cheltenham, Edward Elgar).

Zukin, S. and DiMaggio, P. (eds) (1990), *Structures of Capital: The Social Organisation of the Economy*, Cambridge, Cambridge University Press.

9
Instituting economic processes in society

Mark Harvey

Introduction: epistemological openings

This chapter has as its objective the explication of an 'instituted economic process' approach within which theories of historical economies can be developed. In doing so, it proposes an epistemology (the first section), an ontology (the second section), and a causality (the final section) – in that order, hopefully with some internal consistency. Let us start with epistemology, and in particular a reflection on the relationship between conceptual frames, historical circumstances, and epistemic 'tools', the investigatory practices of research activity. The choice of the term 'instituted economic process' is historically loaded: it is taken from Karl Polanyi's (1957) mature summation of work that was scientific and at the same time deeply conditioned by his political orientation to the turbulence of his life and times (Randles, 2003).[1] A flurry of recent conferences, and much recent academic literature, has put the work of Karl Polanyi at the centre of attention. When the likes of George Soros[2] and Joseph Stiglitz (Stiglitz, 2001) combine with Hollingsworth and Boyer (1997), Fred Block (Block, 2003), Michael Burawoy (Burawoy, 2003) and Giovanni Arrighi (Silver and Arrighi, 2002) to adopt, adapt or appropriate strands of Polanyian thought, it is perhaps worth asking why, why now, or even why again, given a Polanyian vogue following the events of 1968? Collapses in capital markets, turbulence in currency markets, the emergence of a debate on the efficacy of the most advanced and powerful nation states and economies in relation to globalisation of markets, systemic institutional flaws in corporate and market governance, and the fact that all of these are crises within capitalist economies and societies, rather than between capitalist and non-capitalist alternatives, are amongst some of the principal stimuli behind the rush for Polanyian conceptual framing. New conditions for thinking in Polanyian ways have emerged. Dilemmas on the place and scale of the specific causality of economies in relation to scales and scopes of societies, cultures and polities, so central to Polanyi himself, present themselves now if in strikingly new forms.

There is no doubt that structural crises are fruitful conditions for thinking about fundamental assumptions: there is an historical specificity of circumstance to the *Great Transformation* and to current contributions to that political and intellectual tradition. So there is a key relationship between historical circumstance and the reproduction and development of conceptual frames. Additionally, however, a critical conceptual leverage was provided by the specific epistemological and methodological 'tools' developed by Polanyi and his contemporary economic anthropologists. It was the use of these 'tools' in the world of his day that produced *The Great Transformation* – and significant subsequent developments of his analytical framework. The conceptual and empirical character of this book about the 'specific civilisation' of nineteenth-century Britain is inconceivable without the contrast with primitive, archaic and pre-modern societies (Polanyi, 1968, 1957).[3]

By creating contrasts between geographically and historically distant cases, Polanyi was able to explore a central dilemma of the place of the economy in society, whether the economy is embedded or disembedded, and more fundamentally, whether there are specifically historical rather than universal economic causalities. Post hoc, having lived through the turbulence of his times and researched into both their 'origins' *and* distant societies and economies, Polanyi eventually distilled the question he had been asking himself in this way:

> The instituting of the economic process vests that process with unity and stability; it produces a structure with a definite function in society; it shifts the place of the process in society, thus adding significance to its history; it centres interest on values, motives and policy ... The human economy, then, is embedded and enmeshed in institutions, economic and non-economic ... *The study of the shifting place occupied by the economy in society is therefore no other than the study of the manner in which the economic process is instituted at different times and places* [emphasis added]. (Polanyi, 1957, pp. 249–50)

And this is the answer he had earlier provided for nineteenth-century Britain:

> All types of society are limited by economic factors. Nineteenth-century civilisation alone was economic in a different and distinctive sense, for it chose to base itself on a motive only rarely acknowledged as valid in the history of human societies, and certainly never before raised to the level of a justification of action and behaviour in everyday life, namely, gain. The self-regulating market was uniquely derived from this principle. (Polanyi, 1944; 1957, p. 30)

In his account of the rise and decline of the Hundred Years of Peace, therefore, the Polanyian method, generating empirical contrasts,[4] supported his conceptual framework: there was no disembodied economic causality standing above historical institutions, only historical causalities of specifically instituted socio-economic configurations. So, if for Marx the laws of capitalism were distinct from those of previous modes of production, hence a causality only operative within an historical time-frame, a Polanyian anthropological stance radicalises that idea further by exploring the possibility of a variety of differently instituted capitalist economic causalities, as well as the shifting place of economic processes in different societies.

Likewise, therefore, this current development of the concept of 'instituted economic process' has been based on the generation of new empirical material, using contemporary historical and comparative methodologies, giving critical epistemic leverage additional to the changing historical perspectives that create a bridge with a certain span between the shores of Polanyi's own times and ours (a layering of relatively proximate periods of capitalist crises). This redoubles the distance from Polanyian formulations, whilst recognising continuities. Through a wide range of empirical projects undertaken in conjunction with colleagues at the Centre for Research on Innovation and Competition,[5] this development has created some 'clear blue water' with the original concept. On the basis of various empirical research probes into contemporary capitalisms (food provision and historical transformations of the tomato,[6] genomics and bioinformatics,[7] taxation and welfare regimes,[8] labour markets,[9] construction and housing,[10] the interdependence of markets and structuring of capital markets,[11] European markets for mobile telephony[12]) a more elaborated, and in some ways quite distinct, 'instituted economic process' approach has been developed. The anthropological epistemological stance shared by these studies is to take historical transformations as the point of departure, rather than to posit some general axiomatic initial conditions that set a single and closed system of capitalism in motion from a given historical starting gate. This combination between the social reproduction of (diverse, even conflicting) conceptual frames from particular historical 'platforms' and the generation of new empirics by specifically epistemic tools is encapsulated in a reflexive theoretical epistemology of 'relational realism' (Harvey, 1999a). Hopefully, progress in the development of conceptual explanatory frameworks – or rather a plurality of progresses – is *possible*. The alternative is hard to contemplate.

Instituting the economic

From the previous section, the key starting point, the anthropological question, is one of whether there is or is not a specifically economic domain within societies, and if there is, what are the historical transformational processes that shift its place within society, and draw more or less sharp boundaries between economic processes, and legal, political, cultural, or social processes. The concept of instituted economic process – and it seems quite clear that Polanyi did ultimately choose this formulation for a reason[13] – makes a critical distinction between institutedness and embeddedness, and in developing the distinction, leads us to discard 'embeddedness', a concept that tends to dissolve the economic into cosier social contexts (Sayer, 2002), and to deny specifically economic causalities. It is argued that, for particular historical periods, it is possible to deploy explanations grounded on specifically economic causality whilst at the same time not treating the economic as an autonomous or independent causal domain, so invoking a non-reductionist causal complexity.

However, a certain amount of controversy and confusion has surrounded these terms and quite naturally, there are different agendas underpinning different interpretations. There are those who have appropriated and developed the concept of embeddedness to considerable effect, notably Granovetter, thus stimulating new approaches to economic sociology (Granovetter 1985, 1992a). Pushed to its extreme, however, his concept has reduced economic institutions to 'congealed social networks', ultimately founded on interpersonal interaction (Granovetter, 1992b; Granovotter and McGuire, 1998). There are others, notably Block and Barber, who have argued that the real strength of a Polanyian perspective is to take its object as 'the always embedded market economy', and to consign the disembedded market economy to academic and ideological discourses (Block, 1990, 2003; Barber, 1995). There are others that wish to go yet further and suggest that drawing any division between the economic and the non-economic is illegitimate, and that 'the terrain of the market is coterminous with the groundwork of society itself' (Krippner, 2001, p. 801). Yet others have argued that Polanyi did contain the seeds of an important distinction, and was opening out multiple possibilities by speaking of the instituting as well as the embedding of economic processes (Sayer, 2002; Harvey, 2002d). It therefore seems probably fruitless, and in any case of doubtful merit, to try to settle issues by textual exegesis of Polanyian works.

Instead, and without claiming Polanyian authority, the following combination of propositions can be made which together form the basis of an 'instituted economic process' approach, freed from the confusions of embeddedness. This 'ground-clearing' provides for the analysis of a specifically economic domain of causality under historical conditions.

1 In historical circumstances, there are specifically economic processes (to be posited later), with distinctive institutions, power, constraints, and causalities. Firms, markets and employees; monopoly power resulting in price escalation in a market; scarcity or exhaustion of resources; and overproduction and underconsumption resulting in market collapse, could be instances of each of these. It is likewise both possible and useful to distinguish processes of economic competition from sporting competition or war, even when either of the latter is pursued for purposes of economic gain: *the specificity thesis.*
2 Many processes are undifferentiated into the economic, social, political, cultural, etc., even in societies where such differentiation has occurred

to a relatively significant degree. In contemporary households, many specifically economic processes may occur (e.g. reproduction of labour), and specifically economic power may be exercised (control over resources including unequal division of labour) but they are relatively less differentiated from other processes than in institutions such as factories or shops, where differentiation is more marked. So the specificity of the economic does not entail the degree of differentiation, or vice versa. Specifically economic processes may be instituted to variably differentiated extents historically and comparatively: *the variable differentiation thesis*.

3 Economic processes, even when historically differentiated, are always dependent on the coexistence of instituted social, political, legal or cultural processes, and are *normally* affected by significant interactions with them, as they may also be by biological and natural physical events. Economies do not exist in a vacuum of law, states, cultures, habits, etc. Specificity and differentiation of the economic does not mean autonomy of the economic: *the interdependency thesis*.

4 Even when processes are institutionally strongly differentiated, it does not mean that they are devoid of a rich admixture of non-economic characteristics. This thesis is an extension of the differentiation thesis, by accepting the idea that differentiation is unlikely ever to result in purity, or total abstraction of the economic. A lot of other things go on at work other than work, even in the most dedicated workplace and in conditions of super-exploitation: *the multiplicity thesis*.

5 To affirm the presence of specific and historic economic causalities is to also affirm the presence of a field for complex interactions between different causal domains as a consequence of interdependency, where the relative weight of the economic in any combination with other causal explanations is a matter of empirical evidence rather than of analytical or *a priori* precept. Although a given research may well focus on the generation of economic explanations as a pragmatic or disciplinary bracketing procedure, many of the most interesting phenomena achieve their richest and most coherent explanation by including the interaction between different causal domains (legal, political, cultural, social, biological etc): *the complex causality thesis*.

By setting out these five propositions in this way, it can be shown that holding a strong version of the specificity thesis is quite compatible with holding strong versions of either the interdependency, or the multiplicity, or the variable differentiation thesis, or all three.[14] If one holds all four, then the complex causality thesis follows. By combining all five, one is enabled to consider economic processes as historically and distinctively instituted, open to analysis in their own right, as part of any integrated explanatory account. Hence, the concept of 'instituting economic processes in society' can then be readily combined with a notion of 'articulation' in order to avoid reducing the social to the economic or vice versa. To take an example from *Exploring the Tomato*:[15] a tomato presents itself on a UK supermarket shelf in 2003. It is possible to analyse it as an economic institution, subject to a historically specific price mechanism, in a specific market organisation, with distinctive modes of competition, and with a distinctively organised exchange process between a type of shopper and type of retail outlet. There are also distinctively economic consequences if these sets of economic relations go awry: firms see their share values, market share or profit margins plummet or are subject to merger and acquisition; shoppers have to increase expenditures of both free labour and transport costs to travel further, and can no longer buy their favourite tomatoes; some tomatoes may have to travel further too or along different distributional routes; old technologies of tomato cultivation are swept aside as new ones enter, displacing people, dislocating local economies. But, to reduce tomatoes to nothing but economic processes, or even to explain these specifically economic processes in a vacuum of law, custom, national cuisine, biology and ecology, as if the economic tomato was *autonomous* from the social, cultural, biological or legal tomato, would do as much damage to an economic explanation, as the denial of the specifically economic would do to a social or cultural explanation. The pragmatism and disciplinary focus that governs one point of entry rather than another into a field of complex causality, does not mean that partial explanations need be blinkered ones.

Four economic processes

So far, the argument has been to establish grounds for the specificity of the economic within a complex of causalities. In this section, an attempt is made to expound a general framework of analysis for processes that are specifically 'economic', the starting point of the empirical approach, laying down its ontology.[16] The following subsection will then deal with the historical 'instituting' and structural change of these processes.

It is quite striking how broad in one sense and restrictive in another Polanyi was in denoting economic process, and here there will be an attempt both to de-restrict, and to specify further economic processes. The first broad point Polanyi makes, however, is critical: 'Process suggests an analysis in terms of motion' (Polanyi, 1957, p. 248).

The fundamental units of analysis (more broadly, ontology) involve transformational activities occurring over time and space, continuously and/or with distinctive types of periodicity or regularity, change or stasis. In short, a process analysis is one of dynamics. But the restriction that follows orients much of the whole economic empirical domain towards exchange, whether in market, pre- or non-market forms including reciprocation and redistribution:

The movements refer to changes in location, or in appropriation, or both ... Material elements may alter their position either by changing place or by changing 'hands' ... Between them, these two kinds of movements may be said to exhaust the possibilities comprised in economic process as a natural and social phenomenon. (Polanyi, 1957, p. 248)

In an earlier paper focusing on the organisation of exchange (Harvey and Randles, 2002), it was argued that this approach gave pre-eminence to capitalism as a market economy, reflected in much economic writing and indeed contributed to by the central thrust of *The Great Transformation*. There is a need to rebalance this analysis to recognise the importance of the non-market dynamics of most advanced capitalisms. Adopting the broader anthropological concept of the organisation of exchanges, the realm of non-market but equally economic exchanges can be embraced. These exchanges involve compulsory or incentivised payments whether mediated by taxation, and insurance, intergenerational pension funds, or other forms of monetary transfer, and in return become institutionally linked to rights to goods and services, some privately and individually appropriated, others socially appropriated as public goods (Harvey and Maier, 2004). In terms of the organisation of exchanges, exchanges organised through non-market institutions have grown dynamically in all advanced capitalisms, forming a significant proportion of all exchange activities in contemporary economies. Indeed, very few 'market' exchanges take place unaccompanied by non-market exchanges. It is hard to find an untaxed entity to exchange. An instituted economic processes account of exchange is able to deal with dual or multiple economies, and so to analyse the *dynamic interaction* between market and non-market processes and differently organised exchange processes. Apart from anything else, it helps to distinguish what is specifically market about market exchanges. The vision of the modern capitalist economy as defined by the 'self-regulated market' ignores the fundamental historical fact of the enormous growth and dynamism of the non-market sectors of the economy, especially during the twentieth century, and hence of non-market organisations of exchange processes. Could the dynamism of contemporary capitalisms be sustained without the continued expansion of public education, research and science institutions or public/compulsory private health services? The key role of knowledge driving innovation is inexplicable in terms of exclusively market economies (Metcalfe, 2001).

If this broadening of analysis of exchange can be seen to be very much within the Polanyian anthropological spirit, the lifting of the second major restriction is more radical, putting exchange processes into a wider analytical framework. Four transformational economic processes are proposed, including, but redefining, Polanyi's original two. To argue that there are four rather than two general types of 'motion' obviously runs the same risk of picking two in the first place: why six not four? So, the four are provisional, and reasons have to be given both for selecting them, and for restricting their number. The four processes are:

- *Transformations of qualitative characteristics of objects and activities.* Broadly, this constitutes production and provisioning, by use of labour, technology, knowledge, including the qualitative transformation and reproduction of labour itself.
- *Transformations of appropriation through exchange*, whether reciprocal or redistributive, equal or unequal. Broadly this involves processes of exchange of rights of ownership, individual, collective, or social. This involves the instituting of economic property of different forms.
- *Transformations of activities and objects in place and time.* Broadly this involves movements of people, objects, activities across space and over time, under the general rubric of distribution.
- *Transformations of use.* Changes from use in production to use in end consumption, where objects and activities may be qualitatively transformed, but are no longer involved in further changes in appropriation.

The rationale for positing these four transformational processes is that they are each distinct one from another, and that together, however differently configured in relation to one another, they form a basis for economic reproduction and/or growth. Clearly, it is possible to subdivide each into sub-processes, in ways that are suggested later. So, for example, innovation processes may occur within any of the four processes, as may competitive processes, even if, in the literature concerning capitalist processes, most emphasis, possibly undue emphasis, has been accorded to innovation in production, and market competition for exchange. But, the mutual dependence of the four economic processes forms the basis of economic specificity, and hence, it is argued leads to basing causal explanations on distinctively economic norms, institutions, motives, and activities. Each of them taken separately are not intrinsically economic. Only when put together as ongoing processes do they become so, forming the basis of a *relational* ontology of the economic: relations are primary and constitutive of beings/entities.

Building a sandcastle in itself is not an economic production, but tenuously becomes so when sandcastle sculptures for tourists generate an income for the sculptor. Likewise, appropriation by war rather than exchange would fall outside economic processes, however much war might be motivated by economic interests, if only because continued use of war-as-primary-appropriation tends to destroy the goose (production) that lays the golden egg, unless and until military force is replaced by state polity (as in colonisation). Further, subsistence or hunter-gatherer economies may weakly differentiate processes of production, appropriation, consumption, and distribution in institutional terms, but nonetheless even there the processes remain clearly analytically distinguishable. Because both production and consumption involve qualitative transformation of actions or objects, even the distinction between them is blurred except in combination with exchange and distribution, as an exclusively self-provisioning Robinson Crusoe economy suggests. In some circumstances, institutions for exchange can be at the same time institutions for distribution (wholesale markets). In other cases, distribution can be sharply differentiated from exchange (e.g. call centres, Ch. 11; supermarkets, Harvey et al., 2002). Some activities, such as walking the dog, can be performed as work under employment relations, hence economic, but may also be a non-economic cultural activity in other circumstances (Glucksmann, 1995). Movements of people over space and time may be of all different kinds, but when linked to processes of distribution of goods, trade, or hunting for game and bringing it back to a settlement for collective consumption, these movements become distinctively economic movements. Finally, there is the negative testing of the mutual dependency of these four processes: remove one, and the others suffer. Harvest failures, oil blockades, production stoppages of whatever kind, collapses in consumer confidence and demand, or systemic underconsumption, can on their own account then induce considerable disruption in the other three interrelated processes. This mutual interdependency of the four processes underpins specifically economic constraints and causalities.

So each of these four transformational processes has their distinctive characteristics – they are mutually unsubstitutable and indeed have their own dynamics – but each is mutually dependent on the others (see Figure 9.1). For this reason, there are different historical configurations of instituted economic processes and changes in one process domain affect processes in others. The choice of this ontology of processes, including their relationality, distinguishes this approach from theories whose primary ontology is of actors/agents (individuals, firms, groups, etc.) and their contexts (other actors, selection environments, structures, ecologies, etc.).

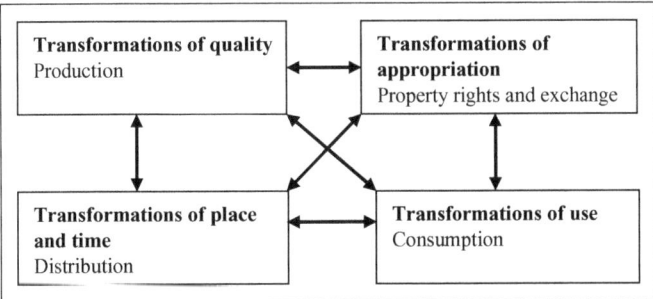

Figure 9.1 Configurations of four instituted economic processes

The articulation of economic and non-economic processes: the example of the wage

Without as yet having turned to the analysis of the instituting of economic processes, there can be little doubt that the various forms of the wage are both pivotal and centrally significant to various forms of contemporary capitalisms. In this section, it will be used to exemplify both the specificity of the instituted economic processes involved, and the fact that these are inextricably articulated to law, taxation, politics and the state. On the one hand, in terms of economic specificity, the wage relation is an organised form of exchange (Harvey and Randles, 2002) of money for labour services, between two or more classes of economic agent, direct and indirect employers of various kinds and employees, differentiated by varieties of employment relations and status. Further, in terms of the connections to other economic processes, it is also clear that this exchange enables the use of labour in production processes, on the one hand, and a transfer of the means of purchase of commodities and services for consumption on the other. As with other organised exchanges, the wage is a particularly central vehicle for taxation, and as such, the different ways that taxation is construed through the wage in different capitalisms are critical economic underpinnings for defining flows of resources into the public and private domains, both for public and private production, and for public and private consumption. The way that market and non-market economic flows are instituted is an important constitutive element of defining boundaries between public and private sectors, as well as flows across those boundaries in health, education, pensions, employment protection, and so on. If one simply takes the variety of institutions for resourcing pensions, one way of instituting these flows supports capital markets with pension funds, now a very significant proportion of capital markets (Blackburn, 2002). Other, European continental ways preclude all but the most minimal development of pension funds (Clasquin et al., 2004; Myles and Pierson, 2001; Myles, 2002). But, all these various modes of instituting pensions involve a combination of market and non-market processes to ensure serial intergenerational exchange, rather than reciprocal intragenerational exchange (Samuelson, 1954). This describes some of the economic specificities of flows through the wage. It is also clear, from current evidence, that crises in these flows are distinctively economic crises, whether one considers the collapse of Enron, or the resourcing of continental social insurance systems.

But the wage relation is also a legal relation, both in terms of employment law and in terms of taxation law. The distinction between contracts for service and contracts of service is essential to defining what is employment and what is not, hence what is a wage and what is not (Deakin, 2001; Deakin and Morris, 1998; Freedman, 2001; Hodgson, 1999, Ch. 10; Harvey, 2001, 1999b). These legal arrangements differ at their core in different capitalist economies. The exchange between wage labour and capital, so central to capitalisms, have different forms of contract. What is exchanged is different and how the exchange links both to the use of labour time in production and to out-of-work time is different in different legal frameworks. Likewise, taxation, although clearly an economic resource flow, is an institution whose existence is predicated on legislation. Different types of tax and insurance regime attached to the wage are distinct political and legal instruments, normally quite different from employment status legal implements. Moreover, major changes in both employment status legislation and in taxation legislation, often contradictory, mean the wage is an historically evolving legal and taxation institution, also interacting strongly with changing economic processes. Last but not least, the politics of the wage and taxation, industrial relations around the wage, and major social conflicts around the wage, suggest that the wage is also a thoroughly political institution.

Where does this lead in terms of embeddedness and the institution of economic processes? It points strongly to the disadvantages of adopting a concept of embeddedness if in so doing significant differences of process are blurred or conflated. Saying that the wage is an embedded exchange does not get very far beyond saying that the wage is never exclusively economic. But to say that the wage is never exclusively economic, does not mean that it does not have specifically and historically instituted, economic processes flowing through it. Further, legal instruments on status are quite different from legal instruments on taxation. Indeed the political and legal processes involved have their own and distinctive dynamics, the one related to judicial process, the other closely bound to budgetary processes of the state. Finally, the politics of the wage, the forms of organisation around those politics, and the historical dynamics of those politics, also have their own specificity. The concept of embeddedness often fails the question of what is embedded in what, the legal in the political, the fiscal in the legal, or just the economic in a mush of all of these.

The story of the wage could be retold across the span of the economy, in terms of contract law, corporate law, anti-trust and competition law, intellectual property law, and so on. Economic processes can never be disarticulated from legal or political processes. That is the strength of a concept of instituted economic process, and the weakness of a concept of embeddedness. The former recognises a specificity in relation to other specificities – and the shifting character and place of those specificities. The latter tends to conflate and dissolve specificity, motivated primarily by a negative argument against the idea of the autonomy, exclusivity, or absolute differentiation of an economic realm and those economists locked within it.

The view that arises from this argument is therefore one of complex causality, of the interaction between different dynamics rather than reduction or subordination to one or other. Just as the dynamics of each of the four economic processes cannot be collapsed into each other, so when dealing with articulation between economic and non-economic processes,

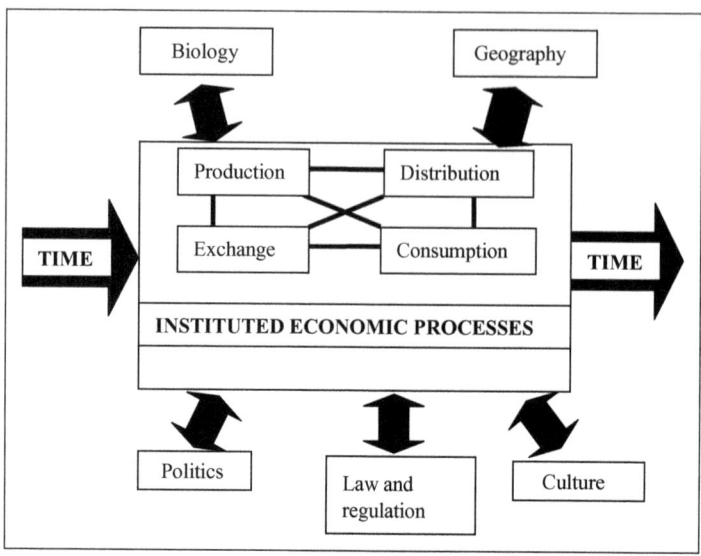

Figure 9.2 The interaction of four multiple causal domains

it becomes necessary to explore the complex interaction between their different dynamics. These interactions in turn constitute distinctive dynamic processes in their own right.

In Figure 9.2, the central focus of this chapter is on instituted economic process. The bold arrows represent interactions between different causal domains. But by placing instituted economic processes at the centre for this analysis, it is in no way intended to privilege these processes and their causal specificities over others. A different focus could adopt any of the other causal domains as central, or indeed, more ambitiously attempt to bring together the interactions between many complex domains – as in the study of the tomato. An analysis of the formation and destruction of markets for GM tomato in the US and UK, for example, demonstrated that biological, legal-contractual, and political processes combined with economic and innovation processes to produce distinctive outcomes for two GM tomato products (Harvey et al., 2003; Harvey, 2004).

Instituting, de-instituting and historical change

Taking the epistemological stance that analytical starting points are historical and from a vantage point in history, there can be no search for 'absolute beginnings' for an institutional analysis. Remote instituted economic processes, such as those brought to the fore by an anthropology of 'primitive' societies, serve most effectively as static points of contrast. Assumptions about the place of economy in society can be shaken to their foundations by such comparisons. Nonetheless, those societies clearly did not spring from nowhere, and, however hidden, had history. *The Great Transformation*, however, as the title suggests, is not about static institutions, or about economic processes that, once instituted, continue to 'run on ruts' forever. Indeed, the book is an analysis of both stability and instability, of institution and de-institution, and of permanent tension – the double movement of creative-destructive markets and countervailing regulation. Moreover, the 'Great' transformation was also a process of changing pre-existing configurations of economic processes, articulated with pre-existing legal, political, and cultural processes of the preceding epoch.

For the sake of simplicity, therefore, 'instituting' can be seen as a process of historically changing pre-existing instituted processes, whereas 'instituted' processes are those that may endure over shorter or longer periods and involve dynamic processes of reproduction, and for economic processes specifically economic reproduction. As in a Marxist framework, however, reproduction can be 'simple' or 'expanded', the former referring to the maintenance of a given level of production, exchange, distribution and consumption through existing institutional arrangements, the latter to the dynamics of growth in scale and scope. Instituted economic processes can be manifest in enterprises, markets, industrial divisions, separation of public and private spheres, consumption practices, households, as well as in 'intangibles' such as economic concepts, knowledge, habits, norms, rules and motives. Dynamic processes, such as innovation, competition, the interaction between supply and demand, can also be shown to be instituted differently within different configurations. In this kind of analysis, perhaps two things need to be emphasised. Whilst it is important to stress the 'ubiquity of habits and rules' (Hodgson, 1997, 2003), an IEP approach requires an analysis of the economic force of specifically economic rationales, habits, and motives. The economic motive for gain has already been referred to, but one can view with the same perspective business strategies as taught and reproduced in business schools or accounting and auditing procedures such as those that have recently become severely destabilised, inviting transformation and re-institution. Recently, Swedberg (2003) has put 'interest' at the heart of his economic sociology, and economic interest too can be seen (here in a non-Weberian sense) to be instituted. Economic concepts, such as equating the economy with the market economy, have endured through many different manifestations, and can be seen to be almost Kuhnian paradigms influencing much governmental policy making. To be sure, many economic norms, concepts, habits may be articulated with non-economic, moral, political or religious attitudes (Weber, 1976). The call for transparency and accountability both has distinctively economic content enshrined in company law, and is articulated with democratic political rhetoric. Thus, firms, public enterprises, markets, transport infrastructure, schools, hospitals, and households can to varying degrees be seen to be manifest institutional expressions of distinctively economic processes over a certain historical period. *Economic* habits, rules, norms, concepts and strategies are clearly also necessary for the reproduction of economic processes, not just habits, etc. in general. The tendency of some economic sociology to ascribe economic stability to some generalised social inertia-loving principle by those who benefit most from it (Fligstein, 2001)[17] presents considerable difficulties for any historical explanation aiming to embrace transformation and institution, stability and instability. Economic habits, motives and reasons, etc., are as vulnerable as any other economic institution, and economic stability, in this light, can only be sustained by dynamic reproduction.

But, secondly, any perspective on instituted economic processes has to see stasis, even dynamic simple reproduction, as an exception in contemporary capitalisms. To exemplify this, let me turn again to an example from the tomato research, the bottle of Heinz tomato ketchup or the can of Campbell's tomato soup. In some ways these are supreme examples of expanded reproduction of instituted economic processes. Both companies were formed in 1867 and both still exist. Both the ketchup and the soup were launched as products in the first decade of the twentieth century. They retain a similar shape, and their commercial design trades on their status as classics that have now endured for a century, quite a record for a manufactured commodity. Both were revolutionary at their time, pioneering mass production for mass consumption and flow-line assembly production, long before Ford motor cars. Moreover, they were part of an innovation process that revolutionised logistics and distribution; supply chain management; the character and organisation of retail outlets; marketing and market research; and consumption and household cooking practices. They established transnational markets very early in the twentieth century, and arguably were amongst the first global manufactured consumer products. Although some of the main parameters of the instituted economic processes of production and business organisation of branded manufactured goods (including extended chains of exclusive suppliers of various inputs), consumption, marketing and retailing have endured, there has been process of expanded reproduction and capital accumulation over many decades radically extending the scale and scope of these processes. Moreover, behind the static façade, almost everything about the product has changed: the bottles and cans, and certainly the tomatoes, have very little in common technologically or qualitatively with their early twentieth-century forebears. Recombinant DNA technology is deployed to hybridise new dedicated ketchup or soup tomato varieties. New forms of processing and heat treatment are involved, and the taste has changed. As hamburgers and fast-food outlet developed, instituted patterns of consumption of these goods, in terms of shopping for and eating these products, also changed. So, even this relatively continuous configuration of production–exchange–distribution–consumption as a platform for expanded reproduction is not quite as unchanging as might appear.

However, this configuration itself has now been disturbed and challenged in radical ways with the growth of supermarket driven, own-label production, where styles and rates of innovation, types of product, structure of markets and marketing, systems of distribution, patterns of shopping and consumption, have been radically redesigned. Chilled fresh tomato soups, a proliferation of tomato sauces, a variety of tomato concasses on pizzas, have all been generated from a very different industrial configuration of production, but also new distribution, marketing, and consumption patterns. In the UK in particular, but increasingly in many other European countries, the branded manufacturers' access to market is being squeezed at the expense of the outputs from this new configuration of instituted economic processes.

If ketchup and soup demonstrated continuities of instituted processes over the long term, in the domain of bioinformatics at the cutting edge of biotechnology, high levels of turbulence and fluidity of markets, shifting boundaries between public and private sectors, and transiency in what is tradable and what is not tradable (e.g. genome sequence data), can be found (McMeekin et al., 2004). New classes of economic agent, dedicated bioinformatic companies, software and algorithm tool producers, genomic and proteomic sequence data providers have been found to rapidly change their products, services and business strategies. In spite of a potentially integrated science and technology platform, major rifts have opened up in pharmaceutical and agribusiness companies and markets, splitting many life science companies down the middle. The landscape of enterprises, as well as of product and capital markets has become more like a seascape, currents dividing and combining rapidly beneath a turbulent surface of new entrants and quick exits, in which even some of the major players seem at risk of being submerged (McMeekin and Harvey, 2002). Moreover, regulatory and trading environments in Europe as a core OECD region, as well as distinctive new innovation pathways in emergent economies, suggest the possibility of major shifts in geopolitical gravity towards Brazil, China, India and elsewhere (Harvey and McMeekin, 2005). This contrast in tomato ketchup and bioinformatics demonstrates that the instituting of economic processes is dynamic, requiring much more than mere routinisation or habituation, and is ever-vulnerable to de-instituting counter-forces.

In an *'instituted economic process'* framework, the key twin aspects of structural change and reproduction (stable or expanding) are necessary to counter a stability- or equilibrium-oriented view of economies in society. The focus of the term 'instituted', therefore, is that dynamic processes are historically instituted in space and at different scales, local, global and regional. There are multiple historical starting points with intersecting pathways: no single defining or original arrangement; no one essence of capitalism; no unique abstract capitalism; no un-instituted economy.

Instituted economic causal explanations

By adopting four economic processes (Figure 9.1) and relations between economic and non-economic processes as the fundamental unit of analysis (Figure 9.2), and then combining to them processes of structural change and reproduction, a type of causal explanation is also implied. From what has already been argued, it is clear a position of complex causality is being advanced in the sense of there being both specific causalities and an interaction between different specific causalities, without any overarching causal explanatory framework. This is so at two levels. Within economic causality, the four processes are irreducible to each other: it is a model where, for example, changes in consumption cannot be seen as directly inducing changes in production, or vice versa. Each process in the relational configuration has its own dynamic, impacting on the others, but not generating the specific changes in any or all of them. Then, at the level of the interaction between economic and other causalities, where there is also radical interdependence, non-economic and economic causalities interact to produce complex outcomes. Biological causes, for example, are radically different from economic causes. But biological events, from the Black Death to BSE, and indeed biological processes involved in the food system including human consumption, can have immense consequences for other causal domains including the economic, without accounting in biological terms for the nature of these effects. The disease Black Death may have played an arguably more or less significant role in disrupting feudalisms, but offers little by way of explanation for the development of capitalisms. Conversely, changes in global climate and ecology may be more affected now than at any other historical time by economic activity, but it is the property of gases rather than of economies as such that brings about those changes. The result is a complex interaction of causalities between socio-economic and natural processes.

The concept of complex causality as defined here in terms of the interaction of specific dynamisms at different levels and the absence of any overarching causal system at any level, does entail a principle of indeterminacy and non-reductive causality, without abandoning causality to 'uncaused causes', such as agency, creativity, or indeed giving up on causal explanation in the face of complexity or particularity of individual micro-processes (Hodgson, 1999, pp. 141–3). The moment one treats events *as if* they were uncaused (*ibid.*, p. 148) is the moment one gives up seeking explanation, rather than a demonstration that some process is intrinsically inexplicable.[18] It is possible to reject entirely causal models of mechanistic determinacy, and embrace contingency and indeterminacy, without abandoning the quest to develop better explanations.

So, instituted economic processes are structured but not (fixed and closed) structures. It would be a mistake to treat processes as free-floating and entirely fluid. The whole analysis has been in terms of how processes are instituted in relation to one another in specific ways at specific historical times and at different geographical scales. Processes are both structured and relational, and can therefore be described as open-structured processes. Interactions between dynamically related structured processes, inducing tensions and increasing incompatibilities, are critical to the process of structural change, of the destabilisation of pre-existing instituted processes and the generation of newly structured processes. The example of the conflict between mass-produced brand manufacturing configuration and supermarket own-label configuration is a small case in point. It is a non-adaptive or non-evolutionary account of change, inasmuch as at a fundamental level there is no category of novelty originators to be distinguished from a category of environments: no exogeneity/endogeneity dichotomy. The presence of multiple different trajectories of many different 'capitalisms', points to the development of many different scales of interaction between 'open-structured processes', a constant source of new tensions and incompatibilities, inducing further historical transformations. In this light, there are immanent and emergent causalities of capitalisms, rather than an unchanging or singular abstract set of laws of capitalism, a unique generative structure, of which historical instances are empirical expressions. This concept of complex causality, therefore, is quite remote from systems causality, whether closed or open. It is a type of causal explanation that is complex, structural, non-reductionist and indeterminist.

Conclusion

Having begun with history, let me end with history. The Polanyian concepts of instituted economic process were developed in a particular time and place, conditioned in part by the turbulence and displacements of the time, and in part by the particular epistemological and conceptual tools available and deployed in various ways. To understand 'our times' was then seen as an attempt to understand 'the origins of our times' through comparative anthropology and history. The epistemological processes are themselves open to transformation, and various transmutations of Polanyian thought have emerged with tensions, conflicts, partial resolutions created under the very different circumstances of our times.

This chapter can be situated in that process. There is a certain consistency or reflexivity between the way of looking at these epistemological processes and the way of looking at instituted economic processes. Researching by means of particular methodologies and conceptual frames, from the vantage point of institutions situated in given places and times, can be seen as an open but structured process with specifically epistemic dynamics. There needs to be a view of how scientific epistemic processes are articulated with economic processes, and indeed how a complex causal analysis might account for this distinctive kind of interaction between diverse causal domains. An explanation of instituted conceptual novelty is of a similar kind to that of instituted economic novelty.[19] In organising the chapter around epistemology, the structure – some would say ontology – of empirical domains, and causality, an attempt has been made to lay some groundwork for the further development of an instituted economic process approach, to combine elements of continuity with elements of transformation within a shared history.

Notes

1 This Chapter was presented at the first conference to focus on Polanyi's work to be held in the United Kingdom, at CRIC in 2002.
2 '[*The Great Transformation*] is a brilliant analysis of the problems of globalisation as they developed in the nineteenth century – the problems we have today are not new.' Soros, interview, Observer, 6 May, 2001.
3 To demonstrate the centrality of the anthropological contrast, Polanyi compares a redistributive and reciprocating 'primitive' economy with the market economy of nineteenth-century Britain. In the first: 'Symmetry and centricity will meet halfway the needs of reciprocity and redistribution; institutional patterns and principles of behaviour are mutually adjusted. As long as social organisation runs in its ruts, no individual economic motives need come into play ... *The economic system is, in effect, a mere function of social organisation* [emphasis added]' (Polanyi, 1944, p. 49). '*Instead of economy being embedded in social relations, social relations are embedded in the economic system* ... For once the economic system is organised in separate institutions, based on specific motives and conferring special status, society must be shaped in such a manner as to allow that system to function according to its own laws. ... A market economy can function only in a market society [emphasis added]' (Polanyi, 1944, p. 57).
4 Block argues that there are many inconsistent historical interpretations within *The Great Transformation*, and that in some important instances, Polanyi can be shown to be empirically mistaken. But he argues also that for Polanyi the questions were rightly empirical ones, motivated by his central problematic concerning the institution of self-regulating markets (Block, 2003).
5 The Centre is funded by the ESRC, and resides in the University of Manchester.
6 Harvey et al. (2003); Harvey (2002a, 2002c, 2002d, 2004).
7 See McMeekin and Harvey (2002) and McMeekin, Harvey and Gee (2004).
8 See Harvey and Maier (2004).
9 See Harvey (2000) and Harvey (1999b).
10 See Harvey (2002c).
11 Randles (2002) and Chapter 14.
12 Mina (2003) and Chapter 13.
13 As Krippner (2001) has noted the term 'embeddedness' only appears twice in *The Great Transformation*, where it is also not indexed. In *Trade and Market*

in the Early Empire the half preface for 'Institutional Analysis' suggests that 'embeddedness' is one aspect of that analysis: 'Neither time nor history have provided us with those conceptual tools required to penetrate the maze of social relationships in which the economy was embedded. This is the task of what we will here call institutional analysis' (2001, p. 242). Block also provides an illuminating discussion of the ambiguities and tensions within Polanyian texts (Block, 2002). See also Barber (1995).

14. Of course, given that the first four propositions stand independently of each other, it does not follow that one is obliged to hold the specificity thesis as a consequence of holding any or all of 2, 3 and 4. The remainder of the chapter offers persuasion to do so.
15. *Exploring the Tomato* (Harvey et al., 2003) was the outcome of a CRIC research project that took the tomato as an empirical probe into major transformations of twentieth-century capitalism, especially to understand the reconfigurations of production, exchange, distribution and consumption.
16. Ontology is taken here to mean the kinds of entities that constitute the reality being analysed. In the view of a relational realism, these are constituted by real interactions between theories (or conceptual frames), methodological practices and realities independent of them, and although *a priori* reasoning is involved in theory making, the gains made by it are the greater the stronger its connections are with real epistemic interactions with the real independent world.
17. 'The theory of fields implies that the search for stable interactions with competitors, suppliers, and workers is the main cause [*sic*] of social structures in markets' (Fligstein, 2001, p. 18). 'When successful, actors produce social relationship that have the effect of creating stable markets, that is, situations where incumbent firms who take one another into account in their behaviour are able to reproduce themselves on a period-to-period basis' (*ibid.*, p. 18). And again: 'The theory of fields assumes that actors try to produce a "local" stable world where the dominant actors produce meaning that allow them to reproduce their advantage'(*ibid.*, p. 29).
18. 'Human agency is neither uncaused nor generally predictable' (Hodgson, 2003, p. 171).
19. An instituted conceptual novelty could be compared with Metcalfe's view of 'correlated' knowledge (Metcalfe, 2004).

References

Barber, B. (1995), 'All Economies Are Embedded: The Career of a Concept and Beyond', *Social Research*, 62(2), pp. 387–413.

Blackburn, R. (2002), *Banking on Death or Investing in Life: The History and Future of Pensions,* London, Verso.

Block, F. (1990), *Postindustrial Possibilities: A Critique of Economic Discourse,* Berkeley, University of California Press.

Block, F. (2003), 'Karl Polanyi and the Writing of the Great Transformation', *Theory and Society,* 32, pp. 275–306.

Burawoy, M. (2003), 'For a Sociological Marxism: The Complementary Convergence of Antonio Gramsci and Karl Polanyi', *Politics and Society,* 31(2), pp. 193–261.

Clasquin, B., Moncel, N., Friot, B. and Harvey, M. (eds) (2004), *Wage and Welfare: New Perspectives for the Analysis of Changes in Employment and Social Rights in Europe*, Brussels, Peter Lang.

Deakin, S. (2001), *Employment Protection and the Employment Relationship: Adapting the Traditional Model*, London, Institute of Employment Rights.

Deakin, S. and Morris, G. S. (1998), *Labour Law*, London, Butterworths.

Fligstein, N. (2001), *The Architecture of Markets: An Economic Sociology of twenty-first Century Capitalist Societies*, Princeton, Princeton University Press.

Freedman, J. (2001), *Employed or Self-employed? Tax Classification of Workers and the Changing Labour Market*, London, Institute of Fiscal Studies.

Glucksmann, M. (1995), 'Why "Work"? Gender and the "Total Social Organisation of Labour" ', *Gender, Work and Organisation*, 2(2), pp. 63–75.

Granovetter, M. (1985), 'Economic Action and Social Structure: The Problem of Embeddedness', *American Journal of Sociology*, 91(3), pp. 481–510.

Granovetter, M. (1992a), 'The Sociological and Economic Approaches to Labour Market Analysis: A Social Structural View', in M. Granovetter and R. Swedberg (eds), *The Sociology of Economic Life*, Boulder, Westview Press.

Granovetter, M. (1992b), 'Economic Institutions as Social Constructions: A Framework for Analysis', *Acta Sociologica*, 35, pp. 3–11.

Granovetter, M. and McGuire, P. (1998), 'The Making of an Industry: Electricity in the United States', in M. Callon (ed.), *The Laws of the Markets*, Oxford, Basil Blackwell, pp. 147–73.

Harvey, M. (1999a), 'How the Object of Knowledge Constrains Knowledge of the Object: An Epistemological Analysis of a Social Research Investigation', *Cambridge Journal of Economics*, 23(4), pp. 485–501.

Harvey, M. (1999b), 'Economies of Time: A Framework for Analysing the Restructuring of Employment Relations', in A. Felstead and N. Jewson (eds), *Global Trends in Flexible Labour*, London, Macmillan.

Harvey, M. (2000), 'Systemic Competition between High and Low "Social Cost" Labour: A Case Study of the UK Construction Industry', in L. Clarke, P. de Gijsel and J. Janssen (eds), *The Dynamics of Wage Relations in the New Europe*, London, Kluwer Academic.

Harvey, M. (2001), *Undermining Construction: The Corrosive Effects of False self-employment*, London, Institute of Employment Rights.

Harvey, M. (2002a), 'Markets, Supermarkets and the Macro-social Shaping of Demand: An Instituted Economic Process Approach', in A. McMeekin, K. Green, M. Tomlinson and V. Walsh (eds), *Innovation by Demand: An Interdisciplinary Approach to the Study of Demand and Its Role in Innovation*, Manchester, Manchester University Press.

Harvey, M. (2002b), 'Privatisation, Fragmentation and Inflexible Flexibilisation: The UK Construction Industry from the 1970s', in P. Philips and G. Bosch (eds), *The Construction Industry: An International Comparison of Construction Industries*, London, Routledge.

Harvey, M. (2002c), 'Competition as Instituted Economic Process', in S. Metcalfe and A. Warde (eds), *Market Relations and the Competitive Process*, Manchester, Manchester University Press.

Harvey, M. (2002d), 'Productive Systems, Markets, and Competition as "Instituted Economic Process" ', in J. Michie, J. Rubery, B. Burchell and S. Deakin

(eds), *Systems of Production: Markets, Organisations and Performance*, London, Routledge.
Harvey, M. (2004), 'The Appearance and Disappearance of GM Tomato: Innovation Strategy, Market Formation and the Shaping of Demand', in S. Vellema and K. Jansen (eds), *Agribusiness and Environmentalism*, London, Zed Press.
Harvey, M. and Randles, S. (2002), 'Market Exchanges and "Instituted Economic Process": An Analytical Perspective', *Revue d'Economie Industrielle*, 101(4), December, pp. 11–30 (also as CRIC Discussion Paper, no. 51).
Harvey, M. and Maier, M. (2004), 'Rights over Resources', in B. Clasquin, B. Friot, N. Moncel and M. Harvey (eds), *Wages and Welfare: New Perspectives for the Analysis of Changes in Employment and Social Rights in Europe*, Brussels, Peter Lang.
Harvey, M. and McMeekin, A. (2005), 'Brazilian Genomics and Bioinformatics: Instituting New Innovation Pathways in a Global Context', *Economy and Society*, 34(4), pp. 634–58.
Harvey, M., Quilley, S. and Beynon, H. (2002), *Exploring the Tomato: Transformations in Nature, Economy and Society*, Cheltenham, Edward Elgar.
Hodgson, G. M. (1997), 'The Ubiquity of Habits and Rules', *Cambridge Journal of Economics*, 21(6), pp. 663–84.
Hodgson, G. M. (1999), *Evolution and Institutions: On Evolutionary Economics and the Evolution of Economics*, Cheltenham, Edward Elgar.
Hodgson, G. M. (2003), 'The Hidden Persuaders: Institutions and Individuals in Economic Theory', *Cambridge Journal of Economics*, 27(2), pp. 159–75.
Hollingsworth, J. R. and Boyer, R. (eds) (1997), *Contemporary Capitalism: The Embeddedness of Institutions*, Cambridge, Cambridge University Press.
Krippner, G. (2001), 'The Elusive Market: Embeddedness and the Paradigm of Economic Sociology', *Theory and Society*, 30, pp. 775–810.
McMeekin, A. and Harvey, M. (2002), 'The Formation of Bioinformatic Knowledge Markets: An "Economies of Knowledge" Approach', *Revue d'Economie Industrielle*, 101(4), pp. 47–64.
McMeekin, A., Harvey, M. and Gee, S. (2004), 'Emergent Bioinformatics and Newly Distributed Innovation Processes', in J. Laage-Hellman, M. McKelvey and A. Rickne (eds) (2004), *The Economic Dynamics of Modern Biotechnologies: European and Global Trends*, Cheltenham, Edward Elgar.
Metcalfe, J. S. (2001), 'Institutions and Progress', *Industrial and Corporate Change*, 10(3), pp. 561–86.
Metcalfe, J. S. (2004), 'The Entrepreneur and the Style of Modern Economics', *Journal of Evolutionary Economics*, 14(2), pp. 157–76.
Mina, A. (2003), 'The Creation of the European Market for Mobile Telephony: Overview of an Instituted Process', *International Review of Sociology*, 13(2), pp. 435–54 (revised for this volume, Chapter 13).
Myles, J. (2002), 'A New Social Contract for the Elderly', in G. Esping-Andersen (ed.), with D. Gallie, A. Hemerijk and J. Myles, *Why We Need a New Welfare State*, Oxford, Oxford University Press.
Myles, J. and Pierson, P. (2001), 'The Comparative Political Economy of Pension Reform', in P. Pierson (ed.), *The New Politics of the Welfare State*, Oxford, Oxford University Press.
Polanyi, K. (1944/1957), *The Great Transformation: The Political and Economic Origins of our Time*, Boston, Beacon Press.

Polanyi, K. (1957), 'The Economy as Instituted Process', in K. Polanyi, C. M. Arensberg and H. W. Pearson (eds), *Trade and Market in the Early Empires*, New York, Free Press.

Polanyi, K. (1968), *Primitive, Archaic and Modern Economies: Essays of Karl Polanyi*, New York, Anchor Books, Doubleday.

Polanyi, K., Arensberg, C. M. and Pearson, H. W. (eds) (1957), *Trade and Market in the Early Empires*, New York, Free Press.

Randles, S. (2002), 'Complex Systems Applied? The Merger that made GlaxoSmithKline', *Technology Analysis and Strategic Management*, 14(3), pp. 331–54.

Randles, S. (2003), 'Issues for a Neo-Polanyian Research Agenda in Economic Sociology', *International Review of Sociology*, 13(2), pp. 409–34.

Samuelson, P. (1954), 'The Pure Theory of Public Expenditure', *Review of Economics and Statistics*, 36(4), pp. 387–9.

Samuelson, P. (1958), 'An Exact Consumption-loan Model of Interest with or without the Contrivance of Money', *Journal of Political Economy*, 66(6), pp. 467–82.

Sayer, A. (2002), 'Markets, Embeddedness and Trust: Problems of Polysemy and Idealism', in S. Metcalfe and A. Warde (eds), *Market Relations and the Competitive Process*, Manchester, Manchester University Press.

Silver, B. J. and Arrighi, G. (2002), 'Polanyi's "Double Movement": the Belle Epoque of British and US Hegemony Compared', *Politics and Society*, 31(2), pp. 325–55.

Stiglitz, J. (2001), *Foreword: The Great Transformation: The Political and Economic Origins of our Time*, Boston, Beacon Press.

Swedberg, R. (2003), *The Principles of Economic Sociology*, Princeton, Princeton University Press.

Weber, M. (1976), *The Protestant Ethic and the Spirit of Capitalism*, trans. Talcott Parsons, 2nd edn, London, Allen & Unwin.

10
Labour markets as instituted economic process: a comparison of France and the UK

Nathalie Moncel

Introduction

The labour market is arguably the place of economic exchange that is the least understandable through neoclassical tales of market functioning, i.e. a place of exchange organised through price mechanism. First and foremost, one must consider the specificity of the exchange that takes place in the labour market in comparison with other markets, such as commodity or capital market.

- The product is inseparably connected with the seller.
- The market transactions and actual exchange are distinct events and the latter one continuous over time in the context of ongoing employment relationships.
- Labour as a commodity is not produced and exchanged in order to make a profit but to reproduce itself.

All these 'market imperfections' have been more or less integrated in recent neoclassical developments of labour economics (Perrot, 1992; Leclercq, 1999). Implicit contracts, the efficiency wage, insider/outsider models are all recent propositions that search to tackle labour market imperfections. The temporal nature of the exchange between workers and firms implies that labour market transactions are characterised by a high degree of uncertainty, incomplete information and informational asymmetries. Recent theoretical developments focus on information as a key feature of labour market functioning. Regarding the strength of norms of equity and fairness in wage determination, some mainstream economists consider the labour market as a social institution.[1] But, analysis is still centred on rational behaviour of economic agents and the functioning of the market itself is less questioned. Indeed, it is assumed to operate through price mechanisms but with certain limits:

> One important difference between the labour market and the market for fish is that the performance of the worker depends on the price paid for his

services... Because the wage rate enters the story in this double role, as a productive factor as well as a simple cost, it is not available simply to balance supply and demand in the usual efficient way. It cannot perform both functions perfectly. (Solow, 1990, pp. 33–4)

In order to develop some elements for an alternative understanding of labour markets and how they function, we propose here to consider the commodification of labour, at the core of capitalist economies, as an instituted economic process in the way that Polanyi used this notion:

Process suggests analysis in terms of motion. The movements refer either to changes in location or in appropriation, or both... The instituting of the economic process vests that process with unity and stability; it produces a structure with a definite function in society; it shifts the place of the process in the society, thus adding significance to its history; it centres interests on value, motives and policy. (Polanyi, 1957, pp. 248–50)

Being instituted, labour markets do not function in a universally similar way. They differ according to societal conditions of labour commodification. Moreover, if one considers labour markets do not exist without being instituted, the process of institution becomes the focus of analysis in order to understand the mechanisms that underlie labour market functioning. This approach suggests three directions which structure the three sections of this chapter.

First, institutionalisation involves the formation of labour supply and labour demand. Two major difficulties arise related to the entity exchanged on this market. Because of the temporal differentiation between transaction and exchange, the examination of labour demand can only be done through the observation of the allocation and use of labour. Because labour power is inseparable from labour owner, labour supply is to be evaluated through labour availability and mobility. Given that a main feature of labour market is the existence of differentiated patterns of labour allocation, use and mobility, the issue is to identify those factors that create this labour market segmentation which are external labour market functioning. Thus, employment structures are determined by and within the firms; labour force production depends quantitatively and qualitatively on familial, educational, and welfare systems; and labour markets establish various rules for allocating differentiated individuals into positions in productive systems.

Second, in the neoclassical framework, the economic process is assumed to be a price-regulated process and economists currently try to take into account institutions, rules and norms that support individuals' supposedly rational economic behaviour. The opposite analytical approach is taken here: the question is how the economic exchange process is instituted, in terms of market rules and institutions, at which level, and how they condition economic agents' actions.

Last but not least, this approach involves reconsidering the wage as the outcome of a set of social norms and rules and interactions of actors that entail exchanges as differently instituted forms. There are different monetary evaluations, not a simple market price. The wage expresses the way labour is recognised in a capitalist system through monetary resources flows. In this way, the connection between use and reproduction of labour is essential to the analysis of wage determination and the question is to understand how the financing of the reproduction of labour has been instituted through modern wage relations and in different ways according to societal configurations.

The chapter applies this framework to compare France and the UK, in order to highlight the set of institutional arrangements and societal structures that institute labour markets. The comparative approach developed here relates to the one developed by the societal effect school (Maurice et al., 1986). The starting point is to consider how differences between countries reflect societal coherences between micro- and macro-level and then to search for the mechanisms and elements of this coherence. From a societal effect perspective, there are no universal employment and wage-determination systems as these depend on the social construction of the actors and the space in which they act within a given societal arrangement. In this way, comparative analysis is an integral part of the theoretical framework and interpretative process. This comparative approach differs from the functionalist approach that assumes a universal theoretical scheme can explain each national configuration (e.g. the pure and perfect competitive market functioning); and from the cultural approach which, to simplify, explains differences by cultural trends. The objective is to analyse the way labour markets are instituted respectively in each country in order to constitute two contrasted societal employment systems. In this chapter, we present the main elements of comparison rather than a comprehensive analysis of each employment system:

- the formation of labour supply and demand;
- the regulation of the exchange;
- the determination of the wage.

The argument is that each of these core elements of employment systems are institutionalised differently in the two countries, and that together they demonstrate a radically different form of market, where the monetary expressions, what is being exchanged, and how the exchanges are organised co-vary and institute different market forms.

But in bringing this introduction to a close, it is worth stating some basic data relating to the two systems, to demonstrate the relevance of the comparison. According to basic macro-level indicators, France and the UK seem to be quite comparable countries. Their populations are approximately the same size as are their gross domestic products. It is well known however that labour markets have different performance in France and in the UK. Cyclical trends of employment are much stronger in the UK than in France. The two countries' unemployment figures are strongly contrasting (Table 10.1): after

Table 10.1 Activity, employment and unemployment evolution in France and the UK

	France				UK			
	1985	1990	1997	2000	1985	1990	1997	2000
Population aged 15–64	34825	35733	37125	37740	36706	37018	37571	38260
F	17736	18141	18829	19069	18372	18489	18672	18992
M	17088	17592	18295	18671	18333	15207	18897	19268
Activity rate	68.9	68.9	68.5	68.9	74.7	77.8	76.2	75.4
F	57.8	59.5	61.5	62.6	61.9	67.0	68.0	68.0
M	80.4	78.7	75.7	75.3	87.6	88.6	84.4	82.2
Employment rate	62.0	62.9	60.1	61.7	66.2	72.4	70.8	71.2
F	50.7	52.6	52.7	54.8	55.0	62.6	63.9	64.5
M	73.9	73.5	67.7	69.1	77.3	82.1	77.7	79.3
Unemployment rate	10.1	8.9	12.4	9.5	11.5	7.1	7.0	5.5
F	12.5	11.8	14.4	11.5	11.0	6.6	6.0	4.9
M	8.3	6.7	10.7	7.8	11.8	7.4	7.8	6.0
Long-term unemployment	46.8	44.8	39.6	–	48.1	35.5	38.6	–

Source: Eurostat, European Labour Force Survey (selected years).

Table 10.2 Determination of the share of GDP going to compensation of employees (average annual growth rate)

	75–82	82–91	91–98
France			
Share of GDP to compensation	−0.4	−1.2	−0.4
Compensation of employees	2.3	1.4	0.9
GDP	2.7	2.3	1.6
Real wage	1.9	1.1	0.9
Productivity	2.3	2.0	1.6
UK			
Share of GDP to compensation	−1.3	0.8	−1.6
Compensation of employees	0.4	3.7	1.0
GDP	1.5	2.6	2.5
Real wage	1.2	2.6	0.4
Productivity	2.2	1.6	1.9

Source: Husson (1998).

the recovery break by the end of the 1980s, unemployment grew continuously in France till 1997 whereas it decreased in the UK.

Another major difference concerns the share of GDP going to employees' compensation which has fallen continuously in France since the beginning of the 1980s (from 76 per cent to 67 per cent in 1998) whereas it has followed cyclical trends in the UK and at the end of the 1990s stands close to the level at the beginning of the 1980s (63 per cent) (Table 10.2). This situation seems paradoxical: the UK is said to have the most deregulated labour market in the European Union, and one could have expected wages share to have fallen in order to increase employment volume as predicted by traditional labour economics framework.

If one examines these trends, the main factor explaining this difference is the growth of real wage that was much higher during the 1980s in the UK than in France. Here again, the feature does not fit the mainstream account of labour market functioning and it even contradicts it, because wage moderation has been stronger in the country with a higher increase in unemployment. The issue raised by these paradoxes are addressed by looking at different processes of wage determination in the two countries, crucial to the understanding of labour market functioning. We now turn to the three core institutional aspects of market processes.

The formation of supply and demand of labour

Neo-classical labour market theory addresses the issue of the formation of labour supply and demand in terms of cost. To simplify, the level of labour supply depends on individual preferences between leisure and work under a budget constraint; and the level of labour demand depends on labour costs as inputs integrated in production functions. The explanation of labour allocation, how people are allocated to jobs and vice and versa, is limited to market process as it assumes that relations between individual and job characteristics are significant on their own, resulting from price determination in the labour market, i.e. the exchange between demand and supply either according to an efficient price or fair price.[2] Employment is a quantitative variable and an empty concept and labour mobility has no other meaning than being a labour market clearing mechanism.

However, empirical observations have shown that the allocation of labour within employment structure is marked by differentiation reflecting segmentation both on the supply and on the demand side. The question is therefore to understand how these segments are produced and maintained and how interactions between segmented groups of economic agents allow for a wide spectrum of employment forms and conditions and for different forms of segmentation between and within sectors and countries (Rubery, 1999).

Differentiation in labour supply

Labour supply is differentiated according to gender, age, class, family structure and ethnicity. Educational and training systems as well as welfare systems contribute to shape the labour force and condition the availability to work. Youth participation in employment is highly conditioned by the training system, and women's employment should be analysed with regard to welfare provision for childcare. The comparison between labour force evolution in France and in the UK illustrates some societal mechanisms of labour supply segmentation.

Firstly, youth unemployment has been a main feature of labour market functioning, a scientific as well as a social problem. Since the beginning of the 1980s, although France displayed higher rates of youth unemployment than the UK, one must be careful in comparing performance, as Table 10.3 shows. Indeed, youth unemployment rate in France in 1997 was twice as

Table 10.3 Youth labour force supply: 1997

Youth (age 15–24)	France	UK
Unemployment rate (% labour force)	29.2	14.2
Unemployment ratio (% pop. aged 15–24)	10.1	9.4
Participation in education		
15–19	92.9	70.6
20–24	43.9	24.3

Source: Eurostat, Labour Force Survey.

high as the youth unemployment rate in the UK. But the unemployment ratio, which expresses the number of youth employed to the total youth population, is quite similar in both countries; more or less one out of ten young people are unemployed at the same time. The explanation relies on different participation rates in education that entail a lower presence of young people on the labour market in France. Consequently, it appears that unemployment is not a worse social problem in France than in the UK, as the same proportion of young people is involved. Unemployment rates depend on youth participation in the labour market and labour market selectivity towards young labour force.

Secondly, different patterns of women's employment highlight the importance of social structures in explaining the formation of labour supply. Women's employment rate is higher in the UK than in France, and the figures for 1994 show a difference up to 8 points. But female employment has a very different profile in each country, more concentrated on part-time, and mainly short part-time in the UK. According to Jane Lewis (1992), such different patterns can be explained by historically constructed welfare regimes shaping women's forms of participation in the labour market. The British welfare state is characterised by a strong male breadwinner model with a firm dividing line between public and private responsibility. Women primarily get access to part-time jobs and the lack of childcare and maternity rights tend to restrict employment access for mothers. By contrast, France is characterised by a 'modified' male bread-winner model that allowed women to enter the labour market less strongly but with predominantly full-time employment. Table 10.4 illustrates this situation.

Finally, labour supply formation also depends on participation in economic activity. However, inactivity does not have the same meaning in each country as can be seen from Table 10.5. Inactivity rate is lower in the UK than in France, and this is mainly due to youth involvement in education and early-retirement schemes that are both more pronounced in France. But within the inactive population, people willing to work are much more numerous in the UK. Several explanations can be given. Unemployed people are discouraged from registering as unemployed as rules are

Table 10.4 Women's participation in France and the UK: 1994

Participation	France	UK
Employment rate	51.1	59.9
% mothers in employment	59.0	53.0
% women employees working part-time	28.3	43.8
% employed mothers as part-time employees	32.2	66.0
% female employees short part-time	8.3	23.7

Source: Rubery et al. 1998.

Table 10.5 Inactive population willing to work

	France		UK	
	Total inactive	Willing to work (%)	Total inactive	Willing to work (%)
16–24	4224	4.0	1893	30.7
25–44	2211	19.1	2781	37.9
45–59	2509	8.3	2461	26.4
60 and over	10999	0.4	10047	2.7
Total	19943	4.2	17182	14.9
(% aged 16)	(43.8)		(37.4)	

Source: LFS spring 1997, Enquête Emploi Mars 1997.

more strict and difficult to fulfil in the UK. This also explains the dramatic rise in the number of disabled people since the 1990s in the UK. Contrary to the unemployed claiming JSA which decreased by more than 1 million (from 2.117 million to 954,000), the number of people on sickness and disability benefits has continued to grow between 1995 to 2000 from 2.719 to 2.954 million (DSA, 2001). As a matter of fact, disability rate among people of working age is higher than the unemployment rate, respectively 8 and 3 per cent in November 2000.

Segmentation of labour demand

Labour demand is segmented according to employment structures which are determined by firms in relation with their productive organisation and institutional context. It has been shown that similar functions in similar industrial sectors may be organised in different ways in different countries. Typically, for manual workers in industries, institutional context has influenced the emergence of internal labour markets in France (ILM) and occupational labour markets (OLM) in the UK. According to Marsden, an OLM is:

> a labour market in which workers have access to jobs of a particular type in many firms, this access usually being based upon the recognised diploma or qualification, or on the recognition of the workers' peers', and an ILM 'may be said to exist for a particular position in an organisation when the employer regularly seeks to fill vacancies occurring in it from among its existing employees'. (Marsden, 1997, p. 415)

These two types of market organisation differ according to social structures that not only sustain but enable and explain specific ways of labour market functioning, notably training and educational systems, industrial relations, and skills and mobility recognition within productive organisations (see Table 10.6). These structures are the result of historical and

Table 10.6 Occupational labour market vs. internal labour market

	OLM	ILM
Labour mobility	Inter-firms, for same skill level, weak role of tenure	Intra-firms, for promotion, strong role of tenure
Skill transferability	Craft-based	Firm-based
Training	Normalised apprenticeship	Specific to a firm
Labour organisation	Craft or professional level	Firm or sectoral level
Collective bargaining	Centred on skill rules	Centred on firm rules
Youth integration	Regulated with specific status through apprenticeship	Selective entry on unskilled positions

societal features that interact and determine labour allocation and mobility. Originally developed by the school of 'societal effect' (Maurice et al., 1986), such an approach to the labour market as a social construction considers that relations between employees and employers are not solely determined by technology but they are part of the relation between work and society constructed by the educational system, the organizational relations domain and the industrial relation domain. Labour mobility is inscribed in a mobility system related to the interactions between these three dimensions. For instance, the value of diploma or degrees depends on how it affects an individual's level of entry and chance of moving up in professional hierarchy which usually results from collective bargaining agreements about skills recognition and transferability.

Considering labour market as an instituted economic exchange process is close to this general analytical framework articulating social dimensions that give rise to labour market outcomes. However, the ILM/OLM typology has been elaborated during the 1980s and concerned only a very particular segment of the labour market (industrial manual workers). One of the major changes in employment structure has been the decline of manufacturing organisations and the rise of service sector organisations. According to Rubery:

> The reshaping of labour markets arise out of changes in the nature and form of competition, changes in organisational forms and changes in the associated power relations between capital and labour; the independent role of competitive factors, organisational factors and industrial relations factors in shaping the new patterns of employment cannot be clearly identified because of the interrelationships between these developments. (Rubery, 1999, p. 2)

Research has identified patterns of 'flexible segmentation' in the service sector, including an internalisation of secondary market jobs such as part-time and fixed-term contracts, and an externalisation of high-skilled high-paid jobs through sub-contracting (Gadrey, 1991). It seems that such a fuzzy configuration corresponds indeed to the heterogeneity of service activities that provide both low-skilled jobs (e.g. waiters, guards, cleaners) and high-skilled jobs (e.g. finance, engineering, research, advertising).

Productive restructurations arguably entailed structural changes in labour market organisation but they are not the only drivers of changes, for transformations within educational systems and industrial relations also impact on labour market evolution. In this way, it is clear that in France ILMs have been destabilised through the increase of non-stable employment forms and the entry of highly educated young people at intermediate levels of occupation (Verdier, 1996). In the UK, the weakness of trade unions and the withdrawal of apprenticeship system through industrial decline both participated to the shrinking of OLMs (Ashton et al., 1990).

Youth employment in the two countries provides an interesting test case. Because they are new entrants in the labour markets, young people directly confront changing structures of employment and are over-represented in service sectors and precarious forms of employment in all European countries (Lefresne and Fondeur, 2000). But changing conditions of transition from school to work are also deeply influenced by other institutional settings. Integration used to be regulated according to the dominant organisation of labour market functioning (OLM versus ILM). But, as unemployment rose, governments have developed labour market policies targeted towards young entrants in the labour market and implemented during the 1980s in the UK and during the 1990s in France. Addressing the collapse of apprenticeships in the UK and stable employment shortage in France, these schemes have modified youth employment conditions and their competitive position within the labour force (Moncel, 1998).

These programmes could be considered as experiments in a massive shift to labour market policies acting on labour supply through positive discrimination. Indeed, other categories of the workforce are now implicated by similar kind of policies (long-term unemployed, lone parent, aged workers, etc.) that aim at promoting employability through training schemes and/or lowering labour cost through subsidies to employers or compulsory contribution exemption.[3] For this reconstructed labour force, firms save a part of the labour cost (more usually a part of the reproduction cost of labour: training, welfare and wage), which is supported by government intervention. Positive discrimination actions create distinction between groups of labour suppliers and therefore competition conditions with other labour supply are changed. Labour market policies and other public interventions also influence labour demand by acting on labour cost for specific skills or employment forms.

In France, the main important interventions are the partial exemptions of social contributions that concern employment paid up to 1.7 times the minimum wage and linked to the working time reduction law;[4] the development of employment-cum-training schemes: and aided-employment within the public sector.[5] In the UK, labour market activation experienced totally different kinds of public policies schemes: social policies act through fiscal policies which mainly include exemptions of national contributions for jobs under the low earnings level (2.5 million employees in 1998, EOC) and in-works benefits that complement low income and are now mainly tax credits (Working Family Tax Credit).[6]

In both cases, these measures tend to support the development of low-skilled, low-paid jobs mainly in the service sector. As a result, one can notice a double trend: there is an up-skilling process in terms of occupational structure,[7] and an increase in low-skilled and more precarious jobs.

To conclude this first section, societal characteristics of labour supply and demand formation show how essential it is to integrate extra-market institutions in the explanation of labour market functioning. This also could lead us to consider that there is no commensurability between what is exchanged on the French and the British labour markets. At least, statistical indicators must be interpreted with caution as they are related to realities with different meanings. The same could be said while considering the conditions of exchange.

The regulation of exchange

The regulation of labour market exchange is linked to the necessity to reduce uncertainty and to regulate the power relationship between supply and demand. It occurs through actors, rules and structures that are specific to each societal configuration.

On the demand side, employers determine the structure of employment and are in competition to recruit workers. The degree of competition depends on a firm's position in the productive system and on its skills requirement and employee retention. On the supply side, workers are in competition to get access to jobs according to their skills and individual characteristics. The relationship between demand and supply is based on mutual dependency and power. Indeed mutual dependency in capitalist societies is linked to the fact that labour reproduction depends on its purchase for use in production and capital reproduction and growth depend on the valorisation process through production. It also follows that the power relationship between labour and capital is asymmetrical. The question is therefore how these relationships are regulated in order to be stabilised.

Wage exchanges are shaped by institutional structures at several levels and according to different forms within sectors and countries. Comparing France and the UK, the most critical differences are evident in the complex area of industrial relations that underpin the wage exchange process. Organisations, functions and issues related to unionism provide historical backgrounds that differ dramatically between France and the UK, both countries appearing as a stereotype of industrial relations model, Anglo-Saxon versus Latin (Slomp, 2000).

Levels of collective bargaining

In the UK, the traditional system of so-called free collective bargaining (voluntarism) is centred on productive units. Until recently and even under the growing influence of employment laws due to the implementation of EU social regulation, one cannot talk about a uniform territorial system. Britain is still very different from the legislative French system of employment relations where collective agreements are usually signed at a national level, and at the firm level these agreements act as a minimum legally binding floor that permits no less favourable conditions.

British unions are predominantly circumscribed by their wage-bargaining role, and cannot be characterised as social partners in the continental European manner. They are present in relatively few national institutions where they usually hold only an advisory role. By contrast in France unions are deeply involved in wage regulation, especially through national bargaining about wage but also occupational and skill classification, working time, and participation and co-management of social security funds according to the 'equal representation' principle of social partnership.

The scope of collective bargaining

Collective bargaining around wage formation differs widely between the two countries. In France, it includes classification grids that define the wage-scale for each level of qualification. These scales are used to determine both the direct and indirect part of the wage. They apply to the national workforce as a whole because collective agreements are legally enforced on all firms, whether they take part in the collective bargaining or not. Qualification, as a politically decided attribute, is thus central to workers' social status.

In the UK, social security is mainly funded by general taxation: national insurance contributions are set by the government in annual national budget with no union negotiating input. Collective bargaining on wages deal with pay rates and fringe benefits and are usually at the firm level. The relationship between labour demand and supply is one more of direct power relations between workers and employers than in France where the state underwrites bargaining. Till the end of the 1970s, British unions were quite powerful and managed to establish collective bargaining for wages and conditions of employment in many sectors and regions. Two decades of Conservative government diminished this power, reducing union recognition and rights to strike, also excluding unions from participation in collective bodies (Wages Councils and Industrial Training Boards).

The contrast between the UK and France is well demonstrated by the role and function of the national minimum wage in the two countries. In the British employment system where the contract remains the main institution, the introduction of a minimum wage and the Employment Relations Act in 1999, constitute a recent and exclusively *governmental* innovation, in relation to which trades unions and employers at most acted as lobbying interests. In France, the minimum wage constitutes the basic starting point for the wage-scale hierarchy, and so is an integral part of the tripartite collective bargaining system. The level at which it is set is increased within this bargaining framework. In the UK, the National Minimum Wage is set below and outside any collectively bargained rates, and is a tool of social policy, part of a package of wider measures, such as the introduction of the Working Family Tax Credit and the reform of the National Insurance, aimed at improving incentives to work, support for low-paid families and thus making work pay (Low Pay Commission, 2000).

The contrast in the instituted wage exchange processes in France and the UK – *how* the price is determined, and *what* is purchased – could scarcely be sharper. Globally, there is in France a territorial homogeneity of wage determination underpinned by the state, whereas in the UK the system is more decentralised, regulated at site, establishment or professional level. The link between qualification and price is institutionally fixed in France, whereas contingent and variable in strength in the UK. For an employee in France, moving from one job to another, one place to another, one sector to another, one remains always within the same wage framework. For an employee in the UK, each shift may involve confronting a different – nonetheless instituted – wage determination situation, with only a state-instituted minimum wage floor.

Institutional differences of employment contract

Employment protection regulations differ widely between France and the UK, in ways that can only be briefly discussed here. It forms part of the comprehensive Labour Code in France whereas British labour law is traditionally characterised by a deliberate policy of abstentionism by the state and reliance on case law. But for the exchange process, one of the most significant differences lies in the nature of the employment contract.

Under French law, temporary employment and fixed-term contracts remain the exception to the rule that normal contract of employment is the contract for an indefinite period. Conclusion of fixed-term contracts is limited to certain circumstances (temporary increase in workload, replacement of an absent employee, work which is temporary by nature...) and such contracts are renewable only once. By contrast, in the UK there are no statutory restrictions on entering a fixed-term contract of employment; this type of contract being assimilated with employment contract for an indefinite period. The only differentiation arises with the increased employment rights acquired after two-year qualifying period (extended by the Conservative government in 1986).

Employment forms, working time and wage patterns: the impacts of labour exchange regulation

Forms and degrees of regulation arguably influence the form and the degree of differentiation of employment forms, working time and wage patterns, for they condition the exchange between employers and employees in terms of amount of labour and wages. Thus changes in regulation lead to changes in patterns of exchange.

In the UK, the decline of manufacturing accelerated in the 1980s led to a massive loss of male full-time jobs. The new jobs created, mostly in the service sector, were predominantly filled with women, very often part-timers. The political and economic processes of restructuring and the active encouragement of entrepreneurship led to a significant increase in self-employment. The spread of flexible forms of employment reduced protection of the workers. The remarkable proportion of workers not covered by social security entitlements is due to restrictive eligibility rules about length of service hours and continuous service.

Given the traditional regulation of employment relation in France, one of the most important developments to have occurred in the French labour market since the 1980s has been the increasing part of fixed-term contracts and temporary work (Table 10.7). Nevertheless, the main employment form is still the full-time open-ended contract, even if it has constantly declined. Another trend is the growth of part-time work in the early 1990s, whereas France seemed to be late in comparison with others Northern or West European countries. Indeed, since the mid-1980s, part-time work has contributed to employment growth more in France than in the UK (Hoang-Ngoc and Lefresne, 1994). Hence, comparing the two countries, one notices that flexibility is attained through different means and different temporalities. Part-time and self-employment are the main features of the British labour market flexibilisation whereas in France fixed-

Table 10.7 Non-standard employment forms in France and in the UK

	1991	1995	2000
Self-employment			
France	9.7	8.5	7.4
UK	13.0	13.4	11.8
Part-time			
France	12.3	15.8	16.9
UK	22.6	24.9	25.0
Fixed term contracts			
France	9.3	11.4	13.8
UK	5.0	6.3	6.2

Source: Eurostat, LFS.

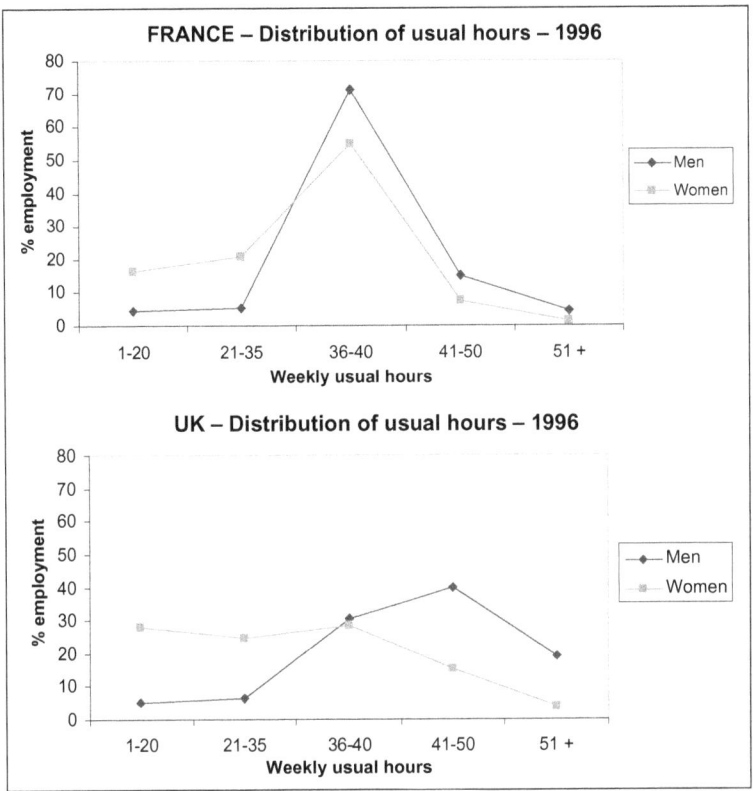

Figure 10.1 Working time patterns
Source: European Labour Force Survey, 1996.

term contracts and temporary jobs have been used to ease manpower management.

However, it is quite difficult to compare part-time development between two countries which present very contrasted working time patterns. Linked to the absence of working time regulation till recently, there is a much wider spread of hours worked by part-timers in the UK than in France (Figure 10.1). The same can be said for wage distribution, where the level of income inequalities is higher within the UK than in France. Here again, lack of regulation and deregulation policies since the 1980s, are expressed in a wide distribution of wages (Figure 10.2).

The market and non-market components of the wage

One of the key features of an IEP approach is that it treats the wage as an integrated institution, involving both commodity purchasing power of disposable income, and the social wage necessary for the broader sustain-

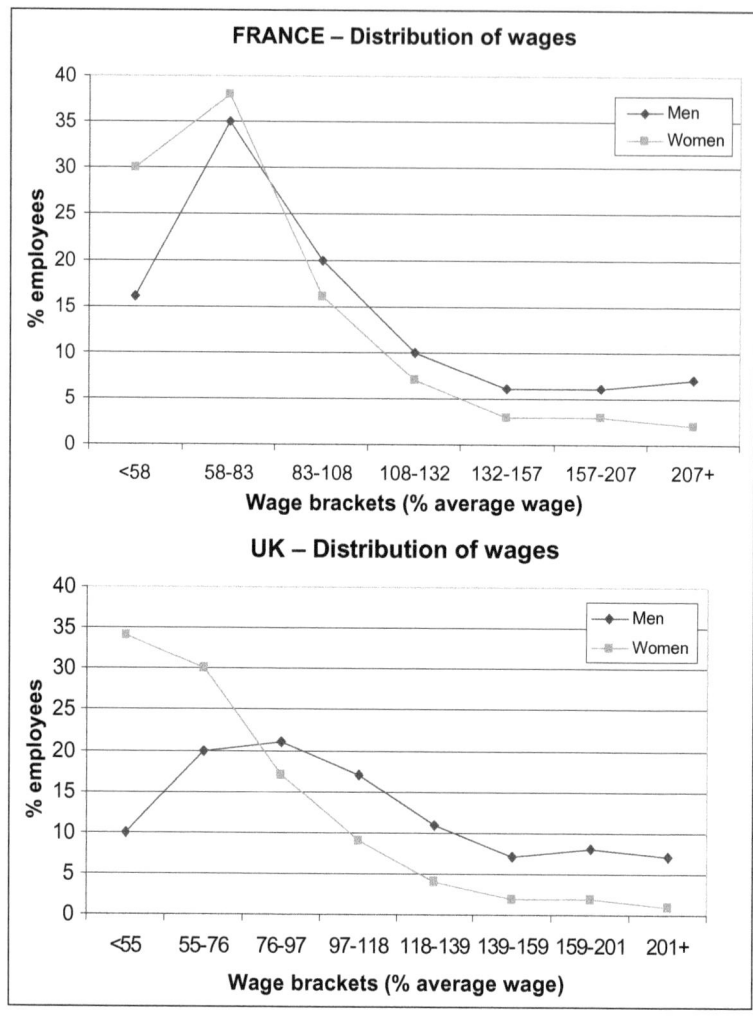

Figure 10.2 Wage distribution
Source: Eurostat, Structure of Earnings Survey.

ability of the labour force (Picchio, 1992). From a historical point of view, employment regulation includes an institutionalisation of resource flows for out-of-work time involving a 'de-commodification' of labour. This process involved political actors (state, unions and employers associations) and resulted in the implementation of welfare states. Social security schemes have been developed during the period of emergence of the wage relation linked to industrialisation. They therefore represent a twin counterpart of employment regulation. Indeed, the wage corresponds not only to the simple remuneration of a productive task, but defines a specific mode of integration into society, through social security provision. Far from being a price, the complex wage appears to be a bundle of rights defined by political institutions and actors of wage relations (Friot, 1998). As Deakin notes:

> The 'contractualisation' of the employment relationship was associated with the gradual spread of social legislation in the fields of workmen's compensation, social insurance and employment protection... Contractualisation had two central aspects: the placing of limits on the employer's legal powers of command... and the use of employment relationship as a vehicle for channelling and redistributing social and economic risks, through the imposition on employers of obligations of revenue collection, and compensation for interruptions to earnings. (Deakin, 2000, p. 4)

Titmuss was the first to underline the constitutive relation between social protection and employment relationships in his essay about the social division of welfare in the UK. He showed that there were different systems of welfare that operate in different social spheres to meet similar needs. 'Social' welfare is identified to publicly provided funds and services (Social Security, local authority housing, the National Health Service, and the personal social services for instance). 'Fiscal' welfare consists of allowances and reliefs from tax which 'through providing similar benefits and expressing a similar social purpose in the recognition of dependant needs, are not, however, treated as social service expenditure. The first is a cash transaction; the second an accounting convenience' (Titmuss, 1958, p. 44). The third system of welfare is 'occupational' welfare that includes a whole range of welfare services provided by particular employers, and can be assimilated to fringe benefits. Discussing the growth of these three different systems of welfare, Titmuss observed that the division of welfare derives not from any differences in intended function or aim but 'from an organisational division of method, which, in the main, is related to the division of labour in complex, individuated societies' (Titmuss, 1958, p. 42).

This division of welfare takes a specific form in each country and globally two dominant logics of resources socialisation oppose the continental model based on socialisation of resources through the wage and the British model based on socialisation primarily by taxation. Here we are concerned not so much with the different welfare systems as such (Esping-Anderson, 1990), but with how the two main logics of socialisation are linked to the degree of formalisation of employment relationship. In Great Britain, for reasons related to the tradition of collective laissez-faire in industrial relations, the normative force underlying the emergence of the contract of employment was a conception of social citizenship (Deakin, 2000). In France, the employment relationship is more regulated at a collective level, including the regulation of the socialised wage (direct wage and social contribution) through collective agreements on skills and social partners involvement in social security funds management. Rights and obligations are largely defined through collective negotiations and the 'equal partnership' principle between employers and employees. This social construction of employment relies on the model of an abstract collective worker (Friot, 1998).

The difference in the way a part of wages is socialised is of critical importance when considering how the labour market is instituted. Indeed, it reflects the degree and the involvement of social actors in the regulation of exchange. It also indicates how the modern wage relation has integrated the question of the total reproduction of labour through resources that flow through the wage and sustain social security. The post-war decades appear to constitute a period of stabilisation of the modern wage relation, which emerged in the nineteenth century, and can be identified with the male breadwinner model. The end of the twentieth century has seen the destabilisation of this relationship in advanced countries as a result of economic change (decline of industry and extension of service sectors, technological innovation, increasing global competition, employment flexibilisation, etc.). The crisis of unemployment now seems to be a wider problem that involves political choices in terms of distribution and redistribution.

Indeed current transformations in social security schemes are explicitly related to employment issues in France as in Great Britain (Figure 10.3). Social contributions represent a smaller part of the social security funding in the UK (one-third) than in France where they contribute up to two-thirds of the financing of social security in 1998. This part has steadily declined during the 1990s due to policies aiming to reduce labour cost in order to promote employment growth. In the same period, government contributions have doubled and now represent one-third of the total funding. There is not such development in the UK concerning the global structure of social security financing. But the role of social assistance has dramatically increased up to more than one-third of social security expenditures as a consequence of tightened entitlements to social contributory benefits. At the same time, a broad fiscal restructuring is taking place through a switch from direct to indirect taxation and a shift from public to private reproduction system (private pensions, private medical provision, and private financing of higher education).

Both systems have undergone deep changes since the 1980s but following ways reflecting the different societal configurations of the links between work and welfare. And these transformations interact with the employment system functioning. In the UK, fiscal reforms tended to enhance women's and low-pay, part-time work, and privatisation of many public services destabilised employment forms in these sectors (Rubery, 1999). In France, reforms in welfare financing relied on targeted reductions or exemptions of social contributions and employment subsidies, which entailed a diversification of employment forms from the point of view of the nature of

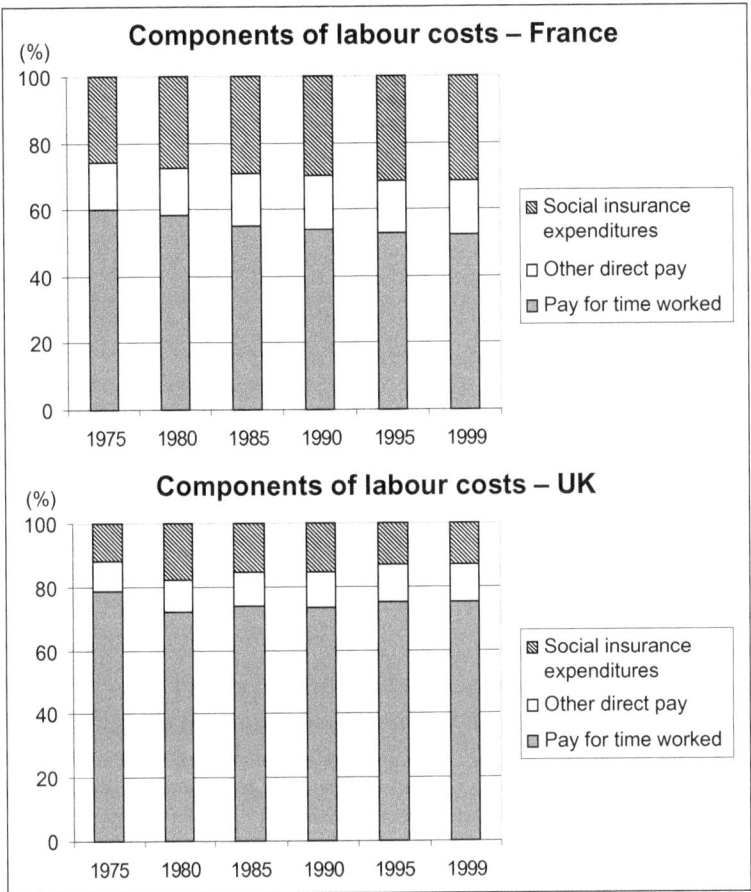

Figure 10.3 Labour cost components
Source: US Department of Labor.

resource. Indeed, several reforms have contributed to enhance labour market flexibility and they also have transformed the source of financing of workers' resources: a part of the direct labour costs or the employers' social contributions have been reduced and replaced by taxation financing employment or social security.

An 'instituted employment system'

To conclude, we have sketched an analytical framework in terms of 'instituted employment system' in order to distinguish, identify and represent the organised set of structures, agents and mechanisms that contribute to the use and circulation of labour force linked to the process of

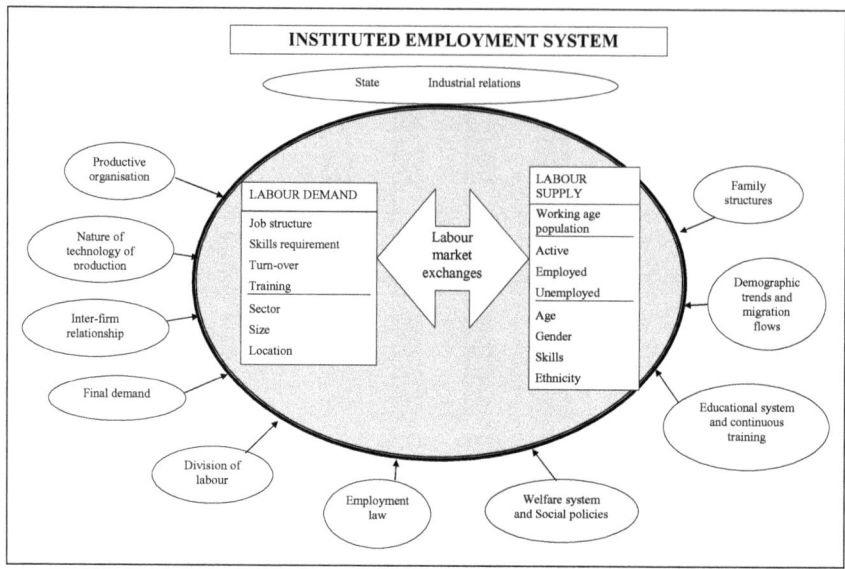

Figure 10.4 The instituted employment system

reproduction of labour (Figure 10.4). More precisely, the employment system articulates demand and supply of labour, which are both structured and interact through a set of relationships based on resource and labour flows. Labour demand has a dominant role on labour supply through the control of the division of labour and the management of labour uses. The dynamic of the employment system is created by interactions between sub-structures conditioning, on the one hand, the labour demand and related to production (organisation of the productive process, division of labour, skills requirement, industrial relations, sectoral patterns of production, final demand for products), and, on the other hand, the labour supply the formation of which is related to the reproduction sphere (educational and training system, family structures, welfare provisions) external to market process.

The employment system incorporating labour markets is institutionally structured rather than an individual behavioural phenomenon. These institutions condition the behaviour of economic agents because their temporality is both more extended and broader in scope than any one of the agents. This does not preclude that economic agents act according a relative independence toward the structures and contribute to modify them. Moreover, this approach assumes that the dominant relationships occur between *classes* of economic agents, i.e. between workers and employers, rather than simple aggregates of the individuals within them. The question is therefore to characterise the relationship between these classes of economic agents and also the role of non-economic agents (public intervention, laws etc.). Thus, an IEP approach goes beyond the separation between micro and macro levels and aims to understand the articulation between different scales of institution.

This analytical framework seems fruitful for refreshing traditional issues of labour market functioning. For instance the question of labour market equilibrium that underlies debates about unemployment is shifted towards a consideration of the institutional conditions that assure employment system sustainability and adaptability. The analysis highlights those mechanisms and dynamics that create conditions for labour supply and demand formation as well as exchange regulation. In a broader perspective, issues about wage determination embrace not only disposal income and purchasing power, but also those resource flows that sustain social rights in most of the European welfare regimes. Major debates from political economy are reintroduced within labour market analysis. Finally, the traditional question of convergence versus specific trends between countries can be addressed in a richer way than through benchmarking listings and indicators. In the case of France and the UK, one can observe a double trend.

- There is obviously a convergent trend towards a model of decentralised bargaining and flexible wage determination process, and an increasing public intervention towards fiscal support for employment:
- However, specific and contrasting institutional features are still strong for employment patterns (especially of young people and women), and industrial relations systems.

Rather than a convergence, one can suggest that these are path-dependent evolutionary trends, constrained by political macro-economic choices within the dynamic of the European integration. This arguably entails structural destabilisation of employment systems and the emergence of new segmentation processes. The changing nature of workers' wage resources, market and non-market, constitutes one of the major aspects of labour force segmentation articulated with the traditional ones.

Notes

1 According to Solow's (1990) book title.
2 The Job Matching theory tries to evaluate the conditions of a good match. It is one of the most refined versions of rational economic calculation on the labour market as it supposes that the worker decides to take and stay in a job or not knowing the possibility of wage increase, his reservation wage, the wage distribution of available jobs, and the probability to get another job.
3 Such policies are put on the fore by the European Employment strategy established since the 1990s (Luxembourg Summit, 1997) and that aims to promote employment growth by improving employability, entrepreneurship, adaptability and equal opportunities.
4 Contribution exemption induces a labour cost reduction up to 12 per cent of the total labour cost and the receipt loss for social security is supposed to be

compensated through tax transfer. This measure concerns 70 per cent of employees in private sector.
5 Roughly 2 million active people have been in employment schemes per year since the 1990s (Barbier, 2001).
6 In 2000, just under 5.0 million people of working age were claiming a key benefit, 14 per cent of working-age population (DSS, 2001).
7 Concerning skills however, the measurement is all than simple through statistical categories as one can see through the current process of renewal of the socio-occupational classification in each country. This aims to introduce IT linked professions and to appreciate differences in skills levels and requirements in the group of clerical occupations and personal services.

References

Ashton, D., Maguire, M. and Spilsbury, M. (1990), *Restructuring the Labour Market: The Implications for Youth*, Cambridge Studies in Sociology, Macmillan.
Atzmuller, R. (1999), 'The Labour Market and Employment in the UK', in M. Harvey and R. Atzmuller (eds), *On Labour Markets, Social Security and the Pension System in the UK*, UK Report for the TSER Network 'La construction sociale de l'emploi', Barcelona, 21–3 October.
Barbier, J. C. (2001), *Welfare to Work Policies in Europe: The Current Challenges of Activation Policies*, Centre d'Etudes de l'Emploi, Document de travail, no. 11, November.
Deakin, S. (2000), 'The Many Futures of the Contract of Employment', paper prepared for INTELL 5, Faculty of Law, University of Toronto, 22–4 September.
Department of Social Security (2001), *Client Group Analysis: Quarterly Bulletin on the Population of Working Age on Key Benefits – November 2000*, National Statistics, First Release, Analytical Service Division.
Equal Opportunities Commission (1998), *Low Pay and National Insurance System: A Statistical Picture*, EOC Research Findings.
Esping-Anderson, G. (1990), *The Three Worlds of Welfare Capitalism*, Cambridge, Polity.
Evans, Martin (1998), 'Social Security: Dismantling the Pyramids?', in H. Glennerster and J. Hills (eds), *The State of Welfare: The Economics of Social Spending*, 2nd edn, Oxford and New York, Oxford University Press.
Friot, B. (1998), *Puissance du salariat: Emploi et protection sociale à la française*, Paris, La Dispute.
Gadrey, J. (1991), 'Les systèmes d'emploi tertiaires: de la segmentation flexible aux approches typologiques', in J. Gadrey and N. Gadrey (eds), *La gestion des ressources humaines dans les services et le commerce*, Paris, L'Harmattan.
Hoang-Ngoc, L. and Lefresne, F. (1994), 'Les règles d'utilisation du temps partiel dans les régimes d'accumulation français et britannique', *Revue de l'IRES*, 14, pp. 145–72.
Husson, M. (1998), 'Convergence des modèles de régulation?', *Revue de l'IRES*, 28, autumn, pp. 63–82.
IRES (2000), *Les marchés du travail en Europe*, Paris, La Découverte, Collection Repères.
Leclercq, E. (1999), *Les théories du marché du travail*, Paris, Editions du Seuil.

Lefresne, F. and Fondeur, Y. (2000), 'Les jeunes, vecteurs des transformations des normes d'emploi?', *Travail et Emploi*, 38.
Lewis, J. (1992), 'Gender and the Development of Welfare Regimes', *Journal of European Social Policy*, 2 (3), pp. 159–73.
Low Pay Commission (2000), *The National Minimum Wage: The Story So Far*, Second Report, HM, February.
Marlier, E. and Ponthieux, S. (2000), 'Low-wage Employees in the EU Countries', *Statistics in Focus*, theme 3–11/2000, Brussels, Eurostat.
Marsden, D. (1997), 'Institutions and Labour Mobility: Occupational and Internal Labour Markets in Britain, France, Italy and West Germany', in R. Brunetta and C. Dell'Aringa (eds), *Labour Relations and Economic Performance*, London, Macmillan.
Maurice, M., Sellier, F. and Silvestre, J. (1986), *The Social Foundations of Industrial Power- A Comparison of France and Germany*, Cambridge, MIT Press.
Moncel, N. (1998), 'Analyse comparative de l'emploi des jeunes en France et en Grande-Bretagne', *Revue de l'IRES*, 28, autumn, pp. 121–43.
Perrot, A. (1992), *Les nouvelles théories du marché du travail*, Paris, La Decouverte.
Picchio, A. (1992), *Social Reproduction: The Political Economy of the Labour Market*, Cambridge, Cambridge University Press.
Polanyi, K. (1957), 'The Economy as Instituted Process', in K. Polanyi, C. M. Arensberg and H. W. Pearson (eds), *Trade and Market in the Early Empires*, New York, Free Press.
Rubery, J. (1999), 'The Shaping of Work and Working Time in the Service Sector', Communication at the *International Working Party of Labour Market Segmentation*, 21st Conference, Bremen, Germany, 9–11 September.
Rubery, J., Smith, M., Fagan, C. and Grimshaw, D. (1998), *Women and European Employment*, London, Routledge.
Slomp, H. (2000), *Les relations professionnelles en Europe*, Paris, Editions de l'atelier.
Solow, R. (1990), *The Labor Market as a Social Institution*, Cambridge, MA, Basil Blackwell.
Titmuss, R. M. (1958), *Essays on 'The Welfare State'*, London, Unwin University Books.
Verdier, E. (1996), 'L'insertion professionnelle des jeunes "à la française": vers un ajustement structurel?', *Travail et Emploi*, 69, la Documentation Française, pp. 37–54.

11

Telephone transactions: instituting new processes of exchange and distribution

Miriam Glucksmann

Polanyian perspectives on telephone transactions

Call centres have been one of the most rapidly expanding forms of business organisation and work in recent years for the sale and purchase of goods and services of all kinds, the transfer of information, and a plethora of other transactions between providers and users, sellers and buyers, and organisations and individuals. They represent a new and distinctive vehicle for the organisation of exchange.

This chapter aims to demonstrate the potential of a Polanyian-inflected approach towards the organisation of exchange for exploring the shifting place of call centres and their workforces in the wider processes of which they are part. A prime concern is with the institutedness of call centre operations and variation in the divisions of labour associated with them. Such a perspective yields rather different insights than one which considers them as self-standing institutions.

Call centres are primarily concerned with exchange and distribution, the two economic processes highlighted by Polanyi (Polanyi 1957, p. 248). Operating in a wide variety of contemporary industries and diverse markets, they frequently combine exchange and distribution in novel ways. Clearly Polanyi could not study twenty-first-century industrial forms. But neither did he explore in any depth differences between market institutions nor the relationship between exchange and distribution in market societies. My objective is as much to extend the scope of a Polanyian perspective as to highlight its continuing relevance to present day developments.

In doing so, however, it is not necessary to subscribe to Polanyi's assumption that movements of appropriation and of location constitute the only economic processes. Although firmly concentrated on exchange and distribution, I suggest that call centres forge the link between these and the processes of provision and production on the one hand and consumption on the other. In other words, they intermediate between and are to be understood as part of an integral overall process comprising production or provision, exchange, distribution and consumption. For such reasons too, although call centres could be described as 'embedded' in a wider organisational network, in the sense of being inseparable, this would not provide an adequate analytical means for demonstrating their diversity or the specificity of interrelationships. An instituted economic process paradigm (viz. Chapters 1 and 9 of this volume) may have greater potential for the analysis of telephone transactions, especially if it can treat production, distribution, exchange and consumption as comprising a mutually interdependent configuration.

The thrust of argument is to develop a relational conception of the call centre as one phase in an integral process of production or provision through to consumption, that relates upstream to production and distribution, and downstream to delivery and consumption. Since the configuration of an overall process is likely to vary according to the field or type of activity, it follows that call centres may be positioned differently in the diverse areas with which are associated. The intermediary function they perform, and significance of this role, may be quite different in different processes. Similar considerations apply to the workers and work done in call centres, which may also occupy a different place in a varying overall division of labour.

The chapter has five sections. The first briefly reviews dominant depictions of call centre employment and key findings from UK research. In the second, I elaborate the analytical framework for approaching the interconnectedness of call centre activity, building on recent writing in economic sociology and cultural economy. The central analysis occupies the following two sections. Five stylised 'call configurations' undertaking a variety of transaction processes are contrasted in the third in order to ground the arguments of institutedness, variation and shifting place. Consumers and changes in the work of buying and selling are brought to centre stage in the fourth. Here the example of telephone sales is used to focus on one part of the process, exploring how the call centre mode of organising exchange affects the sales interaction for both buyers and sellers. The final section highlights some distinctive temporal and spatial features of telephone transactions, suggesting that time and space are also instituted characteristics of call centres.

Portraying call centres

A wealth of empirical data detailing the internal workings of call centres, their managerial strategies and labour process, the gender, age and national profile of call workers and their conditions of employment have supplied material for heated debates concerning 'surveillance versus resistance', work degradation and the relevance of an electronic panopticon.

Since call centres first came to public prominence much commentary has portrayed them in a unitary manner, frequently invoking the spectre of the hi-tech factory where workers are subjected to electronic surveillance far more intrusive than any supervisor.[1] Visually, large numbers of operators are depicted sitting at workstations, facing a computer screen, fingers on keyboard, headset on their ears and talking into a mouthpiece. They look as if they all are doing exactly the same.

However, this generic appearance can be deceptive, obscuring variations in the types of exchange between operator and caller, and in the actual work undertaken. Attention focuses centrally on customer service representatives but telephone operating cannot be understood in isolation from other jobs with which it is linked. Script writing, software development, electronic file updating, packing and delivery are all tasks which complement those of telephone operator, down or upstream of the call, which presuppose or are presupposed by it.

It is now widely recognised that rather than there being a 'call centre industry', call centre operations are characteristic of a wide range of industries from retail banking and financial services, to health, public administration, transport and communication. In each field the 'old' telephone technology is articulated with new technologies integrating computer and telephone and customised to serve particular functions. Similar considerations apply also to those operating the technology: they conduct differing activities, enjoy varying degrees of knowledge, training, and discretion in dealing with clients/customers, thus contradicting the appearance of identical clones. Supplying train information differs from conducting remote medical consultations, and technical support for computing systems differs from selling theatre tickets.

Call centres have developed rapidly since the 1990s, extending from financial services and the utilities in the early 1990s to most parts of the private sector and increasing parts of the public sector. At the same time they have evolved from relatively simple call handling to cover the full spectrum of marketing, selling and serving. Operations may be in-house or outsourced to dedicated call centre firms to which business is sub-contracted. The UK has witnessed the growth in outsourcing specialists, who handle accounts for a number of companies ranging across industries and provide different services to customers in different sectors. 'In-sourcing', whereby a company commissions a specialist service provider to carry out its operations in-house, is also on the increase.

Numbers of those employed in actual call work are difficult to establish, the common problem of official occupational classifications being too aggregated, exacerbated by such rapid change that categories are often unable to keep pace with reality. The most widely accepted figure is around 440,000 full-time equivalents employed nationally (IDS, 2001, p. 14; Labour Force Survey, May 2005), with 581,000 agent positions (DTI, 2004), still qualifying the UK as the 'call centre capital of Europe' (Poynter, 2000, p. 151). Despite ever-increasing international outsourcing of call centre work from the UK since 2000, especially to India[2], employment growth within the UK remains buoyant and the UK is still a net exporter of IT and call centre services (Abramovsky et al., 2004; Heckley 2005, p. 378). It is also problematic to calculate shifts into call centres of jobs previously done in other ways and so answer the crucial question about the substitution of one type of work by another, rather than expansion of one category considered in isolation.[3]

The dominant profile of call operators in Britain is female and young. Around two-thirds are women (Industrial Relations Services, 2001; LFS, 2005), suggesting that employers recruit on account of presumed 'feminine' characteristics, primarily aptitude for communication and personal skills (Belt et al., 2002; Stanworth, 2000). While a similar gender balance obtains across Europe and North America, a quite different pattern is evident in India and other remote locations. Here men form the bulk of the workforce, implying that factors other than employers' gendered assumptions are also at stake (notably the cost of educated labour). The relative youth of call centre employees internationally is striking. Sixty-three per cent are under thirty in the UK (IDS 2001, p. 14) while many Indian centres stipulate that applicants must be under 25 (Payal and Das, 2002).[4]

Monitoring and surveillance are dominant themes in the literature on call centres, many writers viewing penetration of ICT into the customer interface, performance targets, scripting, subdivision and fragmentation of tasks, the minute monitoring of qualitative as well as quantitative criteria as evidence of new frontiers of managerial control in service work. But such methods are not uniformly applied, much depending on the market segment and customer relationship aimed for (Kinnie et al., 2000). Nor do they rule out resistance, whether union activity or informal sabotage (Bain and Taylor, 2000). Researchers highlight the emotional labour of call operating work, and tension between mechanistic repetition and the requirement to actively engage with the caller, project a 'smiling' persona, and manage feelings (Callaghan and Thompson, 2000; Taylor et al., 2002). The premium on vocal and locutional competencies and capacity to enact stylised conversations 'naturally' (Cameron, 2000) demonstrates not only the corporeal and aesthetic aspects at call operating work complementing the emotional, but also how organisations 'make-up' (Du Gay, 1996) the embodied dispositions of employees in a quest for markers of market differentiation.

Analytical framework: an instituted economic process framing of 'TSOL'

I want to propose a perspective towards call centres that can position them within the overall configuration of production/distribution/exchange/consumption of which they are part. The value of this would be to facilitate recognition of the variable geometry of a total process, where some stages may be combined or separated depending on the core activity and kind of intermediation undertaken. It would provide the possibility of recognising the plural and variable role of call centres in differing operations and their varying significance to the rest of process, in terms of both organisation and labour.

This may be achieved by tying an instituted economic process approach into a 'total social organisation labour' framework. The latter was developed to explore the nexus of interconnections between work of different kinds performed in differing socio-economic spaces, or linkages between different sorts of work and occupations undertaken at the different stages of a process of production considered in its entirety (Glucksmann, 1995, 2000a, 2000b, 2006). Previously I have deployed the TSOL to look at historically changing social divisions of labour within and between the commodity and non-commodity sectors of the economy. Here, that perspective is broadened from a focus on work and labour to a wider concern with the various parts or phases of the process in which that labour is conducted. By mapping out the parts and determining their interconnections, a more adequate explanatory framework can be provided, that throws into relief differing ways in which organisations of work are instituted.

In recent years a concern to outline contrasting configurations (e.g. Harvey et al., 2002) or research the linked stages of an integral process (e.g. Cockburn and Ormrod, 1993; Du Gay et al., 1997) has been steadily gaining ground in economic sociology and cultural economy, simultaneously with attempts to analyse the social and cultural in the economic and vice versa (e.g. Lash and Urry, 1994; Ray and Sayer, 1999; Du Gay and Pryke 2002), often as part of a project to overcome conceptual boundaries between the study of consumption and production, for example by thinking in terms of 'systems of provision' (e.g. Fine et al., 1996; Warde and Martens, 2000).

The framework being developed here benefits from these initiatives, and in particular the instituted economic process paradigm elaborated elsewhere in this volume. Developing beyond its Polanyian inspiration, the approach developed by Harvey and colleagues (Harvey et al., 2001; Harvey and Randles, 2002) considers production, distribution, exchange and consumption as a relational complex of four distinct but mutually dependent and interrelated processes. It focuses on each of these four along with the relations between them 'which are inherently a source of variation'(Harvey et al., 2001, p. 59), how they are instituted, and how relations between them become stabilised so as to form distinctive configurations enduring over a given space and time.

The advantage of applying a framework like this to the various domains of telephone transactions is to draw attention away from the call centre as an autonomous unit (though it may be just that in the case of outsourced call centre providers) and towards links between the call and other stages in the configuration, an analysis that could not be accomplished by a labour process approach alone. In terms of labour, attention draws away from call operators as a homogeneous or self-contained group, and towards variability in call operating and all other jobs presupposed by the call, that is, linkages between call operating and its surrounding occupational tasks, which may well also include those of the consumer.

The *processual* perspective brings into sharp focus that call centres are instituted as part of a larger process which shapes and is shaped by the particular sector they inhabit and functions they undertake. It also highlights the significance of time, and provisional nature of particular instituted modes of process. As call centres have been subject to frequent and rapid change, their manner of institution is not permanent but also changes over time. This aspect is particularly evident with respect to jobs: while the expansion of call centres is instrumental in the disappearance or decline of some occupations, it is also associated with the growth of others and with the emergence of entirely new ones. For instance, the demands of transport logistics, script writing and database management are new or of enhanced significance. Gradually these become consolidated into new occupations, contributing to reshaping of the division of labour.

The *relational* emphasis of this approach foregrounds interconnections linking call operators and call centres to others. While sectoral variations in business/activity will shape the precise nature of functions and organisational interconnections, call centres all interdepend with other sites in a more or less complex network. As in other frontline service work, operators are located in a relational web encompassing both the business and client, and a range of other workers. Even if they are not in direct contact, their work presupposes that of the others in the overall process of provision. Relationality acknowledges both the configurational variety of call centres and the variability of their place and function in the whole.

The division of labour comprises a third comparative dimension, relevant at different levels and scales of analysis, from the individual workplace, through the business or organisation, to the wider level of the industry and sector. In the first it concerns jobs, occupational structure and hierarchy, and how such divisions mesh with those of gender, age and ethnicity. The transformation of tasks, including those of the consumer, has effects for the division of labour. At the level of overall process, there will be divisions of labour between call operating and all the work undertaken up or downstream of the centre. Comparison of industrial sectors can reveal differing shapes of divisions of labour and variations in the place of call centres within them. Further complexity enters the picture if operations are outsourced to free-standing organisations independent of the main producer/provider, especially when these are located in distant parts of the world. In this scenario, industrial and organisational divisions of labour enmesh with global divisions of uneven development. Then, gender and age may intertwine with job allocation differently in India or the Philippines, unscrambling associations that reinforce each other in the metropolis.

An instituted economic process framing is thus intended to enhance the capacity of the 'total social organisation of labour' framework. Approached this way, neo-Polanyian perspectives add a new dimension to the analysis of call centres and other contemporary developments in work.

Call configurations

This section distinguishes diverse 'call configurations' in order to illustrate variation in instituted configurations of exchange and distribution, draw attention to how call centres transform established relations between the distribution and exchange of a good, and point to the emergence of new forms and phases of intermediation. Looking systematically at variations in exchange and distribution assists thinking about the place and significance of the centre, call and operator in different overall processes of provision-to-consumption. I am not presenting a typology, nor a comprehensive or fixed list, and the dimensions singled out for consideration are not the only possible ones. Presenting existing empirical configurations is, rather, a device for exploring different ways of instituting distribution and exchange, and the ramifications flowing from particular modes of institution.

Five configurations (there could be many more) are outlined on the basis of the kind of transaction undertaken: providing information to callers; connecting consumers to third parties; selling goods/products over the telephone; selling services; supplying emergency services and helplines. In practice these activities overlap and call centres may undertake more than one. Distribution and exchange transactions vary along a number of dimensions: they may be combined or separated; free or traded; the call may be intermediary or not; the operation may be complementary or stand-alone; the centre may be in-house or outsourced; the service may be in the public or private sector. In addition to these 'supply side' considerations, the organisational shape and practical activity of call centres are also generated by differences in demand by end-users as well as skills and activities of consumers (to be considered in the next section).

Each case contrasts the call centre with the previous mode of transaction and maps its place in the overall configuration and the operator in the wider occupational structure. The oversimplified accompanying diagrams are intended to indicate the diversity of 'shapes' of configuration. Each takes the caller – operator dyad (Figure 11.1) as its starting point.

Providing information to callers

This grouping includes directory enquiries, train timetable, NHS Direct, cinema programmes, local authorities and other information providers. Some interact more with callers than others but none involves the operator in putting the caller in contact with a third party (Figure 11.2). In this sense the encounter is both direct and not intermediary. The grouping is

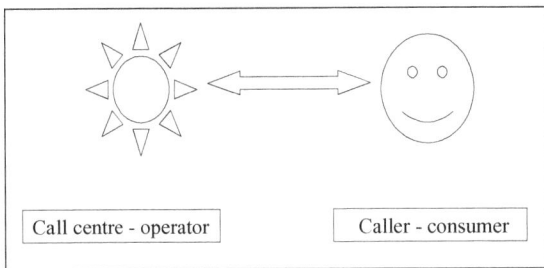

Figure 11.1 The caller-operator dyad

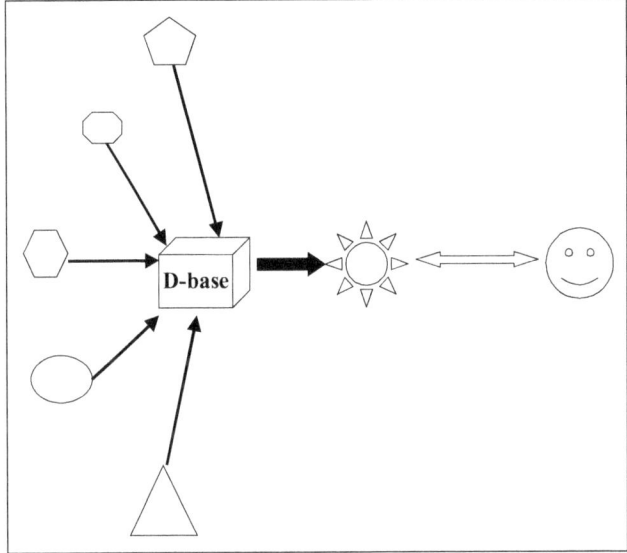

Figure 11.2 Providing information to callers

characteristic of both private and public sectors. Since the information is supplied free to the caller, the prime function is distribution rather than exchange, a new mode of delivering services to recipients.

This is the most independently self-standing transaction of the five, and least transformed from its previous mode of operation. In many cases, telephones had been in use for decades. The shift from switchboard to call centre primarily implies an extension of the scale of operation, the speed and automation of call handling, and frequently geographical concentration into a small number of large centres from a large number of smaller locally dispersed exchanges, sometimes combined with outsourcing to remote locations. NHS Direct, however, represents a new type of service, deploying new technologies for rapid response to medical queries.

The call represents the end-point of the operation, and the operator is the sole point of contact between caller and organisation. All other stages in the information 'supply chain' occur prior to the call, the operation presupposing extensive pre-compiling and coding of information. This implies the key role of information coders, inputters, and script writers in the overall occupational structure, complementing frontline operators. Operators' level of skill and training, and realm of discretion reflect the type of information handled, and the extent to which they are expected to interpret questions and interact with the caller. Rail enquiry and NHS Direct operators would be at opposite ends of a continuum here, the majority of the latter being trained nurses, appointed on the basis of pre-entry qualifications, while the former, recently outsourced to India, undergo limited on-the-job training.

The case of NHS Direct is instructive indeed. A new distribution service, it demonstrates the innovative potential of call centres to disseminate medical advice in a completely novel way. By providing a service additional to those already in existence, it is also instrumental in creating an expanding public economy of information of this kind, as evidenced by exponential growth in its use.

Connecting consumers to third parties

This comprises a wide range of services (car breakdown, telephone repair, water leak, gas service) organised through a call centre for an agent to attend a particular destination. The operator intermediates between customer and service agents, and may be linked to a roving or on-call workforce of technicians or engineers.

Here the shift to call centre operations may consolidate into a single encounter several phases of the earlier mode of working, which would typically have involved return calls or letters, and time delays. Now the operator directly accesses the work sheet of another section of the workforce, making an appointment while the caller is on the line, thereby also speeding up response time and providing a simpler and smoother process of coordination. The operator may undertake some work previously undertaken by clerical workers. Call centre and operator are positioned at a nodal point at the centre of a network connecting them both with the caller and with service engineers, and their prime role is to intermediate between the two parties, rather than make a sale, or impart information. Unlike the first case, the call is neither an end in itself nor the end-point of the operation. Rather, it represents the point of access for the caller and for the organisation to initiate and action the request. Operators' work involves switching between multiple databases relating to callers, service agents, prices and so on, and a (limited) familiarity with the nature of the business (e.g. can you smell gas?). However, call handling comprises only one of many occupations required for the accomplishment of the whole operation, and is not self-standing. Without engineers there would be no call operators.

The contrast between call centre and a roving workforce which are so integrally linked in the operational network is instructive, the same technology facilitating very diverse developments in the spatial organisation of work. While operators become increasingly concentrated in large fixed units, the trend for engineers is the diametric opposite, to become 'independently located' (Felstead et al., 2005), working on their own from home and van, and relying on phone and modem contact with the call centre to tell them about their work schedule, and supply parts. As depots have disappeared, and engineers rarely see each other, the analogy of node and spokes becomes an increasingly apt characterisation of call operators' and engineers' relationships between themselves and to each other.

The main activity of this grouping is co-ordination and intermediation, involving distribution of parts, assistance, and personal details and information travelling in both directions between callers and operators and along numerous routes between operators and the agents and sources they call up (Figure 11.3). However, although its primary function is distribution, this service is not normally free (with the exception of gas leaks and other public dangers) but predicated on callers' prior purchase of membership or a contract conferring entitlement. Differentiation of exchange from distribution facilitates their allocation to different parts of the business organisation, or the selling off or outsourcing of one, other or even both to an independent transacting service. When this happens the demand for distribution or transaction services is strengthened, consolidating the creation of intermediate markets.

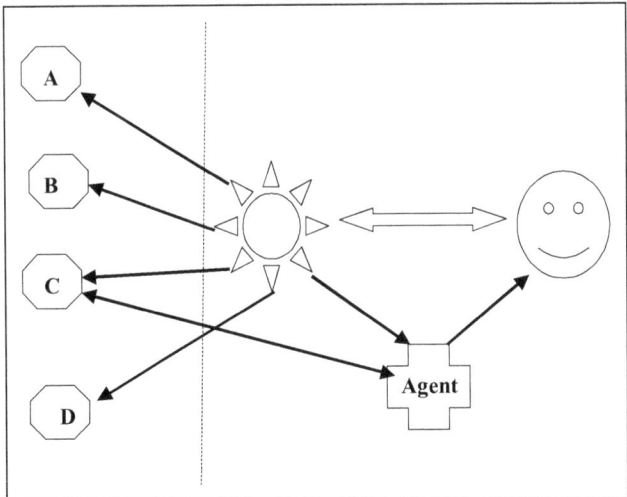

Figure 11.3 Connecting consumers to third parties

Selling goods and products

This kind of transaction, in contrast to the first two, combines exchange with distribution. The goods could be anything from washing machines to computers, books, household goods and clothing. The call effects the final exchange of buying/selling, and initiates the process of delivery to the consumer. But it also presupposes the prior distribution of products from sites of manufacture to warehouses. The call centre is linked downstream to production, advertising and marketing, and warehousing, and upstream to delivery and the final customer (Figure 11.4).

The centre is positioned more straightforwardly than in the previous cases in a sequence of linked stages connecting production to consumption. It is dedicated to making the sale, the work of the operators analogous to that of sales assistant in a shop, clinching the transaction. In companies which introduce telephone sales as an alternative to shops call operators are likely to replace shop workers, performing basically the same exchange function in an altered mode. The operator takes the order, answers queries about details of the product, makes the credit/debit card transaction, and forwards the order to the next link in the warehouse/delivery and billing chains.

In this mode of selling delivery becomes a responsibility of the seller: goods are transported to consumers rather than consumers coming to shops and taking home their purchases themselves. Exchange entails distribution, in that the selling of a good includes selling its delivery. When goods are bought by telephone, warehousing, packing and transport assume

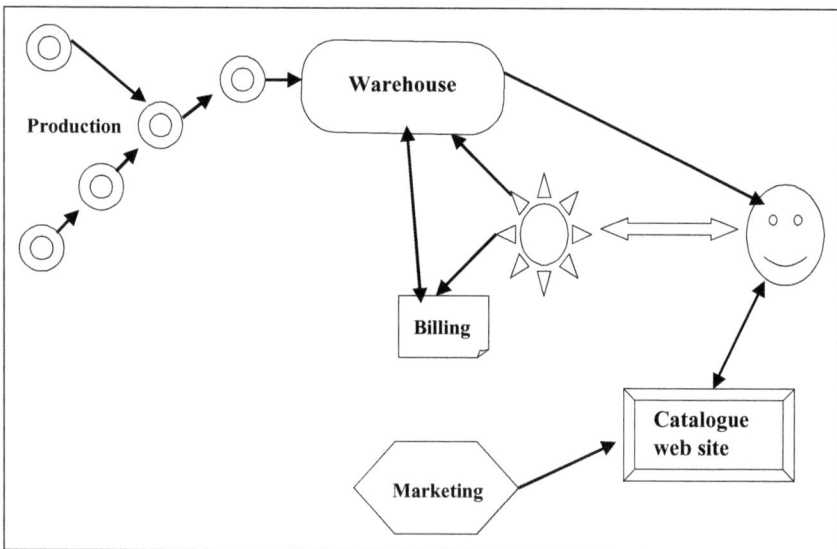

Figure 11.4 Selling of goods or products

increasing importance as essential components of the transaction, even if contracted out to the burgeoning delivery services sector. Alteration in the overall occupational structure is thus likely to accompany the growth of telephone sales, notably expansion of those engaged in warehousing, logistics and transport.

Store catalogues (paper and/or on-line) also become important as adjuncts to the exchange process since companies rely on customers being familiar with the range of stock. So the shift to telephone sales involves new modes of advertising and marketing goods, transforming the work of those engaged in such tasks and their significance in the division of labour.

The nature of the goods being sold will affect not only the detailed organisation of the whole operation but also levels of discretion and product knowledge of sales staff. The particular market segment targeted by companies will affect whether speed and volume of sales are prioritised against establishing customer loyalty. For example, clothing firms targeting the lower end of the market may place operators under time pressure (so many sales per hour) and undertake less training while the reverse obtains at the higher end: operators have greater discretion and time to discuss customers' questions if the aim is to establish loyalty and confidence in the firm.

The exchange transaction is always linked to the activities it follows and precedes, and so whether it is undertaken in-house (as implied here) or outsourced to an independent sales company, similar considerations apply to the contrast between telephone and 'real' shopping and the division of labour. Further implications for the 'call encounter' of telephone sales are discussed in the following section of the chapter.

Selling services
This comprises a large and diverse group including financial services, banking and insurance, the sale of airline and rail tickets, package holidays and car hire, and museum tickets. Like the last case, call centre operations are linked upstream to the production, marketing and advertising of the respective services and downstream to delivery and consumption, the density and length of such connections depending on whether the call operation is conducted in-house or outsourced to a separate transacting business.

Given the complexity of phases and stages of a 'service supply chain' the call centre might best be visualised as positioned variably within a network or along a set of interlinked chains. The work of the call operator is similar to that of the telephone salesperson of goods and products, and again the call centre is geared towards the final transaction between buyer and seller. Similar considerations apply to the need for adjunct product information, and to variations in target market and associated pressures on staff.

This class of business has been especially amenable to outsourcing, a considerable proportion of call operators being employed by stand-alone outsource firms rather than directly by the company whose services they are selling. This involves the removal of one side of their activities from the original service provider, in a process of disintermediation with consequent loss of employment, and the formation of a new self-standing business to whom the selling service is subcontracted. Call centres specialising in ticket sales are a good example of such new transacting services: museum X and theatre Y close down their in-house ticket sales and contract them to an outsourcer specialising in selling tickets for them and many others. The creation of call centre operations, whether in-house or outsourced, is frequently directly associated with a contraction of high-street outlets for banks, insurance companies and travel agencies with consequent job loss (viz. Beynon et al., 2002).

In addition to outsourcing, the selling of services has been also particularly amenable to remote location, perhaps because distributing them is simple compared with material goods, involving little more than letter post, reference numbers, or database adjustments. The outsourced company for a British firm may be in India or Ireland rather than the original employment in Leeds or London, or for a French firm in Morocco, or for an American in South Asia or the Caribbean (EMERGENCE, 2001; Huws et al., 2001). Indeed hardly a day goes by in the UK without reports of another business transferring call centre operations to India, to the dismay of trades unions. In Figure 11.5 the differing lengths of the two lines connecting caller and operator symbolise geographical distance.

Dedicated intermediary firms are particularly characteristic of this grouping, demonstrating again how the transfer to call centre operations stimulates the formation of a new market, in this instance for transaction rather than distribution. The shift of process thus institutes new phases and forms of intermediation.

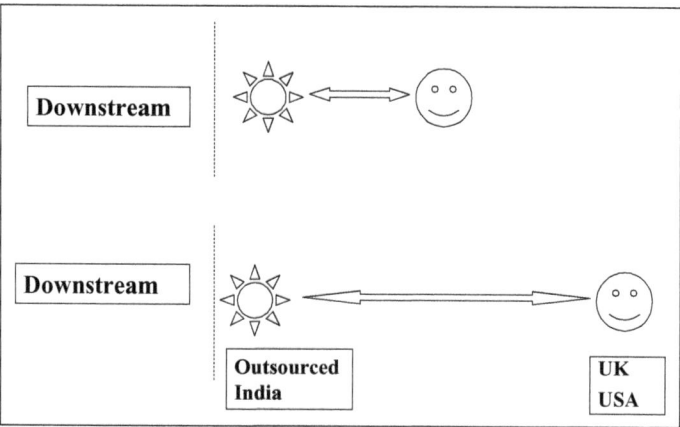

Figure 11.5 Selling services

Emergency services and helplines.

Like some information providers, and unlike sellers of products or services, emergency helplines are usually a public service provided free to the caller (Figure 11.6). They deal in non-traded transactions, unlinked to profit-making business activity (the internal market aside), and are funded by the state, charities or voluntary organisations. The entire operation is geared to a quite distinct aim than transactions discussed so far. Both centre and operators must comply with externally regulated standards and assume responsibilities which might be of a life and death nature. Prime examples in the UK are 999, Samaritans, or ChildLine. So although emergency operators undertake similar telephone answering work to other call centre workers, both centre and workers occupy a very different (non-) economic space. The centre is connected with third parties (ambulance, fire station, police, social and welfare services) to whom calls for action are passed. 999 centres are positioned to call on police, fire and ambulance services and in this respect intermediate between the caller and the service they require; other helplines act as contact points for social and legal services.

Since urgency and accountability distinguish such operations from a straightforward information provider it would be misleading to consider operators as fulfilling primarily a mediating role given the responsibility and decision-making devolved to them in responding to the call. This activity is also distinguished by high levels of confidentiality and specific training to respond to emergencies. In common with many other call centres, however, the trend is for large regional operations to replace local ones.

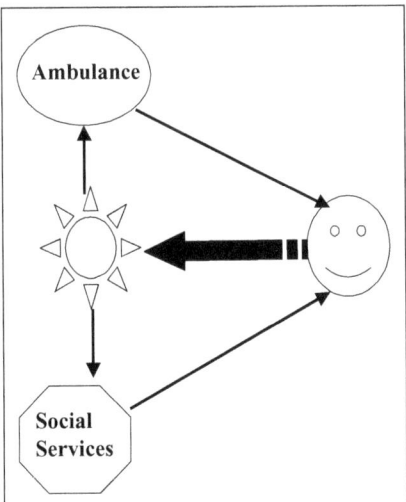

Figure 11.6 Emergency services and helplines

Instituting exchange and distribution

These five contrasting stylised cases demonstrate that call centres form a part, rather than the whole, of an organisational ensemble, accomplishing one stage in a complex series of interconnected activities. The configurations of 'provision-to-consumption' vary greatly. Diverse transactions are undertaken by call centres, and they occupy a shifting place within differing overall processes. This is not to deny commonalities across call centre operations or labour processes but rather to suggest that a focus on outward similarities masks significant differences.

Call centres specialise in the key Polanyian processes of exchange and distribution, but organise and institute these in diverse ways, which cannot be understood without also considering their connections to provision/production and consumption. Call centres establish new and diverse relationships between the distribution and exchange of goods and services, and create new markets for intermediary transaction services, notably for selling selling and for selling distribution. There is no unitary or homogeneous form of distribution or exchange. Moreover, the process of instituting new phases and forms of intermediation is ongoing rather than finished, as is their relation to the processes of production and consumption.

Polanyi's formulations were arguably undeveloped with respect to how movements of appropriation and location develop historically and how processes of market formation relate to each other. An implication of this discussion of call centres is to problematise such processes and add a stronger focus on relationality. If exchange and distribution and their interrelationship are variable and subject to change, as in the case of call centres, then they cannot be taken as given. By contrast, the concern with non-market instituted modes characteristic of neo-Polanyian instituted economic process approaches is particularly helpful for thinking about developments in the public or non-profit sectors, including NHS Direct and the emergency services. Exchange and distribution have been transformed also in non-market domains, and public equivalents of new markets established, involving new organisations of provision and linkage between providers and recipients.

'Call encounters': shopping and retailing by telephone

The consumer assumes prominence in this section which turns in greater detail to reconfiguration of the 'final exchange' between customer and seller through telephone sales. Exploration of the sales encounter has direct relevance to the analytical framework proposed here. From a TSOL perspective, the 'work'[5] of buyers and sellers connects differing socio-economic modes (market paid and non-market unpaid). Their engagement also links the processes of exchange and consumption, instituting in a distinctive manner this intersection of a wider economic process. In other words, the encounter can be viewed as a social organisation of labour occurring within an instituted economic process that comprises production/provision, distribution, exchange and consumption.

Brief as it may be, the encounter between operator and caller lies at the heart of call centre retail as the front-end of a multi-faceted technological-organisational complex which underpins it. The feasibility of telephone selling depends not only operators undertaking specific tasks but also on callers bringing particular competencies and knowledge to the transaction. Understanding what goes on between buyer and seller thus involves more than the dynamics of the call itself. But conversely, the call also crystallises many of the differences between the organisation of 'final exchange' in shops and by telephone.

Although distance shopping is not new, contemporary remote retail is far more than an updated equivalent of mail order. Some of the best-known old established British mail order companies like Freemans, Littlewoods and Grattan have switched from hard copy order forms and the post to call centre operations. These are now far outnumbered by other organisations which have established call centres for sales purposes, many of which would not previously have been thought of as 'retailers' in the conventional sense, such as the financial and other services of the fourth grouping above.

The history of shops and shopping (e.g. Jefferys, 1954; Davis 1965; Kingston, 1994; Humphery, 1998; Bowlby, 2000; Zukin, 2004) reveals how closely developments in the organisation of retail are accompanied by distinctive service relationships as well as new forms of packaging, display and advertising. Traditional grocers, department stores, high-street chains and supermarkets are distinguished from each other not just by store engineering and the different ways products are marketed and presented, but also by the nature of the interaction between sales worker and prospective customer. The 'work' of shopper and seller are mutually shaped, altering in relation to one another, and according to the particular exchange interface. If varying modes of exchange or types of selling presuppose acculturation of customers and the acquisition of appropriate skills, then restructuring of the 'shopper' role will be an integral element of the historical transformation of retail. So how is the 'work' of shopping and selling transformed with the shift from face-to-face to call centre remote retail? What new skills are required and how are the practices and experiences of shopper and sales staff altered?

Selling on the telephone
Although several stages of 'real' shopping are rolled together in telephone sales, other stages become differentiated. Distribution (of material goods) is dissociated from exchange, as outlined earlier, with warehouses and distribution centres complementing the telephone, whereas shops are sites for both distribution and exchange. In one scenario, customers normally undertake the transport of purchases; in the other, goods are stocked in

large facilities distant from the call centre, from where they are collected, packed and dispatched to the customer by post or delivery van. The different elements of work associated with sales are reconfigured and redistributed. Employment grows in stock control, warehousing, driving and haulage with the increased importance of logistics. But traditional sales assistants decline as their tasks are specific to a spatial environment that combines display with sales. In high street fashion chain stores, for example, this includes modelling the goods, acting as an embodied advert, as well as fetching and carrying clothes for customers to try on, answering questions, folding and tidying items after customers have handled them, unpacking deliveries and keeping the store clean, in addition to clinching the sale at the cash register (Pettinger, 2006). This range of tasks contrasts sharply with the more focused 'job description' of the telephone equivalent, the call operator working for a telephone clothing company. Here shelf filling is done by fork lift truck at the warehouse, the need for tidying is removed as there is no customer handling of the goods, advice and information to accompany the display are supplied primarily by catalogue. Arguably, only the till element of sales assistants' work is done by the operator.

Telephone selling thus involves a specific form of 'assisted' self-service where the work of finding out about products falls on the customer, and presentation and display are collapsed into verbal and pictorial descriptions. Compared with shop assistants, operators undertake minimal 'serving' activities, but concentrate on effecting the sale. Nevertheless, many companies emphasise and compete in terms of the quality of their customer 'service'. Even though they do not rely on physical manner, dress, style and bodily comportment to 'look the part', disembodied call operators must still 'sound the part'. Interactive service work of this kind may entail both emotional labour and conscious work on diction, tone, fluency and honing conversational and interpersonal skills in order to establish rapid rapport with callers and carry this through to the desired conclusion. Many call centres train operators extensively in how to use and vary their voice to produce particular feelings and influence the emotional ambience of a conversation (Callaghan and Thompson, 2000, p. 15). Aesthetic labour, in terms of locution, and the pressure to project charm, personality and enthusiasm combine with managerially imposed and electronically measured performance targets for speed and sales to produce a job with very different contours from that of the traditional shop assistant.

Like other service workers, call operators are involved in a triangular relation, facing two directions at the same time, towards their manager or employer and their customer/caller. Analysing the complexities of encounter between pre-war department store sales workers and their employer and customer, Susan Porter Benson (1988) highlights the continually shifting sets of alliances (two against one or each against the other). In her examples, the shop worker related face-to-face with both manager and customer on the shop floor, and was subject to personally imposed managerial control. Such relations would inform any analysis of 'class' relations of sales workers and their employers. By contrast, the call operator faces an 'impersonal' and spatially remote customer, while in close proximity to adjacently seated colleagues. Despite working under the supervision of a team leader or manager located close by, managerial control is effectively mediated and imposed by technological means. The specificity of this set of connections would be important to analysing the broader employment and 'class' relations of call centre work.

Call versus mall

Turning to the other side of the encounter, how do telephone transactions contrast with buying in a shop for the customer and what is required of them? It goes without saying that remote shopping presupposes access to a range of material resources, including the telephone network and finance by credit or debit account. For the shopper the focus on final exchange pares down remote retail to the acts of buying and parting with money. And in turn this presumes that the customer has already acquired product knowledge, prior to initiating the call. So, while telephone sellers work simultaneously with computer and telephone, customers also often consult a website or virtual catalogue for product information, the computer complementing the telephone for them as well.[6]

In malls or high streets similar product shops are often situated close together, enabling customers to browse displays in various shop windows and reduce 'search costs'. The location acts as a portal onto several possible shops which themselves benefit from being grouped in proximity and attracting customers who may not have decided in advance which brand or shop to patronise. All they need to have decided is the range of shops to look at.

Telephone shopping, by contrast, requires greater direction and deliberateness, much of the decision having been made in advance of the call. The customer takes the initiative, based on pre-existing familiarity with brand and company, and sufficient knowledge of the goods, models, designs, sizes, colours and so on, preferably with appropriate code numbers, to make a final choice. When products cannot be examined in reality, touched or tried on, consumers need to consult material catalogues or websites, gaining a new 'research' task in the process. Speed and fluency in answering questions and imparting information are further skills required by this mode of shopping which presumes decisiveness when confronted with choice.

The TSOL of remote retail

The call encounter represents the focal point of a new configuration where a distinctive mode of selling meets a distinctive mode of buying. Remote retail involves reconfiguration both of the transaction and the broader process of which it is a part. Operators concentrate on the work of final exchange, unlike the wider range of tasks normally undertaken by shop assistants, and they are positioned at a particular point in a rearticulated chain of interconnected stages. For both parties, the telephone dissociates and recombines elements of other modes of shopping, demanding skills, knowledge and work specific to this form.

The introduction of call centre selling shows how different modes of retail are accompanied by a different overall 'social organisation of labour' in which some jobs are created, or become more central, while others diminish in importance. As the links connecting production, distribution, exchange and consumption are transformed, so too is the work undertaken at the points of intersection. Appreciating how the re-organisation of final exchange by telephone sales pares down and fragments shop sales work relies on seeing this change in the context of many others occurring both upstream and downstream of the call.

Call time and places

Time and space are integral, frequently intertwined, dimensions of telephone transactions. Continuing with the example of remote retail, I now consider these briefly, suggesting that temporal and spatial dimensions of the transaction are also instituted, but differently for the parties concerned, and from earlier modes of selling and shopping.

Though calls are conducted in real time, the experience and significance of temporality for the employer differs from that of the operator or customer. For businesses, the global telephone network provides the possibility of 24/7 operations, and the cost advantages of adjusting shift size at more or less busy times. Firms may deploy remotely located labour routinely, at night or particularly busy times. Based thousands of miles away, Indian call centre workers undertake exactly the same work as their metropolitan counterparts but for a fraction of the wages, and because of the time difference, firms avoid the higher pay rates of unsocial working hours. This practice, pioneered in the late 1980s by offshore data processing companies operating in the Caribbean (Pearson, 1993; Freeman 2000) and emulated by US medical insurance companies for remote transcription of case notes in India and elsewhere (Sinclair-Jones, 2001), secures an obvious range of flexibilities for the firms concerned. The tendency for offshore labour to be more highly educated but paid less than their metropolitan counterparts has continued into the call centre era. Operators in Bangalore, for example, are frequently male graduates or masters in business administration, for whom call centre jobs represent long-term, high-status work that is well paid, relative to other local opportunities.[7]

For firms engaged in remote selling, it does not matter whether the operator is in the same town as the buyer or the other side of the globe, in Jamaica, Vietnam or India. Similar considerations apply to the connection between final exchange and other activities up and downstream of the call. Almost infinite variability in spatial location is possible, the only condition being that the goods or services can be physically delivered to the customer.

From the perspective of the shopper rather than business, time/space considerations are somewhat different. The caller, of course, has no way of knowing where operators are, especially as those overseas are trained to behave culturally as if they were local to the caller. Shopping by phone involves no special expedition, gives instant contact and saves travel time. It can be done wherever, at home, work, on the move with a mobile phone and whenever is convenient, spontaneously, and simultaneously with, or in the gaps between, other activities or tasks. Those with restricted mobility or access to transport can do it when they were otherwise unable to. By using the telephone, shoppers are able not only to 'save' time but also to 'shift' it, through enhanced control over the sequencing and scheduling of activities (viz. Warde, 1999; Southerton et al., 2002). Thus, instead of going into town or to a shopping centre and doing all the shopping in one go so as to avoid repeated journeys, it can be separated and done in no particular sequence, but as and when a suitable time slot arises (for example, TV adverts or while the meal is cooking or waiting at a bus stop).

For the customer, remote buying involves not just instantaneous time (Urry, 2000, p. 126) but also a form of de-materialised travel, 'placelessness' (*ibid.*, p.158) as it can be conducted from (almost) anywhere. This is especially so with mobile phones, whose proliferation transforms public spaces into sites for mobile communication (Mäenpää, 2001, p. 107) including shopping. At the risk of sounding like an advert, when the travelling is done by the telephone, time can be both saved and shifted as spatial location becomes insignificant.

However, although shoppers may not be constrained by space or time, the purchased goods and services often are. Dissociation of purchase between buyer and seller is often combined with a seemingly contradictory necessity for the buyer to be available at a fixed address and time to receive the goods. Limitless flexibility in making calls thus contrasts with the inflexibility of waiting for delivery, confounding Baumann's characterisation of the ideal consumer society where 'the consumer's satisfaction ought to be instant', by taking the 'waiting out of wanting and wanting out of waiting' (Baumann, 1998, p. 25).

Temporal and spatial flexibility in the exchange may thus conflict with rigid space/time requirements in distribution, when the customer, having already concluded the purchase, is less able to exercise leverage, especially if the delivery is outsourced and the line of responsibility unclear.

For operators, different aspects of temporality are again to the fore, with extreme monitoring of their speed, the same technology that delivers instantaneous global communication being deployed to minutely measure call handling time, down time, call waiting time in milli-fractions of a second (viz. Bain and Taylor, 2000). When linked with payments by results and sales targets, there is potential for tyranny by the clock far in excess of the most Taylorist factory regime. The levels of stress resulting from time pressure are widely recognised as a prime cause of the high turnover rate amongst call centre employees (e.g. IDS, 2001; TUC, 2001) and a central focus of resistance and trade union activity. However, evidence is also accumulating of employers' recognition of the drawbacks of obsessive speed, not only for staff recruitment but also, at the high value end of the market, for service quality and the resultant volume of sales.

Although geography might be 'history' for employers and to some extent for customers, the spatial circumstances of call operators, like the temporal, have far more traditional resonances. Theoretically centres could be established 'anywhere', but in fact the characteristics of local labour markets are prime considerations in location decisions. They tend to be concentrated in particular regions or towns with a ready supply of 'appropriate' labour (Huws et al., 2001). At some times this might be Glasgow or Leeds, and at others Manila or Delhi, prompting concern at the long-term 'threat' of offshoring to metropolitan jobs.

Within call centres, the spatial organisation of work is also far from revolutionary. Operators may be concentrated together in large numbers in quasi-factory conditions, likened in popular and some academic discourse to the 'dark satanic mills' of early industrialisation. Speaking with customers who may be thousands of miles away, they spend their working day immobile, physically attached to headset and computer, sitting in rows or circles with tens or hundreds of others. Restrictions on leaving their position, along with time pressure, figure high in the list of complaints (TUC, 2001).

Thus, despite erosion of earlier temporal and spatial barriers to selling and shopping, telephone retail displays features resembling earlier labour processes. John Urry has observed that '[c]apital's freedom from time and culture's escape from the clock are both decisively shaped by the new informational systems' (Urry, 2000, p. 126). Yet remote retail is not really typical of characterisations of either 'old' or 'new' economy. Telephone transactions do not de-couple buying and selling from the constraints of time and space, but rather re-articulate them through different temporalities and spatialities. When conducted by telephone, distinct patterns of instituted temporal and spatial co-ordination connect provision/production, distribution, exchange and consumption.

Conclusion

Telephone transactions create new forms of intermediation between provision/production, exchange, distribution and consumption, instituting these socio-economic processes in distinct ways and varying configurations. Despite superficial similarities, call centres and call-operating work are heterogeneous, engaged in different businesses, particular tasks and positioned variously, so that it is misleading to conceive of either generic call centres or work. New links are established between the phases and dimensions of an overall economic process, and between different socio-economic forms of labour.

I hope to have demonstrated the fruitfulness of a neo-Polanyian instituted economic process perspective for analysing this important contemporary development. When tied in with a 'total social organisation of labour' approach it provides a powerful means of understanding new interactions and separations between work and workers across socio-economic space. The only way of understanding transformations in the division of labour and 'TSOL' is through their articulation with transformations of instituted economic process in general, and in particular, as demonstrated in this chapter, of exchange and distribution. Changes in the nature of the work of exchange and of distribution are articulated with changes in the work of production, provision and consumption.

Notes

1 See Taylor and Bain (1999) for a critique of this view.
2 Upwards of 100,000 were employed in India in 2002 (BBC Radio 4, 15.7.02). See further discussion in the final section and note 7 below.
3 Case study evidence is the most helpful source. For example, the proportion of employees at Bankco, a major British clearing bank, working in call centres increased from 9 to 38 per cent between 1993 and 1998 (Beynon et al., 2002, pp. 45–6).
4 In contrast to call centres generally, part-time working predominates in telephone retail (to be explored later in the chapter). Large mail-order companies employ the bulk of their staff on contracts of 20 to 24 hours per week (IDS 2001, p. 33). This probably accentuates further the distinctive gender and age profile of UK call centres.
5 There is no space here to develop the argument for consumption 'work'. Nevertheless, self-service (in whatever form) clearly shifts tasks from paid occupations to end consumers.
6 Many organisations provide both internet and telephone facilities for purchasing their services and goods, sometimes offering discounts for using the internet rather than the more labour-costly telephone sales. E-commerce and telephone sales are therefore complementary and interconnected both for sellers and for buyers who increasingly confront a multiple choice or combination of shopping modalities between shops, telephone and web.
7 It would be easy, given considerable attention in the UK media, to overestimate the significance of Indian call centres and operators (currently 100,000 employed in India compared with over 400,000 in the UK (see note 2, and IDS, 2001). But a clear potential exists for massive extension not only of outsourcing (technical support for computers, preparation of legal documents and contracts, engineering and architectural drawing) but also of an increasingly complex international division of labour in call centre work, bolstered by the temporal and spatial advantages (Huws et al., 2001).

References

Abramovsky, L., Griffiths, R. and Sako, M. (2004), 'Offshoring of Business Services and Its Impact on the UK Economy', *Advanced Institute of Management Research (AIM) Briefing Note*, available at www.aimresearch.org/portnews/Articles/081104Offrpt.pdf.
Bain, P. and Taylor, P. (2000), 'Entrapped by the "Electronic Panopticon"? Worker Resistance in the Call Centre', *New Technology, Work and Employment*, 15(1), pp. 2–18.
Bauman, Z. (1998), *Work, Consumerism and the New Poor*, Buckingham, Open University Press.
BBC Radio 4 (2002), 'India Calling: How May I help You?', 15 July.
Belt, V., Richardson, R. and Webster, J. (2002), 'Women, Social Skill and Interactive Service Work in Telephone Call Centres', *New Technology, Work and Employment*, 17(1), pp. 20–34.
Benson, S. P. (1986), *Counter Cultures: Saleswomen, Managers, and Customers in American Department Stores 1890–1940*, Chicago, University of Illinois Press.
Beynon, H., Grimshaw, D., Rubery, J. and Ward, K. (2002), *Managing Employment Change*, Oxford, Oxford University Press.
Bowlby, R. (2000), *Carried Away: The Invention of Modern Shopping*, London, Faber and Faber.
Callaghan, G. and Thompson, P. (2000), 'Proceeding to the Paddling Pool: The Selection and Shaping of Call Centre Labour', *Open Discussion Papers in Economics*, 15, Buckingharm, Open University.
Cameron, D. (2000), *Good to Talk? Living and Working in a Communication Culture*, London, Sage.
Cockburn, C. and Ormrod, S. (1993), *Gender and Technology in the Making*, London, Sage.
Davis, D. (1965), *A History of Shopping*, London, Routledge & Kegan Paul.
DTI (2004), *The UK Contact Centre Industry: A Study*, report produced by CM Insight, ContactBabel and Call and Contact Centre Association for the Department of Trade and Industry, available at www.dti.gov.uk/ewt/contactind.pdf.
Du Gay, P. (1996), *Consumption and Identity at Work*, London, Sage.
Du Gay, P. and Pryke, M. (eds) (2002), *Cultural Economy: Cultural Analysis and Commercial Life*, London, Sage.
Du Gay, P., Hall, S., Janes, L., Mackay, H. and Negus, K. (1997), *Doing Cultural Studies: The Story of the Sony Walkman*, London, Sage/Open University Press.
EMERGENCE (Estimation and Mapping of Employment Relocation in a Global Economy in the New Communications Environment), Newletters, 2000.
Felstead, A., Jewson, N. and Walters, S. (2005), *Changing Places of Work*, London, Palgrave.
Fine, B., Heasman, M. and Wright, J. (1996), *Consumption in the Age of Affluence: The World of Food*, London, Routledge.
Freeman, C. (2000), *High Tech and High Heels in the Global Economy: Women, Work and Pink Collar Identities in the Caribbean*, Durham and London, Duke University Press.
Glucksmann, M. (1995), 'Why "Work"? Gender and the "Total Social Organisation of Labour" ', *Gender, Work and Organisation*, 2(2), pp. 63–75.

Glucksmann, M. (2000a), *Cottons and Casuals: The Gendered Organisation of Labour in Time and Space*, Durham, Sociology Press.

Glucksmann, M. (2000b), 'Retailing: Production and Consumption's Missing Relation', *Economic Sociology European Electronic Newsletter*, 1(3), pp. 12–16, available at www.siswo.uva.nl/ES.

Glucksmann, M. (2006), 'Shifting Boundaries: the "Total Social Organisation of Labour Revisited" ', in J. Parry, R. Taylor, L. Pettinger and M. Glucksmann (eds), *A New Sociology of Work?*, Oxford, Basil Blackwell.

Gronow, J. and Warde, A. (eds) *Ordinary Consumption*, London, Routledge.

Harvey, M. and Randles, S. (2002), 'Markets, the Organisation of Exchanges and "Instituted Economic Process": An Analytical Perspective', *Revue d'Economie Industrielle*, 101(4), pp. 11–30.

Harvey, M., Quilley, S. and Beynon, H. (2002), *Exploring the Tomato: Transformations of Nature, Economy and Society*, Cheltenham, Edward Elgar.

Harvey, M., McMeekin, A., Randles, S., Southerton, D., Tether, B. and Warde, A. (2001), 'Between Demand and Consumption: A Framework for Research', *CRIC Discussion Paper*, no. 40, University of Manchester, ESRC Centre for Research on Innovation and Competition.

Heckley, G. (2005), 'Offshoring and the Labour Market: The IT and Call Centre Occupations Considered', ONS *Labour Market Trends*, September pp. 373–85.

Humphery, K. (1998), *Shelf Life: Supermarkets and the Changing Cultures of Consumption*, Cambridge, Cambridge University Press.

Huws, U., Jagger, N. and Bates, P. (2001), *Where the Butterfly Alights: The Global location of eWork* (IES Reports, no. 378), Institute for Employment Studies.

Incomes Data Services (2001), *Pay and Conditions in Call Centres 2001*, London, Incomes Data Services Limited.

Industrial Relations Services (2001), *Call Centres 2001: Reward and Retention Strategies*, London, IRS/CCA.

Jefferys, J. B. (1954), *Retail Trading in Britain 1850–1950*, Cambridge, Cambridge University Press.

Kingston, B. (1994), *Basket, Bag and Trolley: A History of Shopping in Australia*, Melbourne, Oxford University Press.

Kinnie, N., Purcell, J. and Hutchinson, S. (2000), 'Managing the Employment Relationship in Telephone Call Centres', in K. Purcell (ed.), *Changing Boundaries in Employment*, Bristol, Bristol Academic Press.

Labour Force Survey (2005), 'Employment status by Occupation and Sex', London, Office for National Statistics.

Lash, S. and Urry, J. (1994), *Economies of Signs and Space*, London, Sage.

Mäenpää, P. (2001), 'Mobile Communication as an Urban Way of Life', in J. Gronow and A. Warde (eds), *Ordinary Consumption*, London, Routledge.

Payal, B. and Das, M. (2002), '1-800-Globalization: Call Centre Outsourcing to India', mimeo, Maxwell School of Citizenship and Public Affairs, Syracuse University, New York.

Pearson, R. (1993),'Gender and New Technology in the Caribbean: New Work for Women?', in J. Momsen (ed.), *Women and Change in the Caribbean*, London, James Currey.

Pettinger, L. (2006), 'On the Materiality of Service Work', *Sociological Review*, 54(1), pp. 48–65.

Polanyi, K. (1957), 'The Economy as Instituted Process', in K. Polanyi, C. M. Arensberg and H. Pearson (eds), *Trade and Market in the Early Empires*, New York, Free Press.

Poynter, G. (2000), ' "Thank You for Calling": The New Ideology of Work in the Service Economy', *Soundings*, 14, spring, pp. 151–60.

Ray, L. and Sayer, A. (eds) (1999), *Culture and Economy after the Cultural Turn*, London, Sage.

Sinclair-Jones, J. (2001), 'e-Medicine and e-Work: The New International Division of Medical Labour?', *Health Sociological Review*, 10(1), pp. 19–30.

Southerton, D., Shove, E., and Warde, A. (2002), 'Harried and Hurried: Time Shortage and the Coordination of Everyday Life', *CRIC Discussion Paper*, no. 47, CRIC University of Manchester.

Stanworth, C. (2000), 'Women and Work in the Information Age', *Gender, Work and Organization*, 7(1), pp. 20–32.

Taylor, P. and Bain, P. (1999), ' "An Assembly Line in the Head": Work and Employee Relations in the Call Centre', *Industrial Relations Journal*, 30(2), pp. 101–17.

Taylor, P., Mulvey, G., Hyman, J. and Bain, P. (2002), 'Work Organisation, Control and the Experience of Work in Call Centres', *Work, Employment and Society*, 16(1), pp. 133–50.

Trades Union Congress (2001), *Telework: The New Industrial Revolution?*, TUC available at www.tuc.org.uk/work_life.

Urry, J. (2000), *Sociology Beyond Societies: Mobilities for the Twenty-first Century*, London, Routledge.

Warde, A. (1999), 'Convenience Food: Space and Timing', *British Food Journal*, 101(7), pp. 518–27.

Warde, A. and Martens, L. (2000), *Eating Out: Social differentiation, Consumption and Pleasure*, Cambridge, Cambridge University Press.

Zukin, S. (2004), *Point of Purchase: How Shopping Changed American Culture*, London and New York, Routledge.

12 Instituted economic processes in the telecommunications sector

Andrea Mina

Introduction

In this chapter we interpret and use for empirical investigation the Polanyian notion of *instituted economic process*. This emerges from Polanyi's work (Polanyi, 1944, 1957, 1968) as a distinctive set of insights about a number of fundamental properties of economic systems that constitute an original framework for the analysis of aggregate behaviours traditionally sidelined by orthodox economic accounts.

A first fundamental facet to the notion of instituted process is its dynamic nature. The idea of motion is necessary to capture those mechanisms by which the attainment of observable states is achieved through idiosyncratic sequences and combinations of events. When analysis is aimed at mapping existing differences between systems a comparative-static approach is fully adequate but this hardly allows moving beyond the observation that certain facts are more or less strongly correlated with each other. Causal relations between events are thus likely to remain hidden from view, although it is their very emergence that needs to be explained in the first place. Factors driving to different states are to be found in the process of change and transformation through time of individuals, organisations and the relations between them, so that only a dynamic view of economic systems has the potential to account for the different outcomes of alternative processes of change and to find explanations to the end states of observed developmental paths.[1]

Development implies variation in some characteristics of agents and systems through time. Furthermore, time must be historical time.[2] It is part of Polanyi's legacy that meaningful economic analyses cannot overlook the specific and contingent nature of events, organisations and institutions. It is especially important to recognise that variety and contingency characterise market institutions, in that: (1) there are modes of exchange that are not market-based (Polanyi, 1944); (2) there are different forms of capitalism (Hall and Soskice, 2001; Metcalfe, 2001); (3) there are different sort of markets within capitalistic systems (see, for example, Solow (1990) on the peculiarity of labour markets). Diversity can be observed not only in the variety of agents that interact in the economy, but also in the way these agents interact. In other words, variety exists in the governance and regulation of market processes and modes of governance and regulation are themselves subject to variation over time.

Both internal and external factors can induce variation in socio-economic systems. These factors shape the emergence of novelty in the form of endogenous mechanisms or as exogenous shocks. In the first case, autocatalytic processes of innovation are those creative forces that drive the evolution of the system 'from within'. External shocks, instead, affect the system from outside its boundaries and induce mechanisms of adaptation to changing environmental conditions.[3] Change is both quantitative and qualitative: on the one hand, it entails variation in the relative share of resources appropriated on the basis of differential performance levels (which in turn stem from different endowments in capital, capabilities, power, access to credit, etc.); on the other hand, change implies variation in the nature of these resources (i.e. the way they are generated, their characteristics, their composition, etc.)

Naturally, the presence and emergence of variety pose significant problems of governance that must be overcome to channel innovative forces and co-ordinate collective action in the pursuit of socially relevant goals. This is precisely the role of norms, which function as mechanisms that stabilise imbalances and allow for the achievement and reproduction of ordered patterns. But how do norms come about? This fundamental question is latent in the Polanyian notion of *instituted economic process*. Norms are sources of order and stability because they provide the means for social action and embody rules of continuity over time. Yet norms too change over time and their rate of change arguably depends on their reach, relevance and complexity. The dynamic notion of 'instituting' economic action differs in this respect from a static conception of institutions, whether these are intended as constraints posed to social action or as enabling drivers to change, as found in many neo-institutional strands of research as well as in part of the innovation system literature.

A static notion of institutions is not appropriate when institutions co-evolve with the elements of the system they are supposed to co-ordinate and when these processes occur within the same time frame. If the relative rate of transformation of institutions is of the same order of magnitude as that of other components of the system, then their evolution needs to be fully endogenised. As a consequence, in periods of institutional uncertainty, the notion of 'institution' can be fruitfully replaced by the notion of 'instituting'. 'Instituting' forces are intended as factors whose outcome is the normalisation – or standardisation – of the objects of exchange and of the practices through which economic transactions take place.

In the process of instituting markets, as Harvey and Randles (2002) point out, different classes of agents compete with each other for the allocation and appropriation of resources. Both the notion of competition and the notion of resources need here to be considered in rather broad terms. Competition should not be taken as a given structure but instead as an unfolding process (as suggested in Metcalfe, 2001) in which the use of resources and the rents thereby generated are contended by agents on the basis of different strategies, competencies and factor endowments. Resources include both tangible and intangible assets and their allocation and exchange may or may not be regulated through price-mechanisms. In any economic activity, in fact, market processes co-exist with non-market processes and where the boundaries are set depends very much on the context – historical and geographical – in which markets emerge.

These considerations apply to very different levels of the economy and consequently to different levels of analysis. While they can be easily associated with the macro-level of the overall organisation of the economy, which is typically a matter for political economists, nothing seems to prevent an application of some of the insights Polanyi developed to lower-level systems and analytical units.[4] In this study we focus on the meso-level of the telecommunications sector and attempt to combine elements of dynamic institutional analysis in a perspective of sectoral innovation systems (Malerba, 2004). On this line of enquiry, three Polayian arguments will resonate in this chapter. First, the co-existence and co-evolution of market and non-market transactions in the emergence of new economic activities; second, the interplay between private and public agents in shaping the emergence of new markets; and third, the ever present tension between self-regulation and central planning in defining the social space for economic action.

These issues permeate the development over time of the telecommunications sector, as well as of numerous other sectors based on network technologies, such as railway and electricity supply systems.[5] Network technologies heavily rely on the presence of compatibility standards functioning as the techno-economic 'norms' of large complex systems. Here standardisation, which can occur through market forces or through negotiations in dedicated consortia, is a process through which technical specifications and economic incentives and practices are normalised ('instituted') over time so as to generate a dominant design capable of delivering network compatibility and system co-ordination.[6]

Within the realm of telecommunication services fewer technological developments have transformed the industry as dramatically as the growth of mobile telephony in the 1990s. In this process, the development of new technical standards and the rise of GSM (Global System for Mobile communications) were undoubtedly key events and an analysis of the process that led to the provision of new services is crucial to gain better understanding of the nature, rate and direction of technical change (as well as use of technology) in this and related sectors (i.e. dedicated software). GSM emerged in the 1990s as the world-leading standard for mobile networks among a number of alternative designs. It was developed in Europe through intense co-operative efforts among service providers, equipment manufacturers and regulators, which entailed complex market and non-market processes of knowledge accumulation, recombination and appropriation over an extended period of time. Private and public stakeholders engaged in formal and informal negotiations in which the role of economic incentives, values and perceptions, the relevance of corporate and individual strategies, and the concurrent evolution of the regulatory framework, significantly affected the design, intellectual property, implementation and diffusion of the standard and induced long-lasting effects into the transformation and growth of mobile telephony markets. The purpose of this paper is to revisit from a neo-Polanyian perspective the process whereby GSM emerged through the interplay of innovation, regulation and competition to become a core instituted process in the evolution of modern telecommunication systems.

European telecommunications in the 1980s: institutions and standardisation practices

Until the 1980s, most European telecommunication markets still were state monopolies and large technical infrastructures were planned and managed mainly through public procurement policies. National operators worked with a selected number of manufacturers on the basis of long-term supply contracts and co-operation was achieved by means of quasi-vertical integration of functions (Noam, 1992). With respect to the specification of technical standards, the fact that national markets were protected from external interferences meant that operators often opted for different and incompatible standards agreed locally with their equipment suppliers or developed through joint R&D.[7] Protocols for cross-border communication tended to be devised by specialised technical committees working to guarantee inter-network connections through gateways. On this basis telecoms operators negotiated context-specific agreements on regulation and accounting practices.

The Conference of European Post and Telecommunications Administrations (CEPT), established in 1956 by public service providers, was the arena where international technical and administrative issues were dealt with for the European Region. CEPT was accessible on a voluntary basis, the solution of controversies was consensus-driven (it often required unanimity) and the voting procedure followed national representation. CEPT represented telecommunication operators: it did not include manufacturers (Schmidt and Werle, 1998), was closed to non-European operators (Littler and Sharp, 1990) and did not include consumers either (Hawkins, 1995). As a consequence, also with regard to standard-making activities the organisation tended to maintain the status quo of national monopolies, as most international telecoms consortia did at the time (Rutkowski, 1991).

The creation of the Common Market and the de-regulation of the telecoms sector significantly impacted the transformation of European standardisation practices and standard institutions during the 1980s (Egyedi, 1996). It was in that period that issues of standardisation gained increasing visibility in the agenda of the European Commission because the harmonisation of service markets required the harmonisation of technical standards as one of the necessary, although not sufficient, conditions. Also, the idea of a new telecommunications platform of improved capacity was emerging as a way to foster technological innovations and facilitate entry in all sub-sectors of the industry. Standardisation started to be seen as a viable strategy for delivering such open and inter-operable platform (David and Steinmueller, 1996).

The opening of telecommunications markets constituted a landmark in the evolution not only of the service sector, but also of the related manufacturing base. Equipment manufacturers became exposed to national and international competition and new risks and opportunities emerged for national industries. Very substantial economic interests remained associated with the development of telecommunications infrastructures and the progressive abandonment of direct public procurement practices certainly did not imply disengagement of national governments from the matter. What changed was instead the way in which governments exerted pressures to bend the configuration of telecommunications networks to their own advantage (Davies and Brady, 1998). Standardisation started to figure prominently among the set of viable policy tools that many member states manoeuvred strategically to favour their own manufacturing sectors under the threat of foreign competitors.

Until the 1980s, standards tended to embody existing technical knowhow developed within national borders. Their adoption was limited to the country of origin and international diffusion was rather difficult. In the 1980s, the practice of adapting known technical configurations gradually shifted towards modes of standardisation that encompassed untested solutions for technologies associated with significantly higher levels of uncertainty. One of the consequences of this was that extensive – and costly – stages of research and development were introduced and began to absorb a great deal of resources in the standard-making process.

The divestiture of public companies, the emergence of competitive industrial structures and the progressive exposure of national markets to international competitors not only impacted the nature and scope of technical standards but also the role and governance of the relevant intellectual property rights. In the old framework of state monopolies and quasi-vertical integration of telecom operators and equipment manufactures, incentives to protect the output of R&D activities were relatively few (Noam, 1992; Granstrand, 1999; Bekkers et al., 2002a). Operators carried out research for their own use in the absence of competitors. They were institutionally protected from free-riding on the part of manufacturers as the latter's output market relied on public procurement. Manufacturers also had little incentive to acquire and enforce property rights because: (1) they had no market abroad as foreign markets were also nationalized; (2) they often received preferential treatment as 'national champions' of the local industrial base; (3) where internal competitors were present, they could be forced to license patents at no costs by government intervention.

In the 1980s, however, the tight links that had previously bound equipment manufacturers to service providers were being loosened considerably, the pace of technical change in related ICT domains (computers, switching technologies and software) was accelerating and intellectual property rights became increasingly important for the production of new knowledge and the co-ordination of its exchange. In the changing architecture of telecommunications markets new dynamics began to emerge.

The status quo of mobile technologies in the 1980s

Until the 1980s mobile telephony accounted for a minor share of the telecommunications business, although some of its core technological principles had long been known. The first successful applications of radio communication techniques to commercial telephony services date back to 1946 and were developed in the US by AT&T Bell Labs (Garrard, 1998; Palmberg, 2002). Despite an early start though, the penetration of cellular telephony in the US was rather slow. It is noted in the literature that diffusion of the new technology was hampered: (1) by the relative instability of the regulatory framework of the industry in the phase of liberalisation (Lyytinen and Fomin, 2002); (2) by long-lasting controversies between the two leading equipment manufacturers – AT&T and Motorola – over the cellular design that was to be adopted (Davies and Brady, 1998; Lyytinen and Fomin, 2002); and perhaps also (3) by the initial decision of the Federal Communication Commission (FCC) to favour television services over telephony services in the allocation of radio-frequencies (Meurling and Jeans, 1994).

In Europe national service providers and equipment manufacturers were pursuing the development of various incompatible standards which resulted in highly fragmented markets for analogue services until the mid-1990s. As in the US, the first services generally offered by telecoms operators were automobile-based cellular telephony and personal electronic paging services. The first users typically were business users. Among the many standards that were developed in the 1970s for European national markets, one – the Scandinavian NMT system – was particularly important, not only because it played a crucial role in the technical evolution of mobile technology,[8] but also because it provided a peculiar model of governance for the process of innovation and diffusion, and, as many commentators claim, it was in many respects a precursor of the forthcoming GMS system.[9]

The NMT was the successful result of a series of negotiations, formal state agreements and R&D alliances, started around 1969, between Finnish, Swedish, Norwegian and Danish representatives aimed to harmonise the four national markets. More specifically, the standard was designed to provide access to the network from any Scandinavian country, to allow for automatic connection and to support roaming capability. When introduced in 1981, the first-generation NMT system (NMT-450, installed in automobiles) anticipated the launch of the first North American system.[10] By 1983, NMT was the largest cellular system in the world, with more than 75,000 subscribers (Funk and Methe, 2001). No other European standard gained comparable success since no technical specifications existed for an international mobile telephony market until the development of GSM.

The development of GSM: a core instituted economic process

The process of development of GSM, as Hawkins (1995) suggests, had strong political, economic and technical implications from the very start. From a technical viewpoint, existing knowledge had to be made available and new knowledge had to be jointly created to achieve the desired functions of the network. From an economic viewpoint, an appropriate structure of incentives had to be set up to sponsor the necessary R&D activities, to diffuse the new infrastructures and to promote the new services. From a political viewpoint, the project needed at the same time a transnational centralised drive to co-ordinate it and direct involvement of individual governments, who still controlled monopolistic telecommunications operators and had sovereignty on frequency allocation issues. As a consequence, this process was bound to be highly distributed among a variety of economic agents and deeply embedded in a network of relations within and across groups of agents regulated by a complex set of representation criteria which proved essential to shape the final outcomes.

GSM emerged through the interplay of innovation, regulation and competition at a time when the transformation of the institutional settings of the European economy and the telecommunications sector, combined with the changing nature and role of standards institutions, induced new rationales for action and new frames for co-ordination. Furthermore, unexpected – or at least vastly underestimated – innovation and imitation dynamics in demand and consumption complemented supply-side innovation and imitation and sustained market growth in a typical process of co-evolution.[11]

Technological opportunities and first trials

In 1987 the decision was taken at the World Administrative Radio Conference to put to new uses frequencies in the bandwidth around 900 MHz (Haug, 2002). National telephone operators considered using the new spectrum to provide international mobile telephony services with the prospect of safe monopolistic profits from a core consumer base of business users associated with a relatively price-inelastic demand (Pelkmans, 2001). As a result, CEPT allocated the newly available spectrum to mobile telephony services (Hultén and Mölleryd, 1995).

CEPT also framed the discussions about the standard that was to support the new services. In that context, the Nordic countries applied pressure for the adoption of an improved version of the NTM system, which would have given to their manufacturing base a clear competitive advantage in the infrastructures market. They were confronted with resistance by continental operators and suppliers who were aware of the benefits they could derive from developing locally new technical specifications (Temple, 1987). They were also aware of the risk associated with the project: the costs of developing (or purchasing) new networks were high in the face of uncertain revenues.[12] To resolve some of the issues at stake, in 1982 CEPT assigned to a specialised committee, called GSM (Groupe Spéciale Mobile), the task of setting the technical and operational specifications for an integrated European mobile telecommunication system.[13] The group was based in Paris and included representatives from mobile and radio administrative units and research labs of service suppliers. They soon decided that the new system would work in the 900 MHz frequency area and began to monitor a series of trials where alternative specifications were tested.

In 1984 Germany and France were co-operatively researching on a number of broad-band and narrow-band digital solutions and were later joined by Italy in 1985 and by the UK in 1986. In the same year, technical trials were carried out in Paris on a number of different designs (Temple, 1987). The Scandinavian narrow-band TDMA system, based on Ericsson's technology, performed better than the SEL/Alcatel's broad-band TDMA system but France and Germany strongly supported the broad-band solutions while the UK, Italy and the Nordic countries favoured the adoption of the Nordic system. France and Germany could not stop a first decision in favour of the latter but did manage to halt its implementation in CEPT when it was time to ratify the decision (Ruottu, 1998; Bekkers et al., 2002a). Although a compromise was finally reached, these controversies augmented the uncertainty surrounding the GSM project.

As a response to mounting concerns, the European Commission issued the 1987 Green Paper on the 'Development of the Common Market for Telecommunications Services and Equipment',[14] with a Recommendation and a Directive. The Recommendation stated that all Member States should give political support to the GSM, contribute to the design of the standard and fund the necessary R&D activities.[15] The Directive stated instead that every Member State should reserve the 900 MHz frequency area to GSM.[16] The system would be digital, since digital technology offered an attractive combination of performance and spectrum efficiency, would allow the development of advanced features such as speech security and data communications, which could not be delivered through analogue, and was retro-compatible with the analogue installed base. A digital system would also be easily interconnected with ISDN networks, which at the time were being developed in Europe and in many other regions in the world for land-based telecommunications services.

Shortly after the EC's intervention, the UK authorities decided to further strengthen the commitment of telecoms operators to the project by means of an international procurement procedure. The resulting document – the so-called Memorandum of Understanding – was signed in Copenhagen on 7 September 1987 by network operators from thirteen countries (France, Germany, Italy, Sweden, Norway, Denmark, Finland, Spain, the Netherlands, Belgium, Portugal, Ireland and the UK).[17] The countries committed to the provision of pan-European digital mobile services through GSM networks operative in the 900 MHz frequency area by 1991. They also agreed to reach consensus on the management of administrative procedures and to develop an open, non-proprietary standard for the system.

Institutional transformations and the emergence of a technology club

In the late 1980s, the European Commission was designing the reform of the telecommunications markets. The Commission saw in GSM an opportunity to facilitate the process since the new wireless infrastructure could provide effective alternative access to the telephone network, thus enhancing the chances of competitive entry (Littler and Sharp, 1990). The aim clearly was to parallel the forthcoming competition in the service market with increased competition in the upstream equipment manufacturing sector, since an open and interoperable standard would favour cross-national entry of incumbent and newcomers (possibly also small firms) specialised in the production of different components. Unit costs were expected to decrease, innovation rates to accelerate, and consumer surplus in final markets to increase.

One of the undesired effects of the wave of de-regulation on the GSM project was instead a considerable increase in uncertainty, clearly detrimental to investment. Most telecoms operators had started the GSM project from the safe position of national monopolists, but the looming reform now exposed them to a shock of uncertain outcomes. New risks and opportunities also emerged for equipment suppliers. On the one hand, they were about to lose their status of national champions, hence the direct benefits of public procurement policies; on the other, they had the chance to gain access to new, formerly protected, markets through the new technology. Had they co-operated in the development of the standard, they could have influenced the outcome of the process to their own advantage, at least by preventing the selection of undesired specifications. But if the standard had to be made available to all incumbents and new entrants, they had to find ways to protect their investments. It soon became clear that the role of IPR in the process would be crucial.[18]

At this stage of the project the institutional frame of CEPT implied a number of constraints to the co-ordination of stakeholders. National interests of a minority of operators could heavily influence decisions any time it was perceived that unfavourable options were gaining momentum. Secondly, the decisional power of monopolistic operators represented in CEPT was soon to be weakened by the upcoming de-regulation. Thirdly, although the relative importance of manufacturers was increasing, they were formally excluded from the standard committee. This time, however, their exclusion was not balanced by their close, though informal, co-operation with public operators. CEPT could not guarantee an efficient management of property rights, as manufacturers, and not service providers, held most of the IPRs that were necessary to design the system.

This problem was partly solved when in late 1988 the GSM Permanent Nucleus of CEPT handed over the project to a newly established standard-setting institutions, the European Telecommunications Standards Institute (ETSI), whose mission had been envisaged in the 1987 Green Paper as 'the substantial reinforcement of the development of standards and specifications in the Community'.[19,20] The shift in the nature of the incentives among the agents paralleled the move of the GSM project from CEPT to ETSI, where manufacturers were allowed to exercise formal influence on the project. ETSI was in fact conceived of as a private organisation based in Sophia–Antipolis (France) open to any party (administrators, public and private operators and manufacturers, etc.) with a 'relevant interest' in telecommunications who could join in upon payment of a membership fee. Administrative and technical functions were separated: at the time of the GSM project the former were dealt with in the General Assembly, whose voting required a qualified majority of 71 per cent; the latter were dealt with in the Technical Assembly, whose decisions require a simple majority. Each member had the right to vote for ad interim decisions in the Technical Assembly, while weighted national voting was required for final approvals and dispute settlements in the General Assembly.[21]

As GSM had to be a 'non-proprietary' standard, in ETSI pressure was made on equipment suppliers to make essential IPRs freely available to all manufacturers and to indemnify operators against patent infringements. Manufacturers that wanted to bid for the supply of networks in the countries that had signed the Memorandum of Understanding had to meet these requirements (Cattaneo, 1994; Garrard, 1998). While the second condition was accepted, the first was not. IPR holders were not keen to freely disclose the output of costly R&D activities (Bekkers and Liotard, 1999) and obtained to have the draft procurement revised. The general compulsory licensing policy was revoked in favour of individual contracts to be negotiated between licensors and licensees on a non-discriminatory basis. The problem was that relevant patents and copyrights were not evenly distributed among producers at all (Bekkers et al., 2002b) and the use of bargaining chips became highly strategic. Strategic alliances and cross-licensing were the practices adopted among the few producers of comparable status while licensing-upon-payment was expected to drive agreements between large and small firms. Within this framework, the outcome of negotiation processes was that intellectual property rights were used as an effective entry deterrent and a source of royalty revenues by large manufacturers like Motorola, who held a considerable number of patents, and strategic partnerships were pursued by others, such as Ericsson, to compensate for the minor weight of their core IPRs.[22]

The shift to ETSI did help to speed up these complex negotiations, but it was too late to meet the deadline of 1991 as manufacturers were struggling to reach the R&D targets in time. Simultaneously, the Gulf War was also generating some pessimism among investors (Pelkmans, 2001). The European Commission intervened then again through the Council Resolution 'On the Final Stage of the Co-ordinated Introduction of Pan-European Cellular Digital Land-based Mobile Communications in the Community',[23] which advocated mutual recognition of licences for GSM terminal operation among European countries. Although the resolution reinforced the perception of commitment from the European Commission and sustained the incentives to invest, it still took nearly a year before all terminals could be tested for market approval. At last the final specifications of the GSM standard were made public in May 1991 and later in the same year a pilot GSM network was successfully demonstrated at the International Telecommunications Union's (ITU) exhibition in Geneva. Formal approval for the first terminals was given in June 1992 and soon after the first commercial GSM services were introduced in European markets.

Despite the voluntary nature of the standardisation process, European authorities effectively enforced GSM as a mandated standard. In the European area all telecommunication operators willing to provide cellular digital services could not adopt other standard than GSM (or its later version DCS-1800, which worked in the 1800 MHz area of the spectrum on the same specifications of GSM): telecommunications licences were allocated upon condition that the service be supplied through a GSM/DCS-1800 network[24] and if such condition was not met governments could refuse concession of radio frequencies. Because the regulators bound the provision of the new services to the adoption of GSM networks, the European manufacturing base, which, with Motorola, had developed the relevant technology, enjoyed clear advantages. The policy of constraining the migration from analogue to digital to the adoption of GSM, which in some countries also included financial support to operators intending to purchase GSM networks (Davies and Brady, 1998), considerably favoured the creation at the European level of the internal critical mass that was necessary for profitable large-scale production of equipment. The end result was that by the end of 1993, 32 GSM networks for a total of 1 million subscribers were already on air in 18 areas of the world.

Alternative standards: different outcomes for different processes

The analysis of the instituted process that led to the design and implementation of the GSM standard can explain several features of the growth and transformation of mobile telephony technologies and markets in the 1990s. First of all, GSM heavily influenced the evolution of the market structure in the global equipment industry. As Bekkers et al. (2002b) clearly show, allocation of intellectual property rights and strategic choices by equipment manufacturers in the management of both IPRs and strategic alliances were very important to gain and/or maintain shares in relevant segments of the market (terminals, switching centres and base stations). Suppliers that during the developmental process participated in cross-licensing schemes and actively engaged in strategic partnerships (Nokia, Ericsson, Motorola, Alcatel, Siemens) later dominated world equipment markets. Explanatory seeds of complex processes can often be found in the relative initial conditions. The same consideration applies to patterns of industry growth and of diffusion of technologies. Emergent phenomena cannot be observed independently from the origin and path-dependent evolution of structural characteristics of the units of analysis. One of the consequences is that when standard races take place, the dynamics through which competing solutions emerge contain elements that are essential to understanding the outcomes of the process.

GSM turned out to be a winning standard among a number of viable technical options. In the mid-1980s, for example, cordless telephony and related standards (low-power, low-frequency terminals, operative within a few meters from the home base station connected to the public fixed network) were being developed in the UK for the local market (Hawkins, 1993). Those standards could reasonably be seen as a threat by GSM supporters as they provided an alternative application of the 'mobility concept' that could jeopardise the outcome of the GSM project at a time when the vision of the new service had not yet stabilised around a specific model and demand had not yet been tested. The potential risk was absorbed by ETSI: in parallel with the GSM project, ETSI was assigned the task of developing a new standard for cordless telephony, which was to become the DECT (Digital European Cordless Telecommunications). At the ETSI level, it was possible to control overlaps and stress the potential of complementarities between the two systems.

Only a few years later, a second challenge to GSM came from the so-called PCN (Personal Communication Network) system, which was again developed in the UK (Hawkins, 1993). PCN networks combined elements of cellular telephony (division into smaller areas of the macro-area to cover) and cordless telephony (low-power terminals) and would work over smaller cells. PCN was a direct competitor of GSM, particularly dangerous as its prices aimed from the start to compete with fixed-line service prices. When the first licences for PCN were released in the UK in the early 1990s, however, through the intervention of the DTI, the relevant fees were used to fund research for the development of a new system of increased capacity that would work at higher frequencies (GSM World Association Report).[25] Research activities were carried out in ETSI and resulted in the design of DCS-1800 (Digital Cordless System), based on GSM interface specifications.

Structural features of the GSM standardisation process, however, were even more far-reaching. Not only the development and implementation of GSM marked the emergence of the first pan-European market for mobile telephony, but also considerably affected the patterns of diffusion of digital technology at a global level. Once the majority of European operators and equipment manufacturers were committed to GSM, and being the internal market protected by European-level regulatory interventions, GSM started to be marketed as a world standard and to capture the attention of non-European operators. After two years from its introduction, and with the active support of a powerful consortium of GSM suppliers, the standard started diffusing internationally. The Australian company Telstra first among overseas operators joined the 'GSM club', followed by Indian, African, Asian, Middle Eastern and North American operators. By the end of 1995, 156 operators already served 12 million customers in 86 countries through GSM networks. In October 2002, subscribers to GSM networks were estimated at 763.7 million world-wide (168 countries), accounting for 71.5 per cent of the digital market and for 69.4 per cent of the global wireless market.[26]

At the time when the European standard was diffusing, alternative technologies had also been developed outside the European region, but none of them gained the momentum of GSM.[27] Research on systems technically more advanced than GSM had started in the late 1980s in the US and resulted in the design of CDMA (Code Division Multiple Access) systems. However, in contrast to GSM, the development of CDMA was not endorsed by governmental authorities, and the selection of a standard took place through market forces in the absence of centralised drives or out-of-the-market co-ordination mechanisms.[28] As different and partially incompatible standards were allowed to co-exist, the US market resulted to be highly fragmented, as first-generation European markets had been before GSM. This worked against the creation of a critical mass for a single technology capable of triggering band-wagon effects and no homogeneous internal market for digital mobile telephony and the relative manufacturing base emerged in the US.[29] Japan chose, instead, to develop one single digital system of its own, the so-called PDC, rather than adopt D-AMPS, CDMA or GSM. Despite the good technical performance of PDC and Japan's state-of-the-art skills in terminal equipment production, the European market was strongly focused on GSM and the US market already was too competitive for PDC to easily diffuse outside Japan. Kano (2000), concurring with Fransaman (1999), adds that Japanese suppliers tended to neglect the prospect of global growth and were deliberately oriented to satisfying the (high) internal demand for the new services through their own standard. As a result, this failed to reach international markets.

Final remarks

The development of GSM, jointly with the evolution of the regulatory framework of the telecoms sector in the late 1980s, played a crucial role in instituting the pan-European and global market for mobile telephony infrastructures and services. In this chapter, a focus on the *process* that led to the new technology has been adopted to capture the complex and path-dependent nature of aggregate economic and technological choices that resulted in the wireless sector as we know it today. This process can be said to be *instituted* in a Polanyian sense in that it emerged from dynamics of change and normalisation of economic practices caught in the tension between dispersed and self-regulating mechanisms and centralised government intervention.

In the case of GSM, co-ordination of private and public agents was pivotal to the creation of the new market, and a tension between different missions, rationales and strategies can be observed throughout the entire process. It was the contingent and contextual combination of these contrasting instances that generated an international market for mobile telephony services where no market existed before. Such a market could not have existed had relevant transformations not occurred in the regulatory framework and had supply and demand forces not matched in the process of creating the technology, the need, and the modes of consumption of the new services. This broad process of change, which reshaped the telecoms sector in the 1980s and 1990s, was highly distributed among a variety of economic agents interacting through a number of market and non-market mechanisms of exchange.

With respect to the outcomes of the process, among second-generation standards for mobile telephony there can be no doubt on the supremacy of GSM and the success of European players. This does not imply that GSM was necessarily the best choice. Many commentators argued that North American technologies alternative to GSM were better suited to achieve the functions expected from mobile networks of later generations (among which were the delivery of internet services). Others regretted the dominance of the GSM 'bureaucratic' compromise on the ground that technically superior standards would have emerged if the selection had been left to market forces. This is a contentious point. Had selection been left to market forces, it is not clear that any compatibility standard would have emerged at all (as in the US). At the same time, the economics of standards shows that the outcomes of any standard race may not necessarily be optimal. In fact, they cannot be optimal in all dimensions and for all stakeholders.

It is also important to emphasise that the success of GSM does not imply that the position of European mobile technologies has been once and for all secured with respect to further technological developments. Again, the history of industrial standards teaches that the very advantages gained at any point in time can easily become sources of rigidities at a later stage of the competitive process because the sunk costs implied in heavy investments on one technical option may hamper the generation and/or the acquisition of radically new techniques, new skills and new assets. As a consequence, the costs and benefits of the choice of technologies are not time-invariant and partly depend upon unforeseeable developments in the adopters' preferences and in the technological knowledge that emerges over time in response to newly perceived needs and new visions on how best to satisfy them. In this light, the jury is out on the outcomes of the 'battle of standards' for third-generation mobile networks and associated services.[30]

At a higher level of analysis, the very fact that different processes can produce very different outcomes depending on the time and the context in which they occur provides strong evidence that markets are anything but given. The nature and functioning of markets are emergent properties of the context in which they are born. Moreover, their growth and evolution depend on sets of rules – rules of representation, rules for the allocation of property rights, rules of exchange etc. – which also change over time in response to changing environments. This adaptive process is continuously negotiated in society and is indissolubly linked to the organisation of economic activities. In Polanyian terms, this is an *instituted economic process*.

Acknowledgements

The author gratefully acknowledges comments by Stan Metcalfe, Cristiano Antonelli, Ed Steinmueller, Martin Fransman, Jeremy Howells, Mark Harvey, Sally Randles, Ronnie Ramlogan and all contributors to the 'Karl Polanyi' Workshop hosted at the University of Manchester, 25–8 October 2002.

Notes

1 The reader will find here a substantial affinity with the notion of path dependency as in David (1985) and Arthur (1989).
2 These are also founding principles of many analyses of development processes in the area of evolutionary economics, which offers ground for fruitful dialogue with Polanyian notions. For a broad comparison of perspectives, see Harvey and Metcalfe (2005).
3 Naturally, the difference between the two views heavily relies upon the analyst's choice in drawing the boundary, which is in turn connected to different Kuhnian paradigms across and within the social sciences.
4 A shift to the sector or firm level may be more correctly ascribed to a neo-Polanyian research agenda where the assumption is made that the logical structure of the Polanyian framework remains valid across levels of analysis.

5 See, among others, Chandler (1977), Hughes (1983), David and Bunn (1988), Davies (1996).
6 The literature on the economics of standards is vast and multifaceted. For reason of space we cannot include a full overview of such literature and will refer the reader to the comprehensive reviews in David and Greenstein (1990), David (1995), Schmidt and Werle (1998), Swann (2000) and to the insightful discussions of Antonelli (1994), Foray (1994) and Metcalfe and Miles (1994).
7 At the time, public telecommunications operators heavily invested in extensive research facilities. Formal and informal labour mobility between private manufacturing firms and public research labs was considerable.
8 The NMT was largely based on existing technological knowledge (Haug, 2002). This constitutes a difference with respect to the forthcoming GSM, for which much research and development was instead needed.
9 Detailed accounts of the co-operative process that led to the development of NMT can be found in Hultén and Mölleryd (1995), Garrard (1998), Ruottu (1998), Haug (2002), Lehenkari and Miettinen (2002) Lyytinen and Fomin (2002) and Palmberg (2002).
10 Although both successful, however, neither the North American AMPS nor the Scandinavian NMT had the primacy: the first fully operative network in the world was the Japanese NTT system launched in 1979. In spite of its early start, diffusion of NTT-based mobile services turned out to be below expectations. Pelkmans (2001) argues that the NTT was not as successful as the competing North American and Western European systems because the Japanese internal market was revealed to be limited and because Japanese equipment suppliers were not able to commercialise their heavily protected technology abroad. On the contrary, Lyytinen and Fomin (2002) and Funk and Methe (2001) suggest that NTT did not take over because Japanese producers did not invest enough in capacity expansion since they were pessimistic about potential demand.
11 The social dynamics leading to the formation of the demand for mobile phones and mobile telephony services are an integral part of the process of market growth and transformation and constitute an important research topic in their own right. It is only for reason of space that they cannot receive here the full attention they deserve.
12 It is important to remember that at the time there was no obvious way to foresee the 'mobile frenzy' of the late 1990s.
13 The acronym GSM later passed to the standard itself while the technical committee took the name of SGM (Hawkins, 1993). Interestingly, the first president of the GSM group, Thomas Haug, had been the president of the NMT working group a few years before.
14 COM (87) 290, 30 June 1987.
15 Council Recommendation of 25 June 1987 on the Co-ordinated Introduction of Pan-European Cellular Digital Land-based Mobile Communications in the Community, 87/371/EEC.
16 Council Directive of 25 June 1987 on the Frequency Bands to be Reserved to the Co-ordinated Introduction of Pan-European Cellular Digital Land-based Mobile Communications in the Community, 87/372/EEC.
17 The actual signatures were fifteen, as two independent operators (Cellnet and Racal-Vodafone), as well as the DTI, signed the MoU for the UK (Temple, 1987).

18 For a detailed analysis of the core IPRs of GSM, see Bekkers, Duysters and Vespargen (2002).
19 Green Paper on the 'Development of the Common Market for Telecommunications Services and Equipment', COM (87) 290, 30 June 1987.
20 CEPT was later converted into a European club of Postal and Telecommunications Authorities.
21 For a detailed overview of ETSI, see Besen (1990) and also Bekkers and Liotard (1999).
22 Motorola entered cross-licensing agreements with Siemens, Ericsson Alcatel and Nokia (which held patents in other domains than GSM in which Motorola was interested) but set steep licensing prices for producers that had no patents to exchange, that were seen as direct competitors, or that were not well positioned in the GSM club. As a consequence, both relatively small firms like Talco, Italtel, Cleartone, and Dancall, and large manufacturers like the French Matra and the Japanese firms, were unsuccessful in securing licences (for detailed analyses of Motorola's IPR strategies, see Cattaneo (1994); Garrard (1998); Iversen (1999); Pelkmans (2001); Bekkers et al. (2002b).
23 90/C329/09, 14 December, 1990.
24 Directive 90/388/EEC.
25 It appears that PCN was not considered as able to stand alone in the European market, whose expectations were strongly oriented towards GSM (and DECT); at the same time, furthermore, the fragmentation of the US market for similar networks working in the same bandwidth did not favour the prospect of reaching a critical mass of adopters. As a consequence, large-scale production of equipment was seen as difficult to attain in both markets and serious difficulties in the diffusion of the new services could be envisaged due to excessive consumer costs. Moreover, if heavy investments had been made for PCN, in case GSM had largely prevailed, the cost of incompatibility would have been very high.
26 Source: EMC Statistics, 2002.
27 For detailed comparative analyses of different regional standards, see, for example, Davies and Brady (1998), Kano (2000) and Pelkmans (2001).
28 The Cellular Telecommunications Industry Association (CTIA), which was the body in charge of the approval of the standards relative to the sector and represents both operators and equipment manufacturers (they reach decisions by majority voting), allowed the simultaneous development and diffusion of alternative options. As a consequence, US companies developed at the same time a digital version of the AMPS system (D-AMPS), which used TDMA, was compatible with the analogue installed base and was relatively cheap to implement, and CDMA systems, which were, instead, incompatible with the installed base of AMPS as well as with GSM networks and needed more conspicuous investments (Sorril, 1995).
29 Davies and Brady (1998) also argue that at least two other factors played against CDMA in the 'battle of standards' for second-generation cellular networks. Firstly, the introduction of CDMA systems in the marketplace was considerably retarded by legal disputes between the two pioneers of the new technology, Qualcomm and Motorola, over the relevant property rights. As a result, GSM had time to conquer further market shares in new markets before CDMA was able to compete, thus accelerating the generation of increasing

returns. Secondly, CDMA was 'newer' than GSM and in spite of its technical superiority, when it was launched in the marketplace, it proved less reliable than its rival. CDMA still needed further testing when GSM was already displaying constantly good technical performances in Europe and overseas. In other words, GSM benefited from the rise of externalities in the form of learning dynamics earlier than CDMA.

30 And also on the long-term consequences of the processes through which radio frequencies were allocated in each country, processes – we may say – *instituted* very differently in different European countries and whose relative merit is still an unresolved issue.

References

Antonelli, C. (1994), 'Localized Technological Change and the Evolution of Standards as Economic Institutions', *Information Economics and Policy*, 6(3–4), pp. 195–216.

Arthur, W. B. (1989), 'Competing Technologies, Increasing Returns and Lock-in by Historical Events', *Economic Journal*, 99(394), pp. 116–31.

Bekkers, R. and Liotard, I. (1999), 'European Standards for Mobile Communications: The Tense Relationship between Standards and Intellectual Property Rights', *European Intellectual Property Review*, 21(3), pp. 110–26.

Bekkers, R., Verspagen, B. and Smits, J. (2002a), 'Intellectual Property Rights and Standardization: The Case of GSM', *Telecommunications Policy*, 26(3–4), pp. 171–88.

Bekkers, R., Duysters, G. and Verspagen, B. (2002b), 'Intellectual Property Rights, Strategic Technology Agreements and Market Structure: The Case of GSM', *Research Policy*, 31(7), pp. 1141–61.

Besen, S. M. (1990), 'The European Telecommunications Standards Institute: A Preliminary Analysis', *Telecommunications Policy*, 14, pp. 521–30.

Cattaneo, G. (1994), 'The Making of a Pan-European Network as Path-dependency Process: The Case of GSM versus IBC (Integrated Broad Communications) Networks', in G. Pogorel (ed.), *Proceedings of the Global Communications Strategies*, Amsterdam, Elsevier, pp. 68.

Chandler, A. D. (1977), *The Visible Hand: The Managerial Revolution in American Business*, Cambridge, MA, Harvard University Press.

David, P. (1985), 'Clio and the Economics of QWERTY', *American Economic Review*, 75(2), pp. 332–7.

David, P. (1995), 'Standardisation Policies for Network Technologies: The Flux between Freedom and Order Revisited', in R. Hawkins, R. Mansell and J. Skea (eds), *Standards, Innovation and Competitiveness: The Politics and Economics of Standards in Natural and Technical Environments*, Aldershot, Edward Elgar.

David, P. and Bunn, J. A. (1988), 'The Economics of Gateways Technologies and Network Evolution: Lessons from Electricity Supply Industry', *Information Economics and Policy*, 4, spring, pp. 165–202.

David, P. and Greenstein, S. (1990), 'The Economics of Compatibility Standards: An Introduction to Recent Research, *Economics of Innovation and New Technology*, 1(1–2), pp. 3–41.

David, P. and Steinmueller, E. (1996), 'Standards, Trade and Competition in the Emerging Global Information Infrastructure Environment', *Telecommunications Policy*, 20(10), pp. 817–30.
Davies, A. (1996), 'Innovation in Large Technical Systems: The Case of Telecommunications', *Industrial and Corporate Change*, 5(4), pp. 1143–80.
Davies, A. and Brady, T. (1998), 'Policies for a Complex Product System', *Futures*, 30(4), pp. 293–304.
Egyedi, T. (1996), *Shaping Standardisation: A Study of Standards Processes and Standards Policies in the Field of Telematic Services*, Delft, Delft University Press.
EC (1987), 'Towards a Dynamic European Economy: Green Paper on the Development of the Common Market for Telecommunications Services and Equipment', *COM*, (87) 290, 30 June.
EC (1994), 'Europe's Way to the Information Society: An Action Plan', *COM*, (94) 347 Final, 19 July.
EC Council Directive (1987), *On the Frequency Bands to Be Reserved to the Co-ordinated Introduction of Pan-European Cellular Digital Land-based Mobile Communications in the Community*, (87/372/EEC), 25 June.
EC Council Recommendation (1987), *On the Coordinated Introduction of Pan-European Cellular Digital Land-based Mobile Communications in the Community*, (87/371/EEC), 25 June.
EC Council Resolution (1990), *On the Final Stage of the Co-ordinated Introduction of Pan-European Cellular Digital Land-based Mobile Communications in the Community*, (90/C329/09), 14 December.
Foray, D. (1994), 'Users, Standards and the Economics of Coalitions and Committees', *Information Economics and Policy*, 6(3–4), pp. 269–93.
Fransman, M. (1999), *Vision of Innovation: The Firm and Japan*, Oxford, Oxford University Press.
Funk, J. L. and Methe, D. T. (2001), 'Market- and Committee-based Mechanisms in the Creation and Diffusion of Global Industry Standards: The Case of Mobile Communication', *Research Policy*, 30(4), pp. 589–610.
Garrard, G. (1998), *Cellular Communications: Worldwide Market Development*, Boston and London, Artech House Publishers.
Granstrand, O. (1999), *The Economics and Management of Intellectual Property: Towards Intellectual Capitalism*, Cheltenham and Northampton, MA, Edward Elgar.
Hall, P. A. and Soskice, P. A. (2001), *Varieties of Capitalism: The Institutional Foundations of Comparative Advantage*, Oxford, Oxford University Press.
Harvey, M. and Randles, S. (2002) 'Markets, the Organisation of Exchanges and "Instituted Economic Process": An Analytical Perspective', *Revue d'Économie Industrielle*, 101(4), pp. 11–30.
Harvey, M. and Metcalfe, J. S. (2005), 'The Ordering of Change: Polanyi, Schumpter and Nature of the Market Mechanism', *CRIC Discussion Paper*, no. 70, University of Manchester.
Haug, T. (2002), 'A Commentary on Standardisation Practices: Lessons from the NMT and GSM Mobile Telephone Standards Histories', *Telecommunications Policy*, 26(3–4), pp. 101–7.
Hawkins, R. (1993), 'The Role of Technical Standards in Strategic Planning for New Telecommunication Services: The Case of European Mobile

Communication Systems', prepared for France Telecom Centre National d'Etudes des Télécommunications (CNET), Management Seminar, 8–9 December, Poigny-le-Forêt.

Hawkins, R. (1995), 'Enhancing the User Role in the Development of Technical Standards for Telecommunications', *Technology Analysis & Strategic Management*, 7(1), pp. 21–40.

Hughes, T. P. (1983), *Networks of Power: Electrification in Western Society, 1880–1930*, Baltimore, Johns Hopkins University Press.

Hultén, S. and Mölleryd, B. (1995), 'Mobile Telecommunications in Sweden', in K. E. Shenck, J. Muller and T. Schnoring (eds), *Mobile Telecommunications: Emerging European Markets*, London and Boston, Artech House Publishers.

Iversen, E. (1999), 'Standardisation and Intellectual Property Rights: Conflicts between Innovation and Diffusion in New Telecommunications Systems', in K. Jakobs (ed.), *Information Technology Standard and Standardisation: A Global Perspective*, Hershey, PA, Idea Group Publishers.

Kano, S. (2000), 'Technical Innovations, Standardisation and Regional Comparison: A Case Study in Mobile Communications', *Telecommunications Policy*, 24, pp. 305–21.

Langlois, R. N. and Robertson, P. L. (1992) 'Networks and Innovation in a Modular System: Lesson from the Microcomputer and Stereo Component Industries', *Research Policy*, 21(4), pp. 297–313.

Lehenkari, J. and Miettinen, R. (2002), 'Standardization in the Construction of a Large Technological System: The Case of the Nordic Mobile Telephone System', *Telecommunications Policy*, 26(3–4), pp. 109–27.

Littler, D. and Sharp, B. (1990), 'Prospects for Competition in a Pan-European Cellular Telecommunications System', in G. Locksey (ed.), *The Single European Market and the Information and Communication Technology*, London, Belhaven.

Lyytinen, K. and Fomin, V. (2002), 'Achieving High Momentum in the Evolution of Wireless Infrastructures: The Battle Over the 1G Solutions', *Telecommunications Policy*, 26(3–4), pp. 149–70.

Malerba, F. (2004), *Sectoral Systems of Innovation: Concepts, Issues and Analyses of Six Major Sectors in Europe*, Cambridge, Cambridge University Press.

Metcalfe, J. S. (2001), 'Institutions and Progress', *Industrial and Corporate Change*, 10(3), pp. 561–86.

Metcalfe, J. S. and Miles, I. (1994) 'Standards, Selection and Variety: An Evolutionary Approach', *Information Economics and Policy*, 6(3–4), pp. 243–68.

Meurling, J. and Jeans, R. (1994), *The Mobile Phone Book: The Invention of the Mobile Phone Industry*, London, Communications Week International.

Noam, E. (1992), *Telecommunications in Europe*, New York and Oxford, Oxford University Press.

Palmberg, C. (2002), 'Technological Systems and Competent Procurers: The Transformation of Nokia and the Finnish Telecom Industry Revisited?', *Telecommunications Policy*, 26(3–4), pp. 129–48.

Pelkmans, J. (2001), 'The GSM Standard: Explaining a Success Story', *Journal of European Public Policy*, 8(3), pp. 432–53.

Polanyi, K. (1944), *The Great Transformation*, Boston, Beacon Press.

Polanyi, K. (1957), 'The Economy a Instituted Process', in K. Polanyi, C. M. Arensberg and H. W. Pearson (eds), *Trade and Markets in the Early Empires*, New York, Free Press.

Polanyi, K. and Dalton, G. (eds) (1968), *Primitive, Archaic and Modern Economies: Essays of Karl Polanyi*, New York, Anchor Books.
Ruottu, A. (1998), 'Governance within the European Television and Mobile Communications Industries: PALplus and GSM: A Case Study of Nokia', doctoral thesis, Sussex European Institute, Brighton University of Sussex.
Rutkowsky, A. (1991), 'The ITU at the Cusp of Change', *Telecommunications Policy*, 15(4), pp. 286–97.
Schmidt, S. K. and Werle, R. (1998), *Co-ordinating Technology: Studies in the International Standardisation of Telecommunications*, Cambridge, MA, MIT Press.
Solow, R. (1990), *The Labour Market as a Social Institution*, Oxford, Basil Blackwell.
Sorril, C. (1995), *Global Digital Cellular Communications*, London, FT Management Report.
Swann, P. (2000), *The Economics of Standardization: Final Report for the Standards and Technical Regulations Directorate*, London, Department of Trade and Industry, UK.
Temple, S. (1987), 'Pan-European Cellular Standards Lead the Way', *Telecommunications*, November, pp. 31–3.

13 Corporate merger as dialectical double movement and instituted process

Sally Randles and Ronnie Ramlogan

Introduction

We argue that in order to understand the merger phenomenon it is necessary to analyse the relationally structured positions of different classes of economic agent operating across instituted market and non-market exchange processes, where these instituted exchanges are themselves structurally positioned within an interdependent markets complex and are themselves dialectically co-produced with processes of market regulation. Our chapter thus develops the Instituted Process (IP) perspective to sketch an analytical framework representing the structures and structuring of interdependent markets. It argues that *dialectical exchange-regulation processes* are responsible for instituting particular recurrent behaviours. Further, because the system is necessarily open, these recurrent behaviours and interactions *themselves change* under pressure from other (foreseen and unforeseen) parts of the instituted markets complex. The tensions inherent in the dialectical exchange-regulation process provide a source of dynamism and uncertainty in the instituted markets complex which is therefore *a priori* never totally known, static or predictable.

The analysis develops and extends Polanyi's double movement as a *dialectical double movement* (DDM). Our new insights into the dialectical world of Karl Polanyi draws in part on archive material from the Polanyi Institute which has not, to our knowledge, been previously applied to the analysis of a contemporary case.[1]

We use these ideas to explore the dynamics and transient outcomes evidenced in one particular merger case: that which brought together Glaxo Wellcome and Smith Kline Beecham, finally giving birth to the pharmaceuticals giant GlaxoSmithKline (GSK) in 2000. The merger was finalised after seven long years of negotiations, unanticipated mishaps and delays. This series of events can be looked upon as the empirical outcome(s) of a continuous exchange-regulation dialectical tension. The analysis describes an unfolding situation which is inherently emergent, experimental, restless, and transformative.

The urge to merge

Capitalist accumulation and its reproduction spawns a bewildering array of organisational forms, even within the institution of the 'firm', as many have described and theorised (North, 1990; Penrose, 1959). This scope, indeed the phenomenon of organisational variety is itself *incentivised* as a natural feature of the capitalist reproduction system (Granovetter, 1994).[2] It carries over into firm strategies as an array of organisational options, traditional and novel, which both facilitate and sustain capitalist expansion. So, for example, corporate growth can occur organically through the re-investment of a proportion of surpluses. Alternatively it can occur more rapidly either through acquisition by one entity of the (total or partial) share capital of another or through full scale 'merger' – the intentional dissolution of the ownership structures of two (or more) organisations and their re-institution as a single legal entity. Further, the continuous emergence of new organisational permutations suggests that organisational innovation is itself an important feature of capitalist transformation.

This chapter considers just one of these organisational options: merger, and one example of its expression: the merger which created the pharmaceuticals giant GlaxoSmithKline. Its aim is to shed light on the merger *process* by analysing a single merger through the lens of a Polanyi-inspired conceptual framework coupling the ideas of *dialectical double movement* (DDM) and *instituted process* (IP). We make no comment about whether the merger in question was a 'success' or a 'failure', merely we note that it took place within a larger context of 'merger mania' and towards the end of a period of a merger upswing. We do however note that the management and economics literatures focus rather obsessively on the normative question of success/failure, which after all depend on the underpinning assumptions of what constitutes 'success'. Our start point by contrast is oriented to the political-economy questions of 'what's going on?', 'in whose interests?' and 'who wins/loses'? Our normative objective is to raise questions about the wider economic implications which conditions of mega-merger entrain and in particular the stresses which these conditions place upon the capitalist economic system. Such stresses, we suggest are brought about by interdependent forces and pressures emanating from stock markets, markets for corporate control (arenas where corporate equity is bought, sold, or merged) and, more recently, burgeoning markets for advice about corporate structure (markets for management, financial, and legal consultancy). Such interdependent systems of exchange are countered, we argue, by an ever-present protective regulatory pressure, manifested through the decisions and actions of the state, and also from various market actors themselves, notably the financial markets and from competitors of the merging organisations who seek to counter merger proposals (and industrial restructuring more generally) that are not in their own competitive interests. Whether or not the counter-movement actually brings the merger upswing under control is a matter of empiricism and historical analysis.

Our theoretical proposition provides, we suggest, some explanatory power in the face of a fundamental conundrum identified in the merger literature to date. That is, why we have periodically witnessed intense 'mega merger' activity, when *ex-post* evaluation of mergers according to a range of 'testable' success/failure criteria reveal such a high incidence of merger 'failure' (O'Higgins and Weigel, 2002).[3]

To reflect on the significance of our case study, by the year 2000, *The Economist* reported the record breaking total global value of mergers (and acquisitions) as around 3.5 trillion dollars doubling the 1997 level (*The Economist*, 25 January 2001). This figure reflects the crest of a wave of merger activity worldwide that began in the second half of the 1990s. Contributing to this record level was the value of the second largest merger of all time – the pharmaceutical industry's GlaxoWellcome SmithKline Beecham consolidation creating GlaxoSmithKline (GSK). Indeed, over the previous two decades the pharmaceutical industry appeared to be the spawning ground for a series of large-scale mergers from which these two drug giants themselves emerged.

It goes without saying that the phenomenon of mergers has been extensively studied at different levels of resolution, across a broad range of literatures. This research has provided many invaluable insights from theoretical as well as empirical perspectives but there has been an element of unease about the nature of that understanding. Larsson and Finkelstein (1999) in particular point to the lack of a proper theoretical understanding of what accounts for the success (however defined) or failure of mergers. In their study of American merger activity between 1973 and 1998, Andrade et al. (2001) propose theories encompassing efficiency, agency costs, regulation and diversification as being important to the process while Holmstrom and Kaplan (2001) suggest that improvements in corporate governance and changes in regulation are the important determinants of takeover behaviour. Surveying the various theories Trautwein (1990) expresses dissatisfaction with the state of research and recommends that research in this area should be redirected to explanations that build on decision processes, conflicting goals and ambiguous private information.

In fact, we do know that the propensity to merge, though reaching unprecedented levels in the late 1990s in terms of market capitalisation of post-merged entities has occurred in waves, with the 1990s period representing the fifth such wave in American corporate history, and arguably the first truly 'global' one (*The Economist*, 27 January 2001). On the face of it, these waves appear to be trans-sectoral – they are driven at a level above sector-related consolidation – although it has been suggested that the 1990s wave of mergers in the pharmaceuticals sector lagged consolidation activity in other sectors (Kettler, 2001).

While there have been many systematic studies of mergers there was little attempt until recently to formulate an underlying theory to explain the wave phenomenon. Each wave was associated with a particular unique explanation. The 1960s featured conglomerate mergers in which 'well run and efficient' acquirers built up diversified groups by adding capital and management to acquired firms. This process was reversed in the 1980s. Conglomerate organisation was no longer efficient. Bust-up takeovers in which raiders, financed by bank debt and junk bonds, acquired and unbundled the very same conglomerates assembled in the 1960s were the order of the day. The merger wave of the 1990s featured industry consolidations in similar manner to the mergers of the 1920s that were described as 'mergers for oligopoly' (Shleifer and Vishny, 2001). Explanations of the wave phenomenon vary. Within the framework of oligopoly theory, merger waves result from 'oligopolistic reaction' as large rival firms in an industry counter one another's moves by taking similar courses of action (Knickerboker, 1973; Cantwell, 1992). The most cogent explanation of the wave phenomenon in the recent literature is that waves are created by unexpected industry shocks such as technological innovation, oil prices and deregulation (Mitchell and Mulhern, 1996). Andrade et al. (2001) found deregulation to be a key driver of merger activity in the late 1980s and early 1990s. This they maintain, explains why industry-level takeover activity is concentrated in time and is different over time. Jovanovic and Rosseau (2001) however, contest the deregulation explanation, arguing that it is not well supported by empirical evidence. They put forward the alternative view that merger waves are a response to technological shocks.

Other observers suggest that merger waves occur simply as a 'copy-cat' response to a similar strategy pursued by rival firms; termed *oligopolistic reaction* by Cantwell cited in Meschi (1997). This view chimes with that of writers in economic sociology, where for example DiMaggio and Powell cited in Granovetter (1994) describe a process of *institutional isomorphism*, being the tendency for rival firms to simply follow fashions, including fashions concerning 'appropriate organisational size'. Granovetter describes phases in American corporate history which have swung between 'small is beautiful' to propensities to increase corporate size. He also describes how these propensities are reinforced and given credence by discourses in policy and academia promoting similar 'best size' views, in a self-reinforcing, recursive manner. This may be a credible contribution to the explanation of *general upswings* of merger activity, but it does not explain the peculiarities of individual merger waves, nor does it explain the turning points of waves; for example how, when and why a wave of consolidation activity appears to hit a 'limit' external to the reactions of the individual firms involved in merger activity.

Overall the general conclusion that emerges from various performance-type studies is that the impact of mergers on profitability is in the range of nil to negative. That this is so does not necessarily imply that one cannot find evidence of mergers that have fulfilled the expectations and objective of particular classes agents involved in the merger process. So, we can pose the problem slightly differently to ask which *stakeholders* appear to gain from the merger process, and which lose out? On this question survey evidence reveals that the only group to be consistently shown to benefit from the event are *shareholders of the acquired company*. It has been suggested that this imbalance between the returns to the two different shareholder groups – those of the acquiring, and those of the acquired company – relates to the tendency for acquiring companies to pay a premium over the pre-merger stock market valuation for the acquisition, the cost of which is eventually borne by the acquirers' shareholders (Meschi, 1997).

This paradox – a seemingly incessant 'urge to merge' alongside the absence of conclusive evidence that mergers deliver the 'success' assumed and expected by a range of stakeholders, begs the more fundamental question *'what's going on?'*

In the next section we recap and develop our theoretical framework which is derived from the insights of Karl Polanyi, and indeed draws on archive material from the Polanyi Institute which has not, to our knowledge, been applied to the analysis of a contemporary context before.

The case study which then follows attempts to illuminate this discussion, by using the DDM/IP framework to analyse a particular merger 'event' in some detail, temporally located during a period of 'merger mania'. The analysis focuses on the period 1995 to the end of 2000, when the GSK merger was approved.

Towards a neo-Polanyian theory of dialectical double movement (DDM) and instituted process

Instituted process and interdependent markets

The notion of competition, market formation, and the structuring and restructuring of market and, importantly, non-market exchanges occurring as *instituted process* (IP) has been developed from the writings of Karl Polanyi (Polanyi, 1957) by ourselves and applied to a range of contexts (Harvey, 2002; Harvey and Randles, 2002; Randles and Warde, 2002; Randles, 2002, 2003). IP refers to:

> The tissue of relationships between classes of agents and the unique structure of symbols and techniques that result in the maintenance of their existence. IEP [sic] emphasises the normalisation of individual events into routine practices, but highlights the competitive tensions between classes of agent who consciously and unconsciously construct these relationships. (Harvey et al., 2001, p. 10)

Importantly, *market* exchanges are taken as just one, variously instituted – or regularised – expression of exchange. Importantly also, non-market indeed *non-economic* exchanges are seen to provide crucial underpinnings to various expressions of instituted and socially constructed market exchanges. In certain societies and with increasing prominence market exchanges have come to dominate the organisation of exchange, such that *market systems* have become the dominant societal mode for organising the production, distribution and consumption of resources whether capital, goods or services.

Structurally, we have argued that the 'organisation of exchange' occurs in two stages (Harvey and Randles, 2002). First, it requires the separation of society into different *classes* of economic agent. (These 'classes' are not necessarily exclusive or essentialist, since we all participate in many 'exchanges', both market and non-market depending on the role we are playing at the time.) Second, in order to integrate the economic functions of production and distribution which are a necessary precursor to *some* forms of societal *consumption* (Harvey et al., 2001; Warde et al., 2001) economic and non-economic *exchange relations* become organised across and within these different classes of agent, producing 'frontiers' of exchange – the point of transaction (Harvey and Randles, 2002). The transaction is nevertheless situated within a much wider and influential 'arena of exchange'. This wider arena of exchange contributes to, indeed determines, the terms, conditions, and mutual expectations of what is often a temporally extended *exchange process*. Exchange relations and their resultant and resulting exchange events become routinised over time. That is they manifest as instituted exchanges, visible to the researcher and other constituencies of observers as the regularities of exchange relations.

However, we can extend the Polanyian idea of IP (which arguably does not, in and of itself provide an explanation of either market variety nor dynamic market construction and change) and in so doing we can attempt to inject an explanation of change by considering the interdependencies of systems of market and non-market exchanges, and the outcomes of a continuous dialectical exchange-regulation double movement. That is, we wish to capture the ways in which changes in one market/non-market situation recursively impact on others, causing their particular 'institutedness' to modify. Thus, in this section and in the case which follows we stress that markets can be seen as not only *individually* instituted, but also systemically linked and interdependent. Such a perspective provides a qualitatively different scale of analysis to that which normally pertains when studying in isolation individual markets such as 'markets for corporate control' or 'drugs markets', for example.

We will briefly explore these ideas with the specific objective of hypothesising that market and non-market exchanges become bedded down as systems of institutional regularities, but that the instituted process of exchange formation and change is subjected to forces arising from the *interdependency of instituted exchange systems*. It is these complex interdependencies we suggest, which gave rise to the 'urge to merge' in

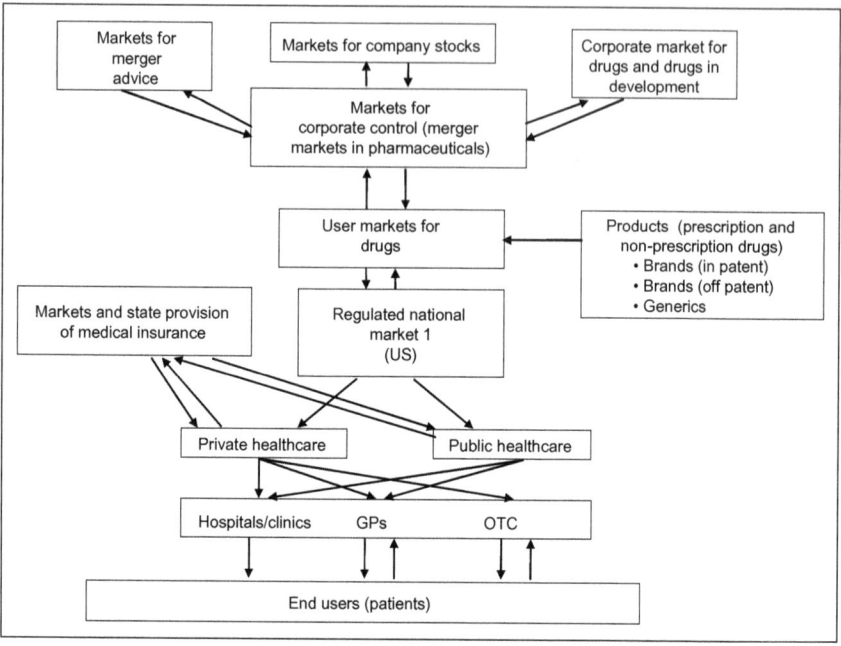

Figure 13.1 Interdependent instituted markets and the merger process

pharmaceuticals and related industries. The main markets which are salient to this particular case are: (1) the changing 'user' markets for drugs; (2) corporate markets for drugs, drugs in development, and market/distribution rights; (3) markets for merger advice; and ultimately (4) markets for corporate control. The interrelations between these markets, taking the particular case of mergers and markets in the context of pharmaceuticals are depicted in Figure 13.1.

Polanyian dialectics and the dialectical double movement

In a series of notes[4] written by Polanyi towards the end of his life he articulates and develops an approach and style of dialectical reasoning which both deepens and extends the market–society double movement of *The Great Transformation*. It is difficult to trace this development to the influence of individual scholars since he does not directly attribute other dialecticians such as Marx or Hegel. Rather, it appears that Polanyi is deploying a method of reasoning derived from his earlier legal and philosophical training, premised on the setting up then knocking down of 'straw men': of argument followed by counter-argument, or case for the prosecution followed by case for the defence. Whether this actually amounts to a thorough and robust dialectical account is questionable. However, the idea of continuous (ontological) tensions existing across and within four meta-domains of analysis: freedom, society, technology, economy, is clearly expressed.

Indeed to begin, we can see that Polanyi invokes in his *tools of analysis* (Polanyi, 1960 in Dalton 1968, pp. 306–10) a methodological dialectic problematising the inherent and irreconcilable tension that arises from:

1 an ontologically essentialist 'whole' interdependent and integrated society as the most basic and fundamental unit of social analysis (but which in epistemic and methodological terms is disabling and inaccessible); and
2 the necessity of disentangling society into constituent sub-systems, of economy, polity, religion (rendering it ontologically inaccurate but enabling its access in epistemic and methodological terms).

In his *tools of analysis* he works hard to come to terms with the problem of disaggregating (economic) phenomena which he holds are in fact ontologically inseparable from their social constitutive origins. He chooses only to *methodologically* disentangle the economy from society as an *approximation* solely to render it analysable, whilst noting at the same time that:

> I am conscious of the inherent limitations of such a treatment particularly from the point of view of general sociology. For the process is embedded not in 'economic' institutions alone – a matter of degree, anyway – but in political and religious ones as well; nor do physical operations exhaust the range of relevant human behaviour, either. But it helps to roughly disentangle the economy from other subsystems in society, such as the political and the religious, thereby make reasonably sure that we know what we mean when we so confidently talk about 'the economy'. (*ibid.*, p. 307).

It is worth continuing a little to see how Polanyi deals with this problem. In ontological terms he decides that society (with economy within) is a tiered, but integrated, structure of systems and sub-systems, parts and sub-parts.

> It must be apparent that just as the economy forms only a part of society, so the economy itself consists of differently patterned parts, each of which may have its characteristic institutions combined with a variety of traits. (*ibid.*, p. 310)

When analytically abstracting economy he decides to do so via the method of abstracting two *approximations* (*ibid.*, pp. 306–10):

- *Approximation 1*: patterns of economic integration (for example reciprocity, redistribution or market exchange) which by themselves or together with the others are capable of integrating the economy ensuring stability and unity; coupled with
- *Approximation 2*: institutions alongside which these patterns of integration are *necessarily* accompanied and through which the economy is organised.

Polanyi stresses that his two approximations provide an analytical framework only. No complete theory (and we could add exhaustive classification) of economic institutions is intended. A wide range of institutional variation is inherent in both the modes of economic integration and in the institutions responsible for their organisation and distinctiveness.

We therefore have some overview of how Polanyi deals with the methodological dialectic – of the necessity to continually flip between an ontology which in his view can only ever be considered in holistic terms, and the epistemic necessity of division into analysable sub-parts. Summarising Polanyi, we can deduce that he recommends the qualified pursuit of analytical procedure which orders levels of analysis as follows:

1. societies as a whole within which are located economic, political and religious (for example) sub-parts;
2. the distinctive place of economies in societies as empirically witnessed in different temporal-spatial settings and as distinguished by characteristic patterns of economic integration;
3. the institutions which characterise, constitute and are responsible for producing the identified patterns of integration at (2); and
4. institutions and institutional variants from other spheres of society (religious, political, and we could add from his other writing ideological and technological, see this section below) having a bearing on the form and organisation of economy.

Moving on, we can identify four themes or objects of substantive analysis which recur during Polanyi's life-work. They are (in no hierarchical order):

- Freedom (F);
- Society (S);
- Technology (T);
- Economy (E).

Evidence can be marshalled to demonstrate that Polanyi often (though by no means always) explores the polarities, oppositions and indeed 'double movements' existing within and between these substantive arenas. Polanyi discusses each object sometimes in isolation from the others, highlighting opposing dialectical tensions internal to it (what we shall call internal dialectics) but often as dialectically related to another of his key themes (which we shall call external dialectics), providing an ontology of coupled relational positions and structures, building to a possible (though incomplete in Polanyi's case) integrated system of dialectical relations. In its completed form (but stating clearly that Polanyi did not, nor may he ever have intended to, complete the process to this logical conclusion) we can portray this diagrammatically (Figure 13.2). We can take a number of these relations to see how Polanyi describes them and thus draw out the intransitive ontological underpinnings.

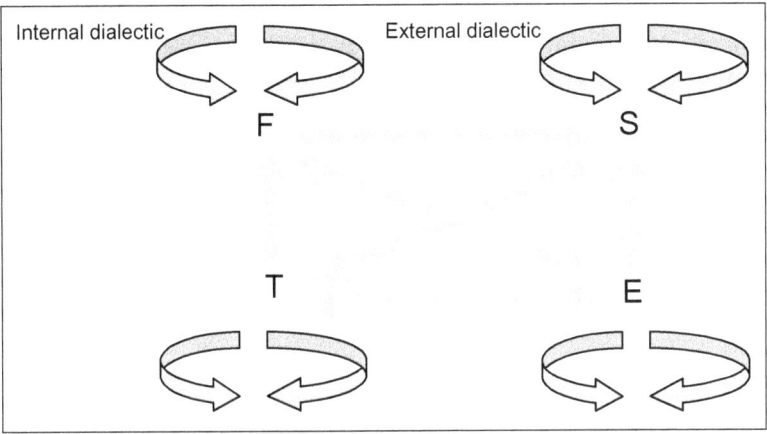

Figure 13.2 Internal and external dialectics of the four key objects of Polanyi's concern and ontological framework

Society and economy

In the internal dialectical relations of society and economy, and the external dialectic which relates economy to society we find the double movement (DM) familiar to most as a central theme of *The Great Transformation* (Polanyi, 1944). This reaches us in two stages. First:

1 economies, even market economies are always and as a rule *embedded* within social relations; *yet*
2 market society exerts a powerful *disembedding* force, cleaving economies from their constitutive social relations.

This we could call the embedding–disembedding internal dialectic of market economies. Second:

1 this disembedding tendency is never realised or complete (unregulated 'free' price clearing markets are a myth, they never actually exist) because
2 society creates within it institutions which underpin and enable the *approximation* to free markets but also institutions which seek to re-embed economy within society, providing welfare and other institutional supports to self-protect against the disembedding tendencies of market society.

This we could call the external dialectical double movement which characterises the relation between (market) economy and society. It is important to note that by re-thinking the dialectical double movement as a meta-physical phenomenon rather than as an empirical one (as it is mainly dealt with in *The Great Transformation*) we remove the necessity to apply arrows of causality or chronologies of action-response. These things are contingent and manifest as specific empirical examples occurring in specific circumstances. That is we remove the need to say that the societal protective response *necessarily follows* or is as a *consequence* of a drive towards market society, or that at the micro-market level regulation *follows* earlier attempts to institute 'un' regulated markets. Rather, forces to regulate markets, and forces to de-regulate markets co-exist, in ontological terms. Likewise these tendencies exist within the market itself, constitutive of the actions of market actors (self-regulation), as well as outwith a particular market (but still constitutive of the market formation and change process) by actors representing interests which intentionally sit outside and monitor/regulate markets, thus shaping and re-shaping the market itself. These multiplexes of motivations, objectives and actions which characterise the positions of different classes of economic agent frequently come into conflict, as the GSK case will illustrate.

Likewise forces to institutionally *disembed* economy from society, such as the push to mega-mergers, a force which potentially threatens the very institutions of capital markets on which corporate buying and selling rests co-exist with forces to *embed* economy in society, such as the merger wave reaching a crest, stalling, and falling back in response to stock market actors and their advisors institutionally recognising the risks to the capitalist system (in terms of concentrated risk and lack of diversity of investment options) that this level of concentration entails.

Freedom and society

The theme of Freedom occupied Polanyi for much of his life (compare Polanyi, 1925, 1943, 1957a, 1957–62). A recurrent theme is Polanyi's reflections on the relationship between freedom (of the individual agent) in the face of the essential location of all individuals in society. He asked the question 'Is a free society possible? (Polanyi, 1943). He proposed with reference to Jean Jacques Rousseau a problem of two parts in perpetual tension:

> First among the moral problems stands that of the double quality of every individual in a free society:
> a) Every human society stands under the law of survival – it behaves in such a fashion as to ensure its survival, irrespective of the will of individuals composing it (and yet).
> b) Every free or legitimate society bases its behaviours on the wills of persons constituting it.

Despite the fact that he eventually decides that Rousseau was wrong, i.e. that individuals cannot 'will' society and need not (cannot) take responsibility or blame for something that both precedes the individual and constitutes the individual, Polanyi nevertheless, both before (in 1925) and much later (in 1957a, 1957–62) places an onus of responsibility on individuals to 'penetrate their situation' by thinking of themselves *as if* they were free of social existence and social constraints (even though they are not and never can be) thereby achieving as close an approximation of such a situation as it is possible to find in a world where separate existence of the individual from society is ontologically impossible. Ultimately he resolves his dilemma by suggesting that 'true freedom' does not equate to freedom *from* society rather freedom *within* society a freedom constituted by powers to recognise and accept the duties and responsibilities that flow from the essentialist condition of individual *as part of* society. He therefore reveals both the possibility of reflexive thinking agents (as the transformative element of his ontology) and the normative optimism of someone who believes that societal 'betterment' is not an unrealistic ambition and can be brought about by the education and mobilisation of individuals.

The relation *between* freedom and society therefore becomes a complex of these dialectical forces and processes in Polanyi's schema. In our pharmaceuticals case, for example, we have the ever-present tension between the freedom of the corporation to engage in commercial drug development activity, and the social constraints originating both from within individual scientists and other employees of the company, and from external regulators alike, to develop those drugs according to prevailing knowledge, safely and responsibly. Phenomena such as whistle-blowing, fraud, or engaging in unethical or misleading business behaviours, can all be seen as substantive outcomes of the freedom-society dialectic.

Freedom and technology

In the trilogy of essays written in or shortly after 1957 which are as yet unpublished[5] Polanyi develops the coupled relations between freedom and technology in 'Freedom and Technology' (FT), technology and economy in 'Freedom in a Complex Society' (FCS) and economics and (technological) society in 'Economics and Freedom to Shape our Social Destiny' (EFSSD).

In the first of the three essays (FT) he begins by returning to the theme of the relation between freedom and society. He briefly reviews moments in American history where different kinds of freedoms were threatened at different points in time, and describes how those threats were over-turned or dealt with by the mobilisation of collective society (as a series of responses very similar in terms of providing a dynamic societal response mechanism to that which he describes in market-regulation terms in the double movement of *The Great Transformation*).

He goes on to discuss the paradoxes of technology and technology – society relations. The technologies he reflects upon are mass media and weapons of mass destruction. The latter he sees as the single most dangerous threat of his time. He couples technologies of mass media and weapons of mass destruction, and links this to the contemporary political climate of the Cold War noting the interdependences within society of political climate and technological development. He is concerned with the Cold War and with the memory of Hiroshima beamed world wide on television screens as a distant, dehumanised mushroom.[6] But a different kind of freedom is required here in the face of a very different kind of threat. He is, in this essay, particularly concerned and pessimistic about the 'silent' (or unrecognised) powers of technology to produce a form of numbing conformism – 'averagism' – both in creating a collective desire for material and (and indeed bodily) homogeneity and in terms of creating a collective inertia in the face of a series of freedom threatening dangers whether direct dangers of weapons of mass destruction, or the unseen dangers of technologies and techniques of mass public opinion and communication.

A familiar 'double-sided' passage follows, which does not negate the positive enabling capacities of technology, but regrets the contemporary absence of attention to its negative potentialities, believing its very invisibility to be a critical dimension of its power. In relating society to technology dialectically then he repeatedly returns to the point that society is in a current/actual *precarious* (unstable) position in its relation to technology.

> But why should a technologically complex society induce fear? Technology is nothing but the material instruments through which man masters Nature; it invests man with power to remove the causes of fear, and to provide him with safety and security. It is the embodiment of freedom; it is a creator of life and the abundance of it. In a hundred ways this is manifest. It is sheer perversity to harp on the secondary and transitory drawbacks of the passing of night, when at last man emerges out of ignorance and helplessness to the daylight of a technological civilisation.
>
> This is perfectly true. But in the meantime – in the transition, we are passing through the narrows of fear because of some actual dangerous effects of technology on our complex society. Such a society is destructible. Its existence is precarious . . . it is quite possible that a big society entering a push button existence may generate fear. A technological civilisation lives in a push button peace. (Polanyi, FT, p. 7–8)

As we draw parallels with our contemporary case located in drug-development and the pharmaceuticals sector, we can recognise a similar context of society–technology dialectical relation. We see on the one hand the instituting of regulation to encourage the positive health-improving capabilities of new drugs through discouraging anti-competition activities of merging oligopolies, and encouraging investment in drugs development and testing. On the other hand we see the society-protecting role of drugs licensing authorities, such as the Federal Drugs Administration, established to limit risks to society (such as deaths during late-stage drugs trials) which the drug-development process entails. Here the regulatory response may be the immediate withdrawal of the drug from trials/the market, a decision which can halt a drug development programme, and through adverse publicity, halt the merger plans of the culpable pharmaceutical company.

Technology – economy – society

In the second of the essays, 'Freedom in a Complex Society' (FCS), Polanyi explores the relation between technology and economy. He depicts market society as being the handmaiden, indeed the product of industrial society (or machine society or technological society) on the grounds that a system of market exchange was *required* or brought into existence as an entire economic integrative system *consistent with* the scale of exchange required for standardisation and efficiency (two essential parameters of machine society). Here in fact he echoes and develops a theme first articulated much earlier in the final chapter of *The Great Transformation* (Polanyi, 1944) and in 'Our Obsolete Market Mentality' (Polanyi, 1947). Unlike *The Great Transformation*, however, he now appears to be giving causal primacy to technology as determining economy in industrialised societies and thus provides causal explanation for the emergence of the particular form of market society. Not withstanding the varied existence of markets in societies and of many types of society where markets play a role in economic integration, he is saying something rather different: that (1) market society is *determined* more than are other societies by the powerfully determining role of markets within it; and that (2) it is (mass and standardising) technologies which provide the determining causal underpinning of market society, thus:

> From behind the problem-veil of market economy questions arise that transcend the economy and are constitutive to a technological civilization. The self-regulating market may well have been the earliest sphere in society to carry those imprints of the machine; efficiency, automatism and adjustment. But not the economy alone, society itself seems to be reconstructed around the machine – taking its forms and objectives from the needs of the machine. For technology does not spin you around as persons to focus our concern entirely on the external; it turns also society itself inside out. The material surroundings, projection of the machine, are not our only artificial environment; this environment comprises also a society, of which the machine itself is the texture. (Polanyi, 1957a, FCS, p. 1)

We therefore discern also a dialectical relation between technology and society in which technology *produces* a particular form of society and economy, but at the same time society *turns itself into* a technological society.

Again we see parallels in GSK case. We witness the simultaneous playing out of technology-drivers to standardise, upscale and internationalise the drug development and marketing process on the one hand. And on the other, market-drivers to achieve organisational scale, cost-reducing standardisation in drugs manufacturing, and improved international reach (particularly dominance of the private – healthcare institutions that characterise the huge US drugs market). These coupled technology-market objectives are shown to be key strategies of the mega-merger outlined below.

Freedom–society–technology–economy

We finally (again reminiscent of *The Great Transformation*) perceive a level of optimism attributed to Polanyi's reflexive agents who he envisages *will* be able to think themselves free of the predicament of their essential socialisation into a technological society. They will therefore, he suggests, creatively design institutions (engage in institutional innovation) to both enable technological society, and protect society from it. Passages here appear to speak to a very modern-day agenda of science–ethics–institution building processes and relations around such technologies as drugs development, genetic modification and nanotechnology. Explicit also in the final passages is the normative concern that technologies are not merely produced for and at the behest of market economy (setting up a relation between technology and economy) but that trade-offs are sought between the freedoms of the market, freedoms of science, and societal self-protection. Although Polanyi does not go as far as calling it such, he alludes to the existence of a technology–society dialectical double movement to parallel the market–society DDM articulated earlier in *The Great Transformation*. He concludes:

> Now, free institutions, I submit are no other than expressions of persuasive principles such as cooperation and competition, which until proof to the contrary should be deemed independent of the technological and organisational aspects of the economy. Freedom finds its institutional expression in the prize set on personality, integrity, character and non-conformity. Free institutions depend upon the valuation set on civic liberties ... The latter are a matter of the total culture of a society and where emphasis lies in such culture is not determined by economic factors. (Polanyi, 1957–62, EFSSD, no page number)

Finally, if we should remain in any doubt that Polanyi viewed the world as essentially constituted through the continuous interrelations of dynamic oppositions, we can refer to one of the latest and most poignant manuscripts at the Polanyi Institute, a letter written to daughter Kari in 1962, not long before Karl Polanyi died in April 1964. In it he writes:

> The development of a world of thought ... *trace it back* from the completed pattern to the origins of the separate strands. This method suits primarily a picture ordered in polarity i.e. in the duality of opposites. No strict polarity is here meant of course, rather a pressing for essential truth, simultaneously in complementary directions. Either direction will possess a continuity of its own, eventually attaining the unity of the final result ... In the middle of the twentieth century, where a variety of valuations caused a veritable ideational vortex, two existential poles and counter-poles attracted the minds. Personality expressed itself in the manner in which duality shaped thinking: fact and value, empiry and normativity, society and community, science and religion. The directions themselves oscillated as they were being tested by life, thought and history. In the retrospect, it appears this polarity formed the permanent axis of my world of thought. (Polanyi, 1962, original emphasis).

The case

The case description which follows describes the interaction of two domains held to be pertinent to understanding the GSK merger, from the perspective of Instituted Process and Dialectical Double Movements. The account: (1) applies the instituted interdependent markets perspective to the GSK case; and (2) describes the competition and drug safety regulatory process and regimes which impacted on the GSK case, revealing these to be dialectically related both internally to the market formation process and externally to market-society and technology–society–economy relations. The case shows how these two dimensions of interdependent markets and regulation each and together, dance a waltz of co-construction. Further, it shows how they are each re-constructed as an outcome of the competitive process, as relations between different classes of economic agent become instituted and re-instituted.

Instituted interdependent markets

The nature and significance of interpreting markets as *instituted* and *interdependent* in the GSK case are hinted at below through brief insights into four markets. They are:

1 *the market for corporate control or 'merger markets'*, showing the merger frenzy to have its economic and societal (risk) related limits;
2 *end-user and intermediate institutional markets* for drugs, themselves undergoing institutional transformation;
3 *corporate market and non-market exchanges* of drugs, drugs in development and market/distribution rights, highlighting the 'hidden' importance of non-market habitual negotiated 'drug-swaps'; and
4 *markets for merger advice*, highlighting the role of 'shadow' finance consultancy and banking firms and their influence on corporate restructuring activity, including mergers.

In fact, it doesn't matter which order we look at these four instituted interdependent markets, since the point of the *interdependency* account is to highlight how changes in one recursively impact on the other three and vice versa.

The market for corporate control or 'merger markets' The GSK merger was finally approved on 20 December 2000. The combined entity had at that date a market capitalisation of around £120 billion; combined sales of around £16 billion; and an estimated 7.3% share of the global pharmaceutical market.

The approval which created this new corporate giant was a significant event in itself. But it was in fact, only one of a spate of large (over £50 billion capitalisation) mergers gaining regulatory approval in the UK in the late 1990s. This produced a concentration of capital ownership unprecedented in corporate history. At the time, in the UK, GSK, together with BP Amoco and Vodaphone, accounted for some 25% of the aggregate valuation of the FTSE 100, and Britain's six biggest companies accounted for 40% of the total value of the FTSE. Such a level of concentration worried the competition authorities. The concern was reflected in changes in their decision making. One outcome was fewer merger proposals successfully negotiating the regulatory process to the point of approval in 2000.[7] Further the costs, in terms of time, legal costs, uncertainty, and consequential business risks of meeting regulators demands was increasing. These trends were not unique to the UK. In the US, note WorldCom's desperate attempt to save its deal with Sprint by pledging $40 billion worth of sell-offs in 2000, a move which is indicative of how the anti-trust environment tightened on both sides of the Atlantic (Prtzelik and Lewis, 2000).

Furthermore, as the merger deals got bigger, the regulatory probes got longer. This has important consequences for merging firms as momentum is lost, internally and externally. During the approval process staff morale declines as jobs and careers become uncertain, and externally information to the financial markets on business performance dries up. Banks advising the corporations are not permitted to publish research with the consequence that analysts following the bid find making forecasts difficult. A pall of uncertainty hangs over the companies and this is exacerbated as the delays continue. Indeed GSK is a case in point, illustrating how the regulatory process both lengthened and became more difficult to negotiate. Potentially, as the merger approval process lengthens and becomes the subject of heightened regulatory scrutiny, potential merger partners will think twice before embarking down this potentially long, costly, and increasingly uncertain road (*Financial Times*, 2000, 13 December). The concentration of so much value in so few hands also created headaches for the stock market, with risk and potential returns insufficiently distributed across a range of companies. Separately, sliding stock values dampened the 'urge to merge' by heightening uncertainty, ushering in a more risk-averse era, and reducing the value of corporate equity – the essential institutional 'currency' with which to pay for acquisitions, hence a key currency of merger markets. Commentators therefore asked whether the merger wave that characterised the 1990s turned, or simply paused.[8]

By comparison, because the share of the global pharmaceuticals market (prescription and OTC medicines) held by each of the largest pharmaceutical companies was still small (at less than 10% per company) relative to other industry sectors such as automotive, industry analysts believed consolidation in pharmaceuticals would continue, and they were correct. So the corporate 'leap frogging' of the late 1990s, as companies competed against each other to combine entities lower down the size league table in an attempt to attain – it appears only temporarily – the title of 'largest pharmaceutical company in the world', continued. Thus, following the

1995 GW merger, the two Swiss companies Ciba–Geigy and Sandoz merged in 1996/7 creating Novartis. France's Rhône–Poulenc and Germany's Höechst group also aspired to, and held briefly in 1999, the title of the world's biggest life-sciences company when they merged to create the next industry giant, Aventis. But Aventis was also subsequently toppled by both GSK and Pfizer. In fact, GSK's aspirations to this title were not only short lived, but were not actually realised as rival Pfizer swallowed up Warner Lambert during the protracted GW–SKB negotiation process, to snatch from GSK the title of pharmaceutical company with the largest market capitalisation.

The point here is that the restructuring in pharmaceuticals in the second half of the 1990s, which featured a frenzy of large mergers was driven in part by a push for 'size' in terms of market capitalisation in order to dominate various institutional buying interfaces and markets. Size also allows large pharmaceutical companies to extend leverage both over an increasingly outsourced manufacturing function, and indeed over smaller biotech companies undertaking drugs-related research and development on behalf of large pharmaceuticals through a series of alliances, joint ventures, and other 'distributed' coalition arrangements.

End-user and intermediate institutional markets for drugs Different national geographical markets display significant differences in the way drugs markets are instituted and regulated. Given the centrality of the US market to the aspirations of GSK, the following discussion focuses on US market for drugs. For example, the process via which 'a patient' comes to take a particular medicine – and not others from the range of possible substitutes – has undergone important changes which are still ongoing. This covers not only which drug is taken, but also who pays, what price is paid, and who bears the cost of the treatment.

In the US, the dispensing of medicines to the general public occurs through a number of routes: (1) through community General Practitioner (GP) prescription followed by dispensary by a local community pharmacist; (2) through the managed care sector into hospitals and clinics for dispensing by hospital doctors and nurses; or (3) via private healthcare institutions and hospitals. In the first case, pharmaceutical companies are pro-actively operating to re-institute the relationship between the patient (consumer), the GP and the pharmacist. Traditionally, drugs promotional effort has been targeted at GPs. Here, a change in the way a sales representative presents the 'message' of a drug's capabilities to the GP (without any change to the actual drug formulation) can have a surprisingly powerful impact on sales.

Increasingly, however, the efforts of sales representative are being supplemented by advertising campaigns used to create a more 'empowered' and 'drugs aware' patient capable and willing to request a particular drug from a busy and pressured GP. It has been shown that GPs will prescribe a drug specifically requested by a patient in 66% of cases (Pilling, 2000). The biggest catalyst of this change in the US occurred when there was an easing of TV advertising regulations in 1997, opening the door to television advertising of prescription drugs. Pharmaceutical companies also increasingly target sales and promotional effort at pharmacists in response to the growth of over-the-counter (OTC) markets for medicines, and in response to government pressure for patients to 'self-treat' minor ailments, with the help and advice of a local pharmacist.

The competitive battle between off-patent branded prescription drugs, and generic substitutes is also implicated in these shifts. Manufacturers of the former argue that generic substitutes do not have to bear the research and development costs that high-margins on patented products are designed to recoup. Generic manufacturers argue that the practice of patent-extension is a competitively unfair method of maintaining high margins. Indeed, where GPs continue to prescribe familiar brand names, generic substitution statutes in the US have been enacted by virtually all states and permit, in some cases require, the dispensing pharmacist to substitute an alternative generic product for the one prescribed. However governmental and other (budgetary) pressures are increasing the propensity for GPs to prescribe cheaper generics.

Pharmaceutical gross margins are also under pressure from the system of rebates through which public medical insurance schemes operate. In the US, pharmaceutical companies are required to rebate the state a portion of their revenue from products dispensed by pharmacies to Medicaid recipients. Medicaid rebates increased for SKB in 1999, reducing net sales and income by $165 million in that year compared to $122 million in 1998 and $94 million in 1997. In general, western societies under pressure to reduce impacts on the public purse of health provision are turning to the profits of the high-margin pharmaceutical industry to bear an increased proportion of escalating health costs.

The all-important managed care sector has grown in the US where the number of members with private health insurance, administered through Health Maintenance Organisations (HMOs), grew from 33.6 million people in 1990 to 105.3 million people in 1998.[9] Here we also see in the US an increasing concentration of buying power in the hands of a smaller number of institutional buyers (SmithKline Beecham 1999). This shift in the structure of institutional buying has produced a corresponding response in the targeting of sales effort on the part of pharmaceutical companies (as witnessed in particular at SKB, prior to the merger). This involves a focusing of effort on 'key accounts' and the provision of a 'one-stop' service to key institutional buyers, enabling them to purchase as wide a range of products from a single pharmaceutical company as possible. In competitive terms this can be seen as an attempt to 'lock out' smaller pharmaceuticals suppliers by nurturing close one-to-one buyer–supplier relationships with key customers in the managed care sector. Clearly, this strategy is only achievable if as full a range of products and product variants as possible can be made available through a single supplier. Further, the 'full range supply' strategy pursued by the largest pharmaceutical companies should not to be confused with full-range in-house drug development, or full-range in-house manufacturing. Rather the strategy (which sheds further light on the rationale for the SKB–GW merger) is to *thicken and thus control the distribution channel*, as a competitive move against rival (smaller range) drug suppliers, whilst *at the same time* organising and co-ordinating at 'arm's length' the drug discovery and drug manufacture stages of the production process via the institution of licences and other institutional agreements.

Research and development intensive pharmaceutical companies are therefore responding to generic competition and other (public) sources of downward pressure on margins in a number of ways including: (1) introducing new ranges of products into as many markets as possible; (2) accelerating the process by which new compounds in development are brought to the market; (3) increasing brand awareness among GPs and consumers of patented products, so attempting to 'shore up' post-patent sales; and (4) increasing targeted sales and marketing effort in the managed care sector.

Taken together these strategies combine a large increase in marketing effort, a widening of the product range and thickening of distribution channels, whilst maintaining organisational, and 'buying power control' over the drug discovery and manufacturing functions. These combined factors can also, crucially, be seen as important drivers of consolidation in the pharmaceuticals sector.[10] Indeed, these strategies for competitively *instituting and re-instituting markets* are furthered through merger. They can be seen as driving mergers and shed considerable light on the period of 'merger-mania' involving trans-national pharmaceutical oligopolies.

Corporate market and non-market exchanges of drugs, drugs in development and market/distribution rights The year 2000 saw the GW–SKB merger delayed on two occasions, embarrassing the two companies and requiring them to retract dates that they had publicly paraded as anticipated dates for final approval. Originally, the merger proposal announced on 17 January 2000 was expected to obtain regulatory approval by August 2000. The first delay arose when the US competition regulator, the Federal Trade Commission (FTC) expressed concerns over two, totally unconnected, treatment areas (herpes and nausea prevention treatments). There followed a series of *intra-industry negotiated swaps*, or non-market exchanges, in some cases occurring across arch-rival pharmaceutical giants. These 'swaps' involved combinations of the exchange of cash for property rights over drugs in development and drugs already on the market. Three SKB products worth £383 million were sold. Kytril the nausea prevention drug for cancer patients (and part of the developing gastro-intestinal stable of

GW–SKB drugs) was sold to Roche. In return, Roche gave up its North American rights to Coreg a drug for congestive heart failure. In addition the Vectavir/Denavir antiviral treatment for herpes, part of the GW–SKB anti-infective portfolio was sold to Novartis. It is interesting to note that in an attempt to prevent anti-competitive behaviour in the industry, anti-trust decisions triggered a series of negotiated exchanges that were far from 'openly competitive'.

Such 'negotiated swaps' are not at all a-typical (Morgan, 2001). Rather, this mixture of market and non-market exchanges which are triggered by regulatory requirements are the 'norm' in merger negotiations, particularly in the pharmaceuticals industry.

On 11 September 2000, GSK was again forced to postpone its anticipated 21 September finalisation date. This time the companies were challenged on a quite different treatment area. The FTC alleged the merger would create unfair dominance of the smoking cessation 'market', by bringing GW's prescription product Zyban under the same corporate umbrella as SKB's OTC products Nicorette gum and Nicoderm patches. This time, GSK lawyers appealed on the grounds that the FTC had inappropriately defined the smoking cessation market, which they claimed was in fact two separate (OTC and prescription) markets. On this occasion the companies' appeal was upheld by the FTC.

This example illustrates the contested nature of market definitions, where the boundaries of where one market merges into another becomes part of the negotiation process between anti-trust regulators and the corporations they scrutinise, with the latter attempting to frustrate regulatory control by arguing for market 'boundaries' which support their own favoured outcome. This raises the question: why did the FTC choose these particular product/market areas to challenge? In fact, it has been suggested that rival Pharmacia and Upjohn wanted to buy SKB's smoking-cessation portfolio, had the FTC insisted that SKB give up its franchise. The origin of the challenge was not therefore the scrupulous analysis by the FTC of the likely impact of the merger on *all of the many* actual and potential markets where GSK could possibly wield anti-competitive post-merger market power. Rather, the challenge came from *within the industry itself* apparently according to the rationale that a rival pharmaceutical company potentially stood to benefit, by buying up products jettisoned as fall-out from the negotiated resolutions taking place between GW–SKB and the FTC. The FTC is therefore revealed in this example as acting reactively rather than proactively, in its policing of the potentially anti-competitive behaviours of firms.

Markets for merger advice No fewer than five investment banking and legal groups advised GW and SKB during the merger process: Goldman Sachs, Morgan Stanley, Cazenove, Hoare Govett and CSFB. Indeed, the final approval and setting of a date which sealed the GSK merger was a lucrative milestone for these companies, triggering as it did £112 million in fees to the advisors. Indeed, league tables of mergers listed by deal size (an indicator of the size and rate of activity in 'markets for corporate control'), and league tables of the turnover of business consultancy groups providing banking and legal merger advice (a proxy of the size, structure and activity in 'markets for merger advice') appear to be closely related. For example Goldman Sachs are said to have made £30 million in advisory fees from GSK alone and the role played by Morgan Stanley Dean Witter triggered payments earning for Morgan Stanley the title of top advisor for global mergers and acquisitions announced in 2000.

Clearly, from the lucrative returns which accrue to investment bankers, legal and accounting teams on finalisation of the merger, there is an economic incentive for advisors to broker successfully as many deals as possible, to the all important approval date which triggers the payment of fees. Merger advisors may therefore be considered an important class of agent who have a vested economic interest in seeing mergers (or indeed demergers and other forms of corporate restructuring) come about. During the particular period that our account focuses on, merger advisors can be seen as stimulating, encouraging and facilitating the 'urge to merge'.

The relationship between on the one hand legal advisors; and on the other the regulatory agencies and regulatory framework is also an interesting one, since as the staff directories of leading legal groups shows, lawyers in this highly specialist field are frequently recruited from, or move into, a policing role within a regulatory agency. Hence we can conjecture that there is a cross-fertilisation of knowledge (and perhaps influence) contributing to the mutual shaping of the regulatory backdrop and the corporate sphere.

The exact nature of the relationship between the largest international merger advisors, their trans-national merging clients, and the regulatory environment is not well researched (Berggren, 2003). Suffice to hypothesise here that there appears to be a *mutual stimulation* and *mutual incentivisation* effect between markets for merger advice and markets for corporate control.

The shifting drug-regulation environment and its recursive impact on markets as dialectical double movement

SKB were in the midst of sensitive merger negotiations with GW when a drug-safety issue caused a regulatory backlash which stalled the merger. Hailed as a future blockbuster to help prepare for post-patent era of SKB's 'superdrug' anti-depressant Paxil, Factive was intended as a prescription drug to treat respiratory tract infections. The drug was not, in fact an SKB creation rather, it was created externally by Korean based L. G. Chemicals and was in-licensed by SKB who acquired worldwide development and distribution rights in 1997. Positioned to play an important role in the joint

GW–SKB portfolio of anti-infectives, Factive failed to win approval from the US Food and Drug Administration (FDA)[11] in December 2000 because of cancer fears associated with the cell-transforming side-effects common to the class of drugs to which Factive belongs, called quinolones. The impact of this rejection was negative publicity ahead of the merger finalisation date, very costly sunk investment which would need to be borne by the post-merged entity, and the prospect of further lengthy and costly trials ahead of resubmission to the FDA. The setback had a negative impact on the merger, with a public backlash, and loss of stock-market confidence in the merging companies.

In fact we see the FACTIVE failure was only indicative of a more significant tightening of the drug approval process in the US. As a result of the increasing number of drugs being associated with high public profile health related side-effects, and even fatalities after launch, the FDA was, at the time, more critically scrutinising drugs during the approval process. Not only the SKB–GW drugs were affected, Warner Lambert's Rezulin for diabetes was also withdrawn and Pfizer's drug approval application Relpax for migraine was held up by the FDA for months. The result was to dis-incentivise lengthy, costly and uncertain radical new drugs development, and incentivise incremental innovation supported by strong marketing effort, the strategy which underpinned the Paxil and Zantc sales. Further, as the SKB 1999 Annual Report notes, the risks associated with over-dependency on single 'blockbuster' successes caused pharmaceutical firms to seek to spread the risks attached to such dependency by developing a 'thicker pipeline' of drugs in development, especially in the late-stage pipeline, a strategy which would see radical innovation discouraged and in its place more effort turned towards incremental adjustment to existing drugs, drug compounds, and methods of taking medicines.

Paradoxically, at the same moment, the merger assessment criteria of the US competition regulator, the FTC widened to incorporate the objective of stimulating and protecting post-merger *new product innovation*. Morgan (2001) has researched the decision criteria and decision processes of the FTC applied to the pharmaceuticals sector between 1995 and 2000. She notes an ongoing debate and shift in policy at the FTC, away from assessing potential mergers on the grounds of final market domination towards the prevention of potential negative impacts on *innovation markets* defined as consisting of 'the research and development directed to particular new or improved goods or processes and the close substitutes for that research and development' (Morgan, 2001, p. 183).

This new mode of merger appraisal is controversial because it is not at all certain it can achieve the objectives set for it. The very objective of taking into account innovative dynamism introduces uncertainty and unpredictability and critics are concerned that concrete merger induced efficiencies today should not be sacrificed for the sake of speculative future returns from protecting and stimulating innovation tomorrow.

More significantly for our account, we see conflicts of motive and regulatory policy producing contradictory outcomes between the US anti-trust and drug-safety bodies respectively. The FTC moved to a set of assessment criteria aimed at protecting and stimulating drug innovation, whilst over at the FDA, heightened drug safety concerns operated in a contrary manner, tightening, lengthening and introducing greater uncertainty into the drug approval process placing safety ahead of innovation and potentially (many would argue legitimately) dis-incentivising radical drug innovation in response to health concerns. The tensions between public safety, the potential welfare gains of drug discovery, and commercial/market success and freedoms are thus revealed as counter-forces, with these interests differently represented in policy terms by different classes of economic agent representing different parts of the market-regulatory system.

This account provides an interesting contemporary illustration of freedom–society–technology–economy dialectical tensions, here theorised as a series of interconnected *Dialectical Double Movements* following the insights of Karl Polanyi.

Acknowledgements

This chapter has been produced as part of the ESRC core funded work of the Centre for Research on Innovation and Competition. We gratefully acknowledge the helpful comments of Eleanor Morgan, Elizabeth Garnsey, Rod Coombs and Stan Metcalfe on earlier drafts. We also thank Peter Allen and Mark Harvey for many helpful discussions. All errors and omissions are the responsibility of the authors.

Notes

1 With thanks to everyone at the Karl Polanyi Institute of Political Economy, Concordia University, Montreal for their kindness enabling us to undertake research at the Polanyi Archives, June 2004, especially to Kari Polanyi-Levitt and Margie Mendell for their assistance and fascinating discussions on the life and work of Karl Polanyi and to Ana Gomez for her help at the Institute.
2 Indeed where organizational demography can be used as one way of analyzing 'varieties of capitalism', e.g. in Grnaovetter's (1994) discussion of Business Groups and their spatial expression.
3 O'Higgins and Weigal have produced a very pessimistic account of ht GlaxoSmithKline merger based on a form of business performance called the Heart of the Business (HOB) Model.
4 Unpublished manuscripts, drafted and re-drafted over the period 1955–1962, 'Freedom and Technology', 'Freedom in a Complex Society', 'Economics and Freedom to Shape our Social Destiny', containers 36, 37, Polanyi Archives, Karl Polanyi. Institute of Political Economy, Concordia University, Montreal, Canada.
5 *Ibid.*
6 Several passages in these essays provide eerily close previews and parallels to the terrorist attacks on the World Trade Center, New York City, and other US targets on 11 September 2001.

7 For example, in Europe Volvo's planned acquisition of Scania was halted in 2000.
8 Prtzelick and Lewis (2000), *Financial Times*, Survey (2000), *Financial Times*, LEX. (2000), *The Economist* (2001).
9 www.pharma.org at 20 January 2002.
10 In fact such strategies are by no means exclusive to pharmaceuticals. Similar accounts of the strategies of large UK retail multiples, (Harvey 1999) and in personal computers, (Sturgen, 1998).
11 The FDA governs the testing, approval, manufacturing, labeling and marketing of drugs and reviews safety and the effectiveness of drugs marketed in the US.

References

Andrade, G., Mitchell, M. and Stafford, E. (2001), 'New Evidence and Perspective on Mergers', *Journal of Economic Perspectives*, 15(2), pp. 103–12.

Berggren, C. (2003), 'Mergers, MNES and Innovation: The Need for New Research Approaches', *Scandinavian Journal of Management*, 19(2), pp. 173–91.

Cantwell, J. (ed.) (1992), *Multinational Investment in Modern Europe*, Aldershot, Edward Elgar.

Dalton, G. (1968), *Primitive, Archaic and Modern Economies: Essays of Karl Polanyi*, Boston, Beacon Press

Financial Times (2000), 'Survey', June.

Financial Times (2000), 'LEX', 13 December.

Granovetter, M. (1994), 'Business Groups', in N. J. Smesler and R. Swedberg (eds), *The Handbook of Economic Sociology*, Princeton, Princeton University Press.

Harvey, M. (1999), 'Innovation and Competitiveness in UK Supermarkets', *CRIC Briefing Paper*, no. 3, CRIC, University of Manchester.

Harvey, M. (2002), 'Competition as Instituted Economic Process', in S. Metcalfe and A. Warde (eds), *Market Relations and the Competitive Process*, Manchester, Manchester University Press.

Harvey, M. and Randles, S. (2002), 'Markets, the Organisation of Exchanges and "Instituted Economic Process": An Analytical Perspective', *Revue d'Economie Industrielle*, 101, 4th trimester.

Harvey, M., McMeekin, A., Randles, S., Southerton, D., Tether, B. and Warde, A. (2001), 'Economic Integration and Practical Consumption: Some Theoretical Considerations', 2nd draft of a paper presented at the European Sociological Association Conference, Helsinki, August.

Holmstrom, B. and Kaplan S. N. (2001), 'Corporate Governance and Merger Activity in the United States: Making Sense of the 1980's and 1990's', *Journal of Economic Perspectives*, 15(2), pp. 121–44.

Jovanovic, B. and Rosseau, P. L. (2001), 'Mergers and Technological Change: 1885–1998', *Working Paper*, no. 01-W16, Department of Economics, Vanderbilt University, Nashville.

Kettler, H. (ed.) (2001), *Consolidation and Competition in the Pharmaceutical Industry*, Office of Health Economics, London.

Knickerboker, F. T. (1973), *Oligopolistic Reaction and Multinational Enterprise*, Boston, Harvard Business School.

Larsson, R. and Finkelstein, S. (1999), 'Integrating Strategic, Organizational and Human Resource Perspectives on Mergers and Acquisitions: A Case of Synergy Realization', *Organization Science*, 10(1), pp. 1–26.

Meschi, M. (1997), 'Analytical Perspectives on Mergers and Acquisitions', Paper no. 5-97, Center for International Business Studies, South Bank University, London.

Mitchell, M. L. and Mulherin, J. H. (1996), 'The Impact of Industry Shocks on Takeover and Restructuring Activity', *Journal of Financial Economics*, 41(2), pp. 193–229.

Morgan, E. (2001), 'Innovation and Merger Decisions in the Pharmaceutical Industry', *Review of Industrial Organisation*, 19(2), pp. 181–97.

North, D. (1990), *Institutions, Institutional Change and Economic Performance*, Cambridge, Cambridge University Press.

O'Higgins, E. and Weigel, J. R. (2002), 'Mega-mergers in the Pharmaceutical Industry: A Strategy or Fad?', paper presented at the SAID World Strategy Congress, University of Oxford, March.

Penrose, E. (1959), *The Theory of the Growth of the Firm*, Oxford, Basil Blackwell.

Pilling, D. (2000), *Financial Times*, 24 October, p. 20.

Polanyi, K. (1925), 'On Freedom', unpublished manuscript, Vienna, Polanyi Archive Ref. 30-1, Karl Polanyi Institute of Political Economy, Concordia University, Montreal, Canada.

Polanyi, K. (1943), 'Jean Jacques Rousseau: Or Is a Free Society Possible?', lecture, Bennington College, Polanyi Archive Ref. 18-24, Karl Polanyi Institute of Political Economy, Concordia University, Montreal, Canada.

Polanyi, K. (1944), *The Great Transformation*, Boston, Beacon Press.

Polanyi, K. (1947), 'Our Obsolete Market Mentality', 'Commentary', 3 February, in R. Swedberg (ed.) (1996), *Economic Sociology*, Cheltenham, Edward Elgar.

Polanyi, K. (1955), 'Freedom and Technology', unpublished manuscript, Polanyi Archive Ref. 36-9, Karl Polanyi Institute of Political Economy, Concordia University, Montreal, Canada.

Polanyi, K. (1957a), 'Freedom in a Complex Society', unpublished manuscript, Ref. 37-3, Polanyi Archive, Karl Polanyi Institute of Political Economy, Concordia University, Montreal, Canada.

Polanyi, K. (1957b), 'The Economy as Instituted Process', in K. Polanyi, C. M. Arensberg, and H. W. Pearson (eds), *Trade and Market in the Early Empires*, New York, Free Press.

Polanyi, K. (1957–62), 'Economics and Freedom to Shape our Social Destiny' (1st draft), 'Economics and the Freedom to Shape our World' (2nd draft), unpublished manuscripts, Ref. 37-4, Polanyi Archive, Karl Polanyi Institute of Political Economy, Concordia University, Montreal, Canada.

Polanyi, K. (1960), 'On the Comparative Treatment of Economic Institutions in Antiquity with Illustrations from Athens, Mycenae, and Alalakh', a published article from 'City Invincible: A Symposium on Urbanization and Cultural Development in the Ancient Near East', reproduced in G. Dalton (1968), *Primitive, Archaic and Modern Economies: Essays of Karl Polanyi*, Boston, Beacon Press.

Polanyi, K. (1962), 'Letter to Kari, Biographical Notes', Ref. 59-2, Polanyi Archive, Karl Polanyi Institute of Political Economy, Concordia University, Montreal, Canada.

Polanyi, K., Arensberg, C. M. and Pearson, H. W. (1957), 'The Place of Economies in Societies', in K. Polanyi, C. M. Arensberg and H. W. Pearson (eds), *Trade and Markets in the Early Empires*, New York, Free Press.

Prtzelick and Lewis (2000), 'Cross Atlantic Consolidation Gains Pace', *Financial Times: International Mergers and Acquisitions*, 30 June.

Randles, S. (2002), 'Complex Systems Applied? The Merger That Made GlaxoSmithKline', *Technology Analysis and Strategic Management*, 14(3), pp. 331–54.

Randles, S. (2003), 'Issues for a Neo-Polanyian Research Agenda in Economic Sociology', Special Collection, M. Harvey and R. Ramlogan (eds), *International Review of Sociology*, 13(2), pp. 409–34.

Randles, S. (2004), 'The Ontology of Karl Polanyi', paper presented at the 8th Annual International Association of Critical Realism Conference, University of Cambridge, England, 17–19 August.

Randles, S. and Warde, A. (2002), 'On Economic Sociology, Competition and Markets', *CRIC Discussion Paper*, no. 53, CRIC, University of Manchester.

Shleifer, A. and Vishny, R. (2001), 'Stock Market Driven Acquisitions', *NBER Working Paper*, no. 8439.

SmithKline Beecham (1999), *Annual Report*.

Sturgen, T. (1998), *Turnkey Production Networks: A New American Model of Industrial Organisation?*, paper presented to the 94th Meeting of the Association of American Geographers Conference, Boston, April.

The Economist (2001), 'The Great Merger Wave Breaks', 25 January.

Trautwein, F. (1990), 'Merger Motives and Merger Prescriptions', *Strategic Management Journal*, 11(4), pp. 283–95.

Warde, A., Harvey, M., McMeekin, A., Randles, S., Southerton, D. and Tether, B. (2001), 'Between Demand and Consumption: A Framework for Research', *CRIC Discussion Paper*, no. 40, CRIC, University of Manchester.

Index

999 service, 221

agency, human, 73, 79–82
Alchian, A., 61
American Ethnological Society, 149
Amin, A., 82
Andrade, G., 256–7
anthropology, 149
Aquinas, Thomas, 124–5
arenas of exchange, 259
Arensberg, C. M., xv
Aristotle and Aristotelianism, 79, 118, 122–6
Arnold, R., xv
Arrighi, G., 163
AT&T, 238
Austen, Jane, 122–6
Austrian school of economics, 68, 136–7, 140
autocatalytic processes of innovation, 234
Aventis, 271
Axelrod, R., 70
Ayres, C. E., 46

Balzac, Honoré de, 27
Barber, B., 114, 166
Bardhan, P., 46
base/superstructure metaphor, 118
Bates, R., 47
Bauer, O., 83–4
Baum, G., 116
Baumann, Z., 227
Bekkers, R., 244

Berthoud, G., 143–4
Black Death, 178
black economy, 120
Block, F., 6, 11, 119, 163, 166
Bohannan, P., xv
Boyer, R., 6, 163
Braudel, F., 30
Braverman, H., 34
Buddenbrooks phenomenon, 50–1
Burawoy, M., 163
Burke, Edmund, 67

call centres, 17, 208–29
Cantwell, J., 257
capitalism, 25–30, 35–6, 93–103, 108, 119–21, 125–6, 169–70, 177–9
Carpi, T., 87
Carr, E. H., 45
caste relations, 49–52, 66
central planning, 103–4
Centre for Research on Innovation and Competition, 165
Chennai families, 50
ChildLine, 221
Christianity, 15, 115–18, 123–6
Ciba-Geigy, 271
civil society, 66, 81, 84, 88, 105
  global, 109
Clark, J. M., 39–40
class relationships, 46–8
climate change, 178
Coase, R., 31–2, 99–100
coffee production, 45, 47

Cole, G. D. H., 14, 36, 83
collective bargaining, 196–7
collectivist policies, 39
Colombia, 45
'command-and-control', 100
Commons, J., 44, 48
communitarianism, 113
complex causality, of, 166, 178–9
Conference of European Telecommunications Administrations (CEPT), 236, 240, 242
Congdon, L., 115
contingent valuation, 100
contracts of employment, 197–8, 201
coordination rules, 69–73
corporate culture, 35
corporate governance, 51–2
cost-benefit analysis, 101
Costa Rica, 45–6
cotton industry, 34–5
culture, 48
customer service, 224

Dalton, G., 135, 148
Deakin, S., 14, 200
deliberative democracy, 87, 102, 108
democratisation, economic, 83–4, 87
deregulation *see* regulation and deregulation
dialectical double movement (DDM), 254–5, 258–9, 269–71
 external, 263
dialectics, internal and external, 262–3
digital technology, 240–1, 245
drug approval process, 276–7
Durkheim, É., 66

ecological economics, 99, 102–3, 108
economic determinism, xii, 82
economic processes, nature of, 9–10, 16–18, 168–76
 see also instituted economic process (IEP)
economic sociology, 12, 43, 73, 114, 141, 150, 166, 175–6

economic, definition of, 120
economics, definition of, 60
economies, 'substantive' and 'formal', 120
Economist, The, 256
'economistic fallacy', 30, 32, 96
educational reform, 85–7
El Salvador, 45
Elson, D., 105
embeddedness and disembeddedness, xiii, xv, 2–18, 26, 32–3, 37, 43, 47, 49, 67, 87, 93–9, 102–9, 114, 120–2, 126, 142, 147–9, 164–6, 173, 263–4
emergency services, 221–2
employment, forms of, 198–9
Engels, Friedrich, 60–1
Enron, 3, 172
entropy, 102
environmental problems, xv, 99–104, 108
epistemic processes, 179–80
Ericsson, 243
ethical issues, 115
European Commission, 237, 241, 243
European Telecommunications Standards Institute (ETSI), 242–5
external shocks, 234
externalities, 100

factory system, 7, 45
family businesses, 50–2
fascism, 116
Federal Communication Commission (FCC), 238
Federal Trade Commission (FTC), 273–7
feminist scholarship, 85
feudal society, 119
fictitious commodities, 7–9, 15–17, 94–5, 102–8, 142
financial crises, 142
Finkelstein, S., 256
First World War, 36, 39
Food and Drug Administration (FDA), 276–7
France, 187–205
Frankel, F., 47

Index

Franklin, Benjamin, 122–6
Fransman, M., 245–6
free-market economics, 99, 101, 108
free trade, xiii
freedom: and society, 264–5; and technology, 265–6
Freire, P., 86
full employment, xiv, 94
Fusefeld, D. B., xv

Galileo Circle, 115, 135
game theory, 63–4
general equilibrium theory, 38
Giddens, A., 113–14
Glaxo Wellcome (GW), 254–6, 264–76
Global System for Mobile Communications (GSM), 235–46
globalisation, xiii–xv, 3, 50–1
gold standard, 2, 8, 29, 138, 142
Goldman Sachs, 275
Granovetter, M., 4–6, 32–3, 145–8, 166, 257
Great Depression, xiii–xiv
Greif, A., 62–3
Guatemala, 45–6
guild socialism, 116, 136, 148–9

habits, 67–8
Harvey, M., 169, 212, 234–5
Hawkins, R., 239
Hayek, F., 1, 64, 68, 72, 136–7
Hegel, G. W. F., 117, 260
Hobbes, Thomas, 33
Hobson, J., 36
Hodgson, G., 32, 44, 48–9, 52, 86, 142, 145, 175
Höechst group, 271
Hollingsworth, J. R., 6, 14, 80–3, 163
Holmstrom, B., 256
Homer, 122–5
Hopkins, T. K., 3
Hume, David, 64, 68, 72
Hungary, 115

'incoherence governance', 80
India, 44–52, 66, 210–11, 216, 220, 226

individualism, 58, 61–8, 73;
  methodological, 61–2, 79, 99–100
  ontological, 61–2
industrial districts, 34
Ingham, G., 66
instituted economic process (IEP), 16–17, 78, 139–40, 144, 150–2, 163–80, 193, 199, 205, 212–14, 222–3, 229, 233–4, 246–7, 254–5, 258–9, 269
instituted employment system, 203–5
institutional analysis, 14, 25, 30–3, 36, 39–40, 43–4; 'old' form of, 48–9, 52–3, 67, 74
  see also new institutional economics
institutional change, 14, 68, 79–85, 88, 150
institutional isomorphism, 257
institutions: as emergent social structures, 67
  objective and subjective, 68
interdependency thesis, 166
internal labour markets (ILM), 192, 194
irrationality, causes of, 37–8

Japan, 34–5
Jessop, B., 6–7
Jovanovic, B., 257

Kano, S., 245–6
Kaplan, S. N., 256
Kenya, 47
Keynes, J. M., 137
Keynesianism, 94, 141
Knight, J., 63
Krippner, G., 147, 166

labour, distinctiveness of, 17
labour costs, components of, 203
labour demand, segmentation of, 192–5
labour markets, 185–205
  imperfections in, 185
  regulation of exchange in, 195–9
  supply and demand in, 189–95, 204–5
labour supply, differentiation in, 190–2

laissez-faire policies, xi, xiii, 94–5, 138, 141
Landes, D., 43, 50, 52
language, 69, 72–3
Larsson, R., 256
law: epiphenomenal conception of, 59–64, 73
 individualist conception of, 63
Lazonick, W., 46
Lewis, C. S., 124
Lewis, J., 191
L. G. Chemicals, 275
liberalism, economic, 35, 82, 94–5, 119
Lie, J., 6

MacIntyre, A., 114, 117–26
MacIver, R. M., xv
Malthus, Thomas, 8
Mannheim, K., 27, 115
market economy, 26, 28, 36, 93, 97
market exchange as distinct from market forces, 106
market failure, 100, 102
market processes, 169
market socialism, 104–5
market society, 26, 28, 39, 93, 97, 120–1
market system, 26, 29–35
 efficiency of, 35–40
markets: institutionalisation of, 9–11, 28–9
 and moral orders, 118–26
 relationship with the state, 66, 74
 see also price-making markets
Marsden, D., 192
Marx, Karl, 16, 27–32, 59–61, 118, 165, 260
Marxism, 46, 58–68, 73, 103, 115–20, 175
mass media, 265
Mauss, M., 26
means-ends relationship, 124
Menger, C., 68, 72
mergers, 254–60, 269–76; advice on, 274–5
Metcalfe, J. S., 235
Mill, John Stuart, 125

minimum wage provisions, 196–7
Mises, Ludwig von, 1, 36, 61, 84, 136–7
Mitchell, Wesley, 36, 40
mobile phones, 17, 235–40, 244–7
money: debasement of, 72–3
 theory of, 10–11, 27–9
moral orders, 118–26
Morgan, E., 276
Morgan Stanley Dean Witter, 275
Motorola, 238, 243
Mouffe, Chantal, 87–8
multiplicity thesis, 166

Nash equilibria, 70
Neale, W. C., xv
neoclassical economics, 48, 108
neoclassical environmental economics, 100–5
neoliberalism, xiv, 87, 94
Neurath, O., 35–6
new economic sociology (NES), 139, 144, 148
new institutional economics (NIE), 44–8, 52–3, 62–3, 72–3
NHS Direct, 215–16, 222
Nietzsche, Friedrich, 113
norms, 234
North, D., 30–1, 46–8, 66
Novartis, 271, 274
Nugent, J., 44–7

occupational labour markets (OLM), 192, 194
oligopoly, 257
outsourcing, 219–20
Owen, Robert, 14, 83, 116

participatory planning, 15, 95, 99, 105–9
patents, 242–3, 272
path-dependence, 44, 102, 205, 244, 246
Pearson, H. W., xv
Peck, J., 7, 142, 145, 147
pension funds, 172
Pfizer, 271, 276
pharmaceutical companies, 272–4
Pharmacia, 274

Polanyi, Karl: citation record, 5
  life of, xi, xv, 2, 15, 115–16, 134–7
  writing style, 135
  Works:
    'Aristotle Discovers the Economy', xii–xiii, xv, 3
    'Behemoth' and 'Uber Die Freiheit', 116
    'Economics and Freedom to Shape our Social Destiny', 265
    'The Economy as Instituted Process', 119–20
    'The Essence of Fascism', 116
    'Freedom in a Complex Society', 265, 267
    The Great Transformation, xi–xv, 1–11, 15, 25, 29–30, 43, 82, 93, 114, 119, 122, 134–8, 145, 164, 169, 175, 260, 263, 265, 267–8
    The Livelihood of Man, 79
    'The Mechanisms of the World Economic Crisis', 85
    'Our Obsolete Market Mentality', 138, 145, 267
    Sozialistische Rechnungslegung, 36
    Trade and Market in the Early Empires (written with C. M. Arensberg and H. W. Pearson), xv, 3, 9, 33
Polanyi-given scholarship, 133, 150
Polanyi-inspired scholarship, 133–4, 144, 150
Polanyi-Levitt, Kari, xi–xv, 134, 137, 143, 268
pollution, 100
Poor Law, xii, 2, 8
Porter Benson, S., 224
Posner, R., 62–3
price-making markets, 27–8, 140
prisoners' dilemma game, 64, 70–1
privatisation, xiv–xv, 94
property rights, 45, 59–65, 99–100

Quine, Willard van Orman, 69
quinolones, 276

Radice, H., 83
Randles, S., 169, 234–5

Rao, M. S. A., 47
Rathenau, W., 36
rationality, formal or substantive, 37–8
Reagan, Ronald, 3, xiv–xv, 141
reciprocity, 149–50
redistributive processes, 9–12
regulation and deregulation, xiv–xv, 3, 8, 11, 18, 94, 141–2, 146, 257, 264–6, 270–1, 275
  of labour markets, 198–9
  in telecommunications, 237, 242
research, need for, 109
Rhône-Poulenc, 271
Ricardo, David, 8, 137
Robbins, Lionel, 38, 137
Roche, 273–4
Roseau, P. L., 257
Rotstein, A., 116
Rousseau, Jean Jacques, 264
Rubery, J., 193
Rudner, D. W., 51
Russell, Bertrand, 36
Ryle, G., 124

Saberwal, S., 51
Sahlins, M. D., 149
The Samaritans, 221
Samuels, W., 73
Sandoz, 271
Sayer, A., 15, 147–8
scarcity, 29–30
Schultz, W., 72
Schweikart, D., 105
Searle, J., 68
secularisation, 118
self-organising institutions, 68–9, 72–3
self-regulating markets, xiii, 1–4, 8–11, 25, 29, 43, 73, 78, 93, 96, 99, 102–9, 138, 145–6, 164, 169
Sened, I., 63–4
shadow economy, 120
Shaftesbury, Lord, 124
shop assistants, 224–6
Silberman, C. S., xv
SKB, 272–6
slavery, 9
Smith, Adam, 15, 68, 72, 119, 137

Smith Kline Beecham, 254–6, 264–75
social anthropology, 82
social learning, 85
social ontology, 67
social ownership, 105–7
social relations, 32–3, 61
social rules, 61, 66–8
social security, financing of, 202–3
social utility, 36–7
socialisation: of the economy, 36
  of the market, 105
  of wages, 201–2
socialism, 35–6, 84, 93–9, 103–8, 118, 126
  centralised, 103–4
  see also guild socialism
societal effect school of labour market economics, 187, 193
'societalised individuals', 79
Solow, R., 185–6
Somers, M., 119
Soros, George, 163
Soviet Union, 80, 103–4
specificity thesis, 166
spontaneous orders, 68–9, 72
Stiglitz, Joseph, 163
structural adjustment programmes, 43
'substantivist' economics, 43
Sugden, R., 61, 63
Swedberg, R., 145, 175

tacit knowledge, 104, 108
Tanzania, 47
Tawney, Richard, 36
taxation, 173
Taylor, C., 79
telecommunications sector, 235–47
telephone sales, 218–19, 222–8
Telstra, 245
Thatcher, Margaret, xiv–xv, 3, 141
Titmuss, R. M., 200
Tolstoy, Leo, 115
total social organisation of labour (TSOL) framework, 212–14, 222, 229

Toye, J., 45
trade unions, 196
transaction costs theory, 31
transformational processes, 170–1
Trautwein, F., 256
tribal societies, 9, 120–1
trust, 49–52

United Kingdom (UK), 187–205
Upjohn, 274
Urry, J., 228
'use value', 120
utilitarianism, 35, 118, 124–6

Vanberg, V., 72
variable differentiation thesis, 166
Veblen, Thorstein, 13, 32, 39, 44–8, 67, 86
Vienna, 86
virtues, conceptions of, 125
voluntary associations, role of, 107

wages, 172–3, 185–9, 195
  market and non-market components of, 199–203
  socialisation of, 201–2
Warner Lambert, 271, 276
weapons of mass destruction, 265–6
Weber, Max, 12–13, 28, 32, 37–8, 116, 120
welfare: 'social', 'fiscal' and 'occupational' systems of, 201
welfare state provision, xiv–xv, 8–12, 86, 94, 137, 141, 200
Williams, Raymond, 86
Williamson, Oliver, 33–4, 62, 66
Wittgenstein, Ludwig, 67
Wohl, C., 135
World Administrative Radio Conference (1987), 239
World Bank, 43
world systems theory, xv
WorldCom, 270

youth employment, 194

EU authorised representative for GPSR:
Easy Access System Europe, Mustamäe tee 50,
10621 Tallinn, Estonia
gpsr.requests@easproject.com

www.ingramcontent.com/pod-product-compliance
Ingram Content Group UK Ltd.
Pitfield, Milton Keynes, MK11 3LW, UK
UKHW021836140426
5217IPUK00021B/1487